Features

Features
Perspectives on a Key Notion in Linguistics

EDITED BY
ANNA KIBORT AND GREVILLE G. CORBETT

OXFORD
UNIVERSITY PRESS

Great Clarendon Street, Oxford, OX2 6DP,
United Kingdom

Oxford University Press is a department of the University of Oxford.
It furthers the University's objective of excellence in research, scholarship,
and education by publishing worldwide. Oxford is a registered trade mark of
Oxford University Press in the UK and in certain other countries

© editorial matter and organization Anna Kibort and Greville G. Corbett 2010
© the chapters their various authors 2010

The moral rights of the authors have been asserted

First published 2010

All rights reserved. No part of this publication may be reproduced, stored in
a retrieval system, or transmitted, in any form or by any means, without the
prior permission in writing of Oxford University Press, or as expressly permitted
by law, by licence or under terms agreed with the appropriate reprographics
rights organization. Enquiries concerning reproduction outside the scope of the
above should be sent to the Rights Department, Oxford University Press, at the
address above

You must not circulate this work in any other form
and you must impose this same condition on any acquirer

Published in the United States of America by Oxford University Press
198 Madison Avenue, New York, NY 10016, United States of America

British Library Cataloguing in Publication Data
Data available

Library of Congress Cataloging in Publication Data
Data available

ISBN 978–0–19–957774–3

Contents

Notes on contributors — vii
Abbreviations — x

1. Introduction — 1
   Anna Kibort and Greville G. Corbett

Part I Key Notions

2. Features: essential notions — 17
   Greville G. Corbett
3. Feature hierarchies and contrast in phonology — 37
   B. Elan Dresher
4. Towards a typology of grammatical features — 64
   Anna Kibort

Part II Perspectives from Syntactic Description and Theory

5. Features in categorization, or a new look at an old problem — 109
   Keith Plaster and Maria Polinsky
6. The definiteness feature at the syntax–semantics interface — 143
   Gabi Danon
7. Features in periphrastic constructions — 166
   Gergana Popova
8. A Minimalist theory of feature structure — 185
   David Adger

Part III Formal Perspectives

9. Features and computational semantics — 221
   Ann Copestake and Dan Flickinger
10. Feature geometry and predictions of locality — 236
    Ivan A. Sag

11. Inessential features and expressive power of descriptive metalanguages 272
Geoffrey K. Pullum and Hans-Jörg Tiede

References 293
Author index 317
Language index 322
Subject index 324

Notes on contributors

David Adger is Professor of Linguistics at Queen Mary, University of London. He is author of *Core Syntax* (Oxford University Press 2003) and co-author of *Mirrors and Microparameters* (Cambridge University Press 2009). He currently edits the journal *Syntax*, and has published widely on syntactic theory and its interfaces with grammar internal systems (morphology, semantics, prosody) and the systems of use (discourse and variation). He is completing a Leverhulme Major Research Fellowship on the grammar–meaning connection, focusing on Scottish Gaelic.

Ann Copestake is Reader in Computational Linguistics in the Computer Laboratory, University of Cambridge. Her research is in computational linguistics, mostly in formal representation issues, compositional and lexical semantics, and natural language generation. She was the original developer of the LKB system, which is a freely available grammar and lexicon development environment for constraint-based linguistic frameworks. She is interested in a range of applications involving broad-coverage text processing. Currently her main research projects concern the extraction of information from scientific texts.

Greville G. Corbett is Distinguished Professor of Linguistics at the University of Surrey, where he leads the Surrey Morphology Group. He is a Fellow of the British Academy, and a member of the Academy of Social Sciences and of the Academia Europaea. His research has focused on the typology of features, as in *Gender* (1991), *Number* (2000), and *Agreement* (2006), all published by Cambridge University Press, and he has recently been developing the canonical approach to typology. He is one of the originators of Network Morphology, and has done fieldwork on Archi, Chichewa, Russian, Serbian/Croatian/Bosnian, and Tsakhur. He currently holds a European Research Council Advanced Grant for work on morphological complexity.

Gabi Danon is a lecturer in the Department of English at Bar-Ilan University. His research focuses on the syntax of nominal features – definiteness, number, and case – and their role at the syntax–semantics interface. He has published in the journals *Linguistics*, *Natural Language and Linguistic Theory*, and *Lingua*, and has co-edited the volume *Current Issues in Generative Hebrew Linguistics* (John Benjamins 2008).

B. Elan Dresher is Professor of Linguistics at the University of Toronto. He has published on phonological theory, learnability, historical linguistics, and Biblical Hebrew phonology and prosody. He is the author of *Old English and the Theory of Phonology* (Garland Publishing 1985) and publications with Aditi Lahiri on the history of West Germanic stress and syllable structure. His recent publications include *Formal Approaches to Poetry: Recent Developments in Generative Metrics* (co-edited with Nila Friedberg, Mouton de Gruyter 2006), *Contrast in Phonology: Theory, Perception, Acquisition* (co-edited with Peter Avery and Keren Rice, Mouton de Gruyter 2008), and *The Contrastive Hierarchy in Phonology* (Cambridge University Press 2009).

Dan Flickinger is a Senior Research Associate at the Center for the Study of Language and Information, Stanford University. He was project manager of the Natural Language Group at Hewlett-Packard Laboratories for ten years, then joined CSLI in 1993 to manage the LinGO Laboratory. He has also worked as consultant and then Chief Technology Officer at the NLP software company YY Technologies, and has been a visiting researcher at universities in Oslo, Cambridge, Saarbrücken, and Melbourne. His central research interests are in wide-coverage grammar engineering for both parsing and generation, lexical representation, the syntax–semantics interface within Head-Driven Phrase Structure Grammar (HPSG), and methodologies for evaluation of semantically precise grammars.

Anna Kibort is a British Academy Postdoctoral Fellow in the Department of Linguistics, University of Cambridge, and visiting researcher in the Surrey Morphology Group, University of Surrey. Her research interests are in morphosyntax and linguistic typology. She is a contributing author in *The Cambridge Encyclopedia of the Language Sciences*, edited by Patrick Hogan (2010).

Keith Plaster is a graduate student in the Department of Linguistics at Harvard University in Cambridge, MA. His research interests include phonology, morphology, and the phonology–morphology interface; the synchrony and diachrony of gender and noun classification systems; and language change. He is currently writing his PhD dissertation on change in morphologically governed accent systems.

Maria Polinsky is Professor of Linguistics at Harvard University in Cambridge, MA. She received her PhD in 1986 from the Russian Academy of Sciences; prior to her arrival at Harvard she taught at the University of Southern California and the University of California, San Diego. Her research interests include language universals and their explanation, comparative grammatical theory, and the expression of information structure in natural language. Her current research projects include the acquisition or loss of categorization in language and the theoretical and processing aspects of ergativity.

Gergana Popova worked as a lecturer at the Department of English and American Studies, Sofia University. She wrote her PhD on the verbal feature of aspect at the Department of Language and Linguistics, University of Essex, and now teaches at Goldsmiths, University of London. Her research interests are in theoretical morphology and morphosyntax.

Geoffrey K. Pullum is Professor of General Linguistics and Head of Linguistics and English Language in the School of Philosophy, Psychology, and Language Sciences at the University of Edinburgh. He formerly taught at the University of California, Santa Cruz, and has been a Fellow at both the Center for Advanced Study in the Behavioral Sciences at Stanford and the Radcliffe Institute for Advanced Study at Harvard. His interests span much of linguistics, including the philosophy of linguistics and applications of logic in formalizing syntactic theories. He also works in descriptive English grammar. His book with Rodney Huddleston, *The Cambridge Grammar of the English Language* (2002), won the Linguistic Society of America's Leonard Bloomfield Book Award in 2004.

Ivan A. Sag is the Sadie Dernham Patek Professor in Humanities and Professor of Linguistics at Stanford University. He is a Fellow of the American Academy of Arts and Sciences and the Linguistic Society of America. In 2005, he received the LSA's Fromkin Prize for distinguished contributions to the field of linguistics. His research focuses on syntax, semantics, and language processing. He is the author or co-author of ten books, as well as over a hundred articles in venues as diverse as *Linguistics and Philosophy* and *Nature Neuroscience*. A member of the research teams that invented and developed Generalized Phrase Structure Grammar (GPSG) and Head-Driven Phrase Structure Grammar (HPSG), his current research primarily concerns constraint-based lexicalist models of grammar and their relation to theories of language processing.

Hans-Jörg Tiede is Associate Professor of Computer Science at Illinois Wesleyan University. He is interested in the application of logic to mathematical and computational linguistics as well as the methodology of linguistics. He has published several articles on the strong generative capacity of proof-theoretical grammars and model-theoretic syntax. A recent survey of applications of modal logic in linguistics, co-authored with Lawrence Moss, was published in the *Handbook of Modal Logic* (Elsevier 2007). A paper on the role of recursion in linguistics, co-authored with Lawrence Stout, appeared in *Recursion in Human Languages* (Mouton de Gruyter 2010), edited by Harry van der Hulst.

Abbreviations

1	first person
2	second person
3	third person
ABL	ablative
ACC	accusative
ACT	actual
ALL	allative
AUX	auxiliary
DAT	dative
DIST	distal
DU	dual
ERG	ergative
F	feminine
FOC	focus
FUT	future
GEN	genitive
HON	honorific
IMPRF	imperfect
INF	infinitive
INS	instrumental
LOC	locative
M	masculine
MID_HON	mid-honorific
N	neuter
NEG	negative
NMLZ	nominalizer
NOM	nominative
NONVIR	nonvirile
OBL	oblique
OM	object marker
PERS	personal
PFV	perfective
PL	plural
POSS	possessive
POT	potential
PRF	perfect
PRIV	privative

PROP	proprietive
PRS	present
PRT	particle
PST	past
PTCP	participle
SG	singular
VEG	vegetable

1

Introduction

Anna Kibort and Greville G. Corbett

Features are fundamental to linguistic description. Linguists frequently turn to them as they try to understand and model the complexity of natural language. From grammars of familiar and less familiar languages, couched in different theoretical linguistic frameworks, to automated language parsers, generators and translators – in all such resources one finds distinctions variously captured with features. We can postulate a feature NUMBER, with the values 'singular' and 'plural', as seen in pairs of forms such as *hat* ∼ *hats*, *loaf* ∼ *loaves*, *child* ∼ *children*, *rhododendron* ∼ *rhododendra*. The feature captures the idea that both the singular and the plural items share information in their respective sets. This information is accessed for agreement purposes: for example, all the plural items are modified by the determiner *these* rather than *this* – even though the plural value of number is realized morphologically in different ways for different lexical items. Other features include CASE (nominative, accusative, dative, ergative, etc.) and PERSON (1st, 2nd, 3rd). Features show consistency across items, and to some extent across languages. Features may also be phonological (specifying, for example, whether a consonant is voiced), morphological (labelling the inflectional class of an item), syntactic (labelling syntactic categories such as phrase types and parts of speech), or semantic (such as ANIMACY).

The notion of feature emerged in inquiries as to the nature of the phoneme, in which Trubetzkoy and Jakobson were prominent; this line of research reached a high point in Jakobson, Fant, and Halle (1952). From then on, the use of features moved out into other branches of linguistics: in the 1960s they were taken into lexical semantics (Katz and Fodor 1963), into syntax (Harman 1963; Katz and Postal 1964; Chomsky 1965) and into morphology (Matthews 1965). A key development was Generalized Phrase Structure Grammar by Gazdar, Klein, Pullum, and Sag (1985); these authors brought together the linguistic work of Stockwell, Schachter, and Partee (1973) with the formal work of Kay (1979) to offer a coherent theory of features.

The impact of features has increased steadily so that today, given a group of linguists of varied theoretical persuasions, the use of features is likely to be something they share. While features appear to be common currency, they also reveal our differences strikingly: we do not understand and use them in the same way. They are therefore a fine topic to put at the heart of a discussion between linguists with different theoretical orientations but common interests. Our discussion – this book – does not just take features as the starting point. We take features to be essential to how we do linguistics, a part of our intellectual infrastructure – one which needs care and work.

There are five issues which recur as we work with features, both throughout linguistics, and in this book. We discuss these below primarily using morphosyntactic features for illustration, though the issues are more general.

Identification Linguists have to establish which features and which values are appropriate for a given language. Sometimes this seems straightforward: 'French has a gender system with two gender values' is an analysis that few would contest. In other instances there have been disputes lasting decades. A notorious example is the long debate on the number of gender values in Romanian. The number of case values in Latvian is a debate of current interest. Definiteness is a particularly difficult feature since the need for it, or not, in various languages is the source of some disagreement. Danon in this volume discusses the specific and challenging question of whether a definiteness feature is required in Hebrew. It is attractive to look for some general yardstick, an external arbiter, to help resolve such instances. However, Pullum and Tiede show in their chapter that there are principled reasons why we cannot expect simple answers when we ask whether postulating a feature in an explicit linguistic description is justifiable or not.

Meaning and function If we believe that a particular feature and its values are justified, how is a linguistic element assigned a particular feature value? How does a speaker of French allot nouns to one or other gender value? What happens with new borrowings? A more sophisticated version of this question is asked in the chapter by Plaster and Polinsky on the gender of nouns in Dyirbal. And the apparently easier features like number conceal tricky problems too, as Copestake and Flickinger demonstrate in their chapter.

Status Our descriptions sometimes imply that instances of feature specifications are all 'on a par', and this would be the simplest situation. And yet we need look no further than basic English sentences like *The girl reads* to see that this is not so. *The girl* is singular for a 'good' reason – there is but one girl. *Reads* is singular because of the rule of syntax requiring it to agree in number with its subject (not because there is a single reading event). This distinction, between inherent and contextual features, is discussed in Booij (1994, 1996), following Zwicky (1986b) and Anderson (1992), and is taken up in Kibort's contribution. Minimalism draws a comparable distinction between interpretable and non-interpretable features, due to Chomsky (1995; also 2001: 4–6), which Adger reviews and develops in his chapter. Distinctions between realization options available to a feature are further used by Kibort to compare different features.

Structure and interactions Within a feature, there are different ways of structuring the values, in terms of the number of values and their relations to each other. This is a recurring theme, discussed especially by Dresher, Corbett, and Adger. The issues are compounded by the interactions of features, seen particularly in the chapters by Dresher and Sag.

Domain And finally, what is the domain of a feature? 'Domain' is a cover term for a set of questions on the structures within which features are distributed and the items which have access to them. Within syntax, the question of 'locality' is a major long-standing issue, and it receives a new treatment in Sag's chapter. The general issue of domain is also at the heart of Popova's chapter, where the operation of features at the syntax–morphology interface is investigated in periphrastic constructions.

There is much more to be understood about features: how they function, within and across linguistic components; and the information they encode, in individual languages and cross-linguistically. Since at the simplest level we use features to make generalizations, to capture similarities, some contributors to our volume focus on this part of the issue: the sorts of feature, their possible types of interaction, the ways in which requirements of identity are modelled, and the structures within which featural information is available or not available. Others focus on the information encoded by features, on what the possibilities are, particularly when we compare across languages. It is important to bring together these two strands: the discussion of the formal properties of features and an awareness of their diverse content in the world's languages. We should do this across the sub-discipline boundaries; thus theorizing about features in morphology and syntax can gain insights from phonology, and vice versa.

To make progress towards these objectives we organized a Workshop on Features in London on 1–2 September 2007, which gathered linguists who had grappled with features within theoretical and applied models and others who had considered the range and variability of features in the world's languages. The Workshop attracted nearly a hundred participants, who took the opportunity to discuss features in a truly ecumenical spirit and were glad to be questioned on the foundations of their theoretical stance on features. This resulted in a congenial atmosphere and fruitful debate.

This volume contains a selection of the papers from the Workshop, grouped into three thematic parts: 'Key Notions', 'Perspectives from Syntactic Description and Theory', and 'Formal Perspectives'. The authors have made a special effort to spell out their assumptions and have tried to identify areas of common ground with other approaches. As a result, the volume contains clear expositions of features from authoritative proponents of different approaches. The selected perspectives represent major areas of linguistic research where features are used.

The first part of the volume, on key notions, opens with a chapter by **Greville Corbett** entitled '**Features: essential notions**', which presents a survey of the use of features in the key components of grammatical description. Corbett advocates sharp definitions: distinguishing features which are at work in particular components (e.g. morphology, syntax, semantics) and at particular interfaces (e.g. morphology and semantics, morphology and syntax) will help us confirm claims that syntax is both phonology-free and morphology-free.

Corbett also discusses the issue of the internal structure of features. He argues against adopting binarity as the universally applicable principle of the organization of feature values, and demonstrates that some systems of values may be better represented by an unstructured (flat) list, while for others we may need the concepts of a facultative value (a value which the speaker is not required to use) and of superclassing (when an otherwise well-established inherent feature value is facultative when it is used contextually in agreement). He discusses the issue of 'inequality' among the values of a feature, bringing in the notion of 'defaults' that has been employed to model different ways in which such inequality manifests itself. He also draws a distinction between inherent and contextual features and recalls three major types of legitimate mismatch between feature values which pose a problem for any syntactic theory that relies on matching feature specifications: agreement with lexical hybrids, constructional mismatches including agreement with conjoined phrases, and agreement within analytical verb phrases (in periphrastic constructions).

Finally, Corbett highlights problems of intra-linguistic and cross-linguistic correspondence of features and values that arise in the construction of an inventory of features and values for a language, comments on standardization attempts with regard to features, and closes on a hopeful note that the work on features has already started moving in a desirable direction, which will eventually enable us to make principled rather than habitual or intuitive choices in our linguistic description, theorizing, and applications.

The following chapter is by **B. Elan Dresher** on '**Feature hierarchies and contrast in phonology**'. Dresher argues that the properties of phonemes that are distinctive in a given phonological system depend on which phonological features are contrastive and which are redundant. He argues that the correct approach to determining contrastive features is not the minimal pairs approach but the contrastive hierarchy, derived by successively splitting the inventory of phonemes by a hierarchy of features. This approach can be compared to the method of establishing the number of morphosyntactic values in a language, developed by Andrej Zaliznjak and the members of the Set-theoretical School – see Chapter 2, Section 2.3.1 for an overview. Hence, Dresher's chapter offers useful insights for theoretical work on grammatical features, as parallels can be drawn between: (i) distinctive phonemes that serve to differentiate words, and inflectional contrasts that serve to differentiate semantic and syntactic functions of words; (ii) distinguishing contrastive features from redundant features based on their function rather than their phonetic characteristics, and distinguishing grammatical feature values on the basis of function rather than form; (iii) applying a hierarchy of features to split the whole inventory of phonemes in a given language into contrastive features, and applying different morphosyntactic contexts to the whole inventory of lexical elements to identify distinctions that we can call 'features' and their 'values' (see Corbett this volume, Section 2.2.1).

Dresher's observation that contrastive hierarchies in different languages may be different even if their segmental inventories look similar echoes the observation about the 'correspondence problem' in grammatical description: for grammatical features too, their values may have different meanings depending on the system of which they are a part, both in terms of the number of oppositions and in terms of the semantics of the values.

Finally, Dresher contrasts active and inert phonological features (Section 3.2.2); a feature is active if 'we have evidence of its existence by virtue of the fact that it plays a role in the phonology (...)'. This is analogous in grammatical description to the distinction proposed between morphosyntactic and morphosemantic features: a feature is morphosyntactic if we have evidence of its playing a role in the syntax through its participation in syntactic agreement or government. This chapter is particularly helpful in reminding us of parallels in the methodology applied in the analysis of features in phonology and morphosyntax.

Anna Kibort's chapter '**Towards a typology of grammatical features**' offers a typology of features that has arisen from a consideration of the descriptive categories that have been found necessary for the grammatical description of the world's languages. The features discussed are those that are identified through morphology – that is, features which express meanings or functions correlating with different forms of inflected words.

Following from earlier work that had been done on types of inflection, and concurring with Corbett (this volume), Kibort argues that for a feature to be 'relevant to syntax' it must be involved in either syntactic agreement or government. She defines a feature as a set of values and the available options for their realization on linguistic elements. Therefore, a morphosyntactic feature – relevant to syntax – is a feature whose values are involved in either agreement or government: in the given language, there must be at least some elements which are targets of agreement or governees bearing a contextually realized value of the feature in question. Values of a morphosyntactic feature may also be realized inherently on controllers of agreement. In contrast, a morphosemantic feature – not relevant to syntax – is a feature whose values are inherent only: they encode regular semantic distinctions, but they are found only on elements which do not act as controllers of agreement. Hence, syntax is not sensitive to and does not need to manipulate the value of such a feature. Furthermore, a purely morphological feature (Corbett and Baerman 2006) – irrelevant to both syntax and semantics – is a feature whose values are inherent only, are not found on controllers of agreement, and additionally cannot be selected by the speaker based on the choice of meaning or function. Hence, the three feature types identified in this way are distinguished on the basis of their available realization options.

After establishing the criteria for recognizing different types of featural dependencies in a domain (i.e. agreement, government, and different types of multirepresentation of a feature value), Kibort applies the criteria to a set of difficult data from Kayardild (Tangkic), an extreme case-stacking language whose case-like inflections have been put forward as possible candidates for agreement in case, tense, mood, and polarity. She concludes that none of the Kayardild phenomena qualify as agreement. Instead, they are either instances of multirepresentation of a (governed) case value in a syntactic unit, or multirepresentation of the value of a morphosemantic feature (semantic case, or TAMP) within a unit for which the value has been selected for semantic reasons. This conclusion has a consequence for the construction of an inventory of possible morphosyntactic features in the world's languages: although number, gender, person, respect, case, and definiteness have been found to participate in syntactic agreement or government, tense, aspect, mood, and polarity appear to be limited to operating at the interface of morphology and semantics.

The second part of the volume focuses on features used in syntactic description and theory. It opens with a chapter by **Keith Plaster and Maria Polinsky** entitled '**Features in categorization, or a new look at an old problem**', which deals with the potential categorization bases used by languages in the determination of the value of the feature of gender. Although the values of gender could, in principle, correspond to any categorization of nouns on the basis of any properties of the referents they denote, most known gender systems are based on comparable formal and semantic distinctions. Plaster and Polinsky argue that the limitations imposed on the inventory of formal and semantic concepts that make up gender values in natural languages are due to learning limitations; formal characteristics relevant for gender determination must be perceptually salient to young children acquiring the language, and semantic concepts used in the determination of gender must be ones to which young children are sensitive (such as 'male', 'female', and 'animate'). To support their point, they analyse a particularly difficult case of noun categorization, that found in Dyirbal (Pama-Nyungan).

Dyirbal genders (noun classes) have been previously analysed in terms of complex conceptual associations (involving, famously, 'women, fire, and dangerous things'; Dixon 1972; Lakoff 1987). However, Plaster and Polinsky argue that many of the earlier proposed concepts and associations are beyond the scope of the understanding of a young learner, and hence would be very difficult for children to learn. On the other hand, the assignment of Dyirbal nouns to genders can be accounted for with a combination of rather straightforward semantic and formal features. The necessary and sufficient semantic features include the basic semantic labels 'animate', 'male', 'female', and 'edible'.

Plaster and Polinsky suggest that the Dyirbal genders arose from a reanalysis of an earlier classifier system: the original number of classifiers was larger than the number of resulting genders, and in several cases several classifier sets merged within a single gender. This merger was facilitated in some cases by formal analogy between the members of different small classes. As a result, there is not necessarily any synchronic conceptual association among all of the items in a given gender; in particular, the smaller subsets within a gender do not need to be radially related to the semantic core.

From the point of view of learnability, the account proposed by Plaster and Polinsky is much more straightforward than one based on attenuated abstract semantic linking. Furthermore, it makes Dyirbal gender assignment directly comparable to other noun classification and gender systems, which typically rely on a combination of simple formal and semantic factors. Crucially, the proposed semantics of the Dyirbal genders is consistent with the semantic underpinnings of gender classifications across the world's languages. Thus, the Dyirbal system emerges as much less exotic than previously thought.

The chapter by **Gabi Danon**, entitled '**The definiteness feature at the syntax–semantics interface**', examines definiteness as found in Hebrew.

Complex genitive constructions in Hebrew, called construct state nominals, are known to give rise to so-called 'definiteness spreading': the definiteness value of the entire construct state nominal, which lacks an independent article, is determined by the definiteness value of its embedded genitive. When the embedded genitive carries a definite article, both the embedded phrase and the entire construct state nominal phrase are always syntactically definite, and hence trigger definite agreement on modifying adjectives. From the semantic perspective, however, when the embedded phrase carries the marker of definiteness, the construct state nominal gives rise to four interpretation patterns, with all possible combinations of the definite and indefinite interpretations for the construct nominal phrase and the embedded nominal phrase.

Danon argues that the differences in the range of interpretations of complex genitive constructions observed in Hebrew vs. other languages point to two different strategies for constructing the meaning of complex nominals: the Hebrew strategy relies on sharing, or spreading, the feature of definiteness, while in other languages definiteness is not present as a feature to be shared. Since definiteness spreading in Hebrew evidently depends on the syntactic structure it is in, Danon argues that it has to be regarded a morphosyntactic feature, and demonstrates that semantic definiteness on its own (i.e. definite interpretation) does not always spread in a construct state nominal.

Finally, Danon tackles the issue of whether definiteness in Hebrew should be analysed as a bivalent feature, or a monovalent feature whose presence alternates with a lack of specification. He adopts the latter approach, arguing that it accounts for various observed asymmetries between definiteness and indefiniteness. The data he discusses are of importance for any framework that sets out to model the behaviour of a feature in the syntax.

Gergana Popova's contribution focuses on '**Features in periphrastic constructions**'. It has been observed in the literature that in periphrastic constructions the morphosyntactic features associated with the expression as a whole cannot be derived easily from the meaning of the constituent parts. For example, in the English present perfect the feature value expressing the 'perfect' cannot be directly associated either with the present tense auxiliary verb *have* or with the participle in *-en*. It is only the combination of the two that can be said to express the perfect tense or aspect. This chapter examines the mismatches of the meaning of feature values associated with the clause (such as tense values) and the values found on analytic forms realizing these values. Examples are drawn from Bulgarian, a Slavonic language with a particularly rich synthetic and analytic verbal morphology, and Popova demonstrates that feature matching in periphrastic constructions is more complex than has been suggested in the literature.

Arguing for a realizational approach to morphology, Popova shows that periphrastic constructions are more amenable to a top-down account, where the construction is a result of the association of a lexeme with some morphosyntactic properties, rather than a bottom-up approach, where the features which are associated with the construction as a whole should be associated first with some or all of its elements. After an examination of some agreement data which are problematic for existing realizational approaches to periphrasis, she suggests a modification of the framework of Paradigm Function Morphology, which allows her to accommodate the difficult data. As linguistic theory struggles to resolve the problem of periphrasis with frequently inadequate devices, Popova's contribution provides an insight into how the construction of meaning in language is apportioned between syntax (sentence structure) and morphology (word structure).

The second part of the volume is rounded off by a chapter by **David Adger** presenting 'A Minimalist theory of feature structure'. While clarifying how features are used in Minimalism, Adger explores the implications, for the featural structure of syntactic objects, of the idea that structure embedding is only a function of Merge – that is, that structure embedding in human language is only ever syntactic. He develops this idea into a fairly explicit proposal for the structure of lexical items and the syntactic trees built up from them. Within such a framework, the feature structures that are the basic atoms of syntax (i.e. lexical items) do not involve embedding of one feature inside another. This 'No Complex Values Hypothesis' stands in stark contrast to any 'lexicalist' theories of grammar, which assume rich featural structure for lexical items, in that almost all the interesting structure is syntactic, although the information which leads to the building of that structure is almost entirely lexical.

Adger's theory involves two types of feature: category features (C, T, V, N, D, etc.) and morphosyntactic features (case, number, person, finiteness, definiteness, etc.), and an account of how these come together to make 'flat'-structured categories which are sets of ordered pairs. Hence, features are ordered pairs, bearing an obligatorily specified attribute and a possibly empty value. Each lexical item consists of a single valued category feature and a number of other features, and the distribution of category features in syntax follows from independently specified hierarchies.

Within such conception, a grammar is a lexicon of items together with a set of operations. The language can be taken as the closure of the operations over the lexicon – this can be viewed algorithmically or declaratively as a specification of constraints on admissible trees. Operations are assumed always to be triggered: the trigger is the presence of an unvalued feature.

Since the No Complex Values Hypothesis imposes restrictions in the analysis of selection and movement, Adger exemplifies theoretical solutions to some problems of non-local dependencies involving agreement or categorial features. Although the proposed theory may not be ultimately 'minimal', it is an explicit feature theory offered within a broadly Minimalist framework.

The third part of the volume offers three different 'Formal perspectives' on features and opens with a chapter by **Ann Copestake and Dan Flickinger** which discusses '**Features and computational semantics**'. The authors argue for the relevance of compositional semantics to modern computational linguistics. They point out that, due to rising demand and technological progress, semantic representations are already being used in the most successful question answering applications, and are introduced in other applications that involve broad-coverage text processing, such as information extraction systems and even machine translation and summarization.

As semantics is increasingly treated as a way of providing a better level of abstraction for forms of matching operations to support the applications listed, certain representation decisions have to be made with regard to features derived from morphology and syntax. The context for these decisions involves: lack of an underlying knowledge base (hence semantic processing is relatively shallow); lack of generally available broad-coverage lexicons with detailed lexical information (hence semantic processing cannot require such information); the necessity to allow for inter-sentential anaphora and text structure (hence these have to be built in the semantic representation, even though they might not otherwise need to); and the need to avoid multiplication of readings (hence the development of underspecified semantic representations). Apart from underspecifiability, computational semantic representation languages must have expressive adequacy, grammatical compatibility (most importantly with syntactic information), and computational tractability.

Copestake and Flickinger exemplify semantic representation in computational grammars with HPSG-based feature structures. These are constructed using Minimal Recursion Semantics (MRS; Copestake, Flickinger, Sag, and Pollard 2005), standard predicate logic augmented with generalized quantifiers and flattened out to represent scope underspecification. This representation is already employed in large-scale DELPH-IN grammars, which are used in information extraction and question answering, as well as machine translation, e-mail response, and ontology extraction. The work on feature sets for DELPH-IN grammars is ongoing, and in their final section the authors discuss English plural marking as an illustration of the issues which arise when trying to link a feature which has been identified through morphology with a formal account.

Ivan Sag's contribution concerns '**Feature geometry and predictions of locality**'. Issues of locality are sometimes left implicit in theoretical discussions; therefore, after illuminating the historical background, Sag surveys the issue of locality of selection (and the related issues of idiomatic expressions, control of overt pronominals, and cross-linguistic variation in lexical sensitivity to filler–gap dependencies). He discusses extensively the issue of locality of construction – the problem of delimiting the syntactic and semantic information accessible to grammar rules. He argues that grammatical theory should provide a characterization of what constructional patterns are in principle possible and claims that, if the only constructional patterns that exist are those involving mothers and daughters, non-local phenomena can be accounted for as involving local encoding and inheritance of grammatical information. All selection being local is a consequence of particular features encoding inherited properties and of employing general principles about how such specifications are inherited.

Sag develops his claims within the framework of Sign-Based Construction Grammar (SBCG), a kind of HPSG – given that it embodies, among other things, signs, linguistically motivated types, type constraints, and a hierarchically organized lexicon – blended with Construction Grammar, as it draws a fundamental distinction between signs and constructs. Two basic principles of SBCG, the Subcategorization Principle and the Head Feature Principle, interact with appropriate lexical specifications and a particular inventory of features to make predictions of locality – a principled circumscription of the domains in which lexical selection and constructional constraints apply. In addition, Sag offers localist analyses within SBCG of a number of phenomena involving non-local grammatical dependencies, such as non-local case assignment in English and in case-stacking languages, various filler–gap dependencies, several phenomena in which a particular argument realized within an expression must be 'visible' to an external entity that combines with that expression, and idiomatic expressions. Other frameworks have not as yet provided explicit hypotheses about how such theoretical issues are to be resolved.

The volume closes with **Geoffrey Pullum and Hans-Jörg Tiede** on '**Inessential features and expressive power of descriptive metalanguages**'. Their chapter is informed by the idea of model-theoretic syntax: the structures of natural language expressions that have to be described can be seen as structures in the model-theoretic sense, and a grammar can be seen as a theory in the logical sense, so that a structure is grammatical if and only if it satisfies (or, equivalently, is a model of) the statements in the grammar. Logics of different power and order can be employed to describe grammatical structures, but as long as they are applied to strings, their descriptive power is relatively weak.

Since the most important structures employed in natural language syntax are labelled constituent-structure trees, Pullum and Tiede apply a series of logics of increasing power to trees, settling on modal logics (rather than the even more expressive weak monadic second-order logic), and relating the model-theoretic approach to the generative approach via the concept of definability. As an example of how grammars of certain specific types can be formalized in certain specific logics, they demonstrate how a basic modal logic is capable of defining the set of all the parse trees obtainable from an arbitrary context-free phrase structure grammar.

Finally, they consider labelling the trees with features instead of atomic category labels. As an example, if each node is allowed to satisfy multiple atomic formulae, each atomic formula corresponds to a binary valued feature. However, Pullum and Tiede demonstrate that, in the context of a particular descriptive metalanguage in which the feature is used, a feature can be considered superfluous if one can eliminate it from the grammar without any loss to the description. They follow this with Kracht's (1997) purely structural definition of uselessness applying to features (informally, a feature is 'inessential' 'if its distribution is fixed by the other features'). When examined from this perspective, features such as GPSG's SLASH and BAR, as well as ordinary morphosyntactic features such as CASE, turn out to be inessential in Kracht's technical sense. Hence they can, perhaps, be regarded only as mnemonics for human-readability of constituent-structure trees. On the other hand, other features which seem superfluous in the intuitive descriptive sense may turn out essential in the technical sense.

Their conclusion is that the distinction between features which are technical artefacts and features which are properly motivated distinguishing properties of linguistic expressions cannot, at least at this stage, be reduced to any formal criterion. We take this to mean that descriptive and typological linguists are not wasting their time trying to capture, even if informally, the distinctions that they find relevant in the description of natural languages. Equally we need to take on board the authors' warning that we cannot study the issue of what features we need without also working on the question of what strength of metalanguage is appropriate for syntactic description.

This concludes the overview of the contents of the present volume. We hope that the volume will inspire more research on features, which is so obviously needed. In signing off, we wish to express our gratitude to all the authors, whose excellent contributions have moved forward the frontier of research on features. We also thank all the participants in the Workshop, as well as our colleagues from the Surrey Morphology Group, for very fruitful discussion of the issues raised.

The Workshop on Features was organized as the dissemination conference during the project 'Grammatical features: a key to understanding language', funded by the UK's Economic and Social Research Council (grant number RES-051-27-0122). We are grateful for this support and opportunity. We also wish to thank the Linguistics Association of Great Britain (LAGB) who supported the Workshop with a conference grant, the most efficient and generous local organizers of LAGB 2007 at King's College London to which the Workshop was attached, Devyani Sharma, Eleni Gregoromichelaki, and Suzanne LaBelle, and – last but not least – Penny Everson, Lisa Mack, and Claire Turner for their careful assistance with proofreading and indexing. Anna Kibort's editorial work on this volume was undertaken while she was generously supported by a British Academy Postdoctoral Fellowship.

Part I

Key Notions

2

Features: essential notions

Greville G. Corbett

2.1 Introduction[1]

Features have been central to linguistics, implicitly or explicitly, from the earliest times. They are 'standard currency': in particular, each of the various syntactic frameworks relies heavily on them. To understand why, one has only to attempt a description of English syntax without features. Rule after rule, or constraint after constraint, would have to be duplicated to allow for singular and plural forms (see Gazdar and Mellish 1989: 218–219 for a comparable demonstration from French). Features thus allow generalizations in syntax; they do so similarly in morphology (Corbett and Baerman 2006). And once we deal with orthogonal features, say case and number, the savings are substantial. Computational work too uses features in numerous applications (see Copestake and Flickinger this volume). While features are heavily used, they are often taken for granted. In fact the level of confusion (much of it not recognized) is considerable. This is a missed opportunity, since features are where different approaches converge. That is why we have put together this volume.

This chapter discusses basic issues, attempting to unpick some of the assumptions commonly made about features. And it includes some of the ways in which the field is moving forward. I hope that as a result linguists will make more conscious choices in the use of features.

---

[1] The support of the ESRC under grants RES-051-27-0122 and RES-062-23-0696 is gratefully acknowledged. I also wish to thank several colleagues for helpful comments: the participants in the Workshop on Features (1–2 September 2007), held in association with the LAGB meeting in London; Matthew Baerman, Dunstan Brown, Marina Chumakina, Patricia Cabredo Hofherr, Anna Kibort, Alexander Krasovitsky, Geoffrey Pullum, and Claire Turner; and two anonymous referees.

2.2 The use of features

As the use of features has expanded and developed, various distinctions have been drawn, and different conventions have arisen. It is worth revisiting these to check which we adopt for good reason and which may have become no more than unjustified habits.

2.2.1 Features for different components

Features are partial descriptions of linguistic objects; as such they allow us to capture regularities in different components. We therefore recognize features which apply within a given component, for example, semantic, syntactic, morphological, and phonological features.

There are also features which have an effect across component boundaries. Perhaps the best known are the morphosyntactic features (Matthews 1972: 162). On a strict definition, any such feature must have a role in both components; that is, morphosyntactic features must have a role in both syntax and morphology; they are not merely the sum of morphological and syntactic features. Such features may be termed 'interface features' (Svenonius 2007a). It is worth sharpening our definitions to distinguish morphosemantic features (with no role in syntax) from morphosyntactic features (which evidently have a role in syntax; compare Stump 2005: 52). Features like tense and aspect are often morphosemantic rather than strictly morphosyntactic.

Provided we can define and distinguish the feature types clearly, we can maintain certain interesting claims. First, syntax is phonology-free (Pullum and Zwicky 1988); that is, syntactic rules cannot refer to phonological features. A rule of the type 'vowel-initial verbs are clause-final' is excluded. And, second, syntax is also morphology-free (Zwicky 1996: 301; Corbett and Baerman 2006); syntactic rules cannot refer to morphological features. A rule of the type 'verbs of inflectional class II are clause-final' is excluded.

2.2.2 The internal structure of features

Some linguists assume that features are binary, while others allow for larger numbers of values.[2] Halle (1957) gives arguments for adopting binary features in phonetics and phonology, but this is unusual; the internal structure of features tends to be assumed rather than argued for. Assuming binarity leads some researchers to decompose feature values. Jakobson (1958) represents a

---

[2] Another possibility is unary features. They are employed mainly in phonology; for discussion of an example of their use in syntax see Warner (1988).

Features: essential notions 19

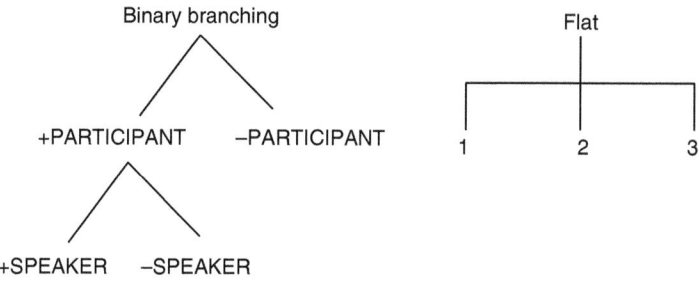

FIGURE 2.1 Feature structures: person

heroic failure in this regard, and there have been some less heroic campaigns since.[3]

When features appear to have more than two values, they can of course be split and be represented by additional binary features. This may mean there are superfluous values; this can be seen if three possibilities are simply represented by two binary features, and the issue is more serious with features with awkward numbers of values like five or nine. Alternatively, a geometry may be proposed in addition, making one feature subordinate to the other. Let us take a simple instance, a three-person system. An account with hierarchical binary branching is given in Figure 2.1, along with the flat structure.

It is often claimed that syncretism provides evidence to support binary branching structures. The branching structure allows of course for all person forms to be different, but also for first and second persons to be syncretic (by reference to the +PARTICIPANT node), or for all three to be syncretic (by reference to the root node). Now there are indeed languages which show syncretism of first and second persons, in the non-singular; these include Burarra, Dogon, and Manchad (Baerman, Brown, and Corbett 2005: 59). But now consider syncretisms like that found in German, where first plural and third plural are identical for all verbs (*wir finden* 'we find', *sie finden* 'they

---

[3] Jakobson's approach, particularly his analysis of case in Russian using three binary features, has been widely discussed and taken further; two examples are Chvany (1986) and Franks (1995: 41–55). There are three difficulties. First, there are further case values not covered by this analysis (see Zaliznjak 1973; Corbett 2008). Second, the analysis is supported by an appeal to syncretism, but does not cover all the actual syncretisms (Baerman, Brown, and Corbett 2005: 210). Third, as Gerald Gazdar points out (personal communication), there are 6720 possible ways to describe eight values using three binary features. In view of this, unless there are principled reasons for postulating particular binary features from the outset, it should not be taken as significant if there is an analysis using binary features which is partially successful.

find').[4] Here we see that the additional structure in the binary branching version is of no value in capturing the syncretism. We need to appeal to a different mechanism. We could specify that the −SPEAKER form is *findet*, and that by default the remaining plural forms are *finden*.

Now let us compare the flat structure. We can treat the syncretism of first and second persons by specifying the third person and having a default form for the first and second persons. For the German example, we can specify the second person form as *findet*, and a default form *finden* (for the remaining two unspecified forms). Thus the flat structure allows us to capture both types of syncretism. The binary branching structure gives no advantage: in the German example the structure is actually superfluous. This means that with small systems like this, the morphology actually provides no argument for a particular structure. The picture becomes more complex and interesting with larger numbers of values (see Baerman, Brown, and Corbett 2005: 59–61, 126–133 for illustration and analysis). It is shown there that attested features with larger numbers of values pose different problems for the two approaches.

My point here is the more basic one, namely that the internal structure of features is something to be argued for rather than merely assumed. Having pointed out an instance where we should have considerable reservations about a hierarchical feature structure, I should stress that, equally, there are instances where there *are* good reasons for postulating internally structured features. Evidence comes from the related issues of facultative values and superclassing.

We talk of *facultative values* when a feature has one or more values which the speaker is not required to use. Thus in Larike (a Central Moluccan language spoken on the western tip of Ambon Island, Indonesia) the number feature has the values singular, plural, dual, and trial; the trial is strictly for three referents. However, the trial need not be used for three referents, nor indeed the dual for two. These values are facultative: in their place the plural may be used (Laidig and Laidig 1990: 93; Corbett 2000: 44–45). The number feature as a whole is not optional: the singular is not used in place of the plural. Here the value which is employed when the facultative value is not chosen, that is, plural for trial and plural for dual, reveals the structuring of the feature values, as represented in Figure 2.2. The arcs indicate the facultative portions of the structure.

---

[4] German is not unique here: for comparable examples from other languages see Baerman, Brown, and Corbett (2005: 59–61).

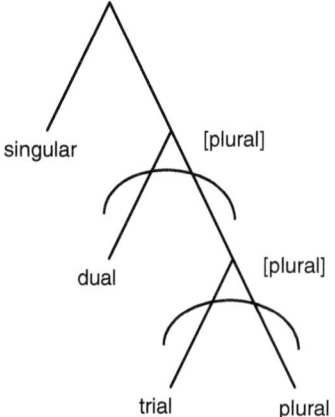

FIGURE 2.2 Facultative number values in Larike

Superclassing is a more restricted phenomenon in that here the choice of use is restricted to agreement. In superclassing, some but not all of the available distinctions are drawn; see the account of Bininj Gun-wok (Mayali) in Evans (1997: 127–140). Superclassing is also found in Jingulu, a non-Pama-Nyungan language of the Northern Territory of Australia (Pensalfini 2003 and personal communication). Like Bininj Gun-wok, Jingulu has four genders: masculine, feminine, vegetable, and neuter. Gender assignment is largely a matter of semantics: nouns denoting male animates are masculine, those denoting female animates are feminine, edible plants are vegetable, and the residue neuter. However, there are additional principles and some instances where the gender value of a given noun is hard to understand. Adjectives agree in gender as follows:

Jingulu (Pensalfini 2003: 160–161, 164–167; Corbett 2006: 151–154)

(1) Lalija   darra-nga-ju   **jamurriyak-a.**
    tea(M)   eat-1SG-do   cooled-M
    'I'm drinking cold tea.'

(2) Wijbirri-rni   **jalyamingk-irni.**
    white.person-F   new-F
    'The white girl is new-born.'

(3) Miringmi-rni   darra-nga-yi   **bardakurr-imi.**
    gum(VEG)-FOC   eat-1SG-FUT   good-VEG
    'I'll eat the sweet gum.'

(4) Jami-rna   dimana-rni   laja-ardu   **ngamulu**   lanbu.
    that.m-foc horse(m)-erg[5] carry-go   big.n   load(n)
    'That horse is carrying a big load.'

The examples we have seen show full agreement, demonstrating the existence of four genders. However, sometimes we find less than full agreement, as in these examples:

(5) Ngamulirni   **jalyamungk-a**   binjiya-ju,   birnmirrini.
    girl(f)   young-m   grow-do   prepubescent.girl
    'That little girl is growing up into a big girl.'

These next were offered by a speaker as alternatives:

(6) **ngininiki**   barndumi   or   **ngimaniki**   barndumi
    this.n   lower.back(veg)   this.veg   lower.back(veg)
    'this lower back'   'this lower back'

These two examples show superclassing, with masculine for feminine in (5), and neuter for vegetable in (6). The choices are not random: these are the possibilities for superclassing. The masculine can also be used as the ultimate default:

(7) **Jama**-rni   nyanyalu-ngkujku,   darrangku   kirdkilyaku.
    that.m-foc   leaf-having.n   tree(n)   bent.n
    'That bent tree is leafy.'

We may represent this situation as in Figure 2.3.

At the lowest level we have full (canonical) agreement. Then at a level up we have superclassing, where only some of the potential distinctions are drawn. And at the top level we have the ultimate default, which is the masculine in this system. Thus we have not only a default value but also a sort of halfway house, which we call 'superclassing'. The point is that we have an optional collapsing of forms. Since the masculine is the ultimate default, the argument depends on the possibility of neuter and of masculine agreement for vegetable nouns. In the case of feminines, there is no way to distinguish the masculine which might be expected for superclassing from the masculine as the ultimate default.

---

[5] The marker -*rni* (where *rn* indicates a retroflex nasal) is indeed an exponent of the feminine, of the ergative, and of the focus, the latter being a recent development from the ergative (Rob Pensalfini, personal communication).

```
                    [MASC]              ultimate default
                    /    \
                   /      \
                  /        \
             [MASC]       [NEUT]        superclassing
             /  \          /  \
            /    \        /    \
         MASC   FEM    NEUT    VEG      canonical agreement
```

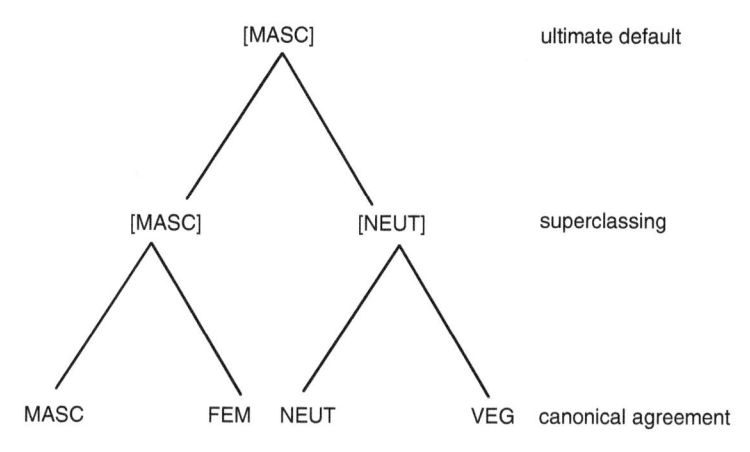

FIGURE 2.3 Gender superclassing in Jingulu

Looked at abstractly enough, the situation could be described as a kind of syncretism. But it differs significantly from the standard examples in respect of the context. For standard syncretism we specify contexts in morphological terms or in morphosyntactic terms; for example, the nominative is syncretic with the accusative in inflectional class II (a morphological context), or in the plural (a morphosyntactic context). In superclassing, the speaker has choices available, unrestricted by grammatical considerations. The choices are: the unique realization for the featural specification and a general default (this much is a common situation), and the third possibility, that is the speaker can mark agreement but not full agreement, reflecting the superclass of the appropriate feature value. And these simultaneous options do not depend on morphological or morphosyntactic context. Thus superclassing represents options available to the speaker, and the structure of those options can be seen as evidence that the values of the feature are structured.

2.2.3 *Feature values are not equal*

Let us now consider instances where, unlike those just discussed, there is no such obvious evidence for structuring. This would appear to be so when a feature has only two values. Yet we still find that the values are not equal. We can see this in at least four ways.

First we can simply look at frequency (see, for instance, Corbett 2000: 280–281 for a compilation of data). In various Indo-European languages, the sources reported always find the singular used more frequently than the plural (typically the singular is used in around three-quarters of the instances).

Second, we look at items which lack a value. We typically find that these exhibit non-random patterns. Thus in English, there are many nouns which do not have both number values. Many abstract nouns like *health*, *wealth*, and *happiness* have no plural; however, many can have a plural when recategorized (*a particular happiness* and *particular happinesses*). Those with no singular, like *scissors*, *binoculars*, and *trousers*, typically denote concrete objects in English. They have no plural; they have half an explanation in that they typically denote paired objects, yet not all paired objects (like *bicycle*, *bigraph*, *dromedary*) behave in this way. The patterns vary across languages, but in general the lack of particular values is not random.

Third, we should consider examples like this:

(8) To err is human.

One analysis of such constructions is that the verb has to agree, and yet there is no controller with the required feature specification. In such circumstances there is a 'least worst' option, which in English is the third person and singular number. Some might wish to attribute the choice to markedness considerations; this is a problematic step (see Haspelmath 2006 for the difficulties with markedness). It is at least worth pointing out that the choice of the feature value differs across languages, sometimes for number (Corbett 2000: 185–186) and often for gender (Corbett 1991: 203–212).

And fourth, we should note the use of 'evasive' feature values. Generally, when a choice between feature values is problematic, one of them is chosen. Thus if there is a choice between masculine and feminine, and the speaker does not know which (for instance, in asking a question), the particular language specifies masculine or feminine. Occasionally a third value is chosen (thus given an awkward choice between A and B, the form used is C). This is an 'evasive' use. For instance, in the Daghestanian language Archi, there are four gender values: gender I for male humans and gender II for female humans; gender III includes most other animates, and some inanimates; and IV has the remaining nouns. The word *lo* 'child' can be used with agreements for I (male human) or II (female human), as we might expect. In addition, the use of gender IV agreements is also possible (this is the gender for abstracts, some inanimates, and rather few animates). This use 'evades' the two obvious genders and so makes no commitment as to the sex of the child. Again the choice of the evasive feature value varies across languages.

Such inequalities are modelled in different ways, notably through the use of defaults. While linguists have rightly embraced the notion of defaults with enthusiasm, we should note that the term is used in rather different senses. We say that by default English verbs form the past tense in *-ed*. This default is then overruled for various exceptional verbs. This is a 'normal case default', according to Fraser and Corbett (1997: 44). Such instances are rather different from the type of default which comes into play to cover various different non-canonical situations (for instance, agreement with controllers which lack the relevant specification, including those which are totally absent, as in impersonals). This type is termed an 'emergency case default' (Fraser and Corbett 1997: 44).

In such instances it is important to be alert to the possibility of smuggling in additional feature values (Stanley 1967: 409–411 is an early warning with respect to this issue). If one is careless, the feature number, for instance, can have the values singular, plural, and unspecified, while apparently being a binary feature. This is something to be alert about when notions like 'valued' and 'unvalued' are introduced.

2.2.4 Features are not equal

Having noted that feature values are not equal, we should also recognize that features themselves are not equal, irrespective of their values. Consider a simple example like *stars shine*. Both subject and predicate mark number, but the feature is rather different for each. *Stars* is plural for good semantic reasons, and if we change number to the singular value, that would equally represent a semantic choice. On the other hand, the plural of *shine* is not motivated semantically. There is not necessarily more than one shining event. Rather, there is a syntactic motivation: the number of *shine* depends on the number of its subject. We may say that the number of the noun *stars* is in the 'right' place and that of *shine* is in the 'wrong' place. The first is an 'inherent' feature, and the second an 'imposed' feature, according to Zwicky (1986b). The term 'inherent' is stable: 'imposed' is often replaced by 'contextual', following Booij's (1996) use in his distinction of types of inflection; Corbett (2006: 123–124) transposes Booij's distinction to the features as such.

It is interesting to note that inherent and contextual features may co-occur on the same item and take different values, as in this example:

(9) Upper Sorbian (Faßke 1981: 382–383; Corbett 1987)
 moj-eho muž-ow-a sotr-a
 my-M.SG.GEN husband(M.SG)-POSS-F.SG.NOM sister(F)-SG.NOM
 'my husband's sister'

The head of the phrase, *sotra* 'sister' is inherently feminine. (According to the conventions of the Leipzig Glossing Rules (see 2.4.1), this is indicated in parentheses since it has no overt marker.) This noun is also inherently singular. It is contextually nominative, as determined by its syntactic position.

The adjective *mužowa*, which is derived from the noun *muž* 'husband', is also feminine, singular, and nominative; these are all values of contextual features: the case value derives from the syntactic position, and the gender and number values are by agreement with the head noun. It is the possessive *mojeho* 'my' which shows the great interest of the construction. It is marked as masculine, singular, and genitive. There is no expected controller to account for these features. Rather we have to say that the possessive adjective *mužowa* is controlling the agreement. We know what the feature values of *mužowa* are, namely feminine and singular – which would not, of course, account for the form *mojeho*. One solution is to suggest that possessive adjectives of this type have both inherent and contextual features of number and gender, and that their values are independent of each other (see Stump 2001: 15–17). In example (9), *mužowa* is contextually feminine and singular (agreement with *sotra*) and is inherently masculine and singular (controlling *mojeho*). Possessive adjectives of this type in Sorbian are always inherently singular; they may be masculine or feminine. Contextually they may take any number (singular, dual, or plural). Case is less clear. I have treated the case of the phrase as being externally determined (rather than as a matter of agreement within the phrase). Either way, the case of *mužowa* and *sotra* is contextually determined. But then to account for the case of *mojeho*, we need to say that *mužowa* governs the genitive (which is plausible at least in part, given that it is formed with a possessive suffix).

The key point, then, is that features may be inherent or contextual, and that the same feature may be inherent and contextual on one and the same item; the values of the features are then independent of each other. This distinction is the essential component of the distinction between interpretable and non-interpretable features within Minimalism.

2.2.5 *Constraining feature structures*

It is evident that there are common constraints on feature structures. We find languages like German, which distinguish gender in the singular but not in the plural, but we do not find a hypothetical language German', with gender distinguished in the plural but not in the singular. Constraints of this type were given by Greenberg (1963: 112–113), and are taken up as Feature Co-occurrence Restrictions in GPSG (Gazdar, Klein, Pullum, and Sag 1985: 27–29).

More recently, 'typing' of feature structures has been introduced. Typing is employed both to state the possible features and appropriate values, and to require that the necessary values are specified. The key reference is Carpenter (1992); this is a demanding read. Alternatively, Copestake offers 'a gentle but precise account' (2002: 3), and Sag, Wasow, and Bender (2003: 59–72) is a helpful exposition.[6] This is a clear point of division between HPSG, which uses typing, and LFG, which does not, relying instead on the notions of completeness and coherence.

2.2.6 Parts of speech modelled with features

When features are mentioned with regard to morphology and syntax, the first to come to mind may well be case, number, and so on. However, part of speech classification is frequently represented in featural terms too. There is explicit discussion in Gazdar, Klein, Pullum, and Sag (1985: 17–18); they refer to Chomsky (1965) as a predecessor (see 1965: 79–86 and 110–111). From one point of view this is fully consistent: features can perfectly well do the job. Features can also represent the projections of these categories in syntax. And yet it may be significant that, when linguists use features like this, a shorthand like NP or DP is often retained too. This preserves the intuition that part of speech categories and subcategories are one type of categorization, and morphosyntactic features are a cross-classification. Thus while it makes sense to use feature notation in both instances, this brings the need to classify the features according to their rather different functions.

2.2.7 The issue of identity

Identities constitute a considerable part of syntax. We need to guarantee identity of feature values across a range of constructions. The early method of managing this was copying. Feature values were simply copied, from controller to target, and thus they were bound to be identical. There are various problems with copying, as pointed out by Barlow (1992) and in Pollard and Sag (1994). For instance, take this Russian example:

(10) Russian
      Ja   side-l-a
      1SG.NOM   sit-PST-F.SG
      'I was sitting' (woman talking)

The verb is feminine in this example; if the speaker were male the verb would be masculine. But the form of the subject pronoun remains the same. In a copying account we require two different subject pronouns *ja* 'I', which are identical

---

[6] A more entertaining account can be found on the website of the book: http://hpsg.stanford.edu/book/slides/.

phonologically, simply so that the feature values which are copied can be different.

For this, and other reasons detailed in the sources above, copying is not used in HPSG and LFG. It was retained in Government and Binding, and replaced in Minimalism by 'checking'. This notion lacks a full formalization; for discussion of the issues see Asudeh and Toivonen (2006a: 409–420), Adger (2006), and Asudeh and Toivonen (2006b).

In other approaches, unification has had a major role. This goes back to work by Kay (1979). A valuable entry into this work is the account in Shieber (1986: 14–16). In HPSG, unification is central. However, it is the identity constraints which matter, since 'unification is but one of the many procedures used to solve systems of identity constraints' (Ginzburg and Sag 2000: 2, fn. 2). LFG uses equality and satisfiability. Unification is a way of implementing equality; thus unification is a submodule in an implementation (Ron Kaplan, personal communication).[7] In such approaches, our example (10) fits well; the subject has the feature values first person and singular, and these unify with (are compatible with) the feature values of the verb, namely singular and feminine.

While constraint-based approaches have had considerable success in using features to handle situations of matching, there are serious problems in those situations where a match might be expected but the feature values do not in fact match. There are two well-established sets of difficult data.

The first concerns lexical hybrids, such as *committee* in different varieties of English (Copestake 1995; Corbett 2006: 211–213). The problem with such hybrids is that their feature specification appears to differ according to the agreement target. For attributive modifiers they are singular (*this committee* is the only possibility, not *these committee). For other targets, both singular and plural may be found.

The choices are not free, but are tightly constrained by the Agreement Hierarchy (Corbett 2006: 207):

(11) The Agreement Hierarchy
      attributive > predicate > relative pronoun > personal pronoun

On the basis of this hierarchy, we can constrain possible agreement patterns as follows:

---

[7] Carpenter (2002) gives a fine overview of constraint-based approaches; he notes how the identities for which agreement is responsible have been one motivation in the development of computational work on language, starting with Colmerauer's early research (1970).

(12) For any controller that permits alternative agreements, as we move rightwards along the Agreement Hierarchy, the likelihood of agreement with greater semantic justification will increase monotonically.

Staying with *committee* and similar items, Table 2.1 shows the results of a large study.

The US data are from the Longman Spoken American Corpus (LSAC), which has five million words, and GB data come from the ten million word section of the British National Corpus (BNC) devoted to spoken language.[8] Attributive position is not included, since only singular agreement is found there, as just discussed. The remaining data are clearly in accord with the constraint given in (11).

To demonstrate that the familiar English example is representative of many others, consider the summary data from a range of languages shown in Table 2.2 (details can be found in Corbett 1991: 226–236; 2006: 214–218). Each of the hybrids listed conforms to the constraint of the Agreement Hierarchy, but each is a problem for straightforward unification accounts.

The second set of problems concerns constructional mismatches; these are constructions which have the same properties as lexical hybrids. That is, the agreements they control depend on the nature of the target. Like lexical hybrids, they are subject to the Agreement Hierarchy. The best-known example is conjoined noun phrases (which typically allow agreement with just one conjunct, normally the nearest, or with all).[9] Other types of constructional mismatches include pseudo-comitatives, syntactic/semantic head mismatches, and default form vs. agreement (Corbett 2006: 208–210, 220–224).

TABLE 2.1 Agreement with *committee* nouns (Levin 2001: 109)

	verb		relative pronoun		personal pronoun	
	N	% plural	N	% plural	N	% plural
US (spoken)	524	9	43	74	239	94
GB (spoken)	2,086	32	277	58	607	72

[8] As the English relative pronoun does not mark number, Levin checked his data and confirmed that singular verbs are normally found with *which*, and plural with *who*. He then counted relative pronouns as singular or plural on this basis, rather than establishing their number each time from the verb. Since relative *that* allows greater choice he included predicates of *that* within the predicate count. These decisions blur the picture somewhat, but there is information for recalculating and reinterpreting his results (2001: 32–33, 55–60).

[9] For a recent analysis of partial agreement in LFG, see Kuhn and Sadler (2007).

TABLE 2.2 The Agreement Hierarchy: a sample of the evidence from gender

	attributive	predicate	relative pronoun	personal pronoun
Chichewa diminutive for human	gender 7	gender 7	gender 7	gender 7 / (GENDER 1)
Serbian/Croatian/ Bosnian *d(j)evojče* 'girl'	n	n	n	n/F
Polish *łajdaki* 'wretches'	non_m. pers	non_m.pers / M.PERS	M.PERS	M.PERS
Konkani young females	f	N	no data	N
Russian *vrač* 'doctor' (female)	m / (F)	m / F	(m) / F	(m) / F
Serbian/Croatian/Bosnian *gazde* 'bosses'	f / (M)	(f) / M	((f)) / M	M

Notes:
1. lower case indicates syntactic agreement, and upper case SEMANTIC AGREEMENT
2. parentheses indicate a less frequent variant

Conjoined noun phrases bring with them the related issue of resolution rules, as illustrated in this classic example:

(13) Slovene (Lenček 1972: 60)
T-o   drev-o   in   gnezd-o   na   njem   mi
that-N.SG   tree(N)-SG   and   nest(N)-SG   on   3SG.N.LOC 1SG.DAT
bosta   **ostal-a**   v   spomin-u.
AUX.FUT.3DU   remain-M.DU   in   memory-SG.LOC
'That tree and the nest on it will remain in my mind.'

The Slovene resolution rules (called into play when agreement is with all conjuncts) determine that two singular conjuncts require a dual target, and two neuters require a masculine target. Hence the masculine dual verb. Recent references on resolution include Dalrymple and Kaplan (2000); Wechsler and Zlatić (2003: 171–195); Corbett (2006: 238–263).

A further identity problem, which has gone largely unnoticed, is that feature values need not match even within a periphrastic construction (Corbett 2006: 86–87). We might have assumed that within a single cell of a paradigm, which is how we may think of a periphrastic form, the values of shared features would be the same. However, this is not necessarily the case:

(14) Czech (Eva Hajičová and Jarmila Panevová, personal communication)
by-l-a   jste   velmi   laskav-á
be-PST-F.SG   AUX.2PL   very   kind-F.SG
'You were very kind' (addressed to a woman)

Such an expression is appropriate for polite address to a single addressee. No pronoun is included, but *vy* 'you' can be included if it is under contrastive stress (*Vy jste byla velmi laskavá*). The auxiliary verb, the clitic *jste*, is second person plural, while the past participle *by-l-a*, literally 'was', is singular. We therefore have a periphrastic verb, and its two parts have different values for number.

2.2.8 Matching across components

Everyone knows that tense does not match time, though there is a relation between them. In many languages it is obvious that morphosyntactic gender corresponds in part to a semantic distinction, but only in part. However, less evident mismatches across components sometimes pass unnoticed. Thus semantic number and morphosyntactic number are not equivalent; here the variation in the semantic value of number with different lexical items is constrained in a principled way by the Animacy Hierarchy (Corbett 2000: 55–57, 83–87). Similarly a morphological distinction may follow a phonological one, but not fully (thus Russian morphological alternations based on the palatalized vs. non-palatalized distinction do not completely follow phonological palatalization). Despite this common knowledge, some make unwarranted inferences from one component to another, perhaps on occasion misled by the similar names of the features. For instance, there has been some excitement about the apparent structuring of feature values based on the evidence of syncretic patterns; however, Baerman, Brown, and Corbett (2005) show that within morphology the possible patterns are extremely varied, and that inferences that morphology directly reflects semantic features and structure are unwise at best.

2.3 The inventory of features

There are several analyses in the literature in which features are sprayed around with disturbing nonchalance. The old warning still applies:

> So linguists fudge, just as has been done in the reflexive rule, by sticking on the arbitrary feature +REFL. Such a feature is a fudge. It might just as well be called +CHOCOLATE, which would in fact be a better name, since it would clearly reveal the nature of the fudge. (Lakoff 1972: ii)

As a counter to this profligacy, there are aspirations at various points in the literature to a list of features and values. It makes good sense to aim for such a list, which would be a simple typology, unless and until it is proved impossible. Such an inventory requires the solution to two problems, the analysis problem and the correspondence problem.

2.3.1 *The analysis problem*

For some languages it is relatively easy to determine the features and their values. In other languages it is a major undertaking; some famous instances have given rise to long-running disputes. A good start on the analysis problem was made by members of the Set-theoretical School, which included scholars such as Kolmogorov, Revzin, Zaliznjak, and Marcus. A careful and sympathetic survey is provided by van Helden (1993); the review of this work, by Meyer (1994), is a good entry point into the literature. Given that a detailed account is available in van Helden (1993), a simplified summary will be given here.

Zaliznjak and others worked out careful and consistent methods for determining the feature and value inventory of a language. A first step is to iterate through lexical items and contexts, so long as distinctions are discovered (see Table 2.3).

TABLE 2.3 The initial stage in establishing features and values (abstract schema)

	Item 1	Item 2	Item 3	...	...	...
Context 1						
Context 2						
Context 3						
...						
...						
...						

Where two items produce identical distinctions, the columns can be collapsed. Thus if two items are *cat* and *dog* in English, they will fit identically into contexts such as *this...* (*this dog* and *this cat* are equally good) or *the... sleeps* (*the cat sleeps* and *the dog sleeps* are both fine). Similarly if two contexts allow identical inventories of items the relevant rows can be collapsed. Consider now a typical instance from Russian, a language where the inflectional morphology has a much greater role than that of English (see Table 2.4).

If we had only the evidence of the first noun *žurnal* 'magazine', we would have to say that the contexts 1 and 3 provided no evidence for different values. However, when we put *gazeta* 'newspaper' in the same two contexts, this provides evidence for distinct feature values (the traditional nominative and accusative). Quite often the result is that the expected features and values are established, but that less clear instances emerge too. In fact, Russian has arguably ten case values rather than the traditional six (see Corbett 2008 for discussion).

TABLE 2.4 Establishing features and values: an example from Russian

	Item 1 *žurnal* 'magazine'	Item 2 *gazeta* 'newspaper'	Item 3	...	...	...
Context 1 *Na stole ležit...* 'on table lies...'	*žurnal*	*gazeta*				
Context 2 *Ona dumaet o...* 'she thinks about...'	*žurnale*	*gazete*				
Context 3 *Ona čitaet...* 'she reads...'	*žurnal*	*gazetu*				
...						
...						
...						

For each feature and especially for each value, we need rules as to when it is used. These are sometimes termed 'assignment rules'. I stress that for each feature and value both justification and assignment rules are required. In work on individual languages one or other may be favoured, according to the difficulty of the issues: thus in one language it may be easy to justify postulating a particular feature, but hard to pin down the rules for its use, while in another determining the number of values of a feature may be the intellectual challenge which has attracted attention.

2.3.2 *The correspondence problem*

In analysing and comparing languages we naturally use similar labels for the features proposed. Yet it is not self-evident that a particular feature (say number) corresponds across languages, and the values even less (Saussure 1916/1972: 161; Gazdar cited and discussed in Zwicky 1986a: 988–989). Yet typological work depends on our resolving these issues. We should continue to attempt to prove cross-linguistic validity of our features, through care about definitions, perhaps within a canonical approach (Corbett 2008). We should also note that the problem has an additional twist: even within a single language, feature values do not always correspond straightforwardly across the elements that carry them. This is shown for instance by gender in Romanian (Corbett 1991: 150–151), or number in Bayso (Corbett 2000: 181–183, based on Corbett and Hayward 1987).

2.4 Practicalities

Since features are shared across sub-areas of the discipline, from the highly theoretical to the most applied, there are practical steps which can have general benefit. There are various steps towards standardizing and generalizing. And then we shall refer to instances of using features in large-scale implementations, which serve as a valuable testing-ground for theories of features.

2.4.1 *Glossing*

Though features are common currency, they can lead to confusion even at the most basic level. Thus we may see PERF used to mean 'perfect' in one paper and 'perfective' in the next, sometimes without even an account of the abbreviations used. At this level the Leipzig Glossing Rules (Comrie, Haspelmath, and Bickel 2004) represent a useful step forward. They give standards for glossing, and propose some standard abbreviations. This is a bare minimum for the discipline.

2.4.2 *EAGLES (Expert Advisory Group on Language Engineering Standards)*

The report on morphosyntactic annotation of this group (Leech and Wilson 1996) represents an early attempt to grapple with the practical issues raised by features. It was restricted to languages of the European Union, which makes it typologically limited, and it does not fully distinguish parts of speech and semantic subcategories from morphosyntax (see 2.2.6 above). It appears that tags which were suggested for particular languages were included without having been rigorously compared with the general set established for a wider range of languages.

2.4.3 *The ISO: Lexical Markup Framework (LMF)*

The International Organization for Standardization (ISO), in particular Technical Committee ISO/TC 37, *Terminology and other language resources*, Subcommittee SC 4, *Language resource management*, worked for several years developing ISO 24613: 2008 'Language resource management – Lexical Markup Framework (LMF)'. The purpose (from the introduction) is this:

Lexical Markup Framework (LMF) is an abstract metamodel that provides a common, standardized framework for the construction of computational lexicons. LMF ensures the encoding of linguistic information in a way that enables reusability in different applications and for different tasks. LMF provides a common, shared representation of lexical objects, including morphological, syntactic, and semantic aspects.

LMF was intended for large-scale applications, and seemed a long way from linguists' main interests. Indeed the linguistic content was insecure. The Committee has taken note of some of the concerns of linguists in the published version.

2.4.4 E-MELD (Electronic Metastructure for Endangered Languages Data) and GOLD (General Ontology for Linguistic Description)

There were two main objectives behind E-MELD: contributing to the preservation of data on endangered languages, and developing the infrastructure for effective collaboration between electronic archives (Aristar Dry 2002). The first objective related to best practice in various areas. So far as it concerned morphosyntactic markup, the direction was not so much to suggest a standard as to ensure that non-significant differences in annotation should not hamper further understanding and analysis. This was consonant with the second objective, and led to initial work on an ontology of linguistic concepts (Farrar and Langendoen 2003).

2.4.5 Inventory of the features

There are references in the literature, usually almost as asides, that there could be an inventory of the features, from which particular languages draw. A list of the features would be the simplest possible typology, and it is surely something we should attempt to achieve. If we discover insurmountable problems we would then reasonably look for more complex alternatives.[10]

2.4.6 Large-scale grammar implementations

While it makes good sense to work out our feature descriptions on the basis of samples of key data, it is also important to ask whether they 'scale up' when used in large-scale applications. There are indeed substantial projects, based on HPSG and LFG. Based on HPSG there is the CSLI LINguistic Grammars Online (LINGO) project (http://lingo.stanford.edu/); this includes the English Resource Grammar (ERG) and the LKB (Lexical Knowledge Builder) grammar engineering system. For LFG there is the Parallel Grammar Project (ParGram), see http://pargram.b.uib.no/. This project includes a commitment to restrict the feature inventory, but the languages tackled so far cover a restricted typological space and so the features and values proposed are somewhat limited.

---

[10] Initial steps towards such an inventory can be found at http://www.features.surrey.ac.uk/.

2.4.7 *Tagging a large corpus*

Similarly, feature sets have to be up to the task of tagging large corpora, including corpora of morphologically rich languages. The IPI PAN corpus of Polish has over a million words, and the requirements for tagging were challenging.[11] The difficulties and analytical choices made are described in Przepiórkowski (2004: 22–37). Such large projects, where a whole corpus has to be accounted for, provide stern tests for feature inventories.

2.5 Conclusion and prospects

Features are central in mainstream linguistics, and they enjoy similar importance in linguistic frameworks which differ substantially in other respects. Features therefore need regular attention, so that we make principled rather than habitual choices in their use. Given their central position, it is not surprising that they bring with them many issues which need debate and resolution. A bright prospect is the bringing together of research into the logic of features, in computational work and some theoretical work, with the work on the substantive semantics of features, which is mainly due to typologists. A second hopeful sign is the 'bottom-up' standardization initiated by the Leipzig Glossing Rules. It is evident that we should know what is intended by others' glossing of examples. We should continue along this path, sharing definitions and conventions wherever possible, so that genuine theoretical differences are highlighted and evaluated.

---

[11] The acronym comes from the name of the host institution (in Polish), the Institute of Computer Science, Polish Academy of Sciences. See: http://korpus.pl/.

3

Feature hierarchies and contrast in phonology

B. Elan Dresher

'[D]ans la langue il n'y a que des différences' [In a language there are only differences]. Ferdinand de Saussure, Cours de linguistique générale (1916/1972: 166)

3.1 Introduction[1]

The notion of contrast has been central to linguistics since Saussure. With respect to phonology, the *Cours* goes on as follows: 'Ce qui importe dans le mot, ce n'est pas le son lui-même, mais les différences phoniques qui permettent de distinguer ce mot de tous les autres' ['The sound of a word is not in itself important, but the phonetic contrasts which allow us to distinguish that word from any other' (Saussure 1986: 116)]. That is, a phoneme is identified not only by its positive characteristics – for example, the fact that it sounds like [e] – but also by what it is not – that is, by the sounds it contrasts with.

The notion of contrast can be understood at several different levels. At the most basic level, it can refer simply to whether two sounds contrast in a language or not. In a language with five distinct vowel phonemes /i, e, a, o, u/, for example, [e] is different from [i], and these vowel sounds alone could

---

[1] An earlier version of this chapter was presented as the Linguistics Association Lecture at the LAGB Annual Meeting 2007, August–September 2007. I would like to thank members of the audience, as well as participants in the associated and partially overlapping Workshop on Features, for stimulating comments. The chapter has also benefited from comments by two anonymous reviewers for this volume. I would like to thank the members of the project on Markedness and the Contrastive Hierarchy in Phonology (Dresher and Rice 2007) for much help over the years; for comments on earlier versions of this chapter I am grateful to Peter Avery, Chiara Frigeni, Daniel Currie Hall, Manami Hirayama, Yoonjung Kang, Sara Mackenzie, Christine Pittman, Keren Rice, Vanessa Shokeir, and Anne St-Amand. This research was supported in part by grants 410-99-1309 and 410-2003-0913 from the Social Sciences and Humanities Research Council of Canada.

serve to differentiate words in the language: a word [pita], for instance, would be different from [peta]. Compare this situation with a language that had only four vowel phonemes /i, a, o, u/, where /i/ is allowed to vary between a sound like [i] and a sound like [e]. In such a language, both [pita] and [peta] may occur, but they are considered variants of the same word, not two distinct words.

This is often what people mean when they talk about acquiring the phonological contrasts of a language; that is, learning that there is or is not a contrast between [i] and [e]. Establishing at least this much is a prerequisite to further analysis, and in all the examples that follow I will assume that we know what the contrasts are at this most basic level.

But there is much more to contrast between sounds, and phonologists have traditionally been concerned with further aspects of contrast. One can study the phonetics of contrast to see, for example, how perceptually salient the difference between sounds is. For example, the contrast between [i] and [u] is more perceptible than the contrast between [i] and [ɨ]. It is reasonable to suppose that good contrasts will be favoured in inventories over poor ones (Liljencrants and Lindblom 1972; Flemming 2004), and this fact could have synchronic and diachronic consequences. This is an interesting topic, which I will refer to as 'phonetic contrast', because it is concerned with the surface phonetics of contrasts between sounds.

However, the study of phonetic contrast has not been the central preoccupation of phonologists or phonological theory since Saussure. On the contrary, an influential current of phonological theory – the mainstream, in fact – has held that the phonetics do not determine the way sounds pattern in the phonology of a language. In the very first issue of *Language*, in the seminal paper that popularized the term 'sound pattern', Edward Sapir wrote as follows: 'And yet it is most important to emphasize the fact, strange but indubitable, that a pattern alignment does not need to correspond exactly to the more obvious phonetic one' (Sapir 1925: 47–48).

Sapir's 'pattern alignment' amounts to the contrastive status of a phoneme, and this is not determined by phonetics. What does determine it? This is the topic of this chapter, what I will call 'phonological contrast'. Phonological contrast refers to those properties of phonemes that are distinctive in a given phonological system. In most theories of phonology, this means determining which features are contrastive and which are redundant.

For example, given that there is a contrast between /i/ and /u/, we want to determine, out of the various ways that these sounds differ, which particular dimension is the one most relevant to the phonology of the language: do /i/ and /u/ contrast with respect to [round], for example, or do they contrast with respect to [back]? Suppose the answer is that they contrast with respect to [back]. Then another question arises about the status of /a/ with respect to this contrast: does /a/ participate in the contrast by being contrastively [+back], or is /a/ outside the contrast, in which case [back] is redundant for /a/? In other words, what is the scope of the contrast based on [back]? If it applies over the entire set of vowels, then /a/ falls within its scope and takes a contrastive value for this feature; if its scope is limited to the non-low vowels, it is not relevant to /a/.

Such decisions are not self-evident. More surprisingly, they have seldom been discussed explicitly. But it is this kind of contrast that has been central to phonological theory for a century because of an abiding intuition that contrastive features are particularly important to the patterning of sound systems. If contrastive features play a special role in phonology, then we need to be clear about what they are and how to identify them.

Before continuing it may be worth returning to the issue of phonetics and sound patterns. Sapir's view that a pattern alignment may deviate from the phonetics was novel in 1925. Fifty years later it had become linguistic orthodoxy. In recent years the tide has shifted again. Much current work in phonology adopts the hypothesis that phonologies of languages are determined by phonetic principles. I will argue that this hypothesis is wrong. Without denying the contributions that phonetics can make to our understanding of sound systems, I will argue that the influence of phonetics, viewed apart from phonological contrast, has been overstated. Therefore, to understand the functioning of phonological systems we need to go beyond phonetics. In particular, I will argue that we need the approach to phonological contrast advocated here.

In this chapter I will first look at how decisions about contrastive features have been made in phonology. I will show that there are two different and incompatible approaches. I will argue that one of these approaches is wrong, and that the other, the contrastive hierarchy, appears to be right. I will then give some brief historical context to situate this approach in the history of phonology. The rest of the chapter will explore some applications of the contrastive hierarchy, arguing that it is indispensable to an account of many phonological phenomena.

3.2 Two theories of contrast

Phonologists have tended to oscillate between two main approaches to determining contrastive features. One approach involves extracting contrastive features by making pairwise comparisons of fully specified phonemes, with a special emphasis on *minimal pairs*. The other approach derives contrastive features by successively splitting the inventory by a *hierarchy of features*, first dividing the whole inventory on the basis of the first feature in the list, then dividing each subset by the other features in turn until all phonemes have been differentiated. Both approaches have a certain intuitive appeal, but they give conflicting results. I will argue that the first approach fails in a wide range of cases, while the second approach works in all inventories.

3.2.1 *The pairwise (minimal pairs) method*

Here is how Martinet (1964: 64) reasoned in arriving at the contrastive specifications for the French bilabial consonants /p, b, m/. Assume that the relevant features are [voiced] and [nasal]. Begin with their full specifications for these features:

(1) French bilabial consonants: full specifications

	p	b	m
voiced	−	+	+
nasal	−	−	+

We observe that /p/ and /b/ contrast only with respect to [voiced]. We will call two segments that are differentiated by a single feature a *minimal pair*. In pairwise comparisons, minimal pairs are particularly useful because the feature that distinguishes them must be contrastive. Thus, [voiced] is necessarily contrastive in /p/ and /b/. Similarly, /b/ and /m/ form a minimal pair contrasting only with respect to [nasal]; their specifications for this feature must also be contrastive. The other feature values can be predicted by the redundancy rules in (2b): /p/ is the only voiceless segment, and it is predictably [−nasal]; /m/ is the only nasal segment, and it is predictably [+voiced].

(2) French bilabial consonants: contrast via minimal pairs

　　a. Specifications that distinguish minimal pairs

	p	b	m
voiced	−	+	
nasal		−	+

　　b. Redundancy rules

　　　　i.　　[−voiced] → [−nasal]　　ii.　　[+nasal] → [+voiced]

The omitted specifications are those that are *logically redundant*, a concept we can define as in (3):

(3) Logical redundancy
 If Φ is the set of feature specifications of a member, M, of an inventory, then the feature specification [f] is logically redundant iff it is predictable from the other specifications in Φ.

A problem with relying on logical redundancy is that in many cases it does not provide a contrastive specification because there are not enough minimal pairs in the inventory. In the inventory in (1), /b/ participates in a minimal pair with both /p/ and /m/. But suppose our inventory of labial consonants consisted only of /p/ and /m/: now every feature specification is logically redundant because each is predictable from the others (4b).

(4) A language with only two bilabial consonants
 a. Full specifications

	p	m
voiced	−	+
nasal	−	+

 b. Redundancy rules

 i. [−voiced] → [−nasal]   iii. [+nasal] → [+voiced]
 ii. [−nasal] → [−voiced]   iv. [+voiced] → [+nasal]

Obviously, it is not possible to omit all these values from a contrastive specification. Some feature values must remain to differentiate the two phonemes. In the absence of minimal pairs, pairwise comparison cannot tell us which feature values are contrastive. We have to decide by some other means which feature takes precedence; in this case, whether voicing or nasality is more important.

3.2.2 *Contrastive specification by a hierarchy of features*

The second main approach to determining contrastive features takes feature precedence as its main property. This approach assigns precedence relations by ordering the features. Jakobson and Lotz (1949) use this method to arrive at contrastive specifications of the French bilabials. They do not begin with full feature specifications; rather, they begin with no features specified. As a first step, they divide the inventory into two sets on the basis of the feature [nasal] (5a). Now, /m/ is uniquely characterized, and only /p/ and /b/ must be further distinguished. The next feature applies only to the non-nasal set (they use [tense] but I will continue to use [voiced]), and distinguishes /p/ from /b/ (5b).

(5) French bilabial consonants: contrast via feature ordering [nasal] > [voiced]

   a. First division (/p, b, m/) based on [nasal]

	p	b	m
nasal	−	−	+

   b. Second division (/p, b/) based on [voiced]

	p	b	m
nasal	−	−	+
voiced	−	+	

In this approach, the ordering of the features is crucial. The specifications in (5b) are the result of ordering [nasal] ahead of [voiced], notated '[nasal] > [voiced]'. In other words, [nasal] has wider *scope* than [voiced].

If we applied the features in a different order we would obtain a different result (6):

(6) French bilabial consonants: contrast via feature ordering [voiced] > [nasal]

   a. First division (/p, b, m/) based on [voiced]

	p	b	m
voiced	−	+	+

   b. Second division (/b, m/) based on [nasal]

	p	b	m
voiced	−	+	+
nasal		−	+

If we were to make the first division based on [voiced], all segments would have a contrastive value for that feature, not just the non-nasal segments as in the previous order; [nasal] would then be relevant only to the [+voiced] set.

We thus have two possible contrastive hierarchies that give us two different sets of contrastive specifications. Though every omitted specification in (5b) and (6b) is of necessity logically redundant, neither ordering omits all logically redundant specifications. On this approach, logical redundancy is simply not the definition of phonological redundancy.

Feature hierarchies and contrast 43

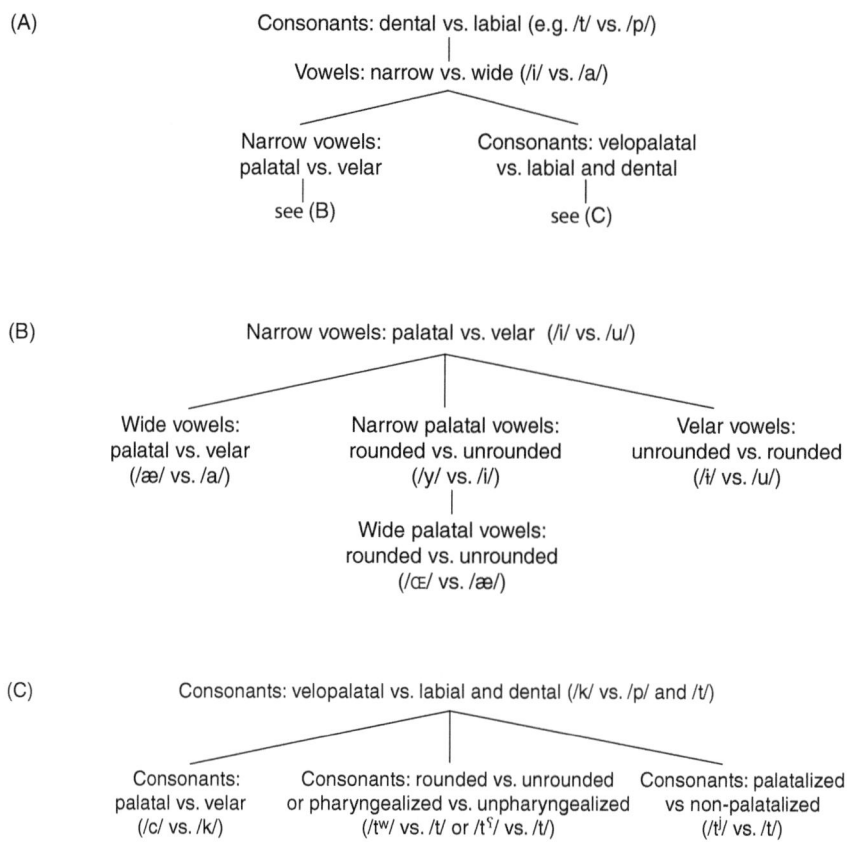

(A) Consonants: dental vs. labial (e.g. /t/ vs. /p/)
|
Vowels: narrow vs. wide (/i/ vs. /a/)
├── Narrow vowels: palatal vs. velar — see (B)
└── Consonants: velopalatal vs. labial and dental — see (C)

(B) Narrow vowels: palatal vs. velar (/i/ vs. /u/)
├── Wide vowels: palatal vs. velar (/æ/ vs. /a/)
├── Narrow palatal vowels: rounded vs. unrounded (/y/ vs. /i/)
│   └── Wide palatal vowels: rounded vs. unrounded (/œ/ vs. /æ/)
└── Velar vowels: unrounded vs. rounded (/ɨ/ vs. /u/)

(C) Consonants: velopalatal vs. labial and dental (/k/ vs. /p/ and /t/)
├── Consonants: palatal vs. velar (/c/ vs. /k/)
├── Consonants: rounded vs. unrounded or pharyngealized vs. unpharyngealized (/tʷ/ vs. /t/ or /tˤ/ vs. /t/)
└── Consonants: palatalized vs. non-palatalized (/tʲ/ vs. /t/)

FIGURE 3.1 Predicted acquisition sequences: oral resonance features (Jakobson and Halle 1956: 41)

Unlike the first approach, this method is guaranteed to yield a well-formed set of contrastive representations in which every segment is distinct from every other one. However, this method requires us to put the features in an order, which raises the question: where does the ordering come from?

Jakobson and Halle (1956) assume that the ordering is basically universal, with certain choices being allowed at specified points. In terms of acquisition, this partially fixed ordering allows for certain developmental sequences and rules out others. They propose the order in Figure 3.1 for the acquisition of oral resonance (primary and secondary place) features. In Figure 3.1, wide vowels are low vowels of high sonority; narrow vowels are high vowels of low sonority; palatal vowels are front, and velar vowels are back. Thus, Figure 3.1 predicts that a height contrast between a high and a low vowel (say, /i/ vs. /a/) must precede the emergence of a contrast between a front and a back vowel (say, /i/ vs. /u/). Further, the latter contrast should emerge in the high (narrow) vowels before it can emerge in the low (wide) vowels. These precedence relations account for why /i, a, u/ is a typical vowel inventory, but /i, æ, ɑ/ is not.

By the same token, the contrast between wide and narrow vowels is predicted to precede the development of a contrast between velopalatal vs. labial and dental consonants (i.e. /k/ vs. /p/ and /t/). But no implicational relation is predicted to hold between the contrast of palatal vs. velar narrow vowels and velopalatal vs. labial and dental consonants.[2]

If the ordering of the features is entirely universal, there is no problem in knowing what it is. But the order does not appear to be entirely universal. Even Jakobson and Halle (1956), who propose a largely universal ordering, still leave room for choices, as shown in Figure 3.1; in a given situation, we have to know which path to take when there is a choice. Later, I will adduce more evidence for cross-language variation in the feature hierarchy. I will adopt the hypothesis that, like other aspects of linguistic theory, the hierarchy of features is subject to parametric variation. It follows that the contrastive hierarchies of different languages may be different, even if their segmental inventories look similar.

There are two separate questions here: (1) How does the learner know what the order is? (2) How do we (those making the analysis) know?

Nobody knows the answer to the first question, the solution of which would amount to attaining an explanatorily adequate theory of phonology. If acquiring a phonology includes acquiring the feature order appropriate to that phonology, then we must assume that learners have ways of determining how the features are ordered in their language, whether we know what these ways are or not. That is, I will let the learners take care of themselves for the rest of this chapter.

The second question is a more pressing and practical one at the moment, one we have to answer or else we cannot proceed. Recall that we cannot simply look at a phoneme inventory and read off the contrasts. So we need at least some informal heuristics for determining feature orderings.

In some cases, the problem is not that difficult. At a minimum, we need enough contrastive features to distinguish every phoneme in an inventory. In those cases where the segments of an inventory fill the entire space relative to a

---

[2] The phonemic oppositions in Figure 3.1 are not given by Jakobson and Halle; I supply them in order to illustrate possible realizations of each contrast. Thus, /t/ vs. /p/ is a likely instantiation of the contrast between dental and labial consonants, but other consonants could serve to illustrate the same contrast (for example, /d/ vs. /b/).

given set of features, assignment of contrastive feature values is relatively straightforward. For example, consider the inventory in (7), where /ɸ/ and /β/ are bilabial fricatives:

(7) Inventory where the phonemes fill the entire feature space

	p	b	ɸ	β
voiced	−	+	−	+
continuant	−	−	+	+

Suppose our theory makes available the features [voiced] and [continuant], and assume that there are no other features that distinguish these segments. Then, all the specifications in (7) are contrastive, without further argument, and the same results will obtain in either ordering of these two features.

A question arises when an inventory is asymmetrical, or there is a choice of potentially distinctive features. Both possible situations are exemplified by (8):

(8) Asymmetric inventory, and choice of distinctive features

	p	b	f
voiced	−	+	−
continuant	−	−	+
bilabial	✓	✓	
labiodental			✓

The inventory in (8) has the three phonemes /p/, /b/, and /f/. Even if we assume, as in (7), that the relevant contrastive features are [voiced] and [continuant], the lack of a phoneme /v/ introduces an asymmetry into the inventory that brings feature ordering into play. If we posit the ordering [voiced] > [continuant], /p/ and /f/ will be contrastively specified for both features and /b/ will be contrastively specified only for [voiced]; if we posit [continuant] > [voiced], /p/ and /b/ will be contrastively specified for both features and /f/ will be contrastively specified only for [continuant].

Another source of variation in (8) is introduced by the place of articulation difference between bilabial /p, b/ and labiodental /f/. The notation in (8) indicates that the place features are privative, meaning that they are either present (✓) in a segment or absent.[3]

---

[3] Another fundamental question arises here, namely, where do the features themselves come from? It has often been assumed, particularly in generative phonology, that the features are innately supplied; Mielke (2008) argues against this view. While this is an important issue, it is largely orthogonal to the questions discussed here.

In such cases, I propose that we determine the feature ordering in each language based on the phonological patterning of the language. That is, we pick the ordering that best accounts for the phonology of that language. More particularly, I will adopt the hypothesis in (9):

(9) Contrast and phonological activity
Only contrastive features are active in the (lexical) phonology. Redundant features are phonologically inert.

To say that a feature is *active* means that we have evidence of its existence by virtue of the fact that it plays a role in the phonology, for example, by causing assimilation, or by participating in other processes or phonotactics that are sensitive to that feature. An *inert* feature is one that may be phonetically present, but which does not trigger phonological processes.

The hypothesis in (9) provides a heuristic for identifying contrastive features: if only contrastive features are active in the phonology, then we can deduce that, if a feature is active, it must be contrastive. The hypothesis is falsifiable since the sum total of contrastive features we posit must correspond to some feature ordering. In a three-vowel system, for example, there cannot be more than two contrastive features. It would be a problem for the theory if three features were found to be active.[4]

3.3 The contrastive hierarchy in phonology: the past

The contrastive hierarchy has roots in the foundations of phonological theory. In this section I will briefly review some early work that uses feature ordering to assign contrast.

3.3.1 *Trubetzkoy*

Though he did not follow this approach consistently, there are places in the *Grundzüge der Phonologie* (published 1939; translated into English as Trubetzkoy 1969) where Trubetzkoy explicitly recognizes the feature ordering principle. For example, he observes (1969: 102–103) that a 'certain hierarchy existed' in the Polabian vowel system, whereby the back ∼ front contrast is higher than the rounded ∼ unrounded one, the latter being a subclassification of the

---

[4] The hypothesis in (9) does not work in the other direction: it is not necessary for a contrastive feature to be active. In the inventory in (7), for example, we would still need to posit two contrastive features even if there were no relevant phonological activity.

front vowels. Trubetzkoy's analysis suggests that the features are ordered into the partial hierarchy: [low] > [back] > [round], as shown in (10):

(10) Polabian vowel system (based on Trubetzkoy 1969)

	[−back]		[+back]	
	[−round]	[+round]		
	i	ü		u
	ê	ö		o
[−low]	e		α	
[+low]		a		

Trubetzkoy's rationale for this analysis is that, in Polabian, palatalization in consonants is neutralized before all front vowels and before 'the maximally open vowel *a* which stood outside the classes of timbre'. We can give formal expression to the notion that *a* 'stood outside the classes of timbre' by ordering [low] before [back]: thus, *a* has no contrastive value for front/back or unrounded/rounded.

Trubetzkoy cites, as further evidence, the fact that the oppositions between back and front vowels are constant, but those between front rounded and unrounded vowels of the same height are neutralizable after *v* and *j* to the unrounded vowels *i* and *ê*. Because [back] is ordered ahead of [round], 'the properties of lip participation were phonologically irrelevant for the back vowels'. That is, they have no contrastive value for [round].

3.3.2 *Jakobson and Halle*

The contrastive hierarchy had its heyday in the 1950s, when it was explicitly proposed by Jakobson and Halle in publications including *Fundamentals of Language* (1956) and Halle's *Sound Pattern of Russian* (1959). Jakobson and Halle (1956: 47) refer to this hierarchy as the 'dichotomous scale', and adduce 'several weighty arguments' in support of the idea that this hierarchical approach to feature specification is 'inherent in the structure of language'.

Despite their arguments for it, they employed the contrastive hierarchy (or 'branching diagrams', as they called it) inconsistently. While they gave conceptual and acquisition arguments for it, they did not present empirical arguments that would connect it to accounts of phonological activity. Perhaps their inconsistency was due to their failure to arrive at a single universal feature hierarchy that could apply to all the languages they studied.

The use of 'branching diagrams' was challenged on various grounds by Stanley (1967), and the contrastive hierarchy disappeared from *The Sound Pattern of English* (Chomsky and Halle 1968) and then from generative phonology. But Stanley remarked (1967: 408), 'There is obviously some kind of hierarchical relationship among the features which must somehow be captured in the theory'.

3.4 Ubiquitous feature hierarchies

The ordering of features into hierarchies is surprisingly pervasive in phonology, even where it is not acknowledged explicitly, and even where one might not be aware of it. To take only developments in generative phonology, for example, feature hierarchies are embedded into markedness theory (Chomsky and Halle 1968; Kean 1980), underspecification theory (Kiparsky 1982, 1985; Archangeli 1984; Pulleyblank 1986; Steriade 1987) and feature geometry (Clements 1985; Clements and Hume 1995).

Feature hierarchies are often implicit in at least a partial way in the practice of phonologists. Consider, for example, the way segment inventories are presented in charts in descriptive grammars. Compare the inventory tables of Siglitun (Dorais 2003),[5] an Inuit (Eskimo-Aleut) language spoken in the Canadian Arctic, and Kolokuma Ịjọ (Williamson 1965),[6] an Ijoid (Niger-Congo) language spoken in Nigeria, given in (11) and (12), respectively. I present them as they are given in the sources (with some changes to the phonetic symbols but not to the arrangement).

(11) Siglitun consonants (Dorais 2003: 62)

	Bilabial	Apical	Velar	Uvular
Stops	p	t	k	q
Voiced fricatives	v	l j	ɣ	ʀ
Voiceless fricatives		ɬ s		
Nasals	m	n	ŋ	

---

[5] I have simplified Dorais's *j/dj* and *s/ch* to *j* and *s*, respectively. As he makes clear, these are variants of single phonemes.

[6] I substitute *j* for Williamson's *y*. Williamson notes that Back = palatal, velar or glottal, Vl. = voiceless, and Vd. = voiced. Williamson mentions that some speakers have a marginal phoneme /ɣ/, but she omits it from the table. I have added it because it appears to be no less marginal than /h/, which is included.

(12) Consonant phonemes of Kolokuma Ịjọ (Williamson 1965)

	Plosive		Continuant				
			Fricative		Sonorant		
					Non-lateral		Lateral
	Vl.	Vd.	Vl.	Vd.			
					Oral	Nasal	
Labial	p	b	f	v	w	m	
Alveolar	t	d	s	z	r	n	l
Back	k	g	(h)	(ɣ)	j	ŋ	
Labio-velar	kp	gb					

Note in particular the different placements of /l/ and /j/ in these charts. The Siglitun chart is not as overtly hierarchical as the one for Ịjọ, but it is clear that the feature [lateral], which presumably characterizes /l/ and /ɬ/, has very narrow scope, confined to making distinctions among apicals, whereas [nasal] is higher in the hierarchy. Thus, in the Siglitun chart /l/ and /j/ are 'partners', as are /ɬ/ and /s/. Apart from the nasals, the other sonorants are not set apart in Siglitun, suggesting that the feature [sonorant] is lower in the hierarchy than in Ịjọ.

The chart for Ịjọ expresses a hierarchy in which the feature [continuant] has wider scope than such features as [sonorant] and [voiced], and [lateral] has wider scope than [nasal]. Now /j/ and /ŋ/ are 'partners', and /l/ stands apart.

Feature hierarchies are pervasive in Optimality Theory (OT, Prince and Smolensky 2004) in the ranking of faithfulness constraints. For example, the tableau in (13) represents an OT grammar in which it is more important to preserve underlying values of [low] than [back]; similarly, [back] is ranked over [round]:

(13) An OT grammar with a feature hierarchy: [low] > [back] > [round]

	/+low, −bck, −rnd/	Ident [low]	*[+low, −bck]	Ident [bck]	*[+bck, −rnd]	Ident [rnd]
a.	[−low, −bck, −rnd]	*!				
b.	[+low, −bck, −rnd]		*!			
c.	[+low, +bck, −rnd]				*	*!
d. ☞	[+low, +bck, +rnd]				*		*

In this schematic example, an input segment /+low, −back, −round/ (say, the vowel /æ/) surfaces as /ɔ/, because, while an input low vowel must retain [+low], there is a constraint against its also being [−back]; and a [+back] vowel is preferably [+round] in this hypothetical example. The point is that any ranking of faithfulness constraints implies a feature ordering.

In the rest of this chapter I will present a series of case studies, drawing on the work of members of our project in Toronto since the mid 1990s. These studies cover different types of phonological processes. They all show the importance of phonological contrast, as instantiated by the contrastive hierarchy. At the same time, they show the insufficiency of purely phonetic approaches to phonological phenomena.

3.5 Vowel harmony (Zhang 1996)

3.5.1 Classical Manchu

The vowel system of Classical Manchu as analysed by Zhang (1996) is given in (14):[7]

(14) Classical Manchu vowel system (Zhang 1996)

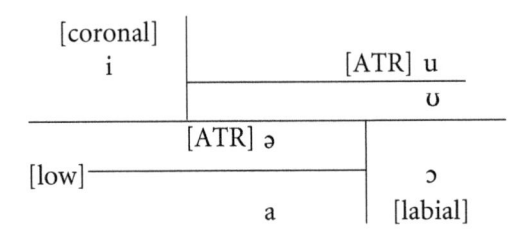

```
         [coronal]
             i              [ATR] u
                                    ʊ
                     [ATR] ə
     [low]                          ɔ
                        a       [labial]
```

Classical Manchu has six vowel phonemes. Zhang (1996) proposes that contrastive specifications are assigned by the feature hierarchy: [low] > [coronal] > [labial] > [ATR]. The first contrast is based on [low], and divides the vowels into [low] (/a, ə, ɔ/) and non-low (/i, u, ʊ/) sets.

The next feature is [coronal] (= [−back]). /i/ is the only non-low [coronal] vowel. As it is uniquely characterized, it receives no further contrastive features. There are no [coronal] low vowels.

Next is [labial] (= [+round]). It has no contrastive work to do among the non-low vowels. Among the [low] vowels it distinguishes /ɔ/ from /a/ and /ə/.

---

[7] This section is based on Dresher and Zhang (2005).

The next feature is [ATR] (= Advanced Tongue Root). It distinguishes /u/ from /ʊ/, and /ə/ from /a/. This feature also accounts for the height differences in these pairs of vowels, as [ATR] vowels tend to be higher than their non-ATR counterparts. /i/ and /ɔ/ are not contrastive for this feature, in this ordering.

The evidence for these contrastive specifications can be summed up as follows:

a. /u/ and /ə/ trigger ATR harmony, but /i/ does not, though /i/ is phonetically ATR.
b. /ɔ/ triggers labial harmony, but /u/ and /ʊ/ do not, though they are phonetically labial.
c. /i/ triggers palatalization of consonants, suggesting it has some relevant feature, which we call [coronal].
d. Alternations /ə/~/a/~/ɔ/ and /u/~/ʊ/ are limited to a height class. We need one height feature, which we call [low].

A more detailed discussion of the harmony facts follows.

All vowels in a word apart from /i/ must agree with respect to [ATR], as shown in (15):

(15) ATR harmony in Classical Manchu

a. /ə/ alternates with /a/[8]

| xəxə | 'woman' | xəxə-ŋgə | 'female' |
| aɢa | 'rain' | aɢa-ŋɢa | 'of rain' |

b. /u/ alternates with /ʊ/

| xərə- | 'ladle out' | xərə-ku | 'ladle' |
| paqt'a- | 'contain' | paqt'a-qʊ | 'internal organs' |

The alternation between /u/ and /ʊ/ is apparent only after back (velar and uvular) consonants (which also alternate, depending on the following vowel). In other contexts, /u/ and /ʊ/ merge at the surface as [u], except for a few sporadic examples. Zhang (1996) assumes that this is a late phonetic rule since it does not affect the behaviour of /ʊ/ with respect to ATR harmony, as shown in (16):

---

[8] The Classical Manchu data are taken from Zhang 1996. See Zhang (1996: 32) for discussion of the transcriptions and phonetic values.

(16) Merger of /ʊ/ to [u] except after back consonants

    a. Underlying /u/: ATR harmony
        susə   'coarse'   susə-tə-   'make coarsely'
        xət'u   'stocky'   xət'u-kən   'somewhat stocky'

    b. Underlying /ʊ/ not after velar/uvular consonants
        tulpa   'careless'   tulpa-ta-   'act carelessly'
        tat'ṣun   'sharp'   tat'ṣu-qan   'somewhat sharp'

In each word in (16b) the vowel that surfaces as [u] patterns with non-ATR vowels; compare the forms in (16a). I suppose, following Zhang (1996), that [u] in (16b) derives from /ʊ/, which merges with /u/ as [u] in these environments.

The vowel /i/ is neutral, as shown in (17). It can co-occur in roots with both ATR and non-ATR vowels and with both ATR and non-ATR suffixes (17a, b), and it can itself appear in a suffix following either ATR or non-ATR vowels (17c):

(17) ATR harmony in Classical Manchu: /i/ is neutral

    a. /ə/ ~ /a/ suffix
        pəki   'firm'   pəki-lə   'make firm'
        paqtṣ'in   'opponent'   paqtṣ'i-la-   'oppose'

    b. /u/ ~ /ʊ/ suffix
        sitərə-   'hobble'   sitərə-sxun   'hobbled/lame'
        panjin   'appearance'   panji-sχʊn   'having money'

    c. /i/ suffix
        əmt'ə   'one each'   əmt'ə-li   'alone; sole'
        taχa-   'follow'   taχa-li   'the second'

Surprisingly, when /i/ is in a position to trigger harmony, it occurs only with non-ATR vowels, as in (18):

(18) Stems with only /i/: suffixes with non-ATR vowels

    a. /a/ in suffix, not /ə/
        fili   'solid'   fili-qan   'somewhat solid'
        ili-   'stand'   ili-χa   'stood'

b. /ʊ/ in suffix, not /u/
   sifi-   'stick in the hair'   sifi-qʊ   'hairpin'
   tṣ'ili-   'to choke'   tṣ'ili-qʊ   'choking'

Despite the fact that it is phonetically an ATR vowel, /i/ does not trigger ATR harmony. This fact is explained if we suppose the contrastive specifications in (14), together with the hypothesis that only contrastive values of [ATR] trigger harmony.

Another vowel harmony process in Classical Manchu is labial harmony (Zhang 1996; Zhang and Dresher 1996; Walker 2001). A suffix vowel /a/ becomes /ɔ/ if preceded by two successive /ɔ/ vowels (19a). Labial harmony is not triggered by a single short or long /ɔ/ (19b), nor by the high round vowels (19c, d):

(19)   Labial harmony in Classical Manchu
       a. pɔtṣ'ɔ   'colour'   pɔtṣ'ɔ-ŋɢɔ   'coloured'
           fɔχɔlɔn   'short'   fɔχɔlɔ-qɔn   'somewhat short'

       b. tɔ-   'alight (birds)' tɔ-na-   'alight in swarm'
           tɔɔ-   'cross (river)'   tɔɔ-na-   'go to cross'

       c. gulu   'plain'   gulu-kən   'somewhat plain'
           kumun   'music'   kumu-ŋgə   'noisy'

       d. χʊtun   'fast'   χʊtu-qan   'somewhat fast'
           tursun   'form'   tursu-ŋɢa   'having form'

As with ATR harmony, only a contrastive feature can serve as a harmony trigger. In this case, only /ɔ/, but not /u/ or /ʊ/, have a contrastive [labial] feature.

3.5.2 *Evolution of Spoken Manchu and Xibe*

This analysis of Classical Manchu is strikingly supported by subsequent developments in the modern Manchu languages. The vowels /ə/ and /u/ undergo changes in their contrastive status, leading to new patterns of phonological activity.

We observed that in Classical Manchu the contrast between /u/ and /ʊ/ is already neutralized phonetically to [u] in most contexts, with surface [ʊ] surviving only after uvular consonants and sporadically in other contexts in a few words. It is no surprise, therefore, to see this neutralization continue to completion in Spoken Manchu, a modern Manchu language descended from an ancestor similar to Classical Manchu. In Spoken Manchu, /u/ and /ʊ/ have merged completely to [u], and the phoneme /ʊ/ has been completely lost.

In a contrast-driven approach to vowel systems, the loss of a contrast in one part of the system could have wider effects. In the Classical Manchu system, the contrast between /u/ and /ʊ/ involves the feature [ATR], just like the contrast between /ə/ and /a/. But with the loss of /ʊ/, the position of [ATR] in the system becomes much more tenuous. The vowel /u/ would now join /i/ as a neutral vowel, occurring with both [ATR] and non-ATR vowels.

Now, the entire burden of the [ATR] contrast would fall on the contrast between /ə/ and /a/. Many languages, however, have these vowels in their inventories without the contrast being due to [ATR]. The contrast between these vowels could more straightforwardly be attributed to a difference in height. Indeed, the feature [low], which is required independently, can serve to distinguish /ə/ from /a/.

Therefore, without assuming that the phoneme /ə/ changed phonetically, the loss of /ʊ/ could have indirectly led to a change in the phonological status of /ə/, from [low] to non-low. This reclassification, in turn, could have influenced the phonetic realizations of /ə/, because in Spoken Manchu it is definitely a non-low vowel. Zhao (1989) characterizes it as a mid-high back unrounded vowel, with an allophone [ɤ]; according to Ji et al. (1989), [ə] is in free variation with a high back unrounded vowel [ɯ]. It is reasonable to suppose that there is a mutual influence between phonology and phonetics in such cases. The phonetics of a vowel obviously influence its phonological representation; but this influence is not simply one-way, and the phonological representation can in turn affect the phonetics, by defining the space within which the vowel can range (short of neutralization).

The change in status of /ə/ in turn has consequences for the specification of /u/. Recall that in Classical Manchu there is evidence that the vowel /i/ is actively [coronal], but no evidence that the vowels /u/ and /ʊ/ are actively [labial], though they clearly are phonetically round. The elevation of /ə/ to a non-low vowel, joining /i/ and /u/, changes the situation. Assuming, as before, that [coronal] takes precedence, /i/ is again specified [coronal], distinguishing it from /ə/ and /u/. But now we must still distinguish the latter two vowels from each other. The most straightforward distinction is to extend the feature [labial], already in the system for /ɔ/, to /u/, as diagrammed in (20):

(20) Spoken Manchu after loss of /ʊ/

[coronal]		[labial]	
i	ə	u	
	a	ɔ	[low]

This analysis thus predicts that the reclassification of /ə/ as a non-low vowel should cause /u/ to become contrastively [labial]. This prediction is borne out in Spoken Manchu, as evidenced by the development of a new phoneme /y/, a front rounded vowel that originated as a positional allophone of /i/ followed by /u/, as well as /u/ followed by /i/ (Zhang 1996). The front feature [coronal] is contributed by /i/, but the round feature [labial] must be contributed by /u/. Further evidence can be found in the related modern Manchu language Xibe, where /u/ participates in labial harmony, unlike Classical Manchu /u/.

3.5.3 Typological surveys of labial harmony

Typological surveys of labial harmony in Manchu-Tungusic, Mongolian, and Turkic languages support the hypothesis that only contrastive features trigger harmony. Zhang (1996: Chapter 6) surveys a number of Manchu and Tungusic languages in China and Russia. We have seen that labial harmony in Classical Manchu is limited to the low vowels. On our account, only the low vowel /ɔ/ is contrastively [labial] in this inventory. The same holds for most Manchu-Tungusic languages, which have similar vowel inventories. A Tungusic example is Oroqen (Zhang 1996), whose inventory is given in (21); again, only low vowels are triggers and targets of harmony.

(21) Oroqen vowel system (Zhang 1996)

[coronal]		[labial]		
i ii		u uu		
		ʊ ʊʊ		
ee	ə əə	o oo		
εε	a aa	ɔ ɔɔ	[low]	

Eastern Mongolian languages have a similar type of labial harmony triggered by and affecting low vowels. An example is Khalkha Mongolian (Svantesson 1985; Kaun 1995), shown in (22):

(22) Khalkha Mongolian vowel system (Svantesson 1985; Kaun 1995)[9]

[coronal]		[labial]	
i		u	
		ʊ	
	ə	o	
	a	ɔ	[low]

---

[9] See Dresher and Zhang (2005) for further discussion of the phonemic values of the Khalkha Mongolian vowels.

Turkic languages tend to have symmetrical vowel inventories. They are typically analysed with three features: one height feature and two place features. A typical example is Turkish, shown in (23):

(23)   Turkish vowel system

| | [coronal] | | non-coronal | |
	non-labial	[labial]	non-labial	[labial]
[high]	i	y	ɨ	u
non-high	e	ø	a	o

Assuming three features, [high], [coronal], and [labial] (or their equivalents), the Turkish vowels exhaust the space of possible values. Therefore, all feature values are contrastive; in particular, [labial] is necessarily contrastive in all vowels that are rounded on the surface.

We predict, therefore, that all round vowels could potentially be triggers of labial harmony in such languages. This prediction is correct, though harmony observes limitations that are not due to contrast but to other factors. That is, having a contrastive feature is a necessary but not sufficient condition for triggering harmony. We find a variety of labial harmony patterns, where high vowels are favoured as triggers and targets, for reasons unrelated to contrast (Korn 1969; Kaun 1995).

In Turkish, for example, harmony triggers can be high or low, but targets are typically limited to high vowels. In Kachin Khakass (Korn 1969), with the same vowel inventory, both triggers and targets of labial harmony must be high, the opposite of the Manchu-Tungus-Eastern Mongolian pattern.

3.5.4 A perceptual-functional alternative?

Kaun (1995) proposes what appears to be an alternative to a contrastive account of labial harmony systems. Closer inspection reveals, however, that her account presupposes a contrastive analysis such as the one presented here.

According to Kaun (1995), labial harmony is governed by a number of constraints. The main ones relevant to the present discussion are given in (24):

(24)   Constraints responsible for labial harmony (Kaun 1995)

   a. EXTEND[RD]: 'The autosegment [+round] must be associated to all available vocalic positions within a word.'
   b. EXTEND[RD]IF[−HI]: 'The autosegment [+round] must be associated to all available vocalic positions within a word when simultaneously associated with [−high].'

Constraint (24a) provokes labial harmony triggered by both high and low round vowels, as occurs (potentially) in Turkic languages; (24b) is meant to account for the Manchu-Tungusic-Mongolian type of labial harmony, which is triggered only by low vowels.

If grammars are permitted to freely rank these constraints, we would have no explanation of the correlation between inventories and type of labial harmony. It remains to be explained why Manchu-Tungusic-Mongolian languages typically use EXTEND[RD]IF[−HI], whereas Turkic languages use EXTEND[RD]. To account for this correlation, Kaun proposes that EXTEND [RD]IF[−HI] is dominant only if there is greater perceptual crowding in the non-high vowels than in the high vowels. To implement this notion in her formal theory, she adopts the convention that EXTEND constraints may operate only on *contrastive* feature values. However, Kaun proposes no theory for identifying which values are contrastive.

The intuitive approach to contrast and the appeal to crowding create unnecessary problems. Yowlumne (formerly Yawelmani) Yokuts (Newman 1944; Kuroda 1967) has height-bounded labial harmony in both high and non-high vowels, though the high vowel space is not crowded; on the contrary, it has optimal separation:

(25) Yowlumne Yokuts underlying vowel inventory

iː i	uː u
aː a	oː o

Kaun (1995: 159) cannot explain why both /u(ː)/ and /o(ː)/ trigger labial harmony since, as she assumes, [labial] is not contrastive in the high vowels. But there is no basis for this assumption. It appears that in Yowlumne the feature hierarchy has [labial] ordered above [coronal]. Yowlumne /i/ is quite different from the /i/ in Manchu-Tungusic and many Mongolian languages. Thus, /i/ is the epenthetic vowel, and does not appear to cause palatalization or other modifications in neighbouring segments. For these reasons, Archangeli (1984) proposes that /i/ is the unspecified vowel in Yowlumne. Only two features can be contrastive in this inventory, and they are [labial] and [high]. Since [labial] is a contrastive feature on both /u(ː)/ and /o(ː)/, it is a potential harmony trigger; crowding is not required.[10]

---

[10] Yowlumne vowel phonology poses another problem to any approach that posits that only contrastive feature values are active. The result of vowel lowering of /iː/ is [eː], which is not an underlying vowel. Since the only contrastive features are [high] and [labial], a further feature is

It follows, then, that if we interpret 'perceptual crowding' literally, the hypothesis that crowding drives harmony is false. The hypothesis can be saved if we interpret crowding relative to the contrastive hierarchy, so that a feature is crowded iff it is contrastive; but then crowding plays no role in the explanation. I conclude that Kaun (1995) does not present an alternative to an account in terms of a hierarchical theory of contrast, but rather implicitly presupposes just such a theory.

3.6 Consonant harmony and similarity (Mackenzie 2005, 2009)

It has been proposed (Hansson 2001; Rose and Walker 2004) that consonant harmony depends on *similarity*. One theory of relative similarity is Structured Specification (Broe 1993; Frisch 1996; Frisch, Pierrehumbert, and Broe 2004). Structured Specification theory derives a similarity metric from the natural classes created by the phonemes of an inventory. Crucially, this theory does not specify certain features as contrastive and others as redundant. The method of computing similarity does weight features differently, however, depending on how much they contribute to creating distinct natural classes. Proponents of the theory consider it an advantage that the similarity metric can take into account the particular membership of an inventory without designating features as contrastive or redundant.

Mackenzie (2005, 2009) argues that the best analysis of many consonant harmony systems does require specifying certain feature specifications as contrastive in terms of a contrastive hierarchy. For then a simple generalization emerges: consonant harmony applies to segments contrastively specified for the harmonic feature.

In Bumo Izon (an Ijoid language), labial and alveolar implosive and plosive stops may not co-occur in a morpheme (Efere 2001). Thus, implosive /ɓ, ɗ/ may not co-occur with plosive /b, d/, though the plosives may freely occur with each other, as may the implosives (26):

(26) Bumo Izon labial and alveolar plosives and implosives (Efere 2001)

	Plosives		*Implosives*	
Labials	búbú	'rub (powder in face)'	ɓúɓaɪ	'yesterday'
Alveolars			ɗɔ́ɗɔ́	'cold'
Mixed	bídé̞	'cloth'	ɗáɓá	'swamp'

required to distinguish [e] from [a]. See Hall (2007, 2008) for discussion and proposals for how to account for such facts.

Feature hierarchies and contrast 59

The velar plosive /g/ and the labiovelar implosive /ɡ͡ɓ/, however, may freely occur with members of both the plosive and implosive series, as shown in (27):

(27) Bumo Izon velar plosive and labiovelar implosive (Efere 2001)

	Velar plosive /g/		*Labiovelar implosive /ɡ͡ɓ/*	
With same	igódó	'padlock'	ɡ͡ɓáɓu	'crack (of a stick breaking)'
With different	dúgó	'to pursue'	ɡ͡ɓódaɡ͡ɓóda	'rain (hard)'
	ɓúgí	'to wring (hand)'		

Why are /g/ and /ɡ͡ɓ/ exempt from harmony? Consider the inventory of oral stops in this language, shown in (28):

(28) Bumo Izon oral stops (Mackenzie 2005: 174, based on Efere 2001)

		labial	alveolar	palatal	velar	glottal	labio-velar
plosive	voiceless	p	t		k		kp
	voiced	b	d		g		
implosive		ɓ	ɗ				ɡ͡ɓ

Intuitively, the labial and alveolar voiced plosive stops each have an implosive 'partner', whereas the velar and labio-velar voiced stops have no counterparts.

Assuming that the relevant laryngeal feature is [glottalic], Mackenzie (2005) proposes that the contrastive hierarchy for Bumo Izon is: place features > [voiced] > [glottalic]. That is, the consonants are first distinguished by place in terms of the place categories shown in (28). Within each place, they are then distinguished by [voiced]. Now [glottalic] is needed only to distinguish the labials and alveolars. The contrastive features assigned to the voiced stops are shown in (29):

(29) Bumo Izon voiced stops: contrastive features (Mackenzie 2005)

	b	ɓ	d	ɗ	g	ɡ͡ɓ
place	lab	lab	alv	alv	vel	lb-vl
voiced	+	+	+	+	+	+
glottalic	−	+	−	+		

The phonemes that participate in implosive harmony are exactly the ones that are contrastively specified for the harmonizing feature, [glottalic]. This is the only clear sense in which /ɗ/ is more similar to /ɓ/ than it is to /g/. It also explains why /g/ and /ɠɓ/ are not sufficiently similar to avoid each other within a word.

As already pointed out by Hansson (2001), the similarity metric of Structured Specification theory makes the wrong predictions in these cases. For example, it rates /g/ as more similar to implosive /ɓ/ than /d/ is, and more similar to implosive /ɗ/ than /b/ is. It thus incorrectly predicts that /g/ and /ɠɓ/ should be the most likely of all the voiced stops to participate in implosive harmony with stops at different places of articulation.

As with vowel harmony, the simplest account appeals to contrastive features as derived by the contrastive hierarchy. No better alternatives have been proposed, to my knowledge.

3.7 Loanword adaptation (Herd 2005)

Patterns of loanword adaptation also provide evidence for the influence of phonological contrast on substitution patterns, when words are borrowed that contain segments that do not exist in the borrowing language. Again, pure phonetic similarity, assuming we had a reliable measure of it, is not sufficient to account for these patterns.

Herd (2005) studies patterns of adaptation of English words into a number of Polynesian languages. These languages have impoverished consonantal inventories, so many substitutions can be observed. Of the main cases he discusses, I will briefly review the adaptation of coronal fricatives into two Eastern Polynesian languages, Hawaiian and New Zealand Māori.

3.7.1 Hawaiian

Hawaiian has a famously small consonantal inventory (30):

(30) Hawaiian consonantal inventory

```
p              k       ʔ
                       h
m      n
w      l
```

All English obstruent coronal segments are borrowed into Hawaiian as /k/, including [s], [z], and [ʃ]; examples are given in (31):

(31) Hawaiian adaptation of English coronal fricatives (Herd 2005)

a. [s] → /k/   b. [z] → /k/   c. [ʃ] → /k/
   lettuce → /lekuke/   dozen → /kaakini/   brush → /palaki/
   soap → /kope/   machine → /mikini/

Note that these segments are not adapted as /h/, which shares with them the properties of being voiceless and continuant, and is thus another plausible candidate. Why is /k/ a better adaptation of these English sounds than /h/? Before attempting to answer this question let us look at how the same sounds are adapted in New Zealand (NZ) Māori, another Eastern Polynesian language with a somewhat similar segmental inventory.

3.7.2 NZ Māori

NZ Māori has both /k/ and /h/, as well as /t/, though it lacks a phonemic glottal stop (32). In this language, English [s], [z], and [ʃ] are borrowed as /h/, as shown in (33). This is surprising, given that /k/ is available, as in Hawaiian.

(32) NZ Māori consonantal inventory

```
p     t      k
f            h
m     n      ŋ
w     r
```

(33) NZ Māori adaptation of English coronal fricatives (Herd 2005)

a. [s] → /h/
glass → /karaahe/
sardine → /haarini/

b. [z] → /h/
weasel → /wiihara/
rose → /roohi/

c. [ʃ] → /h/
brush → /paraihe/
sheep → /hipi/

If substitutions are made on the basis of similarity, these facts are hard to explain. As Herd (2005) points out, if coronal fricatives are more similar to /k/ than to /h/ in Hawaiian, why are they more similar to /h/ than to /k/ in NZ Māori? The relevant notion of similarity must be somehow influenced by the different inventories of these languages. Herd proposes that different contrastive specifications are operative in each language.

3.7.3 *Contrastive specifications of Hawaiian and NZ Māori consonants*

Herd (2005) proposes that the contrastive status of /h/ is different in the two languages. In Hawaiian, /h/ contrasts with /ʔ/. Following Avery and Idsardi (2001), the existence of this contrast activates a laryngeal dimension they call *glottal width*. Glottal width has two values, [constricted] for /ʔ/, and [spread] for /h/.

Herd proposes the feature ordering for Hawaiian (only features relevant to the current discussion are mentioned) shown in (34):

(34) Contrastive hierarchy for Hawaiian (Herd 2005)
[sonorant] > [labial] > glottal width ([spread/constricted])

First, [sonorant] distinguishes /m, n, w, l/ from /p, k, ʔ, h/. Next, [labial] splits off /p, m, w/ from the rest. Then laryngeal glottal width applies to /ʔ, h/. The result is that /h/ is specified for [spread], /ʔ/ is specified [constricted], and /k/ is the default obstruent. Therefore, anything that is not sonorant or labial or laryngeal is adapted to /k/. In particular, [s, z, ʃ] → /k/.

Unlike Hawaiian, NZ Māori has no /ʔ/, so there is no contrast within glottal width. Herd (2005) proposes that, lacking such a contrast, [spread] is not accessible as a contrastive feature. This, and the other differences in the inventories of the two languages, results in a different contrastive hierarchy for NZ Māori (35):

(35) Contrastive hierarchy for NZ Māori (Herd 2005)
      [sonorant] > [labial] > [dorsal] > [dental]

As in Hawaiian, [sonorant] goes first, splitting off /m, n, ŋ, w, r/, and [labial] follows, applying to /p, f, m, w/. Unlike Hawaiian, [dorsal] is also required, to distinguish /k, ŋ/ from /t, n/. It remains to distinguish /t/ from /h/. Herd proposes to use the feature [dental] to characterize the contrastive property of /t/. This feature accounts for why the interdental fricatives [θ] and [ð] become /t/, not /h/. Thus, in Māori /h/ plays the role of default obstruent, not /k/: /h/ is not sonorant, not labial, not dorsal, and not dental. Therefore, [s, z, ʃ] → /h/.

The different contrastive roles played by /h/ in these languages suggests that they have different 'pattern alignments', despite their very similar phonetic realizations. The differing status of /h/, as well as the presence of /t/ in NZ Māori but not in Hawaiian, also account for the very different contrastive status of /k/ in each language: general default obstruent in Hawaiian, dorsal obstruent in NZ Māori.

3.8 Conclusion

To sum up the main points I have tried to demonstrate in this chapter, I first distinguished between phonetic contrast and phonological contrast. I argued that the latter notion is essential because it accounts for a variety of phenomena that cannot be accounted for by phonetics alone.

I showed that phonologists have used two different approaches to assigning contrastive features. Of these ways, the method of making pairwise comparisons of fully specified phonemes is problematic. I supported the view that contrasts are governed by a contrastive hierarchy, that is, an ordered list of features; the contrastive value of a feature depends on its place in the order. We determine what the order is for each language based on phonological patterning, in keeping with the hypothesis that only contrastive features are active in the lexical phonology.

The idea that features are ordered and that contrastive features have a special status is not new, but was either implicit or explicit in phonological theories in the past. Feature hierarchies continue to be ubiquitous in phonological theory and description. The proposal here is not just that feature hierarchies exist but that there is a deep connection between feature ordering, contrast, and phonological activity. These points were supported and illustrated by case studies involving vowel harmony, consonant co-occurrence, and loanword adaptation.[11]

[11] See Dresher (2009) for a fuller exploration of the topics surveyed in this chapter.

4

Towards a typology of grammatical features

Anna Kibort

4.1 Introduction[1]

Classification of linguistic elements according to their inflectional form is a key part of language description, formal syntactic theorizing, and most computational linguistic applications, and has its roots in ancient models. Matthews (1991: Chapter 10; summarized in Blevins 2006: 390) observes that classical grammars approach grammatical analysis essentially as a problem of classification: '[a]n utterance is divided into parts, which are assigned to word classes and then subclassified in terms of their "accidents" or properties.' Such properties, widely referred to as features or categories, express what is shared by different linguistic elements, as opposed to what is idiosyncratic. In contemporary linguistic practice, any such properties may be found labelled as 'morphosyntactic features'. However, if the term 'morphosyntactic' is to be understood strictly as 'relevant to both the morphological and the syntactic component of the language', we find on closer analysis that many such features are not relevant to syntax, though they often encode semantic distinctions.

For a feature, being 'relevant to syntax' requires involvement in either syntactic agreement or government. The features of gender, number, and person are typically involved in agreement, and the feature of case is typically involved in government. If so, these are indeed morphosyntactic features. Conversely, while in many languages the feature of tense encodes regular semantic distinctions, it is *not* required by syntax through the mechanisms

---

[1] The research reported in this chapter was undertaken within an ESRC-funded project (grant number RES-051-27-0122) entitled 'Grammatical features: a key to understanding language'. The support of the ESRC is gratefully acknowledged.

of either agreement or government. On this basis, if in a given language syntax is not sensitive to the tense value of the verb, in hypothesizing the syntactic rules for the language we do not have to involve tense.

This chapter investigates a range of linguistic features which can be recognized through inflectional morphology. It offers a typology of grammatical features – distinguishing between morphosyntactic, morphosemantic, and purely morphological features – as well as clear criteria for their identification. I begin by assuming that what we recognize as features are meanings or functions which are correlated with different forms of inflected words. Section 4.2 discusses some concepts which are essential for the proposed feature typology, including agreement and government, realization and assignment of a feature value, and systematic multirepresentation of a feature value. Section 4.3 describes the construction of a catalogue of possible feature realizations which provides the basis for defining feature types in Section 4.4. Namely, after identifying the feature and its value on an element, I ask where the feature is interpreted, and on this basis establish the method of the realization of this feature value on the element. By comparing and relating different methods by which feature values are realized on different elements, I arrive at a systematic catalogue of possible feature realizations. I then adopt a different perspective and compare features as superordinate categories rather than individual instances of feature realizations. I demonstrate that adopting this perspective allows us to define the three types of grammatical features – morphosyntactic, morphosemantic, and morphological – in terms of realization options available to their values. I also give a brief overview of possible morphosyntactic features which have been found in the world's languages. Section 4.5 contains a summary of the issues discussed in earlier sections, and a heuristic for recognizing feature types in a given language. In Section 4.6, I apply the criteria for recognizing feature types to a set of difficult data and present a case study of Kayardild, an extreme case-stacking language of Australia. Kayardild's case-like inflections have been put forward as possible candidates for agreement in case, tense, mood, and polarity. I examine the phenomena in question and conclude that some of them are better analysed as governed cases, and others as morphosemantic features rather than morphosyntactic features of agreement. Finally, in Section 4.7, I draw conclusions from the preceding discussion for the inventory of morphosyntactic features, and offer closing remarks in Section 4.8.

4.2 Essential concepts for a typology of grammatical features

In this section I set out some concepts which are essential for the proposed feature typology to assist with terminological clarity.

4.2.1 Features and values

In discussion of features, labels such as 'gender', 'person', or 'tense' are often used to refer both to the value of the feature and to the feature as a superordinate category. For example, the term 'gender' is used both for the particular classes of nouns (a language may have two or more genders) and for the whole grammatical category (a language may or may not have the category of gender). Similarly, we refer to an 'inventory of features' (categories, or features as such), while at the same time we talk about 'feature checking' or 'unification of features' in syntax (checking or unifying feature specifications, that is, features and their values). However, it is important to maintain the distinction between 'features' and their 'values' while attempting to construct a taxonomy or typology because the characteristics or behaviour of the feature as such will not be the same as the characteristics of a feature value.

The relationship between the concept of 'gender' and the concepts 'masculine', 'feminine', 'neuter', or between the concept 'case' and the concepts 'nominative', 'accusative', 'genitive', etc., has been referred to with the pairs of terms shown in Table 4.1 (based on Carstairs-McCarthy 1999: 266–267, expanded).

Following Zwicky (1985), I adopt the terms 'feature' and 'value'. Although the concepts 'masculine', 'feminine', 'neuter'; or the concepts 'nominative', 'accusative',

TABLE 4.1 Terms used to refer to features and values

	superordinate	hyponym
Matthews (1972: 162; 1991: 38–40)	category	property, feature
Wurzel (1984: 61)	Kategoriengefüge [complex of categories]	Kategorien [category]
Bybee (1985)	category	(inflectional) meaning
Zwicky (1985: 372ff.)	feature	value
Mel'čuk (1993a)	category	grammeme
Stump (2005: 50)	inflectional category	morphosyntactic property

'genitive', etc., are all 'values', further questions can be asked about the relationships among them. One question concerns the partitioning of the feature space in general between the available values (see, for example, attempts to arrive at definitions of feature values for an ontology of linguistic description);[2] another concerns the structuring within the values available for a particular feature in a particular language (see, for example, the structuring of gender values discussed in Corbett 1991, or the structuring of number values discussed in Corbett 2000).

In the construction of the catalogue of the different types of feature realization, I examine instances of feature values found on elements.

4.2.2 *Features in the components of linguistic description*

A first classification of features that can be proposed is according to the component of linguistic description for which it is justified to use a particular feature: morphology, syntax, semantics, or phonology (see Corbett this volume, Section 2.2.1). A feature operating exclusively within one component, for example morphology, can be referred to as a '(purely) morphological feature', and so on. The term 'morphosyntactic feature' implies that a feature operates across at least two components: morphology and syntax. Features recognized through inflectional morphology are often of this type – examples are gender or person. Typically, such features also correlate with semantic distinctions, so in fact they interface three components: morphology, syntax, and semantics. The aim of this chapter is to suggest a way of distinguishing between the different types of features that involve the morphological component. In Section 4.4.1, I offer definitions of a morphosyntactic, morphosemantic, and morphological feature by referring to the realization options available to their values.

4.2.3 *Agreement and government*

Both agreement and government are concepts that are necessary to describe inflectional morphology. They are both mechanisms which demand the realization of a feature value on an element in a clause or phrase. In agreement, as in *she*(SG) *runs*.SG, the target element (*runs*) carries 'displaced' grammatical information (SG), relevant to another element (*she*) (Moravcsik 1988: 90). In government, as in Polish *piszę książkę* 'write.1SG book.ACC', the governee element (*książkę*) carries grammatical information (ACC) expressing

---

[2] A good illustration is provided by definitions of gender and number values found in the current version of the General Ontology for Linguistic Description (GOLD); see www.linguistics-ontology.org/gold.html.

the relationship it bears to another element (*piszę*), like a 'brand mark'. Thus, in both agreement and government the demand for the specific feature value does not come from the target or the governee but from a 'controller' (in the case of agreement) or a 'governor' (in the case of government). In this way, agreement and government 'share the characteristic of being syntactic relations of an asymmetric type' (Corbett 2006: 8) with regard to the status of the elements which participate in the featural dependency.

However, while the feature value of the target of agreement is determined by the feature value of the controller, the feature value of the governee is determined just by the presence of the governor. Concurring with Zwicky (1992: 378) I assume that while a controller of agreement bears the feature value it requires of its target (the feature values are expected to 'match'), a governor does not bear the feature value it requires of its governee. Therefore, while government is also asymmetric with regard to the possession of the feature specification by the elements, agreement, in contrast, is symmetric. Despite this general principle, note that agreement mismatches may occur for various reasons (see Corbett 2006: Chapter 5), a governor may have the relevant feature specification coincidentally,[3] and also that the presence of a feature value may be covert due to various limitations of inflectional morphology.

4.2.4 *Systematic multirepresentation of a feature value*

Both agreement and government can apply to more than one element in the clause simultaneously, which may result in multiple occurrence of the same feature specification in the domain. In agreement, we find that an element may control a set of targets in the clause (and beyond). For example, in a language which has gender, a head noun may control agreement in gender with an attributive element, a predicate, a relative pronoun, and a personal pronoun. The Agreement Hierarchy (Corbett 1979; 2006: 206–237), which refers to the possible domains of agreement (that is, the controller together with its targets), captures the set of constraints on options available for agreement.

In government, we find that an element typically governs a constituent or unit consisting of one or more elements. The most familiar example of government of a feature over a unit is the assignment of case to (the elements within) a noun phrase. When a noun and its adjectival modifier are in the

---

[3] Corbett (2006: 8, fn. 10) notes that '[for] example, if we have a verb which governs the genitive, a participle formed from it may be in the genitive. The fact that this participle then governs the genitive is still a matter of it being present, and does not depend on its being in the genitive.'

same case, it is because the case value is imposed on both simultaneously. Corbett (2006: 133–135) discusses the possibility of viewing this type of feature multirepresentation as agreement and concludes that it 'will not count as canonical agreement, if we take seriously the issue of asymmetry'. If one accepts the view of syntax which is based on the notion of constituency, when the noun and its modifier are a constituent 'it follows that we have matching of features within the noun phrase resulting from government (rather than agreement in case)'.[4] Note that the same analysis holds for languages which allow more than one case to be stacked – this is an important point for the discussion of Kayardild examples in Section 4.6.

Apart from agreement and government, we find one other mechanism behind simultaneous inflectional marking of the same information on more than one element in the domain: semantic choice. A feature value may be selected for a constituent or an 'informational unit'[5] – e.g. a noun phrase, verb phrase, verbal complex, or the clause – on the basis of semantics, and the inflectional morphology in a particular language may demand that the feature value is realized on several elements which are members of the constituent or unit. In this situation, multiple elements will be expressing the same value of a morphosemantic feature simultaneously. Examples of a semantically imposed feature value which may be realized on several elements simultaneously are: number, definiteness, or semantic case imposed on a noun phrase (see, for example, Givón 2001: 427), or a verbal feature imposed on (the elements making up) a verbal complex.

In all cases where a feature value is selected for and interpreted at the level of a constituent or informational unit, whether due to government or semantic choice, the 'rule' that determines which elements have to realize particular inflections is found in the lexicon in the form of a generalization over the relevant part of speech or a subclass within a part of speech.

It is also possible that simultaneous marking of the same information on more than one element in the clause could be due to a semantic or pragmatic

---

[4] A different conclusion follows for those who accept a dependency view of syntax and treat the noun as the head of the phrase with the adjective depending on the noun (see, for example, Mel'čuk 1993b: 329, 337). Corbett (2006: 133, 135) argues that this would still be less canonical agreement than, for example, agreement in gender because the imposed case value is not inherent to the noun; for those who take a constituency-based view of syntax, government of case over the noun phrase is a better analysis.

[5] Evans (2003: 217), discussing Pollard and Sag's definition of agreement (1988: 237–238) in which they refer to 'objects', suggests instead using the term 'informational entity'. He argues that in this way we can apply it also to situations where tense, aspect, or mood are involved, not just entities such as participants.

choice made for each element individually for the same semantic or pragmatic reason ('what's once true stays true'). In other words, the multirepresentation of a feature value in the clause could be due to coinciding individual semantics of the elements bearing the feature value. A clear example of this type of multirepresentation of a feature value would be a feature of respect whose marking could be justified semantically for every element on which it appears. Corbett (2006: 137) remarks: 'There are...languages where the existence of multiple honorifics suggests an agreement analysis, but where it is not clear that this is justified. It may be argued that each honorific is determined on pragmatic grounds (and that they agree only in the sense that they are being used in the same pragmatic circumstances).'

Finally, some instances of semantically justified multiple marking of information may, arguably, not even be an expression of a morphosemantic feature. This applies to phenomena such as the so-called 'negative concord', where, if the principal marker of information (negation) is there, it requires the presence of the second negation marker. Arguably, the phenomenon does not qualify to be a 'feature' because 'positive' polarity is not information that can be assigned to a value – it is, rather, simply lack of information.[6] Corbett (2006: 29) suggests that where the selection of additional information requires that it has to be repeated somewhere else in the clause, such instances can be termed 'concord'.[7]

The diagram shown in Figure 4.1 summarizes the defining distinctions between agreement and government, and illustrates how syntactic space may be mapped out with features recognized through their realizations on elements in a domain.

4.2.5 Assignment, interpretation, and realization of a feature value

Finally, a terminological note is due on the term 'assignment'. This term is used commonly with reference to verbs which 'assign case' values. It is also used with reference to gender values, as in Corbett (1991), who discusses mechanisms for allotting nouns to different genders; namely, native speakers

---

[6] In order to determine whether such phenomena are indeed not features, or whether they are perhaps less canonical features, we would have to analyse them within a canonical framework. This work is in preparation.

[7] The term 'concord' is sometimes used interchangeably with 'agreement'. The view taken here is that it is worth reserving the term 'agreement' for the featural dependency that involves a controller and a target. Since Corbett (2006: 29) suggests reserving the term 'concord' for a strictly non-featural repetition of additional information in a clause, we are left with no term(s) to refer uniquely to the distributive marking of elements of the expansion of a phrase (whether dictated by government over a phrase or by semantic choice). However, I have not attempted to introduce new terms for the phenomena falling within this range.

| | | Status of elements involved ||
		symmetric	asymmetric
Possession of the feature	symmetric	systematic multirepresentation	agreement
	asymmetric	(no features to manipulate)	government

FIGURE 4.1 Types of featural dependency in a domain

have the ability to 'work out' the gender of a noun, and models of this ability have been called 'gender assignment systems'.

So far, the concept of 'assignment of a feature value' has not been commonly used outside these two situations, even though it might be useful as a general term to refer to the values of any feature. This idea is not adopted for this chapter, but if it were, the locus of 'assignment' of a feature value would correspond to what is referred to here as the locus of 'interpretation' of a feature value. This contrasts with the locus of 'realization' of a feature value, which is where we find the feature value expressed with a particular lexical item. Hence, a case value is 'assigned' to a constituent – which means that it is interpreted at a phrasal level – but it is 'realized' on particular elements (nouns, adjectives) which are members of the constituent.

Note that when a gender value is 'assigned' to a noun, its realization on that element is typically not overt (see also Section 4.4.3), although contextual realizations of gender values on targets of agreement with the controlling noun are overt.

4.3 Constructing a catalogue of possible feature realizations

In order to arrive at a morphosyntactic analysis of a clause such as (Polish):

(1) kupił-em   dwie   ładne
    buy(PST)-M.1SG   two(PL).NONVIR.ACC pretty.NONVIR.PL.ACC
    szklanki
    glasses(NONVIR).PL.ACC
    'I bought two pretty glasses.'

we have to know what inventory of features and values to draw from, that is, which semantic distinctions are grammaticalized as inflectional categories in the language, and how many value distinctions the language makes within each feature.

Establishing an inventory of features and values for a language can be a complex issue. An example of language in which justifying a feature requires careful analysis is Archi (Daghestanian), where the feature in question is person. This language has no phonologically distinct forms realizing person, nor does the standard description of Archi involve the feature person (only gender and number). However, agreement patterns in Archi indicate that this language does require us to recognize a person feature, even though it is a non-autonomous one (Chumakina, Kibort, and Corbett 2007).

There are also many arguments in the literature about the number of values for various features in different languages. Most problems with establishing the number of values arise either when there is conflation of forms realizing two different values (i.e. syncretism), or when different forms realize one and the same value (resulting in distinct inflectional classes, heteroclisis, or deponency).

In an inferential-realizational approach to inflectional morphology, which is adopted here after Stump (2001), the realizations of feature values are identified by establishing a paradigm correlating inflected forms with morphosyntactic properties. The cells in the paradigm of forms associated with a lexeme are regarded as pairings of a stem with a morphosyntactic property (or a morphosyntactic property set), to yield an inflected word form which is the realization of the pairing. Examples of how to establish the paradigm for case in Russian can be found in Zaliznjak (1973) and Comrie (1986), who discuss whether to recognize one or two genitive cases, and whether to distinguish prepositional case from the locative; for further discussion of the locative see Brown (2007). Examples of discussion regarding the paradigm for gender can be found in Schenker (1955), Zaliznjak (1964), and Corbett (1991: Chapter 6) who describes principles for determining the number of genders in a language.

In complex gender systems, with mismatches between the number of agreement classes of nouns and the number of inflectional forms on agreement targets (as in Romanian, which has three agreement classes and two target genders each in the singular and plural), Corbett (1991: 150ff.) argues that a distinction has to be made between controller genders and target genders. However, since target genders are only groupings that capture the pattern of syncretism in agreement forms across the set of targets, when labelling Romanian gender values realized on elements it may be more appropriate to refer to the agreement classes of nouns.[8]

The gender system of Polish poses a different challenge with regard to the number of values, where subgenders ('animate', 'inanimate', and 'personal') have been proposed in addition to the main genders (Brown 1998). Corbett (1991: 163) argues that some agreement classes of nouns can be analysed as subgenders, rather than as full genders, when they control minimally different sets of agreement, that is, agreements differing for at most a small proportion of the morphosyntactic forms of any of the agreement targets. Thus, a subgender is an additional gender distinction within a minimal subset of the paradigm.[9]

Having established the inventory of values to draw from, and identified the feature and its value on the element we are analysing, we can compare the sources of feature specifications found on different elements and begin constructing a systematic catalogue of different types of feature realization. Paraphrasing Zwicky (1992: 369), I am going to find an appropriate place for the differently behaving feature values in an articulated framework of featural dependencies.

4.3.1 *Contextually realized and inherently realized feature values*

Following Anderson's work on inflection types (1992: 82–83), Booij (1994, 1996) distinguishes two types of inflection: contextual – dictated by syntax (e.g. number agreement on Dutch verbs), and inherent – not required by the syntactic context, although it may have syntactic relevance (e.g. number on Dutch nouns, tense on verbs). Corbett suggests that the distinction can be applied to features in general, specifically that it 'concerns the feature in relation to where it is realized' (2006: 123). Therefore, a contextual feature is

---

[8] The controller genders in Romanian are usually called 'masculine' (for class I nouns), 'feminine' (for class II nouns), and the third, disputed gender (of class III nouns, which shares the singular form of inflection with class I nouns and the plural form of inflection with class II nouns) is sometimes called 'neuter' and sometimes 'ambigeneric'. The latter is a useful term provided it is used not to imply that there is no distinct gender but rather that the situation is different from the more common Indo-European three-gender system in that the third gender in Romanian is non-autonomous.

[9] Brown (1998) suggests that the difficult case of Polish masculine personal nouns (often labelled as 'virile' gender nouns) can be analysed as a main gender distinction if we recognize 'masculine personal' as one of the values of the main gender system, and three different values for the subgender of animacy: inanimate, animate, and person. The person subgender can then be analysed as fusing with masculine to create the new gender masculine personal (when it spreads to the nominative case, and from there to agreement targets which do not realize case). After careful consideration of gender agreement in all targets including numeral phrases, Przepiórkowski (2003) offers an alternative hierarchy of Polish genders which includes eleven genders.

one dictated by syntax, while an inherent feature is not required by the syntactic context (for the particular item), although it may have syntactic relevance.

Since both agreement and government are syntactic mechanisms that demand the realization of a feature value on an element in a domain, feature values determined through agreement and government can be regarded as being realized 'contextually'. Such feature values can also be thought of as information that logically originates outside the element on which it is found. In contrast, an inherently realized feature value can be thought of as information that logically belongs to the element on which it is found. Thus, features found on controllers of agreement are inherent features, while features found on agreement targets and on governees are contextual features.

We can now construct a diagram representing the first few subdivisions within the catalogue of possible feature realizations. The diagram includes the inherent vs. contextual distinction, and within the contextual realization distinguishes between feature values determined through agreement and those determined through government (see Figure 4.2).

Examples of contextual features of agreement are: gender – on adjectives, verbs, pronouns; nominal number – on verbs, relative and personal pronouns; person – on verbs, and on nouns in possessive constructions; case – on adjectives in predicate nominal constructions; respect – (honorifics/politeness markers/special agreement) on verbs; and definiteness – (non-autonomous inflection, but possibly agreement effects) on adjectives (see below). An example of a contextual feature of government is 'structural' case on

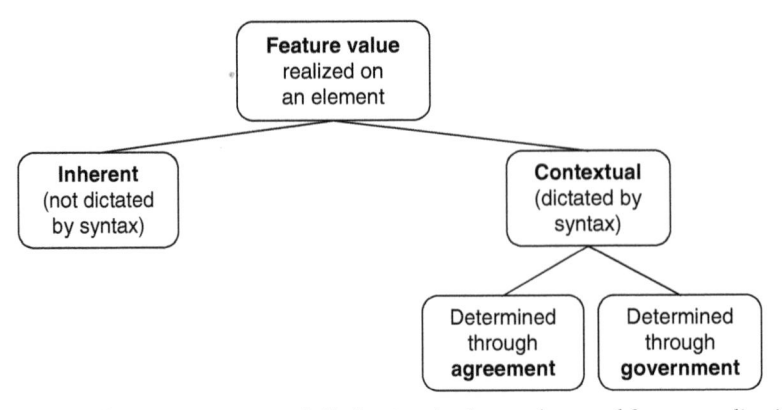

FIGURE 4.2 Inherent vs. contextual distinction in the catalogue of feature realization types

nouns or noun phrases. On the other hand, examples of inherently realized feature values are: gender and number values on nouns, person values on pronouns (and arguably nouns, too – though by default), and tense values on verbs.

The following illustrate the less common features of agreement:

Case – in Polish, the genitive case value on the predicate adjective matches the genitive case value of the quantified noun of the subject noun phrase (Dziwirek 1990: 147; Corbett 2006: 134):

(2) Sześć kobiet był-o smutnych.
 six.NOM woman.PL.GEN was-N.3SG sad.PL.GEN
 'Six women were sad.'

Respect – languages which have agreement in respect include Muna (Austronesian), Maithili (Indo-Iranian), Tamil, and Bavarian German; the following illustrates the use of honorific agreement markers in Maithili (Stump and Yadav 1988; Corbett 2006: 137–138):

(3) tohar bāp aelthun
 your.MID_HON father.HON came.3_HON.2_MID_HON
 'Your (mid-honorific) father (honorific) came.'

Definiteness – in German, definiteness of the determiner dictates the choice of the form of the following adjective ('weak' or 'mixed' inflection). We observe the correlation: definite articles co-occur in the noun phrase with adjectives bearing 'weak' inflection; indefinite articles (and some other elements such as possessive pronouns) co-occur with adjectives bearing 'mixed' inflection; and the absence of an article correlates with the presence of fully inflected adjectives ('strong' inflection) (cf. Corbett 2006: 95–96). Hence, it can be argued that we observe agreement effects (systematic covariance), though the exponence of definiteness on adjectives is non-autonomous.

Thus, a feature value can be realized contextually or inherently. When a feature value is realized contextually, its realization is determined by the syntactic rules of agreement or government. When a feature value is realized inherently, its realization follows only the rules specified by inflectional morphology which require a particular feature to be realized on a particular part of speech or a subclass within a part of speech. A gender assignment system, which classifies nouns into genders on the basis of their inherent formal or semantic properties, is a set of rules specifying the inherent realization of the values of gender.

4.3.2 Fixed vs. selected feature values

A further question that can be asked about inherently realized feature values is whether the particular value is lexically supplied to the element, or whether it has been selected from a range of available values. The following example illustrates the distinction. Both gender and number values are inherently realized on nouns; they logically 'belong to' nouns (in the case of gender) or noun phrases (in the case of number) even when they are used to demand matching agreement on targets. But they are different in that a gender value is *typically* fixed for a particular noun, while a number value is *typically* not fixed but selected from a set of options.[10] (Counter-examples, that is instances of a selected gender value, are multiple-gender nouns such as *baby* which can be assigned any of the available English genders;[11] and instances of a fixed number value – pluralia tantum such as *scissors* or *dregs*).

Furthermore, since inherent feature values are 'not dictated by syntax', they can be found on any elements, not necessarily only on controllers of agreement. Examples include features such as tense, aspect, mood, evidentiality, voice, topic, focus, and other nominal and verbal features which can be expressed through inflectional morphology in various languages. For the majority of these features, the feature value found on the element is a value selected from a range of values available in the language. So, for example, an inflectional tense marker on a verb can be regarded as expressing an inherently realized value of the feature tense, selected from a range of options. Thus, the catalogue of the possible feature realizations can gain another subdivision: that between the fixed vs. selected distinction within inherent feature realization (see Figure 4.3).

4.3.3 Semantic vs. formal basis for the selection of a feature value

Finally, one more distinction can be made within both types of inherently realized feature values, orthogonal to the realization method itself: the distinction between formal and semantic criteria for the selection of a feature value. The distinction between formal and semantic assignment of gender values was proposed by Corbett (1991) to account for the criteria according to which nouns can be allotted to genders. Corbett demonstrates that gender

---

[10] Note that, otherwise, gender and number seem to be more similar than other features, and that is probably why it may be difficult to define their values independently of each other. The difficulty of counting genders in some languages is almost always due to gender's interaction with number.

[11] Note that in English the choice of gender is manifested only in agreement with pronouns.

Towards a typology of features 77

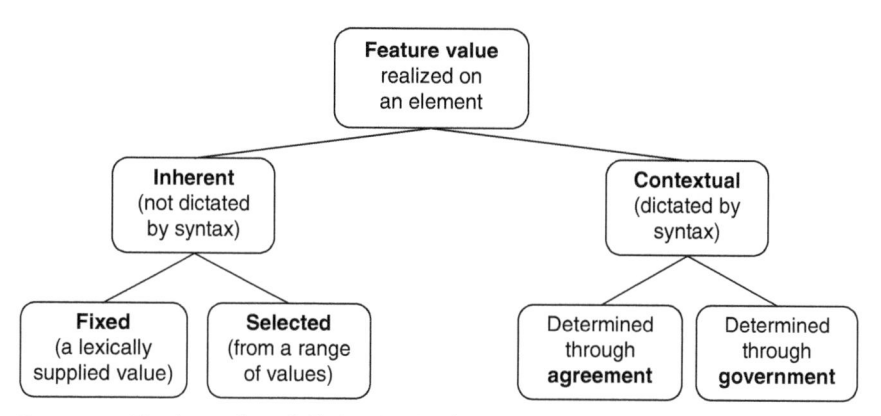

```
                    Feature value
                     realized on
                     an element
                   /              \
          Inherent                  Contextual
       (not dictated              (dictated by
         by syntax)                   syntax)
         /      \                   /         \
     Fixed     Selected        Determined   Determined
  (a lexically (from a range    through      through
 supplied value) of values)    agreement   government
```

FIGURE 4.3 Fixed vs. selected distinction in the catalogue of feature realization types

assignment systems in languages can be semantic or semantic-and-formal – that is, the set of rules that determine the assignment of inherent gender values to nouns refers to the meaning of words, or a combination of the meaning of words and the form of words. There is always some semantic basis to gender classification in any language that has the feature of gender, though gender values can be semantically transparent to a greater or lesser extent.

Within any gender assignment system, the assignment of the gender value to a particular noun can be attributed either to the noun's meaning or to its form. Where the meaning and the form of the noun conflict in terms of gender assignment, semantic criteria may overrule formal considerations (e.g. Russian *djadja* 'uncle', or Polish *mężczyzna* 'man', *poeta* 'poet', etc., have a feminine form and masculine meaning, and they consistently trigger masculine agreement).

This distinction also proves useful when extended to other features, for example number. Among nouns with a fixed value of number, it can be argued that at least some (e.g. English singularia tantum *happiness, poverty,* and other abstract nouns) have their inherent number value assigned on a semantic basis. On the other hand, some others (e.g. English pluralia tantum *scissors, dregs*) are assigned their inherent (and fixed) number value on the basis of form.

In many other instances the formal and semantic criteria for the selection of the feature value coincide (e.g. *Mary* is formally singular and denotes a singular referent). Therefore, the distinction between the formal and the semantic basis for feature selection can be considered an optional subclassification within the catalogue of feature realization types (see Figure 4.4).

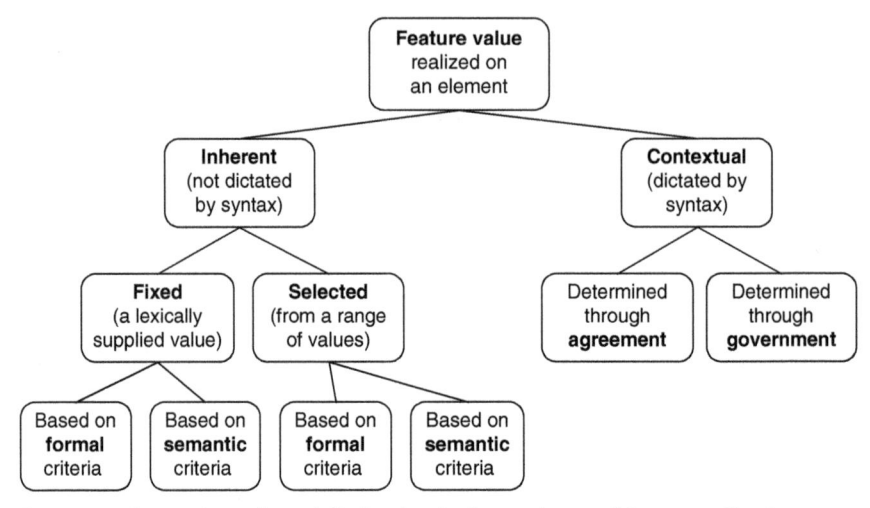

FIGURE 4.4 Semantic vs. formal distinction in the catalogue of feature realization types

4.3.3.1 *Semantic vs. syntactic agreement*   The distinction between semantic vs. formal criteria in the selection of an inherent feature value for an element corresponds to a distinction proposed independently elsewhere, that of semantic vs. syntactic agreement.

We have seen that some controllers with a fixed feature value could be seen as embodying a mismatch between their form and their meaning (e.g. *scissors* or *measles*). However, if they trigger consistent agreement, we may conclude that their form–meaning mismatch is resolved pre-syntactically in favour of one of the values (either the formally determined or the semantically determined one). Hence, such mismatch is invisible to syntax. But there are controllers for which the mismatch is not resolved pre-syntactically. Instead, it is visible to syntax and is carried over to the domain of agreement: such controllers induce more than one type of agreement. Furthermore, there are controllers which trigger variable agreement with the same type of target, and controllers which trigger different agreements according to the type of target. Many complex and fascinating examples of variable agreement, and conditions which favour it, are described in Corbett (2006, also references therein to earlier work).

In his discussion of agreement controllers which induce more than one type of agreement, Corbett (2006: 155–160) refers to the traditional distinction between syntactic and semantic agreement:

> In the most straightforward cases syntactic agreement (sometimes called 'agreement *ad formam*', 'formal agreement' or 'grammatical agreement') is agreement consistent with the form of the controller (*the committee* has *decided*). Semantic agreement (or 'agreement *ad sensum*', 'notional agreement', 'logical agreement' or 'synesis') is agreement consistent with its meaning (*the committee* have *decided*). (...) The terms syntactic and semantic agreement are used only when there is a potential choice. In many instances formal and semantic properties of the controller coincide and so agreement is both syntactically and semantically justified (...). I use the labels 'syntactic agreement' and 'semantic agreement' only when a mismatch gives rise to a potential choice. (Corbett 2006: 155)

Furthermore, Corbett acknowledges that different features may be involved, not just number. Thus, syntactic and semantic agreement are cover terms to describe contrasting agreement possibilities. Controllers which have such possibilities are referred to as 'hybrid' controllers. It has been observed that the availability of agreement options for their different targets, as well as speakers' preferences in the choice of option, are consistent with the Agreement Hierarchy (Corbett 1979, 2006: 206–237).

It is important to emphasize that syntactic and semantic agreement are both instances of agreement. However, in situations when their outcomes would not coincide, syntactic agreement is regarded as more canonical, while semantic agreement is perceived as a 'mismatch' of formal feature values between the controller and the target (Corbett 2006: 24).

4.3.3.2 *Hybrid controllers of agreement*   Typical examples of hybrid controllers are *committee*-type nouns in English which have a choice of agreement options in the predicate: *the committee has decided* – syntactic agreement of the predicate with the noun; or *the committee have decided* – semantic agreement of the predicate with the noun, common particularly in British English (Corbett 2006: 158, and references therein).

Another representative example, illustrating a choice of gender values, involves Russian nouns denoting professions, like *vrač* 'doctor'. This noun (and many others in its class) has the morphology typical of a masculine noun, but can denote a male or a female. Therefore, when referring to a female referent, the noun can trigger either syntactic (masculine) or semantic (feminine) gender agreement in an attributive element, as well as a choice of syntactic (masculine) or semantic (feminine) agreement in the predicate. Corbett reports that in this context most speakers opt for syntactic agreement with an adjective, and for semantic agreement with the verb (2006: 158, and his earlier publications on gender).

For hybrid controllers, there is always a choice of the feature value to control agreement on the particular target. Therefore, I conclude that the feature value is selected from the available range, where the range includes the feature value based on formal criteria, and the feature value based on semantic criteria. The choice of the former results in syntactic agreement, while the latter gives semantic agreement. Note that elements (other than hybrid controllers of agreement) which have their feature value selected from a set of options tend to have the value selected on the basis of semantic criteria. This is true of most count nouns which are assigned an inherent number value, or of nouns for which one can select their inherent gender value (e.g. *baby*), or of many different types of elements that realize a value of a morphosemantic feature such as tense, aspect, mood, evidentiality, voice, topic, focus, and other nominal and verbal features expressed through inflectional morphology.

Recognizing the distinction between semantic and formal assignment can be useful for all features, not just those agreement features which participate in agreement mismatches. Furthermore, this distinction is indispensable when trying to explain agreement patterns (including mismatches) in a systematic way.

4.4 A typology of grammatical features

The sections above complete the account of the ways in which a feature value, recognized through inflectional morphology, can be realized on a linguistic element. I now take a different perspective on features and compare features as superordinate categories. My aim is to distinguish between features which are relevant to syntax (morphosyntactic features) and those which are not (morphosemantic features). Also, I want to be able to relate purely morphological features to the other two types. In order to do this, I define a feature as follows: a **feature** is a set of values and the available options for their realization on linguistic elements.

The three types of grammatical features – morphosyntactic, morphosemantic, and morphological – can now be defined in terms of the realization options available to their values.

4.4.1 *Defining morphosyntactic, morphosemantic, and morphological features*

A **morphosyntactic** feature is a feature whose values are involved in either government or agreement. Since agreement requires the presence of a controller which is specified for the feature value it imposes on the target, the values of a morphosyntactic feature may be contextual (when found on targets and governees) or inherent (when found on controllers of agreement). Hence, a morphosyntactic feature is a set of values which have available to

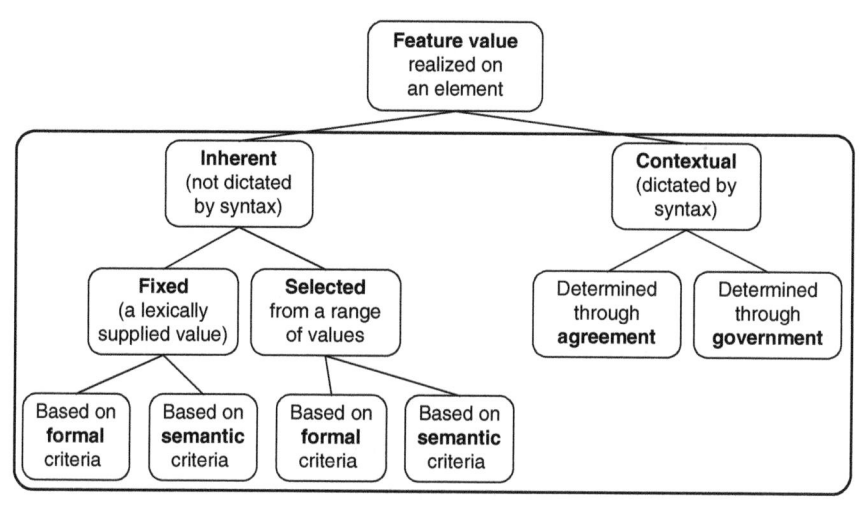

FIGURE 4.5 Realization options available to a morphosyntactic feature

them all of the options identified in the catalogue of realization types, as shown in Figure 4.5.

A **morphosemantic** feature is a feature whose values are not involved in agreement or government but are inherent only. That is, the elements on which the values are found are not controllers of agreement. Because it is not involved in either agreement or government, a morphosemantic feature is not relevant to syntax. Hence, a morphosemantic feature is a set of values which have the realization options shown in Figure 4.6 available to them.

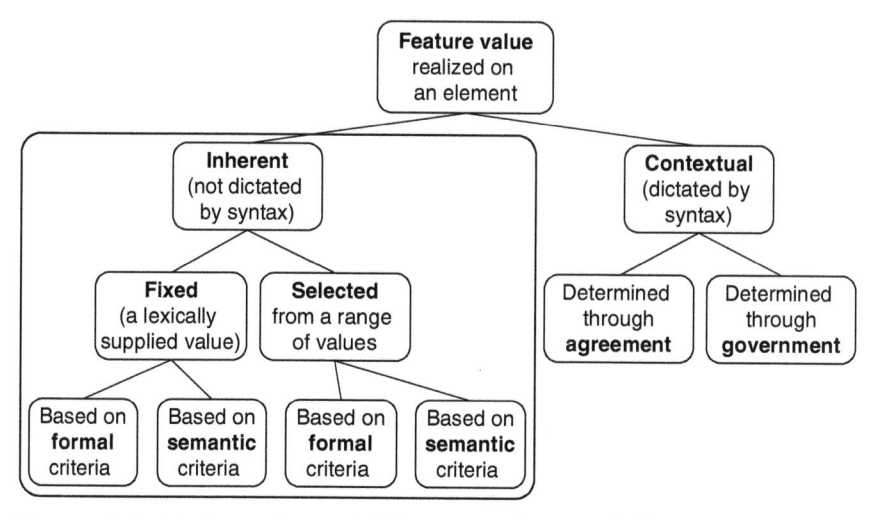

FIGURE 4.6 Realization options available to a morphosemantic feature

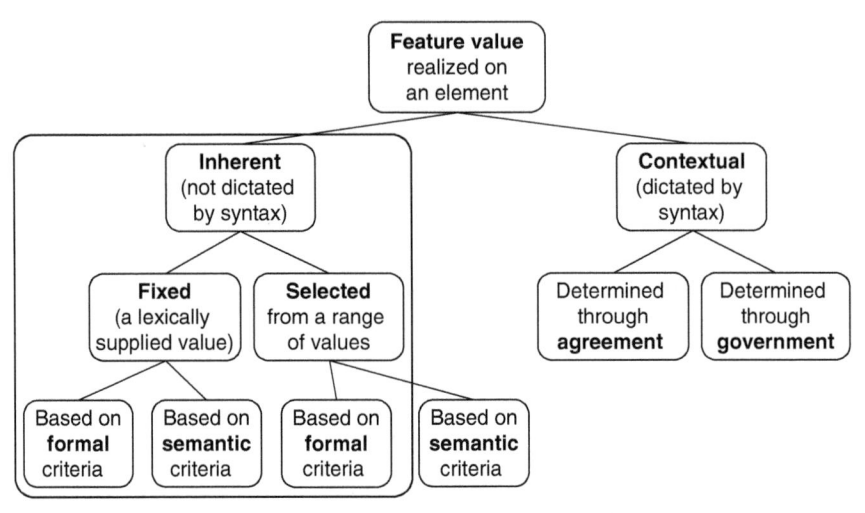

FIGURE 4.7 Realization options available to a morphological feature

Finally, a purely **morphological** feature is a feature whose values are not involved in agreement or government, and are inherent only. Furthermore, the values of a morphological feature do not co-vary with semantic functions (even though there may be instances of free formal variation between values of a morphological feature). Hence, a morphological feature is a set of values which have the realization options shown in Figure 4.7 available to them.

Morphological features have a role only in morphology (hence the possibility of hypothesising 'morphology-free syntax'). An example of a morphological feature is inflectional class (a 'declensional class', or a 'conjugation'). Morphological features can be arbitrary; they may have to be specified for individual lexical items, hence they are instances of lexical features. Alternatively, they may be predictable, to varying extents, from phonological and/or semantic correlations. That is, given the phonology or semantics of a given lexical item, it may be possible to assign its morphological feature value by an assignment rule, rather than having to specify it in the lexicon (Corbett 2006: 122–123; for more on morphological features, see Corbett and Baerman 2006).

4.4.2 *Identifying morphosyntactic features in a language*

The definitions above correspond to canonical morphosyntactic, morphosemantic, and morphological features. No feature in any natural language is expected to have values which are consistently realized in the permitted ways across all relevant elements. However, in a given language, we recognize the feature as morphosyntactic if its values are involved in either agreement or

TABLE 4.2 Morphosyntactic features

	participates in agreement	participates in government
number	✓	
gender	✓	
person	✓	
respect	✓	
case	✓	✓
definiteness	✓	

government for any set of elements. In turn, a morphosemantic feature in a given language is a feature which is inherent only; that is, there are no elements (word classes or lexemes) for which it is contextual.

In the search for possible morphosyntactic features, I have found at least one language (for each feature) in which the features shown in Table 4.2 can be morphosyntactic. However, while some of these are typical features of agreement or government and occur very commonly, others only rarely play a role in syntax. The map in Figure 4.8 shows how they share out the workload in syntax between them.

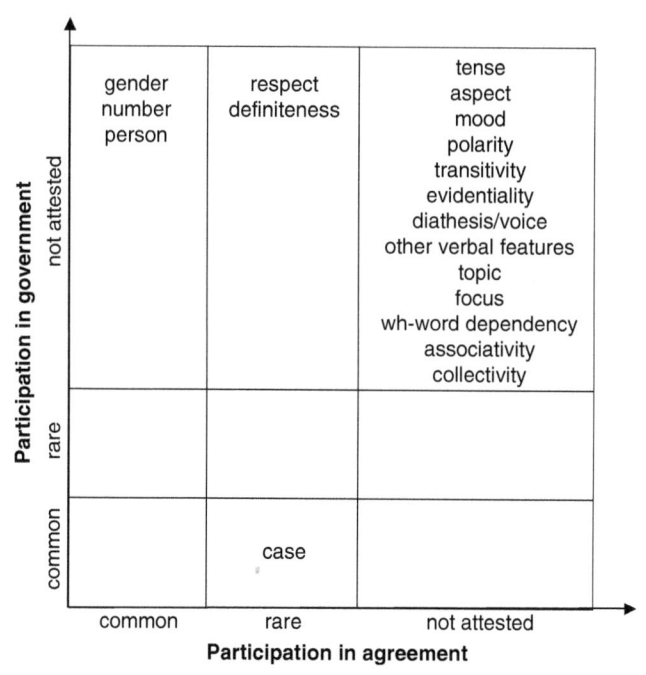

	common	rare	not attested
not attested	gender number person	respect definiteness	tense aspect mood polarity transitivity evidentiality diathesis/voice other verbal features topic focus wh-word dependency associativity collectivity
rare			
common		case	

Participation in government (vertical axis) / Participation in agreement (horizontal axis)

FIGURE 4.8 Participation of various semantic categories in the syntax

The categories which have not been found to participate in either agreement or government are often morphosemantic features.[12]

4.4.3 *Gender and nominal classification*

Gender is perhaps the only feature whose values, when found on controllers of agreement (that is, the gender values inherently assigned to nouns), typically have no overt expression in the majority of languages which have the gender feature. There are languages where gender is marked on nouns of all or most noun classes (Bantu languages, also Berber, especially North Berber – Kabyle, Tashelhit, Tamazight) or on most nouns with the exception of nouns referring to humans (many Arawak languages of South America, e.g. Baniwa and Tariana; Alexandra Aikhenvald, personal communication). However, languages marking genders on nouns are a small minority. Perhaps the fact that gender values are not marked on nouns may be related to the fact that gender is also a feature in which the inherent assignment of the value is predominantly fixed – that is, typically (even though not necessarily), most nouns in languages that have the feature of gender have only one fixed value of gender. Furthermore, the inherent value of gender on the noun is assigned to it on the basis of some specific criterion, semantic or formal. Therefore, in fact, the gender of a noun in a gendered language need not even be specified in the noun's lexical entry, since it can be derived from other information – semantic, morphological, or phonological.

Because of these characteristics, the term 'gender' is most commonly used to refer to classes of nouns within a language which are 'reflected in the behaviour of associated words' (Hockett 1958: 231). This is also the definition adopted by Corbett (1991), who argues that in order to define gender we have to refer to the targets of agreement in gender, which allow us to justify the classification of nouns into genders. In the present typology, it has been possible to retain the special status of gender. However, the position of gender within the typology needs to be clarified in order to enable comparisons with other features.

As defined in Hockett (1958) and Corbett (1991), gender is exclusively a feature of agreement. Hence, the feature is referred to as 'gender' in a language

---

[12] More information, discussion, examples, and references pertaining to each feature can be found on the Grammatical Features website which has been created as an extension to the Features project (www.features.surrey.ac.uk, mirrored at: www.grammaticalfeatures.net). At present, the website already contains articles totalling about 50,000 words plus extensive bibliography, but it is envisaged as a live and ever-growing resource which may, in time, become part of 'Web 2.0' with more direct participation of the community.

if it concerns the classification of the nominal inventory of the language, but only if the inherently assigned gender values found on nouns are matched by contextually realized gender values found on targets of agreement in gender. If a language has a system of nominal classification expressed through inflectional morphology, but the noun classes do not participate in agreement, the classification does not qualify as 'gender'. With respect to syntax, the status of such a feature is similar to the status of tense in most of the familiar languages: an inflectionally marked feature such as tense expresses a semantic or formal distinction, but is not relevant to syntax for the purposes of agreement or government. Syntax does not need to know the value of an inflectional noun classifier or inflectionally marked tense. Therefore, the distinction between inflectional noun classification and gender is that, while the former can only be a morphosemantic feature, gender can only be a morphosyntactic feature.

4.5 Agreement, government, and multirepresentation – summary

In a given language, morphosyntactic features are those features whose values participate in agreement or government. We identify a feature dependency as **agreement** when an element carries grammatical information relevant to another, and as **government** when an element carries grammatical information expressing the relationship it bears to another element. In contrast, morphosemantic features are those features whose values are never found to participate in agreement or government in the given language. Both agreement and government can apply to more than one element in the clause simultaneously, which may result in *multiple occurrence of the same feature specification in the domain*.

Apart from agreement and government, we may find inflectional marking of the same information simultaneously on more than one element in the domain due to **semantic choice**. We find that the same feature value may be realized distributively on the basis of semantics on several elements which are members of a constituent or an '**informational unit**', e.g. a noun phrase, verb phrase, verbal complex, or the clause. In this situation, multiple elements express the same value of a morphosemantic feature simultaneously. It is also possible that simultaneous marking of the same information on more than one element in the clause could be due to a semantic or pragmatic *choice made for each element individually* for the same semantic or pragmatic reason ('what's once true stays true'). In this case, the multirepresentation of a feature value in the clause is due to coinciding individual semantics of the

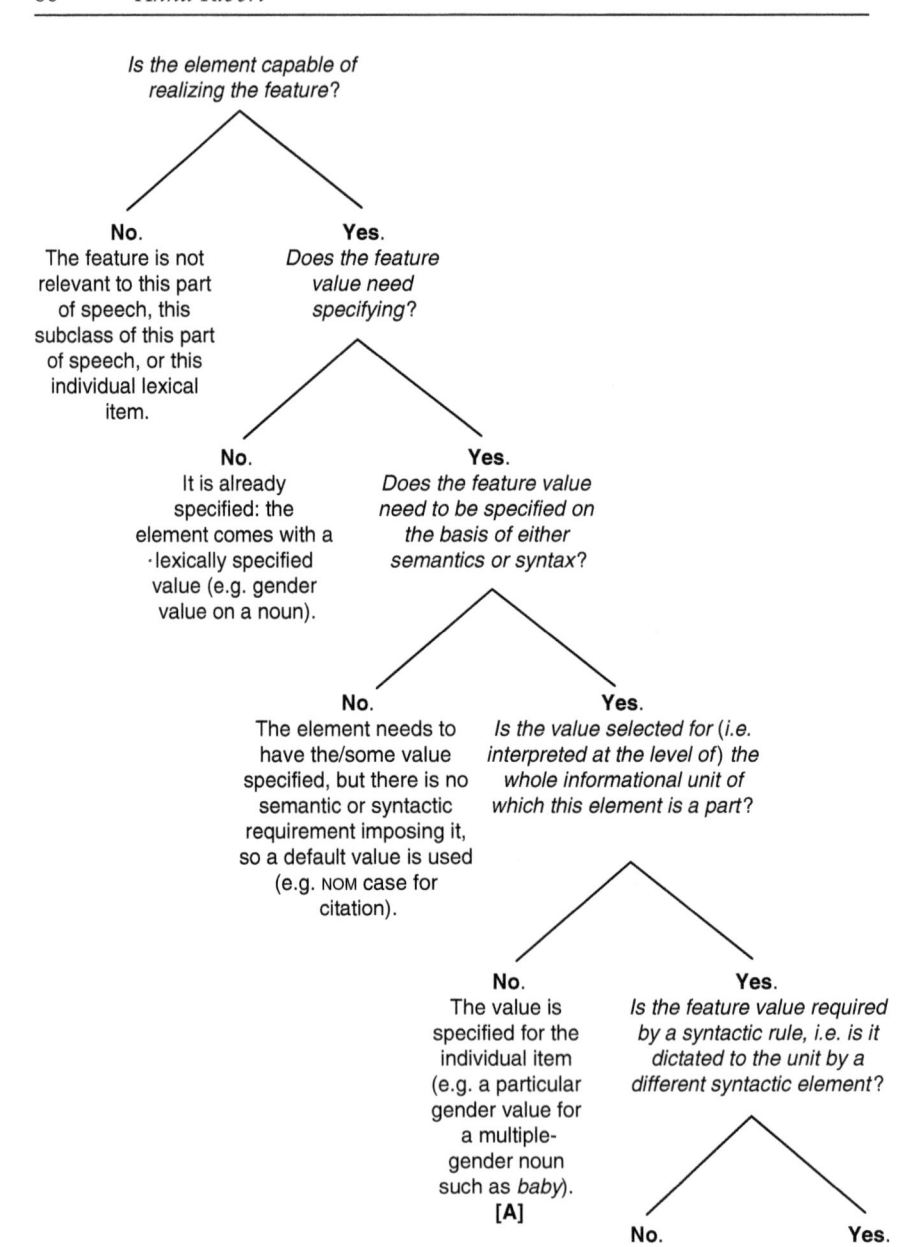

Is the element capable of realizing the feature?

No. The feature is not relevant to this part of speech, this subclass of this part of speech, or this individual lexical item.

Yes. *Does the feature value need specifying?*

No. It is already specified: the element comes with a ·lexically specified value (e.g. gender value on a noun).

Yes. *Does the feature value need to be specified on the basis of either semantics or syntax?*

No. The element needs to have the/some value specified, but there is no semantic or syntactic requirement imposing it, so a default value is used (e.g. NOM case for citation).

Yes. *Is the value selected for (i.e. interpreted at the level of) the whole informational unit of which this element is a part?*

No. The value is specified for the individual item (e.g. a particular gender value for a multiple-gender noun such as *baby*). **[A]**

Yes. *Is the feature value required by a syntactic rule, i.e. is it dictated to the unit by a different syntactic element?*

No. **Yes.**

(Continued)

No.
The value is specified for the unit (including the element) following a semantic/pragmatic choice. The unit may consist of only one element. If there are more elements, they 'do not care' about one another, since their feature specification does not depend on the feature specification of other elements in the unit.
[B]

Yes.
Does the dictating element (normally) have the feature value that it dictates?

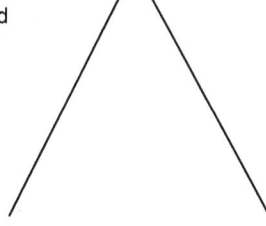

No.
The unit (including the element) is specified for the feature value through government over the unit (e.g. case over noun phrase). The unit may consist of only one element. If there are more elements, they 'do not care' about one another, since their feature specification does not depend on the feature specification of other elements in the unit. There is a governor element somewhere else in the domain which dictates the value to the unit.
[C]

Yes.
The unit (i.e. a set of targets, including the element) is specified for the feature value through agreement. The set may consist of only one element. If there are more elements, they 'do not care' about one another, since their feature specification does not depend on the feature specification of other elements in the set. There is a controller element somewhere else in the domain which dictates the value to the set (N.B. the domain of agreement may be larger than a clause – for pronouns).
[D]

FIGURE 4.9 A decision tree about featural dependencies in a domain

Notes:

Re [A]: Simultaneous realization of a feature value on multiple elements is due to coinciding individual semantics. If truly the same semantic choice is made for each element in the domain individually, it belongs here.

Re [B]: Simultaneous realization of a feature value on multiple elements is due to semantic/pragmatic choice over the unit, not due to the semantics of the individual members of the unit. This includes the realization of semantic case distributively within a noun phrase, as well as instances of distributive realization of feature values at clause level (where the unit is a clause).

Re [C]: Simultaneous realization of a feature value on multiple elements is due to government imposed by the governor over the unit of government. An example is the government of case over a noun phrase.

Re [D]: Simultaneous realization of a feature value on multiple elements is due to agreement imposed by the controller over the set of targets (since 'multiple targets are the same as each other', Corbett 2006: 8).

elements realizing the feature value. (For more detailed discussion of systematic multirepresentation of a feature value in a domain, see Section 4.2.4.)

All possible distinctions in the sources of feature realizations on elements can be ordered along a decision tree about featural dependencies, representing the minimum set of questions that are relevant in the process of combining linguistic elements into phrases and clauses (see Figure 4.9). The first three questions in the tree are relevant to morphology only, and even though the answers in some instances may have some semantic basis, they are not determined by semantic or syntactic choice. The next two questions are relevant to semantics in that the answers to them depend on semantic (or pragmatic) choice. Finally, the last question is relevant to syntax, and both answers invoke a syntactic rule.

Note that Evans (2003: 217, fn. 15–16) refers to situations such as [A] and [B] as 'informational equivalence' where there is 'no directionality'. This corresponds to my notion of 'symmetry in the status of the elements involved in a featural dependency', and 'symmetry in the possession of the feature' (Sections 4.3.3–4.3.4). In situations [C] and [D] there is 'directionality', which corresponds to Corbett's (2006: 8) notion of agreement and government being 'asymmetrical', and to my notion of 'asymmetry in the status of the elements involved in a featural dependency'.

It is also important to note that there may be instances of multirepresentation of a feature value which cannot be clearly identified as belonging to either situation [A] or [B]. Analysing respect by appealing to semantic justification at every element that marks it is perhaps the most convincing. However, certainly with some instances of respect, and probably with many instances of other morphosemantic features (such as tense, aspect, or mood), attempts to argue that the individual element makes sense semantically together with the particular feature value may involve an undue stretching of the semantic interpretation. We can also expect some tricky situations, as with multiple noun classifiers in Daly languages (Australia), which can be seen as the predecessors of agreement systems.[13]

This completes the outline of a heuristic for recognizing feature types in a language. We can expect that in many familiar instances of featural dependencies it will only confirm what is already fairly straightforward to recognize. However, we can also expect to find instances which are not straightforward and require careful consideration. In the following sections I revisit the difficult phenomena found in Kayardild (a highly endangered language

---

[13] I am grateful to Greville Corbett for providing this example.

from the Tangkic family, spoken in Queensland, Australia), in an attempt to classify them with respect to the distinctions identified above. The main objective of the analysis is to establish whether Kayardild does indeed have agreement in case and, even more unusually, whether it does have agreement in the verbal categories of tense, aspect, mood, and polarity (TAMP).

4.6 Agreement, government, or semantic choice – the problem cases of Kayardild

Kayardild presents an extreme example of stacking case-like suffixes emanating from different syntactic levels, with some suffixes changing the word class of their host. Most of these case-like suffixes occur multiply in the clause, lending themselves to be considered agreement phenomena. A detailed description of Kayardild can be found in Evans's (1995) extensive grammar, while problems posed by Kayardild for widely accepted views of agreement are highlighted in Evans (2003). I begin with an overview of case phenomena in Kayardild drawing from Evans (1995), and in the following sections I discuss each type of the multirepresentation of a feature value in an attempt to establish whether it is dictated by **agreement** (as in situation [D] above), **government** (as in situation [C]), or **semantic choice** (as in situation [A] or [B]). My subsections 4.6.1–4.6.6 correspond to the subsections labelled in Evans (2003) as (a)–(f).[14]

Evans (1995: 101–121) identifies five types of functional domain in which Kayardild case-like suffixes operate. In the adnominal domain, a case relates one nominal phrase to another. In the relational domain, a case relates a core argument to the verb or a peripheral argument to the clause as a whole. In the modal domain, a case expresses the mood/tense/aspect of the clause. In the associating domain, a case links a nominal phrase with a nominalized verb. And, finally, in the complementizing domain, a case applies to a whole clause and indicates either that the clause is an argument of the matrix clause or that 'certain marked coreference relationships exist between matrix and subordinate clause' (Evans 1995: 101). Nominals have been found to take up to four cases, in the following order, with the last two types of suffix being mutually exclusive (Evans 1995: 101; see also end of Section 4.6.4 below for some further discussion of the associating and complementizing functions of the oblique case):

---

[14] With special thanks to Nicholas Evans for his timely reading of the Kayardild analysis presented here.

```
                                              S'
                                         ╱────────╲
                                      S ╱          ╲
                                 ╱───────╲          ╲
                        NP(Relational)    ╲          ╲
                   ╱──────╲       ╲        ╲          ╲
          NP(Adnominal)    ╲       ╲        ╲          ╲
                │           ╲       ╲        ╲          ╲
            ADNOMINAL    RELATIONAL  MODAL   COMPLEMENTIZING
```

                         -------------------------------- NOMinative----------------------------------

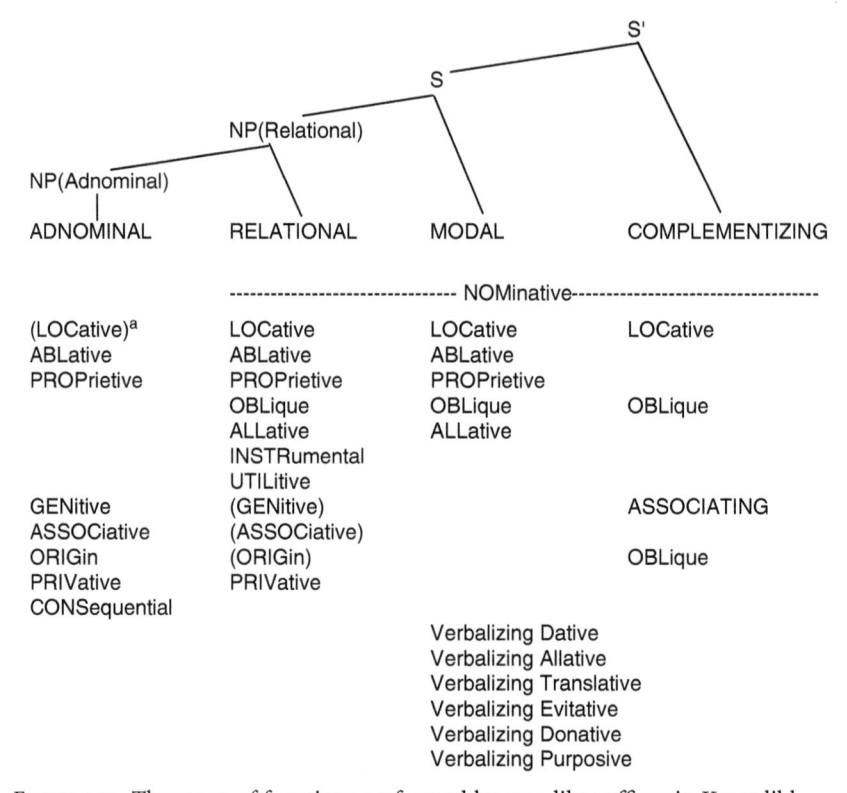

(LOCative)[a]	LOCative	LOCative	LOCative
ABLative	ABLative	ABLative	
PROPrietive	PROPrietive	PROPrietive	
	OBLique	OBLique	OBLique
	ALLative	ALLative	
	INSTRumental		
	UTILitive		
GENitive	(GENitive)		ASSOCIATING
ASSOCiative	(ASSOCiative)		
ORIGin	(ORIGin)		OBLique
PRIVative	PRIVative		
CONSequential			
		Verbalizing Dative	
		Verbalizing Allative	
		Verbalizing Translative	
		Verbalizing Evitative	
		Verbalizing Donative	
		Verbalizing Purposive	

FIGURE 4.10 The range of functions performed by case-like suffixes in Kayardild

[a] Evans (1995: 102) notes that not every entry can be justified here (the reader is referred to Chapter 4 of his grammar for details). Unclear cases are in brackets (the three relational cases in brackets could be treated as either adnominal or relational; the LOCative may only be used adnominally if no other case suffix follows). Furthermore, '[t]he NOMinative is an "elsewhere case", in equipollent opposition to all other cases: it appears only where no relational, modal, associating or complementizing case is assigned.'

(4)   stem + adnominal + relational + modal + associating/complementizing

Each of the five functional domains uses a subset of the common set of case suffixes (Evans 1995: 103). In Figure 4.10, I reproduce a diagram from Evans (1995: 102)[15] which summarizes the range of functions performed by each suffix and diagrammatically relates their morphological order to the syntactic

---

[15] In the original figure, Evans used the term 'verbal case', but in the (2003) paper he changed it to 'verbalizing case', in order to prevent a possible misconstrual of this type of case as a 'case marked on verbs', and to emphasize the way the case-like suffix changes the word class (i.e. part of speech membership) of its host (Evans 2003: 214, fn. 13).

level at which they operate. Verbalizing cases, which make up a different set of suffixes, are

> partly complementary and partly parallel to the normal case system. Core syntactic functions are always marked by normal case, as are 'static' functions like the LOCative; so are all adnominal functions (which are also static). What may be broadly described as 'dynamic' functions, involving change over time (e.g. change of location, change of possession) tend to take verbal[izing] cases. Some dynamic functions, like the allative, ablative and purposive, take either, but the verbal[izing] case is gaining ground. (Evans 1995: 182)

Evans (1995: 103) summarizes the principles of the distribution of case marking in Kayardild in the following way:

> In general case suffixes *appear on all words over which they have semantic or syntactic scope* [emphasis mine – A.K.]. Adnominal and relational cases are marked over entire NPs, and complementizing case over all words in a clause, including the verb [fn. 11: Particles and conjunctions, and pronominal subjects under certain conditions, are excepted (. . .)]. The distribution of modal case is basically all NPs except the subject and some NPs linked to it semantically or syntactically; associating case has a slightly larger domain.

4.6.1 *Multiple case marking*

Among the different types of case-like marking in Kayardild, three types correspond the most closely to familiar types of cases: relational cases, adnominal cases, and verbalizing cases. Roughly, relational cases indicate the core arguments of the verb and some other thematic relations which are interpreted as being in a 'static' relationship to the verb; adnominal cases (also expressing a 'static' relationship) relate one nominal phrase to another; and verbalizing cases indicate thematic relations which are interpreted as being in a 'dynamic' relationship to the verb (see Section 4.6 above for a citation from Evans regarding the terms 'static' and 'dynamic').

All cases are obligatorily marked on all elements of the relevant noun phrases, and when two different cases are assigned to one element, they are stacked. Therefore, we have examples such as (Evans 2003: 207):

(5) dan-kinaba-nguni dangka-naba-nguni mirra-nguni
 this-ABL-INS man-ABL-INS good-INS
 wangal-nguni
 boomerang-INS
 'with this man's good boomerang'

where the 'adnominal' ablative case is not replaced by the following 'relational' instrumental case indicating a thematic relation at clause level.

On the view of case offered here (following Corbett 2006: 133–135), this type of case marking over noun phrases, whether it functions adnominally or relationally, can be treated as assignment of case over a constituent rather than as agreement in case with the head noun. Instances of Kayardild relational cases expressing core grammatical functions can presumably be treated as instances of government of case over a noun phrase (hence, situation [C]), while other cases (relational or adnominal) can be analysed as instances of assignment of case to a noun phrase for semantic reasons, i.e. semantic cases (hence, situation [B]). Verbalizing cases will fall under either of these analyses depending on their function in a particular clause.

Since the constituency view of syntax makes us see these case phenomena as expressing a relation of the whole noun phrase to the predicate or to another noun phrase, it is not necessary to look for a controller of the case value, and indeed there is no element here that would function as the controller of agreement in case.

4.6.2 *Modal case*

Modal cases in Kayardild, formally identical to regular case inflections, are 'tense-sensitive object markers' (Evans 2003: 209, fn. 10) which participate in the expression of particular TAMP meanings. When the relevant TAMP meaning is selected, the modal case has to appear on all noun phrases (and all their component elements) except for the subject noun phrase, various types of secondary predicates on the subject, nouns denoting body parts of the subject, and noun phrases displaying other semantic links with the subject (such as proprietive noun phrases denoting 'private goals', etc.) (Evans 2003: 211).

Modal cases occur only when certain verbal categories are marked on the verb. The verbal categories are expressed on the verb as final inflections which attach to the verbal stem with or without further derivational suffixes (Evans 1995: 253–255). Evans (2003: 208) provides a table summarizing the meanings of the combinations of modal cases with verbal TAMP in Kayardild. In order to make my exposition easier, in Table 4.3 based on Evans's, I have changed the order of columns[16] (otherwise preserving the content of the table):[17]

---

[16] The order of the columns in Evans (2003: 208) is: 'modal case', 'semantic category', and 'corresponding verbal categories'.

[17] Additionally, Evans notes: '(i) Verbal categories listed in square brackets are relatively marked examples where the modal case is independently varied from the verbal TAMP for particular semantic effects. (ii) Modal case forms are cited in their canonical form' (2003: 208).

TABLE 4.3 Combinations of modal cases with verbal TAMP in Kayardild

Verbal categories	Corresponding modal case	Semantic category
ACTual (Affirmative and Negative) IMMEDiate POTential (Affirmative and Negative) [giving 'actual ability' meaning] APPRehensive [giving 'actually occurring undesirable event' meaning]	LOCative {-kiya}	Instantiated
POTential (Affirmative and Negative) APPRehensive [giving 'future undesirable' meaning]	PROPrietive {-kuru}	Future
PAST ALMOST PRECONdition	ABLative {-kinaba}	Prior
APPRehensive DESIDerative HORTative (Affirmative and Negative)	OBLique {-inja}	Emotive
DIRECted	ALLative {-kiring}	Inceptive
IMPerative (Affirmative and Negative) Continuative NOMinalization	Zero	—

In the following example from Evans (2003: 207), past tense verb inflection is used together with the modal ablative (glossed M.ABL) to express the semantic category labelled by Evans as 'prior':

(6) dangka-a   burldi-jarra yarbuth-ina thabuju-karra-nguni-na
     man-NOM   hit-PST   bird-M.ABL   brother-GEN-INS-M.ABL
     wangal-nguni-na
     boomerang-INS-M.ABL
     'The man hit the bird with brother's boomerang.'

And in the following example (Evans 2003: 208), the 'potential' verb inflection is used together with the modal proprietive (glossed M.PROP) to express futurity or ability:

(7) dangka-a   burldi-ju   yarbuth-u   thabuju-karra-ngun-u
     man-NOM   hit-POT   bird-M.PROP brother-GEN-INS-M.PROP
     wangal-ngun-u
     boomerang-INS-M.PROP
     'The man will/can hit the bird with brother's boomerang.'

Although this covariation of TAMP marking on verbs and noun phrases has been considered a strong candidate for an agreement analysis (see Evans 2003, and references therein to Hale 1973, Klokeid 1976, and Hale 1998 on Lardil, also a Tangkic language), a closer look at the table of correspondences reveals that all but one modal cases and some verbal TAMP categories can be re-used in different combinations to yield different semantics. Evans (2003: 210) gives the following examples: holding the modal case constant at the modal proprietive, one can vary the verb's polarity into the negative potential (expressing 'will not/cannot'), or the apprehensive (expressing 'watch out or...'). Or, holding the verbal inflection constant at the potential, one can vary the modal case into the modal locative (expressing 'was able to', i.e. using the modal locative to 'locate', in actual modality, the ability denoted by the verbal potential inflection).

In my view, the fact that the covariation is not fixed but instead the inflections can (to some extent) be mixed and matched to achieve different meanings for the clause – each meaning expressing a particular value of TAMP – should preclude it from being analysed as agreement. As the alternative, Evans (2003: 209 fn. 10, 219–221) considers analysing the phenomenon as government of the noun phrases' case by the verbal inflection. This is prompted by the fact that the verbal inflections and the corresponding modal case inflections are not isomorphic, and by the investigation of the diachrony of this phenomenon: the current constructions originate from 'oblique constructions', that is, subordinate clauses under certain conditions where case was distributed over the clause under government. Problems with this analysis are the following: again, we do not find the expected fixed correspondence between the verbal categories and modal cases; instead, the selected combination of the categories depends on semantics; furthermore, as observed by Evans, 'we would need to relax our definition of government so that it is not seen as stemming just from lexical properties of the governor (...), but can also stem from inflectional values' (2003: 220). Weighing both options, Evans (2003: 221) concludes that, even though the construction appears to be a hybrid between agreement and government, it is easier to see it as the latter by opening the notion of government to allow it to be assigned by inflectional values (e.g. tense) rather than just lexical features (e.g. case frame).

Although without a theory of canonical government it is difficult to assess fully the option of analysing modal case in Kayardild as government, a yet different analysis appears to be plausible. Namely, it is widely accepted that tense, aspect, mood, and polarity are features of the clause, with a value of TAMP normally selected for the clause rather than for an individual element in the clause. Tense, aspect, mood, and polarity are typically morphosemantic features, whose values correlate with different meanings and are dictated by semantic choice. Cross-linguistically, TAMP categories are frequently complex, combining values of the different features (e.g. tense plus aspect, or tense plus aspect plus mood, etc.) into portmanteaux, or distributing the available marking over the verbal complex in a 'non-compositional' way (see, for example, the discussion of periphrastic TAMP in Bulgarian, Popova this volume). It would not be unusual to claim that the TAMP category in Kayardild was expressed in a complex way, that is that two different markers were needed to express one TAMP value, one marker coming from the set of verbal suffixes, and another from the set of modal cases. Since TAMP is a feature of the clause, and since Kayardild has an evident tendency to mark feature values multiply ('on all words over which they have semantic or syntactic scope', Evans 2003: 103), here we once again see the selected value marked on more than one element in the clause in Kayardild.

Therefore, I suggest that the multirepresentation of the modal case component of the TAMP marking in Kayardild is due to the semantic choice of the particular TAMP value for the clause, and to the requirement that in Kayardild TAMP has to be marked on all elements of the syntactic verb phrase (that is, all elements within the syntactic verb phrase have to bear modal case). Hence, this situation falls in category [**B**] along with TAMP in Bulgarian.

4.6.3 *Complementizing case*

Complementizing cases in Kayardild indicate various types of interclausal relation such as being a clausal complement, and they are also frequently triggered by 'odd pivot' conditions (that is, when the pivot shared between clauses is not subject of both) (Evans 2003: 211–213). Furthermore, clauses bearing complementizing case are frequently used independently as a result of 'insubordination', that is the (often conventionalized) ellipsis of the main clause (Evans 2003: 221, fn. 21; 2007). The following examples (from Evans 2003: 212) illustrate the use of complementizing oblique (glossed c.OBL) and complementizing locative (glossed c.LOC):

(8) ngada   kurri-ja,   dangka-ntha   burldi-jarra-ntha
    1SG.NOM   see-ACT   man-C.OBL   hit-PST-C.OBL
    yarbuth-inaa-ntha   thabuju-karra-nguni-naa-ntha
    bird-M.ABL-C.OBL   brother-GEN-INS-M.ABL-C.OBL
    wangal-nguni-naa-nth
    boomerang-INS-M.ABL-C.OBL
    'I saw that the man had hit the bird with (my) brother's boomerang.'

(9) bilda   kurri-ja,   ngakulda   bakiin-ki   burldi-jarra-ya
    3PL.NOM see-ACT   12PL.NOM   all-C.LOC   hit-PST-C.LOC
    yarbuth-inaba-ya   thabuju-karra-nguni-naba-ya
    bird-M.ABL-C.LOC   brother-GEN-INS-M.ABL-C.LOC
    wangal-nguni-naba-y
    boomerang-INS-M.ABL-C.LOC
    'They saw that we all (including you) had hit the bird with brother's boomerang.'

Evans (2003: 212) notes that locative complementizing case is blocked from appearing on pronouns, which therefore default to the nominative (as can be seen in example (9)), but otherwise appears everywhere in the clause. The choice between the complementizing oblique and the complementizing locative (the only two complementizing cases available) is due to semantics: if the subject of the clausal complement is first person inclusive, the clause has to take the complementizing locative case, and in all other instances the clause takes the complementizing oblique. However, with second person subjects either case may be used, and the choice depends on 'subtle factors of solidarity', namely 'C.LOC, with its first inclusive affinities, is used when the speaker wants to group him/herself with the addressee, while C.OBL is used when no such grouping is sought' (Evans 1995: 493–495).

Complementizing case was originally due to agreement of an entire subordinate clause with a case-marked noun phrase antecedent in the main clause, but changes to the main clause case system have obscured this (Evans 1995: 543–549; 2003: 212, 221). In Evans's assessment (2003: 225), this phenomenon receives the largest number of question marks in answer to whether it fulfils Corbett's (2003, also 2006) criteria for canonical agreement. Synchronically, there is no controlling antecedent, and clauses marked for complementizing case can be used independently of the main clause. A government analysis is not plausible either, for three reasons: the possibility of the clauses being independent; the lack of governor in instances of complementizing case assigned under 'odd pivot conditions'; and the fact that the choice of the complementizing case is driven by semantics.

In fact, complementizing cases in Kayardild appear to be analogous to instances of semantic cases, such as the instrumental case in familiar languages which is assigned to a unit (a noun phrase) on the basis of semantic choice. Complementizing cases are, similarly, assigned to a unit (a clause) with which the speaker chooses to express a statement ('complementing information') about some participant in the main clause or in the discourse (including an omitted 'understood' participant). The choice of complementizing case value (oblique vs. locative) is clearly determined by semantics: it depends on the interpretation of the subject of the subordinate clause (and not on any features of the main clause). It has to be marked on all elements of the unit because this is how Kayardild distributes all inflectional information. Hence, I do not hesitate to propose that this phenomenon also falls in category [**B**].

4.6.4 *Associating case*

Associating case is used in connection with nominalizations. The nominalizing suffix is one of two types of inflection in Kayardild that change the morphological word class of the element without changing its syntactic word class. Nominalized verbs are syntactically verbal, but they are morphologically nominal and take normal nominal case inflections (Evans 1995: 89–90). Nominalized verbs may head certain types of dependent clause, or – if they are used in a main clause – indicate continuous aspect (i.e. mark ongoing uncompleted actions).

All noun phrases in a clause headed by a nominalized verb (except the subject and a few noun phrase types linked with it, e.g. secondary predicates on the subject) have to carry an 'associating oblique' case (glossed A.OBL) after any other case suffix they may have (adnominal, relational, and/or modal) (Evans 2003: 213). Examples (from Evans 2003: 213) include:

(10) ngada   yalawu-n-da   yakuri-nja   thabuju-karra-nguni-nja
     1SG.NOM   catch-NMLZ-NOM   fish-A.OBL   brother-GEN-INS-A.OBL
     mijil-nguni-nj
     net-INS-A.OBL
     'I am catching fish with brother's net.'

(11) ngada   kurri-jarra   bilwan-jina   [yalawu-n-kina
     1SG.NOM   see-PST   them-M.ABL   catch-NMLZ-M.ABL
     yakuri-naa-ntha   thabuju-karra-nguni-naa-ntha
     fish-M.ABL-A.OBL   brother-GEN-INS-M.ABL-A.OBL
     mijil-nguni-naa-nth]
     net-INS-M.ABL-A.OBL
     'I saw them catching fish with brother's net.'

Again, the covariation of verbal nominalization and associating case makes the phenomenon available for consideration as agreement. However, as Evans (2003: 222) remarks, the information on the verb and the host noun phrase is 'less obviously of the same type' (the verb is specified as being nominalized, while elements of the noun phrase are specified as taking an associating oblique); the inflection on the verb changes its morphological class form (to nominal), but the inflection on the noun phrase leaves its members unchanged in word class. In my view, while it might be marginally possible to see agreement just in the fact that the verb becomes (morphologically) a noun, and other (target) elements have to agree with it, the key question remains: what do the targets agree in? Kayardild has no gender and the proposed feature has no relation to any independent nominal classification that would need to be proposed for the language outside this construction. There is no plausible agreement feature that could be posited here for the elements to agree in.

Evans (2003: 222) suggests that associating case might be considered an instance of government, 'being a relation between a verbal head and its object(s) and other dependents'; the noun phrase is required to carry an associating oblique 'much in the same way that nominalized verbs in many languages govern the genitive, with the exception that the associating oblique is added on to other cases rather than simply replacing them'. Evans expresses concern about how to account for the process through which the associating case value is distributed through the whole noun phrase – however, as I already argued earlier, on a constituency view of syntax case is governed over a constituent, and it may impose the same feature value simultaneously on all members of the constituent. Therefore, associating case can indeed be analysed as government of case by the nominalized verb over the noun phrase it heads. Hence, it belongs in category [C].

The final question that can be posed with respect to associating case is whether it qualifies to be a feature at all, considering that it appears to have only one value: the associating oblique. In situations such as negative concord, it is reasonable to argue that the phenomenon does not qualify to be a feature because 'positive' polarity is not information that can be assigned to a value – it is, rather, simply lack of information (see Section 4.2.4 above). However, since the value of associating case is imposed by a syntactic rule, rather than being an optional semantic addition, we would want to recognize associating case as a morphosyntactic feature of government, even if the feature appeared to have only one value. Nevertheless, we also observe that the associating oblique is an additional function of the oblique case value which belongs to the set of two values: oblique and locative. Both values participate in the complementizing function, while only one value, the oblique, participates in the associating function. Therefore, despite being glossed here as a unique case (A.OBL), the associating oblique is really an oblique case (OBL) which can be used in an associating function in addition to its other uses.

4.6.5 Multiple TAMP inflection on elements bearing verbalizing case

Multiple marking of elements with verbalizing case in Kayardild was already mentioned in Section 4.6.1. Verbalizing cases express a range of case-like meanings such as beneficiary, direction of motion, purpose, and so on (Evans 1995: 89), and I argued in 4.6.1 that they were best analysed as either instances of government of case over a noun phrase, or instances of choice of a semantic case value for a noun phrase. In this section I discuss a different aspect of the phenomenon of verbalizing case in Kayardild, namely the simultaneous marking of the TAMP category on all elements bearing verbalizing case.

Verbalizing cases are the other type of suffix in Kayardild (the first one being the nominalizing suffix) which changes the morphological word class of the element without changing its syntactic word class. Verbalizing cases attach to each member of the relevant noun phrase, thereby turning each element into a morphological verb. The elements bearing verbalizing case then take the full set of TAMP inflections identical to those found on verbs. They can also take the middle derivational morpheme used in passives and reflexives, and can undergo nominalization using the regular nominalizing suffix or the resultative nominalization. With these suffixes, the verbalized elements are morphologically indistinguishable from verbs, though they continue to occupy their original structural (syntactic) positions (in terms of the ordering within noun phrases) (Evans 2003: 214). The following are examples of clauses with a beneficiary noun phrase marked for verbalizing dative (glossed v.DAT) (Evans 2003: 215):

(12) ngada   waa-jarra   wangarr-ina   ngijin-maru-tharra
      1SG.NOM   sing-PST   song-M.ABL   my-V.DAT-PST
      thabuju-maru-tharra
      brother-V.DAT-PST
      'I sang a song for my brother.'

(13) ngada   waa-nangku   wangarr-u   ngijin-maru-nangku
      1SG.NOM   sing-NEG.POT song-M.PROP   my-V.DAT-NEG.POT
      thabuju-maru-nangku
      brother-V.DAT-NEG.POT
      'I won't sing a song for my brother.'

Multirepresentation of the TAMP inflection in clauses with verbalizing case in Kayardild has been regarded as another strong contender for an agreement phenomenon: agreement in TAMP (Evans 2003: 214–215, 222–223). However, arguing against this analysis Evans (2003: 223) points out that the phenomenon 'lacks directionality' and that 'the category is clausal rather than lexical. In other words, one cannot make a convincing case that the TAMP inflections, on nominals inflected for verbalizing case, are controlled by those on the verb, since an equally plausible account is that both verb and nominals simply reflect, in parallel, the clausal semantics of tense, aspect and mood.' This means that, with respect to both the status of elements involved, as well as the possession of the feature value, the featural dependency is symmetrical rather than asymmetrical. Discussing the same phenomenon, Corbett confirms that the argument as to whether we have agreement in TAMP should run parallel to that concerning the assignment of case to (the elements within) a noun phrase; assuming we adopt the constituency approach to syntax, 'if one believes that tense, aspect, mood and polarity are features of the clause, then marking of these features unusually on items other than on the verb is symmetrical marking and hence not (canonical) agreement' (2006: 139).

Two further arguments corroborate this conclusion. First and more importantly, Evans (1995: 163–164) states that it is possible to omit the main verb in constructions involving verbalizing case. He remarks that this is also allowed with some normal cases, but is more frequent with verbalizing cases. He interprets this as 'being due to the rich semantics of verbal[izing] cases, which often allows the main verb action to be inferred'. An example is (Evans 1995: 164):

(14) ngada   dathin-kiiwa-thu   ngilirr-iiwa-thu
     1SG.NOM   that-V.ALL-POT   cave-V.ALL-POT
     'I will go to that cave.'

If such instances were to be analysed as agreement of the verbalized elements in TAMP, arguably there would be no controller with which the elements could agree. Second, while the categories of tense, aspect, mood, and polarity could plausibly function as features of agreement, the fact that elements bearing verbalizing case can also carry the same nominalization marker (which appears at the same locus as TAMP) as the verb raises the question of what feature that would be.

My conclusion is that the best analysis of multiple TAMP inflection on elements bearing verbalizing case in Kayardild is indeed to regard it as a clausal rather than lexical category, where a particular value of TAMP is selected for the clause following a semantic choice. The multirepresentation of TAMP inflection is due to the requirement that in Kayardild TAMP has to be marked on all elements of the verbal complex, that is, on the main verb together with all other verbalized elements (which are morphologically verbs). (Compare this to the phenomenon discussed in 4.6.2, where all elements within a syntactic verb phrase have to bear modal case.) Hence, this situation falls in category [B].[18]

4.6.6 Multiple TAMP inflection on elements in a verbal group/complex

Finally, Evans (2003: 215–216, 223–224) mentions one more potential site for agreement in Kayardild. This is a construction which involves a more familiar 'verbal group', that is, a sequence of serialized verbs consisting of an obligatory main verb plus up to two further verbs functioning as markers of associated motion, adverbial quantification and aspect. They appear in a fixed order in a single intonational group, and the meaning of the group may be non-compositional. In Kayardild, all verbs in a verbal group take identical values for TAMP, as in the following example (Evans 2003: 223, also cited and discussed in Corbett 2006: 140), where the two verbs of the verbal group match in tense:

(15) niya   kuujuu-jarra   thaa-tharr
     3SG.NOM   swim-PST   return-PST
     'He went off for a swim.'

Note that the verb *thaa-tha* 'return' here means 'go off and V' rather than 'V and return'; therefore (15) could be uttered in a situation when someone has gone off for a swim and not necessarily returned from the swimming yet. Evans emphasizes that the past tense 'is used because of a rule that all words in a verbal group must agree in TAMP, not because it is independently locating "returning" in the past' (2003: 223–224).

Examples like (15), of tense and other verbal features matching within a serial verb complex, are common in serial verb constructions, and the following

---

[18] Alternatively, a case might possibly be made for analysing this phenomenon (or at least some instances of this phenomenon) as situation of type [A], that is, a clause-level feature which is specified for the relevant elements one by one, each time with the same semantic justification. The phrase '[sing] [for-my] [for-brother]' is a verbal group, with the elements other than the main verb bearing a verbalizing case. We may be able to say that negation is specified individually for each element to yield: '[not-sing]', '[not-(do-something)-for-my]', and '[not-(do-something)-for-brother]'. This stretches the semantic interpretation, but probably no more than some other examples of simultaneous marking that we may be tempted to consider to be situations of type [A]. More importantly, this points to the fact that, just as we do not have clear criteria (based on a canonical approach) to distinguish government from agreement, we also do not have any clear criteria to distinguish situation [A] from situation [B] when a feature value is multirepresented in a domain.

sentence illustrates the same phenomenon from Paama (Paamese) (Oceanic, a language of Vanuatu; Crowley 2002: 68):

(16)   ni-suvulu   ni-hiitaa   netano
      1SG:DIST.FUT-climb.down   1SG:DIST.FUT-descend   down
      'I will climb down.'

As suggested by Corbett (2006: 140), in examples such as (15) and (16) it is still possible to view the verbal group as a semantic and syntactic unit, and a TAMP value as being assigned to this unit. This is consistent with viewing a serial verb construction as 'a sequence of verbs which act together as a single predicate without any overt marker of coordination, subordination, or syntactic dependency of any other sort. Serial verb constructions describe what is conceptualized as a single event' (Aikhenvald 2006: 1, though see Baker and Harvey 2010 for discussion of serial verb constructions vs. co-verb constructions).

Therefore, I conclude that the matching of TAMP values in verbal groups, as in (15) and (16), is also better treated as an instance of simultaneous marking of the TAMP value within the verbal group, rather than an instance of agreement of non-head verbs in TAMP with the head verb. I consistently regard TAMP inflection as a clausal rather than lexical category, and view a particular value of TAMP as being selected for the clause following a semantic choice. The multirepresentation of TAMP inflection is due to the requirement that in Kayardild TAMP has to be marked on all elements of the verbal complex, that is, on the main verb together with other verbs in the verb group. As Evans (2003: 223) observes, this looks like a very similar phenomenon to that described in Section 4.6.5, 'except that now it is agreement between straightforward verbs rather than between a verb and nominals whose inflections have converted them into morphological verbs'. (Also, compare this once again to the phenomenon discussed in Section 4.6.2, where all elements within a syntactic verb phrase have to bear modal case.) Hence, I propose that this phenomenon also falls in category [**B**].

Evans (2003: 223) emphasizes that the crucial difference between this phenomenon and TAMP multirepresented in clauses with verbalizing case is that, in some constructions with serial verbs, 'one cannot derive the choice of TAMP inflection on certain non-head verbs directly from the clausal semantics'. Evans attributes this choice to direct agreement with the head verb, but still remarks that the multirepresentation of TAMP in this phenomenon is characterized by informational equivalence and lack of directionality (2003: 217, fn. 15, 218). In response, I repeat the following arguments against an agreement analysis from the discussion of TAMP marking in clauses with verbalizing case: first, TAMP is a clausal not lexical category; and second, the possibility of multiple marking of nominalization in the verbal group suggests that the phenomenon is not agreement because nominalization could hardly be regarded as a feature of agreement.

In the scheme of featural dependencies proposed here, Evans's distinction between compositionality and non-compositionality of the verbal group can be expressed as the difference between situation [A] and situation [B], respectively. That is, any instances of simultaneous marking of a feature value on more than one element which can be justified individually at each element fall in category [A], while any instances of simultaneous marking of a feature value on more than one element which results from the semantic choice of a feature value for an informational or phrasal unit fall in category [B].

4.7 Conclusions for the inventory of morphosyntactic features

All six phenomena of Kayardild discussed above have been considered candidates for agreement phenomena, even though they do not fulfil the criteria for canonical agreement. Since we do not yet have comparable criteria to identify and describe other types of featural dependencies (government, and semantically imposed features), I attempted to identify the space occupied by all these dependencies, and subsequently reanalysed the Kayardild phenomena using the criteria according to which this space is carved up by the dependencies. The intuition behind this decision was that, within the space of featural dependencies, the phenomena which may arguably be regarded as non-canonical agreement are perhaps better analysed as (more) canonical instances of a different featural dependency.

This new look at the problem cases of Kayardild has resulted in my suggestion that:

(a) multiple case marking of relational, adnominal, and verbalizing cases are either instances of government of case over a noun phrase (category [C]), or instances of assignment of case to a noun phrase for semantic reasons (category [B]);
(b) modal case is a component of the TAMP marking, with the particular TAMP value selected for the clause for semantic reasons (category [B]);
(c) complementizing case is a type of semantic case specified for a clause for semantic reasons (category [B]);

(d) associating case is a type of case governed by the nominalized verb over the nominal phrase it heads (category [**C**]);

In all four instances above, multirepresentation of a case value is due to the generalization in the lexicon that nominal elements have to realize all cases they are assigned (that is, in general, 'case suffixes appear on all words over which they have semantic or syntactic scope', Evans 1995: 103).

(e) multiple TAMP inflection on elements bearing verbalizing case is due to a particular value of TAMP having been selected for the clause following a semantic choice, and to the requirement that TAMP be marked on all elements of the verbal complex (so, either category [**B**], or category [**A**] in those instances where the feature value can be semantically justified for every element individually);

(f) multiple TAMP inflection on elements in a verbal group/complex is due to a particular value of TAMP having been selected for the clause following a semantic choice, and to the requirement that TAMP be marked on all elements of the verbal group (verbal complex) (so, typically, category [**B**], though it could be category [**A**] in those instances where the feature value can be semantically justified at every element individually).

These conclusions are consistent with a view of case as a relational feature that expresses a syntactic and/or semantic function of the constituent that carries the particular case value. So, as expected, in Kayardild we find structural (governed) cases and semantic (semantically imposed) cases. But we do not find agreement in case. Agreement in case is rare, and the best examples are found on predicate adjectives, as in the following sentence from Polish (cited in Dziwirek 1990: 147; see also Corbett 2006: 134). Here, the genitive case value on the predicate adjective matches the genitive case value of the quantified noun of the subject noun phrase (the following example is repeated from (2) in Section 4.3.1):

(17) Sześć   kobiet   był-o   smutnych.
      six.NOM   woman.PL.GEN   was-N.3SG   sad.PL.GEN
      'Six women were sad.'

Kayardild presents an extreme example of case stacking (as far as I am aware it is a record-breaker, allowing up to four case markers to be stacked)[19], and the

---

[19] Furthermore, Evans suggests that, theoretically, more than four case inflections could occur, but he has no naturally occurring examples, nor has he been able to elicit any or have such made-up

best explanation for this multirepresentation of case in phrases must be that there is a generalization in the lexicon specifying that nominal elements in Kayardild have to realize all cases they are assigned.[20] Since I have argued that cases in Kayardild are assigned to whole constituents either by government or by semantic choice, there is no need to invoke agreement to account for multiple case marking in Kayardild.

Finally, I have also argued that the assignment of particular tense, aspect, mood, and polarity values in Kayardild is due solely to a semantic choice, and their multirepresentation in the clause or the informational unit (such as a verbal group) is also due to the fact that Kayardild marks feature values on all relevant elements. This conclusion is consistent with the widely held view that tense, aspect, mood, and polarity are features of the clause (rather than being interpreted at the level of lexical items). If this conclusion is accepted, we have to exclude tense, aspect, mood, and polarity from the inventory of morphosyntactic features since their analysis as possible features of agreement can no longer be supported.

Hence, on the basis of cross-linguistic evidence found so far, the only features which qualify for inclusion in the inventory of morphosyntactic features are:

- number (a common feature of agreement)
- gender (a common feature of agreement)
- person (a common feature of agreement)
- respect (a rare feature of agreement)
- case (a rare feature of agreement, and a common feature of government)
- definiteness (a rare morphosyntactic feature, probably of agreement, although this has not yet been established with certainty because we currently lack the criteria to describe [non-]canonical government).

4.8 Closing remarks

Features are a central notion in linguistics, yet very often they are taken for granted, and linguists have not had a commonly agreed-upon inventory of

---

examples accepted; '[t]his is probably due to processing limitations rather than a strict grammatical constraint' (1995: 114).

[20] This does not exclude the possibility of there being exceptions to this general rule, for example regarding some subclasses of elements – for example, pronouns under certain conditions (e.g. as subjects of complement clauses or objects of imperatives) are excepted from case marking.

these basic units of description. The Features Project undertaken in Surrey began to construct such an inventory, focusing on morphosyntactic features. The analysis of feature realization types and considerations of symmetry may provide a new basis for formulating criteria with which to systematize features and establish appropriate inventories for linguists to build on.

Part II

Perspectives from Syntactic Description and Theory

5

Features in categorization, or a new look at an old problem

Keith Plaster and Maria Polinsky

5.1 Introduction[1]

A large body of linguistic literature is concerned with syntagmatic properties of linguistic features: how are features distributed, what is the domain of their operation, what happens when several features compete? All of these issues notwithstanding, it is also important to keep an eye on the paradigmatic aspects of features, and one of the primary questions here has to do with the extent to which linguistic features can and should be taken for granted. This question concerns any set of possible linguistic features, and there may very well be no uniform answer. This chapter examines the content of gender[2] features possible in human language.

We would like to start with an analogy with phonetics. Humans are capable of producing (and distinguishing) a significant number of sounds, but phonological systems around the world are typically constrained by general principles of intelligibility, distinctiveness, or optimal design. This sets in motion a system of checks and balances that allows for significant recurrence of phonetic features across the world's languages.

If we now turn to the category of grammatical gender, gender features can, in principle, be of any kind – nouns in a language can be categorized on the basis of various properties of their denotations, from function to size to colour. But, just as one does not find vowel systems consisting solely of /i/, /y/, and /u/, we do not find gender categorizations based on colour, curly shape, or density. Why? Is it simply because linguists have not been looking closely enough or in the right places, or is it because such systems are impossible?

---

[1] We are grateful to Claire Bowern, Greville Corbett, Mark Harvey, Jay Jasanoff, Anna Kibort, Andrew Nevins, Jeremy Rau, the audience at the Features Workshop at University College London, and two anonymous reviewers for their helpful comments. All errors are our responsibility.

[2] Noun class and gender are different terms denoting the same concept (Corbett 1991: 1); 'class' and 'gender' will be used interchangeably in this chapter.

This chapter is an attempt to revisit this general issue and to argue that, at least with regard to gender classifications, the inventory of features employed by different languages is quite small. The limitations imposed on such an inventory are ultimately due to learnability constraints and perceptual salience. To support this point of view, we will examine a particularly difficult case of noun classification.

Much work on noun class/gender systems has focused on the role of semantics in the assignment of nouns to classes. Sometimes the semantics responsible for noun class assignment is rather straightforward and based on general, superordinate categories such as 'human', 'animate', or 'female', which are known to be foundational in developmental psychology. Sometimes, however, the kinds of semantic categories used to account for noun class composition are of a very culture-specific, complex nature (for an overview of the relevant literature, see Craig 1986; Corbett 1991: 307–324).

Before appealing to complex semantic and cultural information as the basis for noun classification, it is helpful to gauge the extent to which this information is available to speakers, and in particular to those trying to get a toehold in the system. Young language learners do not yet have access to much of the abstract and culture-specific information possessed by adults, and may have substantial difficulties learning a noun classification system based on such knowledge. The idea that gender systems are learned early is strongly supported by the acquisition of gender in Bantu, where the system that needs to be learned is quite complex, with languages continuing the canonical Bantu noun class system generally containing six noun classes paired for singular and plural and another set of approximately six unpaired classes (Katamba 2003). For a number of Bantu languages, it has been shown that gender is learned by the beginning of the third year of life and that both production and comprehension of gender are practically error-free (Kunene 1979; Suzman 1991, 1996; Kapust 1998; Demuth 1988, 1992, 2000, 2003; Deen 2005, 2006; Idiata 2005).

Outside of Bantu, the complex gender systems of German, French, or Russian are also learned early, and this learning is manifested both in comprehension and production (Mills 1986; Karmiloff-Smith 1979; Gvozdev 1961; Kempe et al. 2003; Polinsky 2008).[3] The knowledge of gender is revealed in multiple ways – from the use of correct declension classes correlating with

---

[3] In each of these languages, small subclasses of nouns resist correct gender assignment until an older age, usually 4 or 5. For example, in Russian, certain neuter nouns and feminines ending in a palatalized consonant continue to pose a problem for learners until age 5 (Gvozdev 1961: 442; Smoczyńska 1985: 644; Polinsky 2007). In German, some plural endings (in -e), whose gender assignment is not always straightforward, remain problematic for children up to age 4;0 (Mills 1985, 1986).

genders (cf. Gerken et al. 2005, where English-speaking 17-month-olds were able to distinguish grammatical from ungrammatical Russian words after approximately two minutes of exposure to a Russian gender paradigm) to the correct use of gender agreement (Deen 2006; Kempe and Brooks 2001; Karmiloff-Smith 1979, among others). Crucially, the learning of all these systems relies on simple conceptual cues (animacy, mobility) and salient formal features. For example, the acquisition of Slavic gender is facilitated by the frequent use of diminutives (Kempe and Brooks 2001; Ševa et al. 2007); the diminutives provide consistent *formal* cues, which are further reinforced by regular agreement patterns. Overall, the generalization is that young learners pay attention to the combination of salient formal features of a word *in conjunction* with agreement.

At the same time as young learners are mastering the gender systems of various languages, their abstract thinking lags behind their grammatical competence. Numerous studies show that children in the second year of age are just beginning to develop incipient symbolic reference (Gallistel 1990; DeLoache 1995). Moreover, children in their second and third year of life map words and objects referentially, not associatively (Gallistel 1990; Preissler and Carey 2004; Clark 1993; Gelman and Bloom 2000; Gelman 2000, 2003; Mandler 2004). This in turn suggests that outside of the most frequent items, whose grammatical information is likely to be learned by rote as word islands (cf. Tomasello 1992), the young learner acquiring gender is sensitive to what he or she knows how to identify best – word segmentation, stressed segments, syllabic division, or, in other words, salient formal properties of language (e.g. Hudson Kam and Newport 2005; Weiss and Newport 2006).

To the extent that language change is driven by children acquiring language, we should expect the kind of information to which children have access to play a significant role in the structure and development of a language. If so, gender systems which are based on complex semantic cues and strong meaningful analogies should present an insurmountable obstacle to learning. Either such systems should be learned much later in life and/or prove unstable, or it may be that their inherent structure is amenable to a different analysis, one that does not rely on complex semantic features.

In this chapter, we will take up a particularly well-known case of exotic noun classification, that in Dyirbal, a moribund Pama-Nyungan language of Australia. We argue that the development and operation of Dyirbal gender can be accounted for on the basis of a small number of semantic features andthe morphophonemic similarities of items and their type/token frequency without recourse to complicated semantics. If our proposal is on the right track, this arguably sophisticated gender system does not constitute a counterexample to the general conception that grammatical gender is acquired on the basis of straightforward linguistic cues.

The remainder of the chapter is structured as follows. In Section 5.2, we introduce the composition of the Dyirbal nominal lexicon. Section 5.3 reviews the existing analyses of Dyirbal noun classification. Section 5.4 is a brief survey of our proposal concerning the diachronic development of the Dyirbal genders, and Section 5.5 presents a proposal concerning the synchronic composition of Dyirbal genders such that it could be accessible to a young learner. Section 5.6 takes our reanalysed system to the next step, where this system is further simplified and undermined by loss of agreement cues. Section 5.7 presents our conclusions.

5.2 Data

Dyirbal has four noun classes (genders), which are manifested in agreement with the demonstrative ('noun marker', Dixon 1972). Demonstratives also mark case and differentiate between proximal, medial, and distal deixis. For medial deixis, the gender markers are shown in Table 5.1.

Moving on to the composition of noun classes, Dixon (1972) presents the following list of concepts associated with each class and suggests that such a heterogeneous list might indicate that the noun classification lacks any principled basis. However, he also notes that speakers have little variation in class assignment and immediately assign loanwords to a class. The breakdown of concepts by classes is shown in Table 5.2.

This table shows a complicated system, which poses a serious challenge to any learnability model. Even if we set young learners aside, the storage and access of such a classification system nevertheless seem challenging for an adult speaker. Therefore, accounting for such a system is particularly important for our understanding of noun categorization in natural language. A plausible account should try to explain the principles underlying the system and also make predictions for the classification of new words entering the

TABLE 5.1 Dyirbal noun class markers, medial deixis

	Absolutive	Ergative	Dative	Genitive
Class I	*bayi*	*baŋgul*	*bagul*	*baŋul*
Class II	*balan*	*baŋgun*	*bagun*	*baŋun*
Class III	*balam*	*baŋgum*	*bagum*	—
Class IV	*bala*	*baŋgu*	*bagu*	*baŋu*

TABLE 5.2 Distribution of concepts across noun classes in Dyirbal (Dixon 1972: 307)

I (*bayi*)	II (*balan*)	III (*balam*)	IV (*bala*)
men	women		parts of the body
kangaroos	bandicoots		meat
possums	dog		
bats	platypus, echidna		
most snakes	some snakes		
most fishes	some fishes		
some birds	most birds		
most insects	firefly, scorpion, crickets hairy mary grub anything connected with fire or water		bees and honey[a]
moon	sun and stars		wind
storms, rainbow			yamsticks
boomerangs	shields		
some spears	some spears		some spears
	some trees	all trees with edible fruit	most trees
			grass, mud, stones
			most noises, language

[a] While Dixon (1972) identified *girnyjal* 'honey' as belonging to class IV, Dixon (1984) identifies the noun as belonging to class III.

lexicon. Dixon and several authors after him have proposed a purely semantic account of the Dyirbal noun class system, to which we turn in Section 5.3.

5.3 The semantic account of gender assignment in Dyirbal

The existing accounts of Dyirbal noun classes, proposed by Dixon (1972), Lakoff (1987), Mylne (1995), and Harvey (1997: 19–24), all emphasize the conceptual underpinnings of the classification.

To account for the distribution of concepts across the four noun classes in Dyirbal (Table 5.2), Dixon suggests that class membership in Dyirbal is best explained through the interaction of some basic (core) concepts associated with the various classes and a set of overriding rules. The core concepts are (Dixon 1972: 308):

(1) Core semantic concepts in Dyirbal noun classification
    Class I: animacy, (human) masculinity
    Class II: (human) femininity; water; fire; fighting[4]
    Class III: edible plants (nonflesh food)[5]
    Class IV: everything else (residue)

Although in theory the association between core concepts and noun classes could be quite straightforward, in actuality nouns are assigned to classes subject to a set of conceptually based rules. These rules override the general principles of class assignment listed in (1); in other words, the principles in (1) represent the default conditions, whereas the overriding rules allow for a more fine-grained noun-to-class network, based on more specific conditions.

At this point, we will present the overriding rules followed by examples of their application.[6]

(2) *Rule 1 (Myth-or-belief)*: If a noun has characteristic X (on the basis of which its class membership would be expected to be decided) but is, through belief or myth, associated with characteristic Y, then generally it will belong to the class corresponding to Y, not to X.

For example, most birds are in class II because they are thought to be spirits of dead women. However, willy wagtails, which as birds should be in class II, are instead in class I because they are believed to be mythical men. Several other birds are also assigned to class I based on such mythical connections (Dixon 1972: 308).

---

[4] In a different account, Mylne (1995) suggests that the main opposition is in terms of potency and benign/malign power. This still leaves the account driven by complicated semantics, a feature we are arguing against here.

[5] Such a narrowly defined class is rather surprising given the three other classes which are very inclusive. But note that in Australian traditional culture, 'children must learn from the earliest age to be able to classify plants (and indeed anything else they are liable to put into their mouths as babies)' (Mylne 1995: 390). See also Walsh (1993).

[6] Dixon (1972: 308–310) proposes the first two rules; rule three is proposed by Lakoff (1987: 93) on the basis of Dixon's analysis.

(3) *Rule 2 (Domain-of-experience)*: If there is a basic domain of experience associated with A, then it is natural for entities in that domain to be in the same category as A (Lakoff 1987: 93).

To illustrate, plants tend to be in the elsewhere class in Dyirbal (class IV), but plants that have edible fruit are in class III with the fruit they yield.

(4) *Rule 3 (Important-property)*: If a subset of referents has some particular important property that the rest of the set does not have, then the members of that subset may be assigned to a different class from the rest of the set to 'mark' that particular important property. In Dyirbal, the important property is often [+harmful].

For example, most types of fish are in class I; however, harmful ones (stonefish, toadfish) are in class II. Similarly, harmful (stinging) trees are in class II, with the harmful fish, but all other trees without edible fruit are in class IV.

Following Dixon's analysis, Lakoff (1987) proposes a description of the Dyirbal gender system based on the notion of a radial category. Within a radial category, a particular element that has most of the defining characteristics of that category serves as the prototype. Other elements are assimilated to the prototype on the basis of their perceived resemblance to the prototype, but they do not have to actually share the criterial features of that prototype. The more peripheral members are linked to the prototype through other members, and these links can be motivated by certain principles. Taken together, the members of a category thus form a radial structure, with the most representative, or prototypical, members located at the centre, and with less representative outliers clustered around this hub.

In the case of Dyirbal class II (containing 'women, fire, and dangerous things'), the core is human females (Lakoff 1987: 100–101). The links to the core are achieved in the following manner: the sun is a female deity and is married to the moon (which is in class I, as a male). The sting of the hairy mary grub hurts like sunburn; thus, it is linked to the sun. All items related to fire (fire, matches, and pipe) are linked to the sun as well. The firefly is linked to fire. Stars and light are associated with and linked to fire, and through it to the sun.

Birds are in the female class because they are spirits of dead women. (And some birds are in class I because they are spirits of dead men.) Crickets in myth are 'old ladies' and they are in the female class. Since women are related via myth to the sun, and the sun via domain-of-experience is related to fire, women and fire end up in one class. Since fire is dangerous, other dangerous things should be in the same class. This brings in water and fighting.

So far, we have applied the myth-or-belief rule and the domain-of-experience rule. Now comes the important-property rule (4): because something is 'harmful', it is placed in a separate class from all other members of its subset. Thus, most fish are in class I, but harmful fish are in class II. In other words, noun class distinctions can be used to underscore differences in some critical characteristic (see Zubin and Köpcke 1986 for a similar principle in the analysis of German gender assignment).

Mylne (1995) modifies Lakoff's account to make it more culture-specific and sensitive to the semiotics of the traditional aboriginal society. However, despite these modifications the analysis remains largely semantically driven and expands the notion of the prototype. Thus, theoretically, it is not very different from Lakoff's account. And in another drive towards a more culture-specific account, Harvey (1997: 24) proposes an ontology in which natural concepts such as [human], [force of nature], [edible] are associated with particular environments (air, tree, water, ground), with further classifications built on such associations. While the details of his proposal may differ from the others discussed here, the spirit is very similar: identify a salient concept and build a radial category by various semiotic links to this concept.

If the rules described above applied satisfactorily and if the radial category account were comprehensive and had predictive power, then one could conclude the investigation of the Dyirbal noun classification. However, the rules do not apply in any systematic way and, as they are, seem to act more as after-the-fact generalizations than operational principles (see also footnote 12). The radial-category account fails to motivate the links in an unambiguous and predictive manner. Most importantly, if links between members of a radial category require specific cultural knowledge and often have to be explained at length, it raises the crucial question of learnability: how does a young learner acquire all these links and relations? In our view, the opacity of links inside the presumed radial category suggests that an alternative account would be desirable.

Crucially, in their discussion of the Dyirbal genders, the previous authors rarely mention the actual lexical items occurring in Dyirbal – instead, they deal only with semantic concepts and the referents of the lexical items. In other words, they have not tried to find any connection between the form of the Dyirbal words appearing in a certain class before turning to the words' semantics. Given that learners are known to be very sensitive to formal cues from infancy (Saffran et al. 1996a, b; Newport and Aslin 2000, 2004; Hudson Kam and Newport 2005), and that young learners tend to regularize inconsistent input based on segmental information, it is important to give formal cues the credit they deserve before turning to complicated semantic cues. In addition, if formal cues were shown to fail then the categorizing power of conceptual structure could be validated even more forcefully than in the earlier accounts presented here.

In what follows we will attempt to explain Dyirbal noun classification differently, and our results will be compatible with the very general features that are found in gender systems all over the world. In a nutshell, we will portray Dyirbal as a much less exotic language as far as notional motivation for gender is concerned. In particular, we will argue for a combination of formal and semantic cues in Dyirbal gender assignment, bringing its gender classification much closer to the familiar systems around the globe. Before discussing these issues in Section 5.5, we will briefly address the diachrony of gender classification in Dyirbal.

5.4 Diachronic origins of Dyirbal noun classes

The category of gender in Pama-Nyungan is rare, although there are numerous instances of languages with classifiers. In Plaster and Polinsky (2007), we review evidence from closely and more remotely related Pama-Nyungan languages and show that they have comparable classifier systems which find correspondences in the composition of Dyirbal noun classes.

In addition to the evidence for classifier systems in languages closely related to Dyirbal, Dyirbal itself provides evidence of its former classifier system. Dixon and Koch (1996: 44) note that the Dyirbal gender system is a relatively recent development, as confirmed by the relatively infrequent use of noun class markers in Dyirbal song poetry (see Plaster and Polinsky 2007 for the details of this evidence).

The original classifier system of Dyirbal likely contained many more classifiers that can no longer be identified as synchronic semantic classes. Gender systems can develop from classifier systems through the collapse of a larger number of classifiers into a smaller number of genders, with generic nouns such as 'woman', 'man', and 'animal' serving as class cores (Corbett 1991: 311–312, 317). During the development of the Dyirbal classifier system into the present gender system, different classifiers merged to create each noun class. Although classifiers themselves are semantically based, the composition of the genders resulting from such a merger are not necessarily driven by the semantics of the classifiers; although one may expect classifiers for clearly semantically related concepts (such as 'edible' and 'potable') to merge, semantically unrelated classifiers may merge based on shared formal features or for no currently clear reason (the semantic motivation may have become opaque).

In Plaster and Polinsky (2007), we hypothesize that correspondences between the classifier classes and the resulting noun classes in Dyirbal are as follows:

(5) Dyirbal classifier classes > Dyirbal noun classes

    Class I   [+male], [+edible animate]
    Class II   [+female], [+bird], [+fire], [+fresh water], [+stinging]
    Class III   [+edible non-animate]
    Class IV   everything else

The merger of several of the classes we have identified can be motivated straightforwardly based on the semantic characteristics involved. As we will discuss below, [+male] and [+female] appear to be the semantic cores of classes I and II respectively, and the distinction between animate and inanimate nouns in Dyirbal is strong. All animate nouns fall within classes I and II; while classes I and II contain some inanimate nouns, no animate noun appears in class III or class IV. Accordingly, it appears that animacy was likely a driving factor in the development of the noun class system.

Focusing on *animate* nouns, a merger of the [+male] class with the [+edible animate] class led to the exclusion of those animate nouns that are not edible. Since only two classes, I and II, include animate nouns, this entailed that animates which were not [+edible animate] ended up in class II: any other animals that were not identified as 'edible', including dogs, flies, grasshoppers, spiders, and worms, were placed into class II. Similarly, animates capable of inflicting a harmful sting were placed in class II due to their animacy, and not because they were identified with human females. As non-edible animals, they could not be placed in the other animate class, class I; this left only class II available, and the entire set of [+stinging] items was drawn into class II.

However birds are a problem for this proposal: they are included within the scope of the [+edible animate] classifier, for example, in the closely related language Yidiny, but they are in class II in Dyirbal rather than the expected class I. This may indicate that the merger of birds with human females occurred at an early stage during the collapse of the classifier system, possibly due to formal attraction or analogy, or the early identification of birds with the spirits of dead human females.

One possible attractor for such a merger of birds with human females into a single class is the feminine suffix *-gan*, which is found in a number of languages on the east coast of Australia (see Dixon 1972: 12–13 for references), including Banjalang (Crowley 1978: 37). For example, Dyirbal *jarrugan* 'scrub hen' appears to be derived from the Dyirbal generic noun or classifier corresponding to the Yidiny classifier *jarru*, possibly consisting of *jarru*- 'bird' and the feminine suffix *-gan*. Identification of the ending *gan* with the feminine suffix *-gan* could easily have led to the form being attracted into the class for human females. Other bird names in our sample also contain formal features identified with class II.[7]

In assigning gender to a new noun, a speaker may classify it on the basis of formal similarity with familiar nouns (rather than semantics), especially if the initial or final segments of the noun resemble a pattern that the speaker recognizes as associated with a particular class. In addition to the salient suffix *-gan*, a crucial role in formal analogy belongs to stressed segments. The role of stressed segments in the division of nouns into classes is well known from familiar Indo-European languages; for instance, Latin or French gender assignment can be successfully explained by appealing to stressed endings (Tucker et al. 1977; Corbett 1991: Chapters 2 and 3; Polinsky and van Everbroeck 2003; Lyster 2006). In Dyirbal, the stress is invariably on the first syllable, and we find strong evidence indicating that the initial syllable played a role in creating formal analogy that could facilitate class mergers.

For example, *yimalimal* 'welcome swallow' begins with *yi*-, which is strongly correlated with class II and is the initial syllable of *yibi* 'woman'; all animate nouns in our sample with the initial syllable *yi*- are placed in class II.[8] In addition, several bird names begin with *bi*-, which is also strongly correlated with class II membership, likely due to the association with the form *bibi*, which appears in various Pama-Nyungan languages with the meaning 'woman', 'mother' or '(female) breast' (O'Grady 1998). 'Whistle duck', 'large parrot', and 'white ibis' all begin with *bi*-. We will discuss each of these formal features in detail in Section 5.5, but we would like to emphasize that the

---

[7] Our sample contains 597 Dyirbal nominal forms culled from the following sources: Dixon (1972, 1980, 1982a, b, 1984, 1989, 1990), Dixon and Koch (1996), and Schmidt (1985). In the original lexicon, there are a number of items from the avoidance language (a highly formalized register used for communication across moieties, found in a number of Australian languages), which we did not include in our analysis because avoidance languages are often associated with their special phonology or grammar. In addition, we did not include items that appear only in Dyirbal song poetry. Thus, here we treat only forms from Guwal, the everyday, non-avoidance language. A spreadsheet of the forms used in our sample is available upon request.

[8] As we explain in Section 5.5, although *yirrinyjila* 'dragonfly' begins with *yi*- in the Dyirbal dialect of Dyirbal, the form in the other dialects begins with *wi*-. As a result, in all other dialects the form does not contain the formal feature.

existence and salience of these features was probably the initial motivation for the classification of birds with human females.

Of the *inanimate* classes, the class of edible inanimate items was clearly the most salient, as attested by its status as the sole semantic class found in class III. As with the merger of names for birds and human females, we propose that the merger of fire- and water-related items with the other members of class II was due to existence of formal attractors and not any semantic identification between human females and fire or fresh water. For example, *bugan* 'brush fire' ends in *-gan*, which is identical to the feminine suffix *-gan*. Likewise, *binda* 'waterfall' begins with *bi-*, which we have also identified as a formal feature associated with class II (see Section 5.5).

Formal features allow us to directly account for two of the prime examples for the 'domain-of-experience' rule in (3): *garri* 'hairy mary grub' and *yarra* 'fishing line'. Although we would expect to find *garri* in class I, the default class for animate nouns, it appears in class II. Dixon (1972: 310) explains its classification as due to its semantic association with the sun, noting that 'its sting is said to feel like sunburn'. However, Dixon makes nothing of the exact correspondence between the forms *garri* 'sun' and *garri* 'hairy mary grub', or that this correspondence provides a more direct explanation for the class assignment. Put more directly, we propose that *garri* 'hairy mary grub' is not a class II noun because its sting is similar to the effect of spending too much time in the *garri* 'sun', but because its form is identical to *garri*.

In fact, recognizing that formal attraction led to the placement of both nouns in class II allows us to explain the assignment of *garram* 'garfish' to the same class. Although most fish are assigned to class I, a few fish, including garfish and stonefish, are assigned to class II, which Dixon and Lakoff attribute to the operation of the important-property rule, provided in (4); under their analysis, a subset of fish possess an important property ('harmfulness'), and this property is marked by placing these fish in a different class from other fish. However, while stonefish are, in fact, harmful, garfish are not; no Australian garfish species is known to be dangerous or harmful, although the members of one species are 'described as "pugnacious... but are incapable of inflicting anything like a serious wound"' (Mylne 1995: 395). This and certain other assignments of non-human animates to class II led Mylne (1995) to question Dixon and Lakoff's determination that harmfulness underlies the assignment of these non-human animates to class II.

As noted above, we propose that the Dyirbal [+edible animate] classifier class merged with the class of male humans to form class I. Under this scenario, 'garfish' was originally placed in class I as 'edible', while 'stonefish' and 'toadfish' were excluded from class I as not 'edible', just as 'garfish' bears the 'edible meat' class *minya* in Yidiny, while 'stonefish' and 'toadfish' do not. Accordingly, the assignment of 'garfish' to class II is similarly unexpected.

We propose that the assignment of *garram* 'garfish' to the same class as *garri* 'sun' and *garri* 'hairy mary grub' is due to the phonological shape of the left edge of each word. No other animate noun in our sample begins with *garr-*; all three – the sun being animate by myth – are assigned to class II.[9]

A similar argument can be made for the assignment of *yarra* 'fishing line'. Although, as an inanimate noun, we would expect to find *yarra* in class IV, it is found in class I. This unexpected classification is explained by Dixon as due to the semantic connection between men and fishing. However, the phonological similarity between the actual form for 'man', *yara*, and 'fishing line', *yarra*, more directly explains the class assignment. These forms are identical except for the rhotic in each form. Although /r/ and /rr/ are phonemes in traditional Dyirbal, as shown by the minimal pair in question, the /r/ and /rr/ distinction appears to have been breaking down at the time of Dixon (1972), as shown by consistent dialectal differences in the presence of /r/ or /rr/ word-finally, as in the forms for 'navel', *jujur* in the Dyirbal and Mamu dialects but *jujurr* in the Giramay dialect, and 'urine', *jujar* in the Dyirbal and Mamu dialects but *jujarr* in the Giramay dialect. Thus, we propose that the rhotic distinction was not sufficiently salient to prevent the attraction of *yarra* 'fishing line' into class I on the basis of *yara* 'man'. This proposal receives support from the observation that the distinction between the two phonemes is almost lost in Young People's Dyirbal (YD), the language of the children and grandchildren of Dixon's Dyirbal consultants.[10]

The identification of formal features by speakers may either encourage the reassignment of a noun from its semantically expected class to the class with which the formal feature is associated (as in the case of *garri* 'hairy mary grub', *garram* 'garfish', and *yarra* 'fishing line'), or prevent the reassignment of a noun from a semantically unexpected class – but with which the formal feature is associated – to another, semantically expected class.[11] The result

---

[9] The Dyirbal word *garambarri* 'young alligator' is the only other animate noun in our sample that begins with the sequence *ga-*, but due to its association with the class I nouns *gujagay* 'alligator' and *maybaja* 'alligator' we would not expect its classification to be affected by *garri* 'sun'.

[10] According to Schmidt (1985), the distinction between these phonemes has been fully lost in YD in words except where the distinction is necessary to prevent homophony, as in the case of *yara* 'man' and *yarra* 'fishing line'; otherwise, YD speakers wavered in their realizations of the /r/ and /rr/ phonemes. The weakening or collapse of rhotic distinctions has also been documented for other dying languages (see Schmidt 1985: 193 for references and discussion).

[11] Which of these two forces is more powerful is an interesting question, but beyond the scope of this chapter.

of either scenario is identical: a noun's class matches the formal feature that it carries.

If the origins that we propose for the noun class system are correct, the language documented by Dixon (1972) represents an intermediate stage in the expected development of the noun class system. The semantic criteria for certain classes have changed over time as speakers in general and child learners in particular were faced with the task of identifying the system's underlying principles, as shown by the shift from [+edible animal] to [+non-human animate] as a component of class I. The difficulty of identifying these semantic principles became even more troublesome once reclassifications began to occur on the basis of formal features. An extremely shallow agreement system, where the demonstratives were the only exponent of gender, added to the difficulty of maintaining gender in Dyirbal (compare this shallow system with the pervasive agreement found in Bantu, Northeast Caucasian, or Indo-European gender languages). If given sufficient time, we would expect the number of exceptional classifications in the Dyirbal system to dwindle, and the vast majority of nouns to be classified simply and straightforwardly on the basis of a small number of core semantic classes and clear formal features.

5.5 Motivating Dyirbal noun classifications synchronically

In accounting for synchronic noun categorization we approach it first and foremost from the standpoint of learnability. When faced with the task of determining which noun class to associate with each noun, a Dyirbal child is not able to draw on sophisticated semantic concepts and connections that either adults (seeking to justify the class associations that they have learned)[12] or linguists (seeking to find an underlying order in the system) may come up with. A child has no inherent (or learned) association of women with dangerous things, contrary to Lakoff's account, or as an 'other' and 'associated with the disruption of harmony of living', contrary to Mylne (1995: 387). Since many of the concepts that Lakoff and Mylne identify as underlying

---

[12] Lakoff (1987: 100–101) cites the following speech recorded by Schmidt (1985) from a semi-speaker of Dyirbal as evidence for a connection in the minds of Dyirbal speakers between fire and danger, on the one hand, and women, on the other: 'buni [fire] is a lady...Woman is a destroyer. 'e destroys anything. A woman is a fire.' However, it is impossible to determine whether the speaker possessed this belief prior to being asked, or if the speaker actually relies on the stated association to classify the items. If asked, even English speakers, who possess a minimal gender system, can posit semantic reasons for ships being referred to as 'she' rather than 'it', while in actuality it is merely a matter of custom.

the Dyirbal noun class system are beyond the scope of young children's understanding, the systems posited by Lakoff and Mylne would be nearly impossible for children to learn. Unless we expect Dyirbal children to have memorized all class associations by rote until such time as they could understand the complex concepts and relations posited by the semantic accounts, the existing explanations of the Dyirbal gender system are difficult to maintain.

While complex mythological associations that require rote learning, abstract knowledge, and vast cultural experience are unlikely for a 2-year-old, developmental psychology shows that children under the age of one are able to differentiate such basic categories as 'human', 'animate', 'male', 'female', and 'mobile' (Gentner and Namy 1999; Namy and Gentner 2002; Kellman and Arterberry 1998; Mandler 2004, among many others). Remarkably, these categories match the basic semantic categories involved in gender assignment across languages (Corbett 1991: 7–30, 82–89), and we can reasonably expect such a core to be present in our system. With nouns that fall outside of those semantic cores, one could expect a child to make errors and to reassign the nouns on the basis of some other salient cues, most likely the phonological form of a word. For example, children should learn quickly that males and most non-human animates belong in class I, females in class II, edible items in class III, and inanimate things in class IV. A child faced with the need to determine which class marker to use with *jirrga* 'eel-spear' and *baŋgay* 'spear' would place them in class IV with the other inanimate nouns that the child knows, rather than class I and II, respectively.

5.5.1 *Semantic core*

When we examine the composition of the noun classes in Dyirbal, we find that classes I through III have a well-defined semantic core. This core is reinforced by the fact that nouns denoting the relevant concepts do not appear elsewhere, so the core is in a sense exclusive to the relevant class. Nouns referring to male humans appear only in class I, while nouns referring to female humans appear only in class II. Consumable, non-beverage items other than meat – a more accurate characterization than 'edible', which we use henceforth for the sake of brevity – appear only in class III. Examples are provided in (6):

(6) a. Class I: [+male]
 yara 'man'
 gaya 'mother's younger brother'
 wirru '(potential) husband'

b. Class II: [+female]
bulgu '(potential) wife'
jugumbil 'woman'
gajin 'girl'
c. Class III: [+edible]
jugur 'wild yam'
gabi 'gabi fig'
wuju 'vegetable/fruit food (generic)'

Loanwords from English are also drawn into the relevant classes on the basis of the same semantic criteria, as shown in (7):

(7) a. Class I
bulijiman ~ *buliman* 'policeman'
waybala 'white man'
b. Class II
mijiji 'white woman (missus)'
c. Class III
binarra 'peanut'
gaygi 'cake'
laymun 'lemon'

Thus, any [+male], [+female], or [+edible] nominal will be assigned to class I, class II, and class III respectively.[13] In addition, the majority of non-human animate beings, such as animals, fish, and insects, appear in class I, and in fact comprise the majority of the class I nouns in our sample, while the vast majority of inanimate nouns are placed in class IV. Accordingly, class I appears to be the default class for non-human animate beings, while class IV is the default class for inanimate nouns.

While class III is a limited semantic class, only admitting edible items, and class IV is an elsewhere class, accepting nouns that are not assigned to any of the other three classes,[14] classes I and II contain a variety of nouns that do not fall within the semantic classes identified above. The three smaller semantic classes that we identified in Section 5.4, [+fire], [+fresh water], and [+stinging], account for the classification of certain inanimate nouns to

---

[13] The exceptionless character of these class assignments leads us to conclude with Dixon (1972) and Lakoff (1987), and against Mylne (1995), that masculine and feminine are core features of class I and II respectively.

[14] Due to its elsewhere nature, class IV is by far the largest: of the 597 nouns that we have been able to establish, about 49% belong to class IV.

class II. A decision tree for determining the assignment of Dyirbal nouns based on the above features is shown in (8):

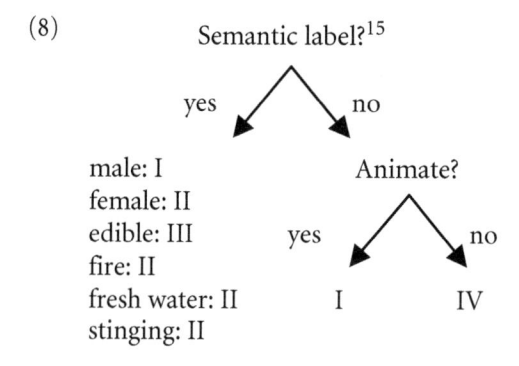

(8)   Semantic label?[15]

```
              yes  /\  no
                 /    \
male: I              Animate?
female: II           /    \
edible: III      yes /      \ no
fire: II
fresh water: II   I          IV
stinging: II
```

While the previous accounts of the Dyirbal gender system sought a synchronic semantic basis for the assignment of every Dyirbal noun to its class, we propose that those nouns whose classification does not follow directly from (8) are classified on the basis of formal features or are remnants of the earlier classifier-based system which have successfully resisted reassignment due to their frequency of use.

5.5.2 Beyond the core: in search of synchronic motivations

Recall that classes I and II contain certain nouns whose class assignment is unexpected. In addition to words for humans, classes I and II contain non-human animate nouns as well as various inanimate items, including the words for 'sun', 'moon', and 'rainbow'. Although class I appears to be the default class for non-human animate beings, certain non-human animate beings appear in class II, including most birds and certain fish. If class I is the default class for animates, any animates found in class II require an explanation. Similarly, we must explain any inanimate nouns placed in either of these classes.

As emphasized by Dixon (1972, 1984) and Dixon and Koch (1996), the role of folklore in Dyirbal culture is undeniable, and we agree that folkloric

---

[15] We separate animacy from the remaining semantic features for two reasons. First, unlike the other semantic features, which could be assigned to nouns not possessing the semantics of the feature (as, for example, in the class assignment of the moon and sun based on their mythological identification as male and female respectively), [+animate] appears not to have been a feature that could be applied to a noun unless its referent truly was animate. In addition, in the event of a conflict between an assigned semantic label and a noun's inherent [+animate] feature, the assigned semantic label determined the noun's class assignment (as in the case of the animals belonging to class II due to their identification as [+female] or [+stinging]).

associations are likely responsible for the class assignment of at least some nouns found in class I or II. The categorization of words denoting celestial objects (stars, planets) is likely due to folklore. As Dixon explains, the moon is the husband of the sun in Dyirbal folklore, and accordingly *gagara* 'moon' is placed in class I and *garri* 'sun' in class II. Similarly, *yamani* 'rainbow' is a man in Dyirbal mythology, and assigned to class I. In addition, according to Dyirbal folklore, birds are the spirits of dead human females, and most bird names are in class II.[16] Similarly, crickets, which were excluded from the class of edible animals that formed class I, are assigned to class II because speakers liken them to 'old ladies'.[17]

Since the telling and retelling of folklore was such a part of Dyirbal society,[18] from an early age children learned the mythological semantic labels associated with these nouns, and this accounts for their gender assignment; it certainly helps in the learning of their gender that these words are few in number and presumably at least some of them are frequent. If certain words were not such an integral part of Dyirbal everyday conversation or storytelling, we would expect them to be susceptible to reassignment to class I, in the case of birds, or to class IV, in the case of inanimate nouns. In fact, these are precisely the reassignments that Schmidt (1985) documented in the language of the children and grandchildren of Dixon's Dyirbal consultants, as we will discuss in Section 5.6.

The situation with the smaller semantic subclasses is similar. To the extent that a child is able to identify that nouns associated with water or fire or that are capable of harmful stinging are placed in class II, the association of these items with class II will remain. Fresh water and fires both played a large role in Dyirbal daily life, and words relating to fresh water and fire do not appear in any other class. As a result, it is easy to believe that children received sufficient input to identify that fresh water- and fire-related items belong in class II.

---

[16] The names of birds follow mythological associations much less reliably than the names of celestial objects or require more extensive knowledge of the avian world. In addition to birds like willy wagtails, which are placed in class I as mythical men, Dixon mentions that certain other birds (like hawks) go into class I because they eat other birds. Rather than being classified as [+male], we suspect that such bird-eating birds may not bear the [+female] label due to their carnivorous conduct, and as a result are placed in the default class for animates.

[17] Again, the question of chronological order arises: were crickets viewed as 'old ladies' before they fell into class II, or did the connection between crickets and 'old ladies' come about later as an explanation for the class assignment?

[18] We would like to thank Mark Harvey for a very helpful discussion regarding the importance of storytelling and folklore in Australian aboriginal culture.

Similarly, the class of 'stinging' items appears to remain a semantic class relevant to noun class assignment, but one that was breaking down at the time of Dixon (1972). The 'stinging' nouns in our sample include:

(9) Animate nouns

bima	'death adder'
gabul	'forest carpet snake'
gadambal	'mangrove crab'
gumbiyan	'echidna'
jaŋgan	'stonefish'
juruŋun	'toadfish'
malayigarra	'scorpion'
marrigal	'chicken snake'
munilan	'chicken snake'
yunba	'water python'

(10) Inanimate nouns

bumbilan	'stinging nettle'
jaŋali	'small stinging tree'
duŋan	'stinging tree'
giyarra	'big softwood stinging tree'

Although not all of the animates that we have identified as possible members of the [+stinging] class are poisonous, each is capable of causing a harmful stinging by biting, pinching, or otherwise attacking a human. For example, although pythons are not poisonous, the water python is a particularly aggressive snake. Similarly, the mangrove crab can exceed two kilos and possesses powerful claws.

We propose that the relevant semantic feature remains 'capable of inflicting a harmful sting' rather than simply 'dangerous' or 'harmful', as Dixon and Lakoff propose, as shown by assignment of 'harmful' nouns to other classes. Many animals assigned to class I are capable of inflicting harm, including crocodiles, alligators, the brown snake (one of the most dangerous snakes in Australia), and the *bujimburran*, a stinking beetle that squirts fluid (and is identified as a 'danger to eyesight') (Dixon 1984: 148). Thus, due to the assignment of all stinging plants and the stinging animate nouns identified in (9) to class II, we posit that [+stinging] is a synchronic classification relevant for class assignment, albeit a weaker classification than the other classifications identified above.

In sum, under the view proposed here, the semantic assignment of gender in Dyirbal was based on the following principles:

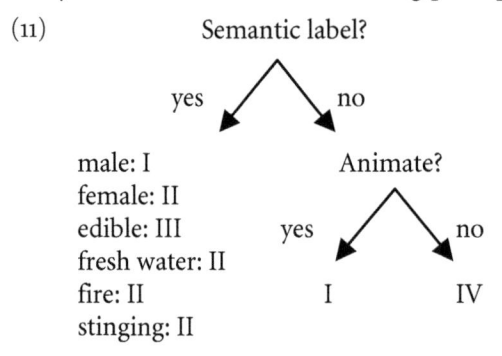

(11)

Semantic label?
 yes / no

male: I
female: II
edible: III
fresh water: II
fire: II
stinging: II

Animate?
 yes / no
 I   IV

The semantic labels match some of the original classifiers that we hypothesized Dyirbal had; the range of these classifiers is also supported by the evidence from the classifier systems of related languages (see Plaster and Polinsky 2007). The development of larger gender classes resulted in the loss or bleaching of semantic motivation for smaller classes, and gradually resulted in a greater role of formal cues. Had Dyirbal stayed healthy as a language and not undergone attrition and gradual death under the encroachment of English, its four-class system may have developed further, with formal cues as criterial factors. Instead, the system underwent a significant reanalysis in Young People's Dyirbal, which we will discuss in Section 5.6 below. Before turning to this new language, however, we would like to discuss the formal cues that were available in traditional Dyirbal.

5.5.3 *Beyond the core: formal cues in gender assignment*

The formal features responsible for class assignment affect only the animate nouns in our sample. That such a restriction would exist is not surprising given the distribution of nouns across the Dyirbal classes. Animate nouns appear only in classes I or II, and both of these classes consist primarily of animate nouns. Inanimate nouns, on the other hand, appear predominantly in class IV. Upon determining that a noun is animate but not inherently male or female, a child learner knows that the noun will appear in class I or II; as a result, the amount of motivation necessary to pull a class I noun into class II will be less than that required to pull an inanimate noun into class II. While formal features that affect both animate and inanimate nouns may also be present in Dyirbal, we have not been able to identify any in our sample.

Yi-. An example of a formal feature that affects only animate nouns is *yi-*, the initial syllable of the Dyirbal word for 'woman', *yibi*. Our sample contains

TABLE 5.3 Dyirbal nouns in *yi-*

Noun	Class	Gloss
yirrinyjila	I	'dragonfly'
yibi	II	'woman'
yigarra	II	'crayfish'
yimalimal	II	'welcome swallow'
yidir	IV	'grass'
yigan	IV	'sky'
yila	IV	'feather'
yilal	IV	'song style'
yilan	IV	'yellow feather in head of white cockatoo'
yimburr	IV	'bad smells'
yinin	IV	'wing of net trap; spirit place'
yiŋgar	IV	'long basket with cone-like mouth'
yirri	IV	'rotting material used by scrub hen to build nest'
yirribarra	IV	'nectar of forest red gum'

Dyirbal words beginning with *yi-*. As Table 5.3 shows, four nouns beginning with *yi-* in our sample are animate: *yirrinyjila* 'dragonfly', *yibi* 'woman', *yigarra* 'crayfish', and *yimalimal* 'welcome swallow'. While *yibi* and *yimalimal* are expected members of class II due to a [+female] semantic label, *yigarra* should appear in class I, the default class for non-human animates. We propose that *yigarra* was drawn into class II due to the identification of animate nouns beginning with *yi-* with class II.

The reason for the resilience of *yirrinyjila* to the formal feature is clear: the form shows vacillation of its initial segment between *y-* and *w-*. While the Dyirbal dialect of Dyirbal shows *yirrinyjila*, the Mamu dialect form is *wirrinyjila*. The same alternation is seen in one of the Dyirbal words for 'firefly', but this time between the Dyirbal dialect and Nyawaygy, a closely related language; the form in the Dyirbal dialect is *yugiyam*, while its cognate in Nyawaygy is *wugiyam*. Thus, it appears that the original form of both 'dragonfly' and 'firefly' began with *w-*, and that the *y-* forms are due to a development within the Dyirbal dialect.

As Table 5.3 also shows, none of the inanimate nouns beginning with *yi-* are drawn into class II; they are all in class IV, as otherwise expected. Since the source of the formal feature – the word for 'woman' – is animate, only nouns that are also animate are affected by the feature. As noted earlier, children from a very early age are able to distinguish 'animate' as a semantic category. Dyirbal shows a clear split of classification based on animacy, so it is not surprising that this split should also affect the operation of formal features.

TABLE 5.4 Dyirbal nouns in *bi-*

Noun	Class	Gloss	Motivation for assignment
bilŋgarriny	I	'little jew-fish'	animate
binyjirriny	I	'small lizard'	animate
bilmbu	I/II	'widow/widower'	male/female
bimu(nyja)	I/II	'father's elder brother/sister (and reciprocal)'	male/female
bijuju	II	'whistle duck'	female
bigi	II	'pig'	*bi-* + animate
bigin	II	'shield'	—[b]
bilmbiran	II	'large parrot'	female
bima	II	'death adder'	*bi-* + animate
binda	II	'waterfall'	water
bingay	II	'white ibis'	female
biyilbiyil	II	'peewee (magpie-lark)'	female
binana	III	'banana'	edible
binarra	III	'peanut'	edible
bigay	IV	'handle of basket'	inanimate
biguny	IV	'(finger/toe)nail'	inanimate
bilayŋgirr	IV	'blanket'	inanimate
bilbara	IV	'main track'	inanimate
bilu	IV	'noise of a horn'	inanimate
birrgil	IV	'frost, wintertime'	inanimate
biyinyji	IV	'fence'	inanimate

[b] Although *bi-* has not attracted any other inanimate nouns into class II, this formal feature could be partly responsible for the assignment of *bigin* 'shield' to class II.

Bi-. A related form for 'woman' provides another formal feature: *bi-*. A widespread word for 'woman', 'mother', and '(female) breast' in the Pama-Nyungan family is *bibi* (including Mbabaram *bib* 'breast', Muluridyi *bibi* 'breast', Ngyangumarta *pipi* 'mother', Northern Nyungar *pipi* 'female breast', Kuku-Jalanji *pipi* 'breast', Kala Lagaw Ya *ipi* 'female, woman, wife'). Although the form is not in our sample, it is widespread in the region and may be related to *yibi*, discussed above. If we examine all of the forms in our sample that begin with *bi-*, we find the forms listed in Table 5.4. The number and variety of nouns beginning with *bi-* is larger than those with *yi-*, so we have also included the motivation for the class assignment of each noun. As expected, all animate nouns appear in classes I and II, and inanimate nouns appear in class III, if edible, or class IV otherwise (with the exception of *bigin* 'shield').

TABLE 5.5 Expected class I: [+male] and [+animate] nouns

Noun	Class	Gloss	Motivation for assignment
bilŋgarriny	I	'little jew-fish'	animate
binyjirriny	I	'small lizard'	animate
bilmbu	I/II	'widow/widower'	male/female
bimu(nyja)	I/II	'father's elder brother/sister (and reciprocal)'	male/female
*bigi	II	'pig'	bi- + animate
*bima[c]	II	'death adder'	bi- + animate

[c] While we identified *bima* 'death adder' as a potential member of the [+stinging] class, we treat it as if it is not a member of the class for the purposes of this section to show that it is doubly marked for assignment to class II.

TABLE 5.6 Expected class II: [+female], [+water], and [+fire] nouns

Noun	Class	Gloss	Motivation for assignment
bilmbu	I/II	'widow/widower'	male/female
bimu(nyja)	I/II	'father's elder brother/sister (and reciprocal)'	male/female
bijuju	II	'whistle duck'	female
bilmbiran	II	'large parrot'	female
binda	II	'waterfall'	water
bingay	II	'white ibis'	female
biyilbiyil	II	'pee wee (magpie)'	female

The class assignment of most animate nouns follows straightforwardly from the semantic labels we have proposed, as shown in Tables 5.5 and 5.6. While the two starred items in Table 5.5 should be placed in class I as non-human animates, both are class II nouns. Dixon states that the assignment of *bima* 'death adder' is 'probably' due to the snake's connection to *gurrburu* 'seven sisters', a constellation also found in class II, noting that the seven sisters are 'believed to be a "death adder in the sky"' (Dixon 1972: 310). Dixon provides no explanation for the unexpected assignment of *bigi*; although *bigi* is a borrowing from English, it should nonetheless be assigned according to the principles applicable to native Dyirbal words, as shown in (7).

As Table 5.5 shows, four animate forms in *bi-* should have been placed in class I, and the actual classifications are split, with *bilŋgarriny* 'little jew-fish' and *binyjirriny* 'small lizard' in class I, while *bima* 'death adder' and *bigi* 'pig' appear in class II. The resilience of *bilŋgarriny* and *binyjirriny*, and the susceptibility of *bima* and *bigi*, to the formal feature is straightforward with the proper definition of the salient feature as being the composition of the entire initial syllable, not just the initial segment. The first syllable of the nouns in class II, *bima* and *bigi*, is *bi-*, while the first syllable of the nouns that were not transferred to class II is not *bi-*; both *bilŋgarriny* and *binyjirriny* begin with a closed syllable. Thus, it is the initial syllable (and not merely the first two segments) that constitutes the relevant formal feature. This is consistent with our proposal that stress (and therefore prominence) is behind the identification of certain formal features (see Section 5.4). By identifying the operation of a formal feature, we are able to explain the assignment of all four nouns without the need for tenuous semantic connections.

Ma-. An additional formal feature associated with class II is the initial segment *ma-*. Our sample in Table 5.7 contains animate nouns beginning with *ma-*. Based solely on semantic labels, *maga* 'rat' and *mawa* 'shrimp' should be assigned to class I; we have posited a [+stinging] label for *malayigarra* 'scorpion' and *marrigal* 'chicken snake', and *marraba* 'bird' is classified according to its [+female] feature.

Again, the relevant formal feature appears to be the initial syllable *ma*; the initial syllable of both forms that unexpectedly remain in class I is bigger than *ma-*, showing that it is the composition of the entire syllable, rather than its initial segments, that acts as the formal feature. However, class I contains two forms whose initial syllable is *ma-* but which resisted reclassification: *mabi* 'tree kangaroo' and *maral* 'snail-like slug'. 'Tree kangaroo' likely remained in class I due to the presence of other kangaroos, including *yunga* 'kangaroo' and

TABLE 5.7 Dyirbal animate nouns in *ma-*

Noun	Class	Gloss
mabi	I	'tree kangaroo'
mandija	I	'milky pine grub'
maral	I	'snail-like slug'
marbu	I	'louse'
maybaja	I	'alligator, crocodile'
maga	II	'rat'
malayigarra	II	'scorpion'
marraba	II	'bird (generic)'
marrigal	II	'chicken snake'
mawa	II	'shrimp'

yuri 'grey kangaroo', in class I. *Maral* similarly may have resisted reclassification due to its identification with the grubs and worms that are placed in class I. Unlike tree kangaroos and slugs, rats and shrimp may not fall as easily into a class of animate nouns identified solely with class I.

Gugu-. Another formal feature that we have identified is the initial disyllabic sequence *gugu-*. Our sample contains only three forms that begin with *gugu-*: *gugu* 'mopoke owl', *gugula* 'platypus', and *guguwuny* 'brown pigeon'. Of these three, *gugu* and *guguwuny* are birds, and accordingly placed in class II as [+female]. *Gugula*, on the other hand, has no semantic basis for assignment to class II, which Dixon was unable to explain. However, the presence of the initial disyllabic sequence *gugu-* in 'mopoke owl' and 'brown pigeon' likely was a sufficiently conspicuous feature of these class II nouns that 'platypus' was also drawn into the class.

While the majority of formal features that we have identified appear at the word's left edge, coinciding with the stressed syllable, at least one right-edge formal feature also appears to exist. We have already hypothesized that suffixes may have played a role in the original merger of small classes (see Section 5.4 above). The role of the feminine suffix *-gan* seems to continue synchronically as well. For example, the assignment of *jaŋgan* 'stonefish' to class II rather than class I, where the majority of fish species are assigned, may be due to the identification of *-gan* with class II in addition to the semantic label [+stinging], as proposed above. Table 5.8 shows all forms in our sample that end in *-gan*.

TABLE 5.8 Dyirbal forms ending in *-gan*

Noun	Class	Gloss
barrgan	I	'wallaby'
burŋgan	I	'termite species'
nuŋgan	I	'larger louse'
bugan	II	'brush fire'
julbungan	II	'woman who entices her promised man'
yalŋgayngan	II	'single woman (beyond usual marrying age)'
jaŋgan	II	'stonefish'
jarrugan	II	'scrub hen'
babuligan	IV	'pub, publican'
balgan	IV	'bark of tree'
jungan	IV	'bull oak'
bugan	IV	'open forest'
girramaygan	IV	'tribal territory'
girramaygan	I/II	'members of tribe'

With the exception of *barrgan* 'wallaby', *burŋgan* 'termite species', and *nuŋgan* 'larger louse', all animate nouns ending in *-gan* appear in class II. While the feminine suffix is clearly present in *julbungan* and *yalŋgayngan*, and likely is also present in *murrgan*, class II contains other nouns in which *-gan* would most likely be perceived but only as a formal segment, without a semantic association with [+feminine]. For example, *bugan* 'brush fire' is unlikely to contain the suffix *-gan*; it is straightforwardly assigned to class II with the other 'fire' words, and the presence of *-gan* may have been immaterial but may have also reinforced the class membership. Similarly, the assignment of *jarrugan* 'scrub hen' could be due to the belief that birds are spirits of dead women rather than the presence of *-gan*; however, this form nonetheless does end in *-gan*, implying class II membership.

If our proposal that *-gan* shifted its association from implying a [+feminine] feature to simply indicating class II membership is correct, the failure of *barrgan* 'wallaby', *burŋgan* 'termite species', and *nuŋgan* 'larger louse' to be assigned to class II deserves an explanation. As animate nouns, these should have been placed in class II due to the existence of the formal feature. First, we propose 'termite species' and 'larger louse' resisted reassignment because they form a small group of closely related insects assigned to class I, all of which are covered by a single avoidance language term, *bayi dimaniny*. Second, the different treatment of *barrgan* 'wallaby', which was not reclassified, and *jangan* 'stonefish', which was, is likely due to the relative frequencies of the forms. High-frequency forms commonly preserve irregularities that less frequent forms do not (Bybee 2002).[19]

In sum, the formal features that play a role in Dyirbal gender assignment fall into two groups: stressed segments (which are word-initial), which seem to play the most prominent role, and at least one salient suffix.

To reiterate, formal features are operative only with respect to nouns that do not bear a semantic label; a noun with a semantic label is classified accordingly. However, formal features do prevent the default class assignment

---

[19] Although we do not have frequency numbers for the Dyirbal words in our sample, certain words would naturally be expected to be more frequent than others; for example, 'sun', 'moon', 'fire', and 'fresh water' are likely among the highest-frequency items as they were part of Dyirbal daily life. Since wallabies were hunted by Dyirbal men as sources of food, we would expect 'wallaby' to be a high-frequency item, mentioned very frequently to, and in the presence of, Dyirbal children. Although stonefish are dangerous, and accordingly Dyirbal children needed to be warned about them, they were likely mentioned with much lower frequency, only to children who had reached an age where they may encounter them, and then only as part of a warning. Thus, we propose that the failure of *barrgan* to be reclassified from the default class for animates to class II despite the presence of the formal feature we have posited is explained by the high frequency of the item.

of animate nouns that do not carry semantic labels. Accordingly, the operation of formal features in noun class assignment may be easily represented using the decision tree in (11) by adding the possibility for assignment of animate nouns based on formal features prior to assignment to the relevant default class, as shown in (12):

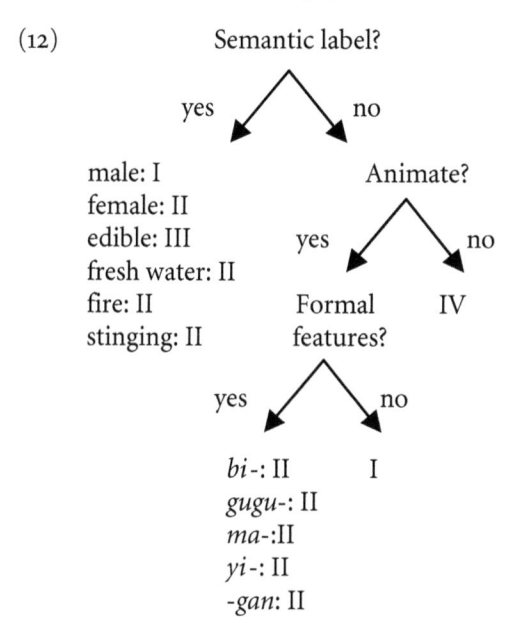

(12)

Semantic label?
- yes →
  - male: I
  - female: II
  - edible: III
  - fresh water: II
  - fire: II
  - stinging: II
- no → Animate?
  - yes → Formal features?
    - yes →
      - *bi-*: II
      - *gugu-*: II
      - *ma-*: II
      - *yi-*: II
      - *-gan*: II
    - no → I
  - no → IV

5.5.4 Preservation of original class assignments

In addition, we propose that a number of animate forms placed in class II are conservative retentions of the noun class assignments that resulted from the merger of the former Dyirbal classifiers. For example, as more fully described in Section 5.4 and Plaster and Polinsky (2007), we proposed that only 'edible' non-human animates were originally placed in class I, and that all non-edible animates fell into class II. To the extent that such items were frequent, and accordingly their class membership was conspicuous to Dyirbal speakers, such items may have resisted later reclassification to class I despite the lack of a clear semantic reason for membership in class II.

Perhaps the best example of such a noun is *guda* 'dog', whose placement in class II is unexplained by Dixon (1972). The dog held a special place in Australian culture and was not included among the 'edible' animals; as a result, it would have been excluded from the set of animals that we propose merged with male humans to form class I.[20] Accordingly, we propose that from the beginning of Dyirbal's four-class gender system, 'dog' was a member of class II along with female humans and the other animate nouns that did not designate edible animals. While the motivation for this assignment would have been unclear to later generations of speakers after class I was reanalysed as the default class for animates rather than the class for edible animals, the frequency with which *guda* appeared in children's input ensured that it would be learned as a class II noun. Not surprisingly, once the frequency of use decreased, *guda* was reclassified as a class I noun in YD, even in the more fluent speakers of Dyirbal that Schmidt (1985) studied.

Although we have accounted for the gender assignment of the majority of the Dyirbal nouns in our sample, some unexplained forms still remain. These forms may also be conservative retentions of classifications that occurred during the merger of Dyirbal's earlier classifier classes, particularly if such items may also have been sufficiently frequent to enable them to resist reclassification – for example, the presence of *jirrga* 'eel-spear', *jumala* 'woomera', *waŋal* 'boomerang', and *warrginy* 'boomerang' in class I may indicate the existence of a class of hunting implements that merged with human males and edible animals to form class I. However, we feel there currently is not sufficient evidence to posit the existence of any such additional classes of items. We will discuss the unexplained forms in the next subsection.

5.5.5 Outstanding forms

We now have accounted for 573 of the 597 nouns in the Dyirbal lexicon that we had available. There is a small number of nouns outstanding (about 4%) whose gender is still unpredictable, as shown in Table 5.9. Although we do not have a definitive account of gender assignment for these nouns we would like to offer some observations.

First, the unexplained class assignments in the sample may be either conservative retentions of the original classes that resulted from the merger of the classifier system or later class reassignments, made by young language learners. However, frequency and formal features, rather than semantic content, are the likely motivators of any retention or reassignment.

Second, as Dixon (1977: 310) notes,

it seems likely that some [class memberships] are WITHOUT EXPLANATION (as would be the case in any natural language: some may have had an explanation in

---

[20] Dixon (1972: 481) notes that 'people in all parts of Australia felt a close relationship to the dog (sometimes including it within the kinship system) and certainly the Yidiny would never have considered eating a dog.'

TABLE 5.9 Unexplained classifications

Noun	Class	Gloss
burrubay	I	'boil'
gubaguba	I	'(type of stripy pearl shell)'
jirrga	I	'eel-spear'
jumala	I	'woomera'
maɲany	I	'boomerang'
mayjala	I	'flash of lightning'
mayjanmayjan	I	'continuous flicks of lightning'
mugay	I	'grinding stone'
waŋal	I	'boomerang'
warrginy	I	'boomerang'
balma	II	'old scrub hen nest'
baŋgay	II	'spear'
buluba	II	'fighting ground'
bulugi	II	'cattle'
bunarra	II	'bow and arrow'
bundiny	II	'grasshopper'
gabu	II	'cup, telephone/telegraph mouthpiece or earpiece'
galabay	II	'beetle'
gawa	II	'cow'
jayari	II	'horse'
lambi	II	'lamp'
nyiyi	II	'noise of birds'
ŋama	II	'shield handle, trigger (on gun)'
warrayi	II	'bony bream'

terms of an earlier stage of the language, but the class assignment has been retained and the explanation lost as the language has altered).

While we have been able to reach earlier stages of Dyirbal to explain certain class assignments that were not predicted by Dixon's classification system and to motivate certain 'myth-and-belief' assignments on a more solid basis, we have not been able to determine the explanation for all items. Nonetheless, our successes demonstrate that the inquiry is worthwhile, and may shed light not only on the linguistic development of the language but also the source of certain pieces of myth and folklore.

Third, there may be additional semantically motivated classes that are difficult to ascertain because of the small size of the sample. For instance, it is feasible that cows, horses, and pigs all formed a coherent small class of domesticated animals, which would explain the assignment of both *gawa* and *jayari* to class II, where *guda* 'dog', the other domesticated animal, is found, and which could have served as an attractor. At the current stage of our knowledge of Dyirbal vocabulary, such proposals are doomed to be speculative. We prefer to leave some items unexplained rather than posit additional classes on the basis of limited data.

5.6 What happens when categorization collapses: noun classes in Young People's Dyirbal

As mentioned above, Schmidt (1985) documented the language of the children and grandchildren of Dixon's Dyirbal informants and identified two groups of speakers: a more fluent group of speakers of traditional Dyirbal, and a less proficient group of speakers of a new variety of the language, Young People's Dyirbal. While the more fluent speakers preserve a majority of the features of traditional Dyirbal, YD has undergone a variety of changes that differentiate it from traditional Dyirbal. Most relevant for this chapter is the simplification of the noun class system into a straightforward three-class system, as set forth in (13). The reanalysis of Dyirbal noun classification was largely driven by the concomitant process of attrition in noun class agreement – with diminishing agreement, speakers had fewer cues that allowed them to differentiate between several noun classes. Such a reanalysis with further simplification based on salient linguistic characteristics is attested in different languages undergoing attrition, for example, in Gaelic (Dorian 1980) and Heritage Russian (Polinsky 2008).

(13) Noun classification in YD (Schmidt 1985: 158)

Category		Class
animate:	masculine	I
	feminine	II
inanimate		IV

Schmidt found that YD speakers classify nouns solely on the basis of the categories set forth in (13), and, as a result, reclassify all nouns whose former classification did not comply with the YD system. For example, YD speakers retain none of the mythological class assignments found in traditional Dyirbal, as shown in Table 5.10.

TABLE 5.10 Noun classification by traditional Dyirbal and Young People's Dyirbal speakers (Schmidt 1985)

	Traditional Dyirbal	Young People's Dyirbal
'man'	I	I
'rainbow'	I	IV
'moon'	I	IV
'storm'	I	IV
'woman'	II	II
'bird'	II	I
'sun'	II	IV
'star'	II	IV

As Table 5.10 shows, in YD all inanimate nouns appear in class IV, despite any semantic associations that caused them to be placed in class I or II in traditional Dyirbal. Similarly, birds appear in class I with all other non-human animate beings. These developments, which occurred over a relatively short period of time, underscore the fragility of the hypothetical mythological associations in noun categorization.

In addition, YD speakers place the formerly [+fresh water] and [+fire] items in class IV rather than class II. This reassignment is expected under our analysis, due to the loss of the more minor semantic labels.

For prior Dyirbal speakers these labels were both relevant and frequent, and as a result children quickly identified the semantic classes and their class assignment. YD speakers are much less likely to hear or participate in conversations about fires than their ancestors, who cooked on fires and slept near fires for warmth. Sources of fresh water are likely no longer frequently mentioned, and water may not be the first beverage that comes to their mind when they are thirsty. Schmidt's YD speakers simply did not receive sufficient input to motivate the extra semantic labels on these inanimate items; as a result, they are placed in the default class for inanimate nouns.

Returning to the system that we proposed for noun classification in traditional Dyirbal in (12), we find that YD has preserved the core of the basic categorization that was present in the traditional system, while eliminating the formal features and removing the more ancillary semantic labels that were relevant to traditional Dyirbal speakers. These abandoned classification devices appear in shaded boxes in the decision tree set forth in (14); the remaining decision tree represents the classification system of the YD speakers:

(14)

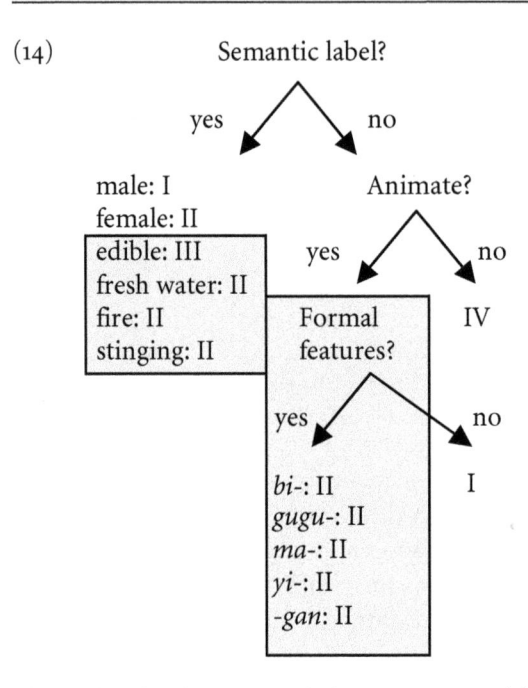

```
                    Semantic label?
                   yes  /\  no
         male: I          Animate?
         female: II      yes /\ no
         ┌──────────┐       
         │edible: III│  Formal      IV
         │fresh water: II│ features?
         │fire: II  │   yes /\ no
         │stinging: II│    
         └──────────┘   bi-: II      I
                        gugu-: II
                        ma-: II
                        yi-: II
                        -gan: II
```

Thus, the development of the Young People's Dyirbal noun class system follows directly from the noun class system of traditional Dyirbal, with the loss of the more ancillary classification devices. The changes seen in the YD noun class system need not be attributed to the direct interference of English or the discontinuation of the traditional Dyirbal worldview, as has been suggested; rather, while the abandoned pieces of the tree were able to be maintained by Dixon's informants, their children and grandchildren did not receive sufficient input to infer the existence of these semantic categories and to identify these formal features.

5.7 Conclusion

In this chapter, we have reanalysed Dyirbal noun classification, which has been previously analysed in terms of radial categories that rely on complex conceptual associations. We have proposed that the assignment of Dyirbal nouns to genders is determined by a combination of rather straightforward semantic and formal features. Crucially, the relevant semantic features are quite similar to what is found in gender systems around the globe; they include the basic semantic labels 'animate', 'male', 'female', and 'edible'. These features comprise the semantic core of Dyirbal classes I through III.

The fourth class, which includes most of the inanimate nouns in the lexicon, constitutes the default gender for nouns that do not bear these labels.

We have also proposed a small subset of minor semantic labels, such as 'water' or 'fire', which identify semantic subclasses within larger classes. The Dyirbal noun classes arose from a reanalysis of an earlier classifier system; the original number of classifiers was larger than the number of resulting genders, and in several cases, several classifier sets merged within a single class. We hypothesize that this merger was facilitated by formal analogy between the members of different small classes. If this proposal is on the right track, it has as an important consequence that there is no synchronic conceptual association among all of the items in a given gender class; in particular, the smaller subsets within a class do not need to be radially related to the semantic core. The overall class membership is motivated only diachronically, and even then not necessarily on semantic grounds.

We have identified several formal cues that play a role in synchronic gender assignment in Dyirbal and may have also affected the merger of smaller classes in the history of the language. Most of these formal cues are provided by the initial syllable, which is where the primary stress falls in Dyirbal; we have been able to connect at least some of these salient formal cues with words that represent core semantic notions. The reliance on prosodically prominent word segments is known to motivate gender assignment in many unrelated languages, including familiar Indo-European languages like French and Latin, so this finding also brings Dyirbal closer to well-known (and rather unsurprising) gender systems. Of course, any reconstruction remains tentative and hypothetical, and, in a linguistically complex and documentally impoverished area such as Australia, the tentative nature of any proposal needs to be underscored; we certainly leave room for doubt in our proposal, but the existing body of data and various cross-linguistic parallels make it plausible.

The development of the straightforward gender system of Young People's Dyirbal directly follows from the explanation of traditional Dyirbal gender proposed herein. While noun classification in traditional Dyirbal involved several semantic and formal features, a noun's gender is determined in YD solely on the basis of the objective, readily apparent characteristics of its referent: masculine animate beings are placed in class I; feminine animate beings are placed in class II; and everything else falls into class IV. The changes between traditional Dyirbal and YD are precisely those that we would expect given the decreasing use of the language in the younger generation.

From the standpoint of learnability, the proposed account of Dyirbal genders is more plausible than one based on attenuated abstract semantic linking. Children show early acquisition of superordinate categories but are less likely to acquire more sophisticated and culture-specific semantic categorization at an early age (Mandler 2004). Children are also known to pay attention to statistical and phonetic cues in their language in the first year of life (Jusczyk et al. 1993, 1994; Saffran et al. 1996a, b; Karmiloff-Smith 1979; Levy 1983; Berman 1985; Smoczyńska 1985; Slobin 1973; Newport and Aslin 2000, 2004). Although adult speakers may offer intriguing generalizations concerning the motivations for gender assignment, there is no evidence that these are any more than after-the-fact rationalizations that speakers of any language often come up with, let alone what children use to assign gender.

Despite its initial appearance, Dyirbal gender does not require complex semantic rules and links; instead, it relies on core semantic categories and independently motivated features such as stressed syllables and salient suffixes, and is directly comparable to other noun classification systems, which often rely on a combination of formal and simple semantic cues (Corbett 1991: Chapters 2 and 3). Even though the language is not yet officially extinct, working with Dyirbal is much like working with a meagrely attested ancient language: we are extremely thankful for what has been preserved (and to Dixon for his many efforts to do so), and we must extract everything possible from the surviving attestations, even if they cannot provide all of the answers we seek. We cannot help but wonder what would have become of the Dyirbal gender system without the drastic impact of the colonization of Australia on the language and its speakers.

6

The definiteness feature at the syntax–semantics interface

Gabi Danon

6.1 Introduction

Cross-linguistically, genitive constructions in which embedding does not make use of a prepositional element have often been noted to display some kind of sharing of definiteness value between the embedded nominal and the larger one within which it is embedded (Longobardi 1996). This is illustrated below with examples from English and Hebrew. In both examples, not only the embedded phrase but also the DP as a whole is interpreted as definite, despite lacking its own independent definiteness marker:

(1) a. John's shirt is wet.

    b. xulcat   ha-yeled   retuva.
       shirt   the-boy   wet
       'The boy's shirt is wet.'

Despite the similarity in interpretation between genitives in these two languages in examples like (1), it has often been noted that there are also systematic differences between Semitic 'definiteness spreading' and the kind of phenomenon observed in English and many other languages (Borer 1999; Dobrovie-Sorin 2003; Alexiadou 2005). In Section 6.4 I argue, following Alexiadou (2005), that the mechanism that gives rise to definiteness spreading in Hebrew is different from the one used in English and most other languages. Specifically, I argue that Hebrew definiteness spreading is a syntactic phenomenon involving sharing a morphosyntactic definiteness feature, while 'definiteness spreading' in other languages is merely a side effect of the semantic composition of a noun phrase, which makes no reference to definiteness as a feature. Furthermore, I argue that a definiteness feature of the kind that makes the Hebrew derivation possible is not available in most languages. This will thus serve as an illustration of the methodological significance of properly characterizing the inventory of morphosyntactic features in a given language, as different feature inventories may give rise to very different syntactic and semantic derivations.

Empirically, the main focus of this chapter is the range of interpretations found in Hebrew construct state nominals. Unlike what has often been claimed in the literature on Semitic construct state nominals, I show in Section 6.3 that the syntax of such nominals systematically allows several interpretation patterns for the same kind of structure. This, I claim, can easily be analysed as the result of a feature sharing operation, in which the syntactic representation is underspecified with respect to the exact locus of interpretation of a shared feature, which is determined at the syntax–semantics interface.

Following Danon (2001), the discussion in this chapter relies on making a clear distinction between a morphosyntactic definiteness feature and semantic definiteness; this distinction is introduced in Section 6.2. One of the central goals of this chapter is to spell out more precisely the properties of the formal encoding of definiteness that allow the morphosyntactic definiteness feature to be properly interpreted at the syntax–semantics interface despite the fact that there is no one-to-one correspondence between nominals marked as [+def] and those that are semantically definite. Specifically, in Section 6.5 I consider several asymmetries between definites and indefinites which favour an asymmetrical analysis of the [def] feature rather than the more traditional view of a symmetrical [±def] feature.

6.2 The morphosyntactic definiteness feature

6.2.1 *The definiteness feature in Hebrew*

Languages vary greatly in how they mark definiteness: among the mechanisms employed to distinguish definite noun phrases from indefinite ones are articles (both definite and indefinite, or only one of these contrasting with lack of an article), case marking, and word order.

In addition to semantically motivated definiteness marking, some languages also employ morphological definiteness marking in places where it has no immediate semantic motivation. Like other semantically motivated classifications, such as number and gender, grammaticalization of definiteness may give rise to occurrences of morphological realizations of definiteness that are triggered syntactically, via agreement. This is the case in Hebrew (as well as in Arabic), where attributive adjectives obligatorily agree in definiteness with the noun that they modify:[1]

(2) a. ha-sefer *(ha-)adom ne'elam.
 the-book the-red disappeared
 'The red book disappeared.'

 b. sefer (*ha-)adom (exad) ne'elam.
 book (the-)red (one) disappeared
 'A red book disappeared.'

Following Borer (1999), Wintner (2000), Danon (2001), and Falk (2006), I assume therefore that nouns and adjectives in Hebrew carry a morphosyntactic [def] feature, such that the distribution of definite articles on adjectives illustrated in (2) follows from the same kind of agreement mechanism as the one behind the more familiar gender and number agreement; alternatively, if we adopt the view in Corbett (2006), the distribution of definite articles on adjectives follows from the same principles as those which determine multiple realizations of case within the same noun phrase in many languages (which, based on the theoretical framework assumed, might be different from the agreement found with gender and number features). Either way, the realization of definiteness on adjectives in Hebrew is determined by the syntactic structure, which is, by definition, the characteristic property of morphosyntactic features.[2]

As is the case with any other morphosyntactic feature, some of its occurrences – specifically, the ones triggered by agreement – are semantically vacuous. Under an architecture of grammar in which the semantic component interprets representations formed by the syntax, there might be at least two

---

[1] An alternative view is that multiple realizations of definiteness within the same noun phrase are not determined by agreement with the noun, but are all realizations of the single syntactic or semantic assignment of definiteness to the noun phrase as a whole; see for instance Corbett (2006: 133–135) and Kibort (this volume). Note that under current Minimalist assumptions (and possibly under the assumptions of other grammatical frameworks), there is no formal distinction between these two views, which would both be analysed using the same formal device. Furthermore, even if we adopt the agreement approach, we should note that not in all languages where articles are doubled in the presence of adjectives is this an instance of agreement; see, for instance, Alexiadou (2005), who argues that article doubling in front of adjectives in Modern Greek is not an instance of agreement.

[2] Sichel (2002) argues against viewing definiteness on adjectives in Hebrew as agreement, on the basis of the fact that the article in complex APs is not necessarily located on the adjective itself but rather could precede the entire AP. This is true only for colloquial Hebrew, which might suggest that the status of the article is currently undergoing some kind of reanalysis. In any case, I believe that the fact that there is an obligatory doubling of the definite article with adjectival modifiers can best be accounted for as agreement.

alternative strategies by which the semantic component would 'know' which occurrence of a definiteness feature should be interpreted:

1. Based on the lexical category of the marked node: definiteness on adjectives is not interpreted; definiteness on nouns is interpreted.
2. Based on independent syntactic encoding: definiteness on adjectives may be marked as interpretable or uninterpretable by the syntax, and/or 'deleted' by the syntactic component prior to transfer to the semantic component.

The theoretical issue involved in choosing between these two approaches is to what extent the syntactic representation determines the interpretability of features. According to the first approach, the syntax is only responsible for 'spreading' features from node to node, but not directly for determining their interpretation; according to the second approach, which is essentially the mainstream view in current Minimalism (Chomsky 2000, 2001), the syntax also actively determines the locus of feature interpretation. We will return to this issue in Section 6.4, where I will argue in favour of the former approach.

Assuming that Hebrew has a morphosyntactic definiteness feature, another important question is to what extent the distribution of this feature on noun phrases overlaps with the semantic notion of definiteness. This is not a trivial question, as even a quick comparison with other morphosyntactic features might suggest. For instance, it has long been noticed that morphosyntactic number marking does not always match semantic number. Some familiar examples are plural pronouns used to refer to singular individuals, as in French *vous* and English 'singular *they*' (see, for instance, Sauerland et al. 2005, Corbett 2006, and references cited there); or the cross-linguistically common use of singular nouns with plural numerals, illustrated below for Hungarian (from Ortmann 2000):

(3) (Az)   öt   nagynéni   sört   isz-ik   /*isz-nak.
    (the)   five   aunt   beer   drink-3SG   /drink-3PL
    '(The) five aunts are drinking beer.'

As noted by Danon (2001), similar mismatches can be found between morphosyntactic and semantic definiteness in Hebrew. For instance, demonstrative adjectives, like other adjectives, may be used with or without a definite article; in the latter case, the noun phrase is semantically definite but morphosyntactically indefinite, as witnessed by the lack of definiteness marking on additional adjectives in the same noun phrase:³

(4) sefer   (*ha-)xašuv   ze   pursam   be   1875.
    book   (the-)important this published in   1875
    'This important book was published in 1875.'

Similarly, semantically definite determiners such as *oto/ota* ('that', 'the same') do not trigger definiteness agreement, and hence do not give rise to morphosyntactically definite noun phrases (see Siloni 2003 and Alexiadou 2005, who discuss similar examples without distinguishing the two notions of definiteness):

(5) ota   tmuna   (*ha-)mefursemet
    same   picture (the-)famous
    'the same famous picture'

Overall, the generalization for Hebrew is that only the following kinds of noun phrase trigger a definite inflection on adjectives (see Danon 2001):

- noun phrases where the noun is marked by the definite article *ha-*
- noun phrases where the noun carries a pronominal possessive suffix
- proper names
- construct state nominals in which the embedded nominal is morphosyntactically definite; this will be discussed in detail in Section 6.3

Clearly, this differs from semantic characterizations of definiteness, which would take into account a broader range of determiners and not merely the definite article. To avoid confusion, I will restrict the use of the notation [±def] to *morphosyntactic* definiteness in the sense defined above.

One way to address this mismatch between formal definiteness marking and semantic interpretation is to assume that morphosyntactic definiteness is only one of the factors used by the semantic component in determining the (semantic) definiteness of a noun phrase; other factors, such as the lexical semantics of other elements in the noun phrase, may override the

---

³ An additional test often used to diagnose formal definiteness in Hebrew is the use of the object marker *et*, which is allowed only in front of formally definite objects. Since one of the claims of this chapter is that morphosyntactic features should be identified based on their relevance to indisputable agreement phenomena, I will not rely on the distribution of *et*; it should be noted, however, that with very few and highly restricted exceptions, the use of *et* overlaps with definiteness agreement on adjectives.

morphosyntactic encoding. In Section 6.5 we will see that with a careful choice of values for the [def] feature we can avoid the need to assume that the formal encoding and the lexical semantics can provide contradictory information; instead, it is possible to show that these two sources of information complement each other.

In what follows, I will therefore make the following assumptions:

- Hebrew has a morphosyntactic definiteness feature which is part of the syntactic representation.
- Although this morphosyntactic feature plays a central role in constraining the semantic definiteness value of a noun phrase, the two notions of definiteness are distinct.

The question is then how exactly morphosyntactic definiteness is handled by the syntax–semantic interface. In the rest of this chapter I attempt to provide a partial answer to this question. I focus on two issues in particular:

1. definiteness spreading in genitival constructions
2. definite/indefinite asymmetries and the formal representation of the definiteness feature.

But before proceeding to introduce the relevant data, I would like to briefly discuss the issue of parametric variation in the availability of the [def] feature.

6.2.2 *A definiteness feature in other languages?*

While there is clear evidence, in the form of agreement, for the presence of a definiteness feature in the *syntax* of Hebrew, in many other languages no such evidence can be found. Taking English as an example, we should note that while this language has definite and indefinite articles, there are no definiteness agreement phenomena, nor any other indisputable *syntactic* phenomena involving definiteness; various familiar 'definiteness effects' might in fact be semantic phenomena, or they may involve only an indirect relation to the formal encoding of definiteness. The question is thus whether we should assume a [±def] feature in the syntax for such a language.

In essence, this boils down to the question of what is meant by the term 'feature'. Under the broader use of this term, a feature is simply a formal way of partitioning a syntactic category (such as NP) into sub-categories; the information leading to this partitioning may be of different kinds, and the partitioning itself may be motivated by requirements of any component of language, as well as by extra-linguistic systems of use, such as computational applications. Under this broader view, there is obviously no reason not to assume that English noun phrases carry a definiteness feature, whose value is determined (in most cases) by the choice of determiner.

A more restricted notion of feature is that of a *morphosyntactic* feature, which is a partitioning of a syntactic category into subclasses that are marked (at least partially) morphologically and that are relevant to syntax, most notably by being involved in agreement operations; see for instance Corbett (2006), Zeijlstra (2008), and Kibort (this volume). For many languages, this covers features such as number, person and gender, which are all involved in overt agreement. Under a slightly broader view, tense and aspect also belong to this class of features; even though most languages do not show overt tense/aspect agreement, it is usually assumed within the Minimalist framework (Chomsky 1995, 2000) that abstract agreement does apply to these features.

Restricting the discussion to morphosyntactic features, there seems to be no reason to assume that a language like English has morphosyntactic definiteness, at least not in the stricter sense that gives rise to overt agreement. In what follows, I will assume that the availability of a morphosyntactic definiteness feature is a parameter that distinguishes Hebrew and Arabic, on the one hand, from most of the other languages that have definiteness marking, on the other hand. I will argue that this distinction gives rise to different patterns of definiteness spreading in complex nominals.

6.3 Definiteness spreading in Hebrew

As noted by numerous authors and illustrated in (1b), the definiteness value of a Hebrew construct state nominal (CSN) is dependent on the definiteness value of its embedded genitive.[4] In this section I will elaborate on the claim made in Danon (2001) that this phenomenon, which I refer to as DEFINITE-NESS SPREADING (DS), is spreading of *morphosyntactic* definiteness; I will discuss data that shows that this syntactic process gives rise to several different semantic patterns in Hebrew CSNs.

6.3.1 *Background: Semitic construct state nominals*

Semitic construct state nominals (CSNs) have been the focus of a large body of research over the last 20 years, with various authors addressing, among other things, issues of word order, hierarchical structure, the nature of nominalizations, the syntax–prosody interface, and the syntax of definiteness

---

[4] The genitive can be a possessor, or may stand in a wide variety of other semantic relations with the head of the CSN.

and articles. In this section I briefly review the properties of CSNs that are relevant to the discussion that follows.

A CSN is a complex nominal consisting of, at least, a phonologically reduced head noun immediately followed by an embedded genitive phrase, as illustrated in (6) below:[5]

(6) [$_{DP1}$ tmunat *([$_{DP2}$ ha-nasi])]
   picture   the-president
  'the picture of the president'

For simplicity, I will refer in the discussion below to the two levels of a CSN as DP1 and DP2, as in (6).[6]

Hebrew has a prefixal definite article, *ha-*, and no indefinite article. Unlike other nominals, a CSN may not have an article attached to its nominal head; attaching the definite article to the head of a CSN leads to ungrammaticality, as in (7a). Free nominals containing the prepositional element *šel*, in contrast, do allow direct attachment of an article to their head, as in (7b):

(7) a. *ha-tmunat   ha-nasi
       the-picture the-president
      'the picture of the-president'

   b. ha-tmuna   šel ha-nasi
      the-picture of   the-president
      'the picture of the president'

The only way of specifying the definiteness of a CSN is via definiteness spreading (DS): the definiteness value of the CSN (DP1) is determined by the definiteness value of the embedded phrase (DP2). One of the central issues in previous research has been trying to derive the special properties of the CSN that have to do with definiteness from other properties of the CSN (see, for instance, Siloni 2003), or vice versa (Borer 1999); for a detailed overview of the literature on DS, see Danon (2008). In this chapter, I am not interested in relating DS to the other properties of the CSN, but focus instead on providing

---

[5] The head noun of a CSN is derived from the base form of the noun by a process of morpho-phonological reduction; the output of this process is not always distinguishable from the free form of the noun, but even when it is not, identifying a nominal as a CSN is still possible due to the construct state's unique syntactic characteristics.

[6] Throughout the discussion I refer to both levels of the CSN as DPs, keeping in mind that it might be the case that at least in some CSNs, the DP layer could be missing from one or both levels; see for instance Borer (1999, 2009), Dobrovie-Sorin (2003), and Danon (2006, 2008).

The definiteness feature

a thorough description of the more intricate and less familiar aspects of DS and their implications for the notion of 'definiteness feature', which has often been used in a somewhat vague sense that should be more clearly defined.

6.3.2 Establishing morphosyntactic feature spreading

The first thing that should be established is that definiteness spreading in Hebrew indeed involves the morphosyntactic definiteness feature and is not merely a semantic issue. In other words, regardless of the semantics of CSNs, we should verify that adjective agreement supports the claim that both levels of a CSN have the same definiteness value.

This has long been known to be the case. As illustrated in the following examples, in a CSN with an embedded definite, an attributive adjective modifying any of the two levels must be definite, as in (8a); and similarly, only indefinite adjectives can modify a CSN with an embedded indefinite, as in (8b):

(8) a. tmunat   ha-yeled   *(ha-)gavoha   *(ha-)memusgeret
picture(F) the-boy(M) (the-)tall.M   (the-)framed.F
'the framed picture of the tall boy'

b. tmunat   yeled   (*ha-)gavoha   (*ha-)memusgeret
picture(F) boy(M) (the-)tall.M   (the-)framed.F
'a framed picture of a tall boy'

As was shown in (5) for simple nominals, adding a semantically definite determiner to a CSN with an embedded indefinite is irrelevant with respect to definiteness agreement – only an indefinite adjective is allowed, despite semantic definiteness:

(9) ota   tmunat   praxim   (*ha-)mefursemet
same.F.SG picture(F).SG flowers(M).PL (the-)famous.F.SG
'the same famous picture of flowers'

It is thus clear that DS involves, at least, 'spreading' of the morphosyntactic definiteness feature of the embedded nominal to the CSN as a whole. In the next section I show that this is not true of semantic definiteness, which does not always spread in a CSN.

6.3.3 Definiteness spreading and interpretation

Unlike what has often been claimed or implicitly assumed, a CSN whose embedded nominal is marked as definite is *not* always interpreted as definite. Furthermore, the embedded nominal itself, the one that carries the definiteness marking, is also not always interpreted as definite. In this section I show that there are four different interpretation patterns that can be found with definite-marked construct states.[7] These are:

1. both the embedded DP (DP2) and the CS as a whole (DP1) interpreted as definite
2. only the embedded DP (DP2) interpreted as definite
3. only the CS as a whole (DP1) interpreted as definite
4. [+def] not interpreted at all within the CS.

6.3.3.1 *Both the embedded DP and the CS as a whole interpreted as definite* In prototypical 'semantic DS', the morphosyntactic definiteness value matches semantic definiteness, such that both levels of a [+def] CSN are interpreted as definite. Thus, the CSN in (10a) could be paraphrased using the non-CSN in (10b), where both DPs are definite:

(10) a. **xulcat ha-yeled** nirteva.
shirt the-boy got-wet
'The boy's shirt got wet.'

b. ha-xulca šel ha-yeled nirteva.
the-shirt of the-boy got-wet
'The boy's shirt got wet.'

This semantic pattern has been taken as the typical case in the vast majority of the literature on Semitic CSNs. However, upon closer inspection it seems that this is only one of several patterns; it is not even clear whether this pattern is statistically the most common one.

6.3.3.2 *Only the embedded DP interpreted as definite* As noted by several authors, most notably Fassi Fehri (1999), Engelhardt (2000), and Danon (2001, 2002), there are predictable cases where a CSN with a definite embedded DP is not interpreted as definite. In the following examples, there is no presupposition of uniqueness associated with the singular CSNs in (11); furthermore, the plural CSNs in (12) allow weak determiners (contra Siloni 2001), which are usually allowed only with plural *indefinites*:

[7] More precisely, there are four possibilities for a non-recursive CSN, that is one whose embedded nominal is not itself a CSN. The discussion below makes the prediction that the number of interpretation patterns would grow exponentially with the depth of recursive embedding, a prediction which I believe to be correct, even though it is extremely difficult to elicit reliable semantic judgements in cases of multiple embeddings.

(11) a. dan   hu   **yelid**   **ha-ir.**
       Dan   is   native   the-city
       'Dan is a native of the city.'

   b. lifney   švu'ayim   ne'ecar   **saxkan**   **ha-kvuca.**
      before   two weeks   arrested   player   the-team
      'A player of the team was arrested two weeks ago.'

(12) šney/   kama   **yelidey ha-ir/**   **bogrey**   **ha-xug**   le-balšanut
     two/   several natives the-city/   graduates   the-department   to-linguistics
     'two/several natives of the city/graduates of the linguistics department'

This semantic pattern is systematically found with [+def] CSNs headed by what we may refer to as 'group nouns' – nouns that denote members in a group or collective. This means that the lexical semantics of the head noun of a CSN is relevant for the kind of reading (definite or indefinite) assigned to the CSN, which suggests that the interpretability of the definiteness feature on each level of the CSN is not determined by narrow syntax, which has no access to lexical semantic distinctions between classes of nouns.[8]

As noted by Engelhardt (2000), similar facts occur with 'non-definite' event-denoting CSNs, which are allowed in environments that disallow definites. This is shown in (13), taken from Engelhardt (2000); (13a) illustrates one environment that is sensitive to definiteness; (13b), then, shows that [+def] event-denoting CSNs are nevertheless allowed in this environment, unlike simple definite event nominals:[9]

(13) a. ruti   mevala   et   zman-a   be-/*ba-   ktiva.
        Ruti   spends   OM   time-POSS.3SG.F   in-/*in.the- writing
        'Ruti spends her time writing.'

---

[8] As pointed out to me by Greville Corbett, by the same reasoning we might conclude that agreement is also outside narrow syntax, as agreement is known sometimes to distinguish between group nouns and other nouns, etc. (see, for instance, Corbett this volume). I believe that this might be true for *some* instances of agreement (so-called 'semantic agreement'), but not for agreement in general.

[9] The preposition *be-* ('in') in (13) changes to *ba-* in front of the definite article: *be+ha* ⇒ *ba*. This does not happen in (13b), where the definite article is on the embedded nominal.

b. ruti   mevala   et   zman-a   be-   **ktivat**   **ha-sefer.**
   Ruti   spends   OM   time-POSS.3SG.F in-   writing   the-book
   'Ruti spends her time writing the book.'

The conclusion at this point is that whether or not a [+def] CSN gets a definite reading depends, among other things, on lexical properties of the head noun. This goes in line with the claim made by Heller (2002) and Dobrovie-Sorin (2003) that semantic definiteness spreading follows from the head noun being interpreted as a function from individuals to individuals; nouns for which this kind of interpretation is not readily available are thus expected to show other semantic patterns.

6.3.3.3 *Only the CS as a whole interpreted as definite* As observed by Dobrovie-Sorin (2000), even the embedded nominal in a definite-marked CSN, which is the nominal carrying the definite article, is not always interpreted as definite. This is illustrated in (14):

(14) a. **ha-mas**   **ha-ze**   yifga   be- **roxšey** **ha-dirot.**
        the-tax   the-this   hurt.FUT   in   buyers   the-apartments
        'This tax will hurt the buyers of apartments.'

   b. **asfan**   **ha-atikot**   **ha-ze**   hu   pošeʻa.
      collector   the-antiques   the-this   is   criminal
      'This antique collector is a criminal.'

   c. **ugat**   **ha-tapuxim**   hayta   meʻula.
      cake   the-apples   was   excellent
      'The apple cake was excellent.'

This pattern systematically appears when the embedded nominal is a non-referential modifier, as in (14c) (see Borer 2009). In many other cases, only pragmatic factors distinguish between this kind of interpretation and the 'double definiteness' reading. Consider, for instance, the contrast between the following two examples:

(15) a. **tmunat**   **ha-nasi**   še-   al   **ha-kir**   hudpesa   be-   hodu.
        picture   the-president   that   on   the-wall   printed   in-   India
        'The president's picture on the wall was printed in India.'

   b. **tmunat**   **ha-nazir**   še-   al   **ha-kir**   hudpesa   be-   hodu.
      picture   the-monk   that   on   the-wall   printed   in-   India
      'The monk's picture/the picture of a monk on the wall was printed in India.'

The only difference between (15a) and (15b) is the choice of embedded noun, which leads to a difference in the salience of the two possible readings. In (15a), world knowledge makes the double-definiteness reading the salient one, since most contexts presuppose a single president and hence an indefinite reading for the embedded phrase is quite unlikely. In (15b), on the other hand, no such presupposition exists in typical contexts, and the reading where the embedded nominal is indefinite becomes more salient. It is important to note that this is no more than a preference, and given the right context the opposite pattern could emerge. Once again, this seems to argue against an analysis in which feature interpretability is uniquely determined by the syntax, and favours an analysis in which the syntactic representation is compatible with multiple interpretations, some of which may be filtered out by pragmatic factors.

6.3.3.4 *[+def] not interpreted at all within the CS* At first, the possibility of having a [+def] CS in which definiteness is not interpreted at all might seem highly implausible. But, in fact, this case is indeed attested, when a construct state serves as a modifier that acquires its definiteness value via agreement with an external node. This is made possible by the fact that a construct state can be headed not only by a noun but also by an adjective, in which case it has the distribution of an AP (see Borer 1999; Hazout 2000; Siloni 2002). This is illustrated in (16):

(16) dan   makir   et   ha-yalda   **arukat**   *(**ha-**)**raglayim**.
     Dan   knows   OM   the-girl   long   the-legs
     'Dan knows the girl with long legs.'

The definite article in the adjectival CS (ACS) is an agreement marker: adjectival CS modifiers must agree in definiteness with the modified noun, just like simple adjectival modifiers. The ACS *arukat ha-raglayim* in (16) agrees with the [+def] feature on *ha-yalda*, and hence the article in the adjectival CS is obligatory.

Given this, it is not surprising that definiteness is not interpreted anywhere within the ACS. This is seen, first, by the fact that the ACS in (16) is semantically equivalent to the relative clause in (17a), in which the noun (*raglayim*) is indefinite.

(17) a. dan   makir   et   ha-yalda   še   yeš   la   raglayim   arukot.
        Dan   knows   OM   the-girl   that   exists   her   legs   long
        'Dan knows the girl who has long legs.'

b. dan   makir   et   ha-yalda   **švurat**   ***(ha-)regel**.
   Dan   knows   ᴏᴍ   the-girl   broken   the-leg
   'Dan knows the girl who has a broken leg.'

Furthermore, an ACS is perfectly acceptable even when the context rules out the possibility of a uniqueness presupposition being associated with the embedded nominal, as in (17b), where the definite-marked *ha-regel* is perfectly felicitous even in a standard context in which every girl has two legs. We thus conclude, following Winter (2005), that definite articles in adjectival CS modifiers may be semantically vacuous.

6.3.3.5 *Summary of the main descriptive generalizations*   We thus have the following generalizations regarding definiteness spreading:

- Morphosyntactic definiteness of the embedded nominal spreads to the entire CS.
- It is not the case that *both* levels in a [+def] CS are always interpreted as definite; a definiteness feature is always interpreted on at least one of the nodes to which it spreads via DS or adjectival agreement, but not necessarily on all these nodes.

At the same time, we should also note that, unless an additional determiner is present, morphosyntactic definiteness of the embedded nominal is a necessary condition for semantic definiteness of the entire CS; hence, we cannot simply dismiss DS as having nothing at all to do with semantics. The theoretical challenge for any analysis of DS is thus to account for the entire range of interpretations and not only for the simple 'double-definiteness' cases. For a detailed discussion of the shortcomings of the various approaches to DS proposed in the literature, see Danon (2008).

6.4 Definiteness spreading cross-linguistically

6.4.1 *Against a unified analysis*

As noted at the beginning of this chapter, phenomena that are superficially similar to Semitic DS can be found in many other languages, such as English (Hazout 1991; Dobrovie-Sorin 2003), Romanian (Dobrovie-Sorin 2003), and Welsh (Sadler 2000). More specifically, it has been noted by Longobardi (1996) that definiteness spreading is typical of preposition-less constructions. A central question is whether these are all instances of the same phenomenon, derived by a single mechanism. Some authors, such as Hazout (1991), Fassi

Fehri (1993), Longobardi (1996), and Dobrovie-Sorin (2003), have argued for a unitary account of DS in all these languages, while others, most notably Alexiadou (2005), have claimed that DS in Hebrew differs significantly from DS in English and other languages. In this section I will provide additional evidence in favour of Alexiadou's claim, and will make an explicit distinction between two kinds of DS: one that is based on sharing the value of a morphosyntactic definiteness feature, and one in which the compositional semantics of a noun phrase makes no reference to such a feature.[10]

Alexiadou (2005) provides several arguments against attempting to unify Hebrew and English DS. Following Siloni (2003), she claims that there is no DS in Hebrew CSNs containing an embedded indefinite, unlike the case in English:

(18) a. ota   tmunat   praxim
        that/same picture   flowers
        'that picture of flowers'
     b. a man's dog

As the possibility of using a definite determiner like *ota* ('that/same') in (18a) shows, the CSN here can only be claimed to inherit the indefiniteness of its embedded nominal in a weak sense that can be overridden by an overt determiner. The English example in (18b), on the other hand, does not allow any definite determiner.[11]

Similarly, Dobrovie-Sorin (2003) argues that there is no *in*definiteness spread in Hebrew CSNs, which differ semantically from English nominals with indefinite possessors:

(19) a. bney   melex
        sons   king
        'sons of a king'
     b. a king's sons

---

[10] Alexiadou (2005) also suggests that what makes DS in Hebrew special is the fact that definiteness in Hebrew is involved in agreement processes. She does not, however, argue for a lack of a definiteness feature in languages other than Hebrew; on the contrary, she refers to a ±def feature that is checked by a determiner in Modern Greek, which is a language that, according to Alexiadou, does not have DS in preposition-less genitives (contra Longobardi's generalization). It is therefore not entirely clear, under her approach, what makes the definiteness feature of Hebrew different from that of other languages.

[11] But see Woisetschlaeger (1983), who argues that phrases like (18b) are in fact definite.

While the English phrase in (19b) refers to the entire set of sons of a king (similar to a plural definite like *the sons of a king*), the Hebrew CSN in (19) is a regular indefinite, which is compatible, for instance, with weak determiners. Dobrovie-Sorin thus concludes that indefinite CSNs in Hebrew are substantially different from English noun phrases with an indefinite possessor; as to definites, on the other hand, she does argue for a unified analysis.

Turning to complex nominals with an embedded *definite* phrase, we can see that the kind of variable interpretation discussed in Section 6.3.3 is not observed in English possessive constructions. First, in the case of group/membership nouns for which lexical semantics makes a uniqueness presupposition quite unlikely, English singular prenominal possessives are pragmatically odd, as in (20a) and (21a); this contrasts with plural possessives, which do not presuppose uniqueness:

(20) a. #The team's player was arrested yesterday.
b. The team's players were arrested yesterday.

(21) a. #The committee's member will submit a report next week.
b. The committee's members will submit a report next week.

What this contrast shows is that the entire possessive DP in these examples is interpreted as definite; since definite singulars, but not definite plurals, presuppose uniqueness, the judgements above are expected if these possessive DPs must indeed be interpreted as definite. Thus, unlike Hebrew CSNs, English possessives with an embedded definite show obligatory semantic definiteness for this class of nouns.

As discussed in Section 6.3.3, Hebrew CSNs with embedded definite-marked nominals do not always have the embedded nominal itself interpreted as definite, as in the example in (14). Not all these CSNs have a grammatical English counterpart in the form of a prenominal genitive, due to the fact that English prenominal possessives are more restricted than Hebrew CSNs in the kinds of semantic relations that they can encode (Borer 1999). Specifically, Borer claims that a depicted entity in a 'picture NP' is not allowed in [spec, DP]:

(22) *the sunflower's picture

However, I believe that this is not entirely accurate, as an *animate* depicted entity does seem to be allowed in this position; for instance, *The president* in (23) can easily be interpreted as being depicted in the picture rather than as its possessor:

(23) The president's picture appeared on the front cover.

TABLE 6.1 Hebrew vs. English preposition-less genitives

		Hebrew	English
Indefinite DP2	Definite determiner allowed for DP1	yes	no
	Maximality entailed for DP1	no	yes
Definite-marked DP2	Indefinite reading of DP1 possible	yes	no
	Indefinite reading of DP2 possible	yes	no

With this in mind, we can see that the embedded nominal in such cases is invariably interpreted as definite, even for nouns that do not carry an inherent uniqueness presupposition based on world knowledge:

(24) The monk's picture on the wall was printed in India.

Thus, *The monk* in (24) seems to have only the following two interpretations:

1. definite possessor
2. definite depicted.

What it lacks is the reading associated with the parallel Hebrew CSN in (15b): the indefinite/nonreferential depicted reading.

We thus conclude that there are significant differences in interpretation between Hebrew CSNs and English possessive constructions: in addition to the differences previously noted in the interpretation when the embedded nominal is indefinite, English also shows no variability in interpretation with embedded definites of the kind shown in Section 6.3.3 to exist in Hebrew CSNs; these differences are summarized in Table 6.1. I thus conclude, like Alexiadou (2005), that the Hebrew and English constructions should not receive a unified analysis.

6.4.2 Two kinds of definiteness spreading

The question at this point is what makes Hebrew CSNs different from preposition-less complex nominals in most other languages. As pointed out in Section 6.2, one thing that distinguishes Hebrew from most other languages is the availability of a morphosyntactic definiteness feature. I propose that this is indeed the source of the difference in interpretation of complex nominals.

If a language has a morphosyntactic definiteness feature, syntactic operations may impose restrictions on the value of this feature across different nodes. I will refer to the notion of FEATURE SHARING, which can be implemented in different ways under all major theoretical frameworks: in LFG and HPSG, feature sharing is simply unification; in Minimalism, feature sharing has been proposed by Frampton and Gutmann (2006) as well as Pesetsky and Torrego (2007) as an alternative to the operation Agree of Chomsky (2000, 2001). Abstracting away from differences between these frameworks, what characterizes feature sharing is the fact that it leads to a situation where, in the syntactic representation, a single feature is 'linked' to two or more nodes.

Let us assume that the process of forming a CSN leads to sharing the definiteness feature of the main and embedded nominal. Following Brody (1997) and Pesetsky and Torrego (2007), I assume the following principle:

Thesis of Radical Interpretability (Brody 1997) Each feature must receive a semantic interpretation in some syntactic location.

Crucially, this does not require the syntax to determine the exact locus of interpretation of a given feature; as long as the syntax ensures that every feature is found on at least one head that is compatible with the feature's meaning, interpretability can be determined at the syntax–semantics interface, where non-syntactic information can also be taken into account. This differs from the mainstream approach in Minimalism, where feature interpretability is established deterministically in the syntactic component by deletion of those instances of a feature that get their value via agreement.

Thus, at the syntax–semantics interface, a CSN with a definite-marked embedded nominal has a single definiteness feature shared between its two levels. According to the Thesis of Radical Interpretability, this feature may be interpreted on either level. Furthermore, if the entire CSN shares its definiteness feature with an additional node, as is the case in adjectival constructs that serve as modifiers, such as (16), interpretation may take place outside the CS, such that neither level of the CS is interpreted as definite. We can thus derive all four interpretation patterns found with a [+def] CS under a feature-sharing approach with no additional stipulation.

For this kind of analysis to be possible, of course, a [+def] feature must be present in the syntax. Following the discussion in Section 6.2.2, I assume that languages with no definiteness agreement phenomena do not have such a feature. This means that the interpretation of a complex nominal in a language such as English cannot make reference to a (shared) definiteness feature, and must be based entirely on 'direct' structure-based compositionality. Such an analysis has been proposed, for instance, by Dobrovie-Sorin (2003), who makes an explicit claim about the semantic relation between a noun and a nominal in its specifier position (namely, she proposes that the nominal in specifier position is interpreted as a function from individuals to individuals). This kind of analysis makes no direct use of a syntactically encoded [±def] feature, while it does depend heavily on having the embedded nominal in a fixed structural position; whatever definiteness value is derived in this kind of analysis is only an indirect semantic property rather than an independently marked feature.

We thus have two alternative ways of deriving the definiteness value of a complex nominal: one that depends on sharing a morphosyntactic definiteness feature, and one that does not. It should be clear that of these two mechanisms, the feature-based one is expected to be typologically much less common, due to its dependence on the availability of a feature that is not found in many languages; the other strategy, on the other hand, should be available universally, since the grammar should always have a way of determining the compositional semantics of any grammatical construction. The prediction is thus that only a language that shows definiteness agreement will have genitival constructions with the semantic properties of Hebrew CSNs.

6.5 The nature of morphosyntactic definiteness

Focusing now on the fact that the definiteness feature in Hebrew is visible to the syntax–semantics interface, we turn to address a question that the discussion so far has put aside: what is the exact nature of the definiteness feature, and specifically, what are the values that it can take? There are essentially two alternatives:

- [def] is a bivalent feature, with possible values [±def].
- [def] is a monovalent (privative) feature, where the alternation is between having a [+def] feature (or, simply, [def]) and lacking it.

In previous work (Danon 2001, 2006), I have argued that the second alternative has some conceptual advantages. While the focus of these works has been on differential case marking, which was argued to relate to presence vs. absence of a [def] feature on direct objects in Hebrew, they also point out the fact that assuming a monovalent [def] feature avoids the problem of having a morphosyntactic definiteness value that contradicts the semantic definiteness value of a nominal. Specifically, this avoids having to posit a morphosyntactic [−def] feature in simple nominals that are morphosyntactically indefinite but get a definite interpretation, as with demonstratives that do not co-occur with a definite article:

(25) sefer   (*ha-)xašuv   ze
     book   (the-)important   this
     'this important book'

The fact that the adjective *xašuv* cannot be marked as definite shows that this noun phrase is morphosyntactically indefinite, which under the bivalent approach would have to be encoded as [−def]; nevertheless, this does not give rise to an indefinite reading.[12] We would thus have the undesirable situation of having a morphosyntactic feature with absolutely no semantic content. This problem does not arise if nominals that are not morphosyntactically marked as definites simply lack a [def] feature, as would be the case under the monovalent approach. Lacking [def] is then not equivalent to being semantically indefinite.

Similar considerations apply to CSNs with an embedded indefinite. Consider again example (18a), repeated below as (26):

(26) ota   tmunat   praxim
      that/same   picture   flowers
      'that picture of flowers'

According to Siloni (2003) and Alexiadou (2005), the fact that the CSN in this example is compatible with a semantically definite determiner like *ota* ('that/same') shows that indefiniteness, unlike definiteness, does not spread from the embedded nominal. If true, this is quite surprising: there is no immediate reason why the two possible values of a [±def] feature would exhibit such a sharp asymmetry in their grammatical properties, which suggests that there is something that this formulation of the facts still misses.

The observation that lack of an article, as in (26), does not entail indefiniteness has, in fact, nothing to do with (in)definiteness spreading: the same determiner as in (26) is also compatible with the basic (non CSN) form of the noun, *tmuna* ('picture'), as shown in (5); this means that lack of a definite

---

[12] Of course, the same issue comes up in the context of other features: singulars can often refer to more than a singleton, morphological present tense is not limited to the (semantic) present, etc. The two theoretical options are either to adopt an asymmetric, monovalent, representation of such features, which would make the syntax–semantics interface relatively 'transparent'; or to assume bivalent/multivalent features, with somewhat more complex rules for determining their interpretation. While the present discussion argues in favour of the former approach, the more important point is simply that this issue has to be dealt with explicitly as part of any theory of features, and that a naive theory under which all features are bivalent/multivalent and every feature value corresponds to one fixed interpretation is inadequate.

article is compatible with both definite and indefinite determiners.[13] Since an adjective modifying the CSN in (26) would obligatorily be indefinite, as shown in (9), it is clear that here the nominal is not [+def]. The monovalent approach, under which this nominal simply lacks a [def] feature, avoids the problem of assigning a morphosyntactic [−def] feature to a nominal that is semantically definite.

In light of this, I believe that although Siloni's and Alexiadou's conclusion that indefiniteness does not spread is true, this way of stating it is somewhat misleading. Spreading in Hebrew is an operation that applies to a morphosyntactic [def] feature, which, I claim, is not present on indefinites; therefore, [−def] does not spread simply because there is no [−def] feature to begin with. The interpretation of a nominal with no [def] feature in Hebrew is thus determined as in languages with no morphosyntactic [def], based on the choice of (semantic) determiner.

A similar conclusion arises from the consideration of another asymmetry observed in CSNs. As discussed above, a [+def] CSN can have any of its levels interpreted as definite, with the other level getting an indefinite reading; in an indefinite CSN, on the other hand, both levels must be interpreted as indefinite, unless an additional determiner is present, as in (26). In other words, definiteness in Hebrew must always be triggered by overt definiteness marking, while indefiniteness is the unmarked 'elsewhere' interpretation. This is best captured by a feature system that encodes definiteness and indefiniteness in an asymmetric way, rather than as the '+' and '−' values of a [def] feature. Under the monovalent approach, formal indefiniteness thus amounts to underspecification, which is compatible with all possible semantic interpretations. Note, furthermore, that viewing indefiniteness as underspecification also straightforwardly predicts the lack of any morphological marking of morphosyntactic indefiniteness in Hebrew, that is the fact that Hebrew has no indefinite article (as opposed to the prefixal definite article).

Adopting the monovalent approach is not without problems, though. One major issue is that, if morphosyntactic indefiniteness is lack of a [def] feature, enforcing obligatory definiteness agreement with adjectives raises some non-trivial technical problems. Under constraint-based approaches to agreement, it is not immediately obvious that statements of equality of features would be valid in this case: when a noun lacks a [def] feature, care must be taken to

---

[13] Here I refer to 'determiner' in the semantic sense, as in Barwise and Cooper (1981), Keenan (1987), and many others; this is not the same as the syntactic category of articles. In Section 6.2 it was noted that as far as morphosyntactic [+def] is concerned, only the presence of the definite article matters. For a more detailed discussion of the syntactic variability of determiners in Hebrew, see Danon (2006).

ensure that constraining the adjective to have the same 'value' for the missing [def] is a coherent statement and that it does not lead to adding a [def] feature to the representation of every postnominal adjective.

More seriously, under the Minimalist approach to agreement, adjectives in Hebrew would probably be assumed to enter the derivation with an unvalued [def] feature, which has to be valued via agreement. This is straightforward under the bivalent approach to definiteness, but not under the monovalent approach, which relies on the possibility of no feature at all. Under the latter approach, we could assume that adjectives *optionally* enter the derivation with unvalued [def], and, if they do, agreement must take place. But this does not rule out the possibility of attributive adjectives with no [def] feature modifying a definite noun, as in the following example:

(27) *ha-sefer   adom   ne'elam.
       the-book   red   disappeared
       (intended) 'The red book disappeared.'

If the adjective is allowed to enter the derivation without a [def] feature, then in (27) there is no unvalued feature to value, and the structure is wrongly predicted to be well formed. What is missing is some way of forcing agreement to be 'maximal': if a modifier *can* agree with the modified element, it *must* do so. This might be a general property of agreement or concord, not limited to definiteness agreement. In fact, the problem of enforcing the presence of agreement features on modifiers is a general problem for any analysis that allows feature underspecification; the same problem would apply, for instance, to analyses of subject–verb agreement under approaches that take 3rd person to be lack of a person feature, as argued on various grounds by many authors. Evidently, what is required is a more fine-grained theory of agreement that takes into account feature underspecification, which is an issue that seems to be gaining increasing interest over the last few years; see, for instance, Harley and Ritter (2002), Béjar (2003), McGinnis (2005), and Adger and Harbour (2007).

6.6 Conclusion

In this chapter I have argued that definiteness spreading in the Hebrew construct state can best be accounted for by assuming a monovalent morphosyntactic [def] feature, which is shared by the two levels of the CSN and interpreted on at least one of the nodes that share it. Following previous work, most notably Alexiadou (2005), superficially similar spreading phenomena in other languages have been shown to have significantly different properties.

Consequently, I argued that, cross-linguistically, there are two distinct mechanisms for definiteness spreading in complex nominals: one based on sharing a morphosyntactic definiteness feature, which is only possible in languages that have such a feature; and one that does not make any reference to definiteness as a morphosyntactic feature.

The definiteness feature in Hebrew has been shown to give rise to various definite–indefinite asymmetries, which, under a traditional approach assuming a symmetric [±def] feature, would pose various problems both to the syntactic analysis and to the compositional interpretation of this feature at the syntax–semantics interface. These problems do not arise under a feature-geometric approach that takes indefiniteness to be underspecification or lack of a formal definiteness feature. Combining the conclusions from the cross-linguistic comparison and from the language-internal analysis of Hebrew, we come to the following view of the relationship between morphosyntactic definiteness and semantic definiteness:

- Nouns (and noun phrases) may either have a [def] feature or lack it.
- Every instance of the [def] feature is interpreted as semantic definiteness on one of the nodes where it is present.
- The interpretation of a noun phrase with no [def] feature, or of a phrase that shares a [def] feature that is interpreted on some other node, is determined by the presence of other semantic determiners or by the compositional properties of the specific construction in which it appears; in the absence of any other factor that induces semantic definiteness, indefiniteness is the default interpretation.

Taking a broader perspective, this chapter has aimed to show that the use of features in linguistic analysis should be subject to careful consideration of the availability and content of each feature in the inventory of a given language. Different languages may have different inventories of morphosyntactic features, and the availability of a given feature could have important consequences in the kinds of grammatical operations that can apply in that language. I have tried to defend the view that not every semantic classification that has overt manifestations is encoded as a morphosyntactic feature, and only those that have clear morphosyntactic realizations should be analysed as features that the syntax can manipulate and that are visible to the syntax–semantics interface.

7

Features in periphrastic constructions

Gergana Popova

7.1 Introduction[1]

There is a long tradition in linguistic studies of saying that (classes of) words in a language are associated with some grammatical categories, or, alternatively, with some morphosyntactic features. Thus, nouns may be associated with number, verbs may be associated with tense, person, and number, etc. The association of lexemes with some features in a language may determine to some extent their morphological form. For example, in English nouns may have different forms for singular and plural, as in singular *dog* vs. plural *dogs* or singular *mouse* vs. plural *mice*; number may also have consequences for syntactic phenomena like agreement (the singular noun has to be premodified by a singular determiner as in *this dog* whereas the plural noun has to be premodified by a plural determiner as in *these dogs*).

Sometimes, however, features seem to be associated not with inflected word forms but with groups of inflected word forms. One often cited example comes from Russian. Russian has past, present, and future tenses and verb morphology reflects these categories. Verbs, however, have different forms for the future tense depending on whether they belong to one or the other of two aspects: perfective and imperfective. For example, the 1SG future tense form of the perfective Russian verb *napisat'* 'write' is the synthetic form *napišu*, but the future tense form of the imperfective verb *pisat'* 'write' is periphrastic. It comprises two forms: an inflected form of the verb 'to be' and an infinitival

---

[1] I would like to thank Bas Aarts, Andrew Spencer, the editors of the volume and two anonymous referees for their comments. I am also grateful to the audience at the *Workshop on Features*, held on 1–2 September 2007 at King's College, London as part of the LAGB annual meeting. The responsibility for all remaining errors is mine.

form of 'write' (for example, the 1SG perfective future of *pisat'* is *budu pisat'* 'I will write'). Since neither *budu* nor *pisat'* in isolation is the future tense form of the imperfective 'write', the feature TENSE with value *future* can only be associated with both these forms. Note that in such groups of forms each element itself can in turn be associated with a set of morphosyntactic features. For example, the form *budu* is itself a 1SG future tense form of the verb *byt'* 'be'.

The existence of such groups of forms which seem to demand an association with some morphosyntactic features in their entirety raises a number of interesting issues. One could indeed question the need to associate periphrastic forms with morphosyntactic features above and beyond the features assigned to the individual elements that comprise them. One could wonder whether the sets of features associated with periphrastic forms are similar in terms of their grammatical status to the sets of features associated with closely linked synthetic forms. A question to ask, then, is whether the TENSE: *future* feature associated with the synthetic form in the Russian example above is similar in status to the TENSE: *future* feature associated with the periphrastic form. Or one could examine the relationship between the features associated with the overall periphrastic construction and the features associated with its elements.

This chapter will explore some of these questions. The data used come from Bulgarian, which almost uniquely within the Slavic language family has a very rich system of periphrastic verbal tense forms. This chapter looks at the data primarily from the point of view of morphology and primarily from the point of view of a realizational morphological framework. The next section introduces a small set of the periphrastic tense forms in Bulgarian and gives some arguments for the choice of a realizational approach to morphology. Sections 7.3 and 7.4 present some arguments for the need to associate periphrastic constructions with (some) morphosyntactic features directly at the level of the construction. Section 7.5 gives an outline of Paradigm Function Morphology (PFM) – the framework which will be used in the chapter. Section 7.6 outlines briefly how frameworks like PFM have been used to assign features directly to periphrastic constructions, and Section 7.7 presents some agreement data which are problematic for existing realizational approaches to periphrasis. Section 7.8 shows that with a minimal modification realizational approaches can accommodate such data.

7.2 Features and verbs

In Bulgarian, as in other languages, lexemes belonging to different word classes are associated with different grammatical categories. Verbs in Bulgarian, for example, are said to inflect for person, number, mood, tense, voice, and aspect (descriptions of the verbal system can be found in Aronson 1968, Stankov 1969, Tilkov et al. 1983, Scatton 1984 amongst others) whereas nouns inflect for number, gender and definiteness (see Tilkov et al. 1983 or Pašov 1994 for some examples). In most cases grammatical categories are closely bound to the morphology of lexemes: for example, a change in the person, number, and tense values of a verb may be accompanied by a change in morphological form. The example in (1) shows a small part of the paradigm of the Bulgarian verb *mislja* 'think'.[2] As can be seen, the different endings of the verb are associated with different values for person, number, and tense (this small section of the paradigm ignores changes in mood, aspect, etc. If all relevant grammatical categories are taken into account, the number of forms increases vastly).

(1)   Present Tense   Aorist Tense
          Singular   Plural   Singular   Plural
    1   *mislja*   *mislim*   *mislix*   *mislixme*
    2   *misliš*   *mislite*   *misli*   *mislixte*
    3   *misli*   *misljat*   *misli*   *mislixa*

In many contemporary linguistic approaches grammatical categories associated with different word classes are expressed via a system of features. Features in turn have values; for example, the feature NUMBER may have the values *singular* and *plural*, the feature GENDER may have the values *feminine, masculine, neuter*. The grammar may declare what feature–value combinations are appropriate for each class of lexemes.

There are differences between the different approaches in whether features are associated with lexemes prior to, or as a result of, some process of composition. To give an example, one way to analyse the 1PL aorist verb form *mislixme* 'we thought' is to say that it is composed of a root *misl* associated with the lexical meaning of the lexeme THINK, and has two further elements: the morpheme *-x-* which is associated with the feature TENSE with value *aorist*, and the ending *me* which defines the values *first* and *plural* for the features PERSON and NUMBER. When the root gets combined with the two other morphemes, the resulting form inherits the lexical meaning of the root and the grammatical content of the morphemes.

---

[2] Bulgarian verbs do not have infinitival forms. Traditionally, the 1SG present tense forms are used as citation forms.

Such a 'compositional' approach quickly runs into problems, however. Without going into detail, one example can be drawn from the paradigm fragment in (1). What morphological element could be associated with the *present* value of the feature TENSE? The only putative candidate is the stem vowel -*i*-, but this stem vowel is present in the aorist forms as well.

Because of the difficulties associated with morpheme-based approaches, an alternative has been developed in works like Matthews (1972), Zwicky (1985), Anderson (1992), Aronoff (1994), Stump (2001). This alternative view entails an association of lexemes with the features appropriate for them which is independent of the construction of their word forms. The change in morphological form, where this occurs, is a reflex of this association, or in other words morphological material 'realizes' some properties of word forms, but morphological material is not a precondition for these properties to be associated with word forms. A detailed defence of realizational approaches is found in Stump (2001), for example.

In many cases the feature sets appropriate for a given class of lexemes are realized by synthetic forms of these lexemes, as in the fragment of the verbal paradigm shown in (1). It can also be the case, however, that morphosyntactic features are associated with a whole sequence of word-like elements. For example, in Bulgarian the feature TENSE traditionally has been said to have nine values: *present, aorist, imperfect, future, past future, perfect, pluperfect, future perfect, past future perfect*. Of the nine tenses, however, only three are synthetic, whereas the others are periphrastic. To illustrate, an example of the periphrastic perfect tense is given in (2):

(2)
	Aorist Tense		Perfect Tense	
	Singular	Plural	Singular	Plural
1	*mislix*	*mislixme*	*mislil/a/o sâm*	*mislili sme*
2	*misli*	*mislixte*	*mislil/a/o si*	*mislili ste*
3	*misli*	*mislixa*	*mislil/a/o e*	*mislili sa*

Unlike the aorist, the perfect tense is not represented by a single synthetic form of the verb but by a combination of two components: a synthetic form of the verb *sâm* 'be' and a synthetic participial form: *pisal/a/o* 'written'. Each of these forms is associated with a set of features of their own. For example, the verb 'be' is in the present tense and has different forms for the different PERSON/NUMBER values (*sâm, si, e, sme, ste, sa*). The participle has different forms for number and in the singular has different forms for the three genders (*mislil* is masculine, *mislila* is feminine, and *mislilo* is neuter). The components in the perfect tense construction have their own syntactic peculiarities.

For example, the present tense form of the verb 'be' is a clitic. It occurs in the Bulgarian verbal clitic cluster and like the other verbal clitics appears preverbally (3a and 3b) unless this puts it in a clause-initial position (3c and 3d) (see Avgustinova 1994, Franks and King 2000, Bošković 2001 amongst others):

(3) a. Učiteljat   e   mislil   dâlgo   vârxu   uroka.
       teacher.the be.PRS.3SG think.PTCP long   upon   lesson.the
       'The teacher has given the lesson a lot of thought.'

   b. *Učiteljat   mislil   e   dâlgo   vârxu   uroka.
       teacher.the think.PTCP be.PRS.3SG long   upon   lesson.the
       'The teacher has given the lesson a lot of thought.'

   c. Mislil   e   dâlgo   vârxu   uroka.
       think.PTCP be.PRS.3SG long   upon   lesson.the
       '(He) has given the lesson a lot of thought.'

   d. *E   mislil   dâlgo   vârxu   uroka.
       be.PRS.3SG think.PTCP long   upon   lesson.the
       '(He) has given the lesson a lot of thought.'

Periphrastic constructions like the perfect tense above pose a number of problems as far as the features associated with them are concerned. On the one hand, they seem to be associated with the same set of features as synthetic forms. For example, the forms *mislixme* 'we thought' and *mislili sme* 'we have thought' are associated with the same set of features (namely MOOD: *indicative*, VOICE: *active*, ASPECT: *imperfective*, PERSON: *first*, NUMBER: *plural*) with one exception: the synthetic verb has TENSE: *aorist* in the set of features, whereas the periphrastic form has TENSE: *perfect* in its set. The feature tense, in other words, is sometimes realized with synthetic forms and sometimes with periphrastic forms.

On the other hand, the periphrastic form consists of elements with a high degree of syntactic independence. In addition, these elements may determine the presence of features which are absent from the feature set of the synthetic forms. For example, as discussed above, the singular perfect tense forms have gender values exactly because gender is a feature appropriate for participles in Bulgarian, whereas gender is generally not expressed by verbal forms.

Like synthetic forms, periphrastic forms have been analysed broadly in at least two ways: as syntactic phenomena whose features get assigned via some kind of composition in the syntax, or as forms of lexemes whose features are given a priori and whose elements can be seen as 'realizations' of these features. (See, for example, Börjars et al. 1997, Sadler and Spencer 2001, Blevins forthcoming, and references therein.)

Ackerman and Stump (2004) propose three criteria for distinguishing periphrases from word combinations whose composition is governed by syntax:

- if an analytic combination has a featurally intersective distribution (there is no one property that is always expressed periphrastically rather than synthetically) then it is a periphrase;
- if the morphosyntactic property set associated with an analytic combination is not the composition of the property sets associated with its parts, then this analytic combination is a periphrase;
- if the morphosyntactic property set associated with an analytic combination has its exponents distributed among its parts, then this combination is a periphrase.

Each of these criteria may help identify cases of periphrasis: there is no requirement for all of them to be fulfilled. The first two especially are relevant to constructions like the perfect tense construction in Bulgarian. It was already mentioned that the tense feature is sometimes realized synthetically and sometimes periphrastically. In other words, this is not a property which is always expressed periphrastically. On the other hand, the features associated with Bulgarian periphrastic tense constructions are not simply a composition of the features associated with the parts of the construction. For example, no part of the perfect tense construction is itself associated with the morphosyntactic feature TENSE: *perfect*. For some features, however, it is the case that the construction and its elements have similar specifications. For example, *mislili sme* is, as shown in (2), the 1PL perfect tense form of THINK. Both the verb *sme* 'be' and the participle are themselves associated with the feature NUMBER: *plural*. In this sense, then, there is multiple exponence of plurality. In singular forms, however, only the participial form is an exponent of gender.

The fact that constructions can be associated with features which are not part of the feature sets associated with their parts, on the one hand, and the fact that constructions can exhibit multiple and distributed exponence on the other, makes realizational analyses especially easy to construct. However, some properties of some constructions pose challenges for realizational approaches.

Since this chapter looks at periphrastic morphology from a realizational point of view, in what follows the focus will be on what problems periphrastic constructions pose for a realizational approach to morphology, though this will be preceded by a discussion which argues that periphrastic constructions are problematic for bottom-up approaches as well.

7.3 Feature assignment: top-down or bottom-up?

7.3.1 Difficulties for bottom-up approaches

Given that periphrastic constructions are composed of syntactically independent elements, one might argue that whatever features are associated with the construction as a whole should be associated first with some or all of its elements. A short example of what this might entail will be given with the future tense construction. The future tense fragment of the verbal paradigm is illustrated in (4):

(4)

		Present Tense		Future Tense	
		Singular	Plural	Singular	Plural
1		mislja	mislim	šte mislja	šte mislim
2		misliš	mislite	šte misliš	šte mislite
3		misli	misljat	šte misli	šte misljat

As is clear from the comparison with the present tense synthetic forms of 'think', one of the elements in the periphrastic future tense construction is the conjugated present tense form of the (main) verb. The other element is the indeclinable particle *šte*, historically a present tense form of the verb *šta* 'want'.

One could imagine a fairly straightforward constructional analysis where the particle *šte* is associated with the feature TENSE: *future* and the main verb contributes feature values for person and number. This is represented schematically in (5):

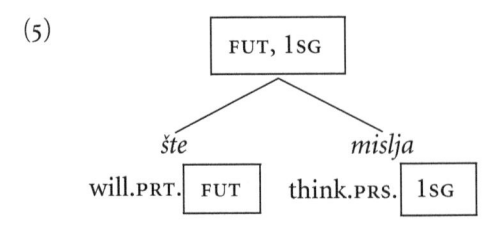

(5)

```
            FUT, 1SG
           /        \
         šte         mislja
    will.PRT. FUT   think.PRS. 1SG
```

There are various ways to ensure that the features associated with the elements of the construction might be shared with the construction as a whole. One way could be some identity relation between a mother node and a daughter node (for example there might be identity between the agreement features associated with the verb *mislja* 'I think' and the agreement features associated with *šte mislja* 'I will think'), or one might use unification to collect the non-conflicting information associated with the daughters at the mother node (a unification analysis for some Bulgarian periphrastic constructions is proposed in Avgustinova 1994).³ Note that using unification would still entail a stipulation that the tense value will be passed up by the particle *šte* rather than by the main verb. An analysis in which the feature TENSE: *future* is associated with the particle *šte*, however, runs into problems. One of the difficulties with the bottom-up approach is illustrated below.

The negated part of the paradigm of the future tense is idiosyncratic. There are two ways of negating the future tense forms and these are illustrated in (6):

(6)   Negated future I   Negated future II

	Singular	Plural	Singular	Plural
1	ne šte mislja	ne šte mislim	njama da mislja	njama da mislim
2	ne šte misliš	ne šte mislite	njama da misliš	njama da mislite
3	ne šte misli	ne šte misljat	njama da misli	njama da misljat

The negated forms could be derived via the addition of the negative particle *ne* 'not' as in the first two columns of (6), or they could be based on the impersonal forms of the verb *njama* 'not have', which is a special fused negated form of the verb *imam* 'have' (historically, these are 3SG present tense forms of the verb). The problem arises in the latter case: there is no particle *šte* in this construction, so futurity will have to be contributed by some other element (possibly the verb *njama*, even though this verb is in fact in the present tense).

Another argument why there should be features that are assigned directly to a construction instead of being propagated up from one or more of its elements comes from the possibility of reinterpreting a construction in the process of language change. The next section describes the so-called inferential construction in Bulgarian which has not received much attention in existing grammars.

---

[3] An anonymous reviewer pointed out that subsumption is another, and possibly better, way of modelling the correspondences between features of constructions and features of their elements.

7.4 The inferential construction and the reinterpretation of periphrastic constructions

According to the available sources the so-called inferential construction (*predpoložitelna forma*) shown in (7) draws on two existing constructions: the future tense construction, illustrated above in (4) and in (8a), and the perfect tense construction illustrated in (2) above and in (8b). The inferential construction has a modal meaning, expressing a supposition on behalf of the speaker. It is possible to use the construction with a present time reference, as in (7a), or with a past time reference, as in (7b):

(7) a. V kâštata **šte** (**da**) e, kâde drugade.
       in house.the PRT   PRT be.PRS.3SG where else
       'He must be in the house, where else could he be?'

   b. **Šte** (**da**) go   e   **napisala**   pismoto.
       PRT   PRT   him be.PRS.3SG write.PTCP.SG.F letter.the
       'She must have written the letter.'

Most authors claim that the inferential form in (7a) is a reinterpretation of the future tense (8a) (see, for example, Pašov 1966, Stankov 1969, Maslov 1982). The construction in (7b) has similarly been linked to the perfect tense (8b):

(8) a. Toj **šte** e   v   kâštata   utre.
       he PRT be.PRS.3SG in house.the tomorrow
       'He will be in the house tomorrow.'

   b. Tja e   **napisala**   pismoto.
       she be.PRS.3SG write.PTCP.SG.F letter.the
       'She has written the letter.'

As can be seen from the examples, the inferential construction with present time reference can be identical to the future tense construction, though the inferential but not the future construction allows the insertion of an optional complementizer *da*. The inferential construction with past time reference is also similar formally to the perfect tense construction, except for the presence of the particle *šte* and the optional complementizer *da*.

There are also semantic links between the inferential construction shown in (7a) and (7b) and the future and the perfect tenses, which are described in existing sources (for example Stankov 1969). The future tense construction has inherent in it the meaning of prediction or supposition and it is easy to see how this might be emphasized. The perfect tense, on the other hand, has the meaning of result. It can be extended to indicate an eventuality which is inferred on the basis of its results without being witnessed by the speaker.

The problem for bottom-up approaches is the following: a group of forms (a construction) like *šte e v kâštata* 'will be in the house' needs to be associated with the feature TENSE: *future*, but, on the other hand, it also needs to be associated with the feature MODALITY: *inferential*. If features are not associated directly with constructions, but are somehow passed on to the construction from the individual elements that comprise it, then the question arises what features could be associated with the same elements to result, on the one hand, in the TENSE: *future* specification, but in some other cases in the specification MODALITY: *inferential*?

One could argue that examples like these are mostly to do with semantic interpretation. The future or modal interpretation (which are very similar in many ways) are both available to the same construction, much like a word can have more than one meaning. We need to find the right semantics for the elements in constructions and then we will be able to show that the right combination of elements will give us the desired semantics, or we need to allow the construction as a whole to have different semantic interpretation in different contexts.

The problem with a purely semantic approach (whatever shape that may take) is that the two constructions are different not just in terms of what meaning they are assigned but also in terms of their morphosyntactic behaviour. Namely, the two constructions have different negation patterns. As we saw in (6), the future tense has two negative forms, of which the form with the fused negated verb *njama* 'not have' is by far the more usual and prevalent and the form with the negative particle *ne* is felt to be archaic. The inferential construction, on the other hand, is negated with the negative particle *ne*, rather than with the verb *njama* 'not have'. Therefore example (9a) can only be the inferential construction, example (9b) can be either the inferential or the future tense construction, and example (9c) can only be the future tense construction:

(9) a. Toj   ne   šte   da   e   v   kâštata.
       he   not   PRT   PRT   be.PRS.3SG in   house.the
       'It must be the case that he is not in the house.'

    b. ?Toj ne   šte   e   v   kâštata.
       he   not   PRT   be.PRS.3SG in   house.the
       'He will not be in the house.'

c. Toj njama da e v kâštata.
   he not-have PRT be.PRS.3SG in house.the
   'He will not be in the house.'

Another formal difference between the two constructions concerns the existence of alternative forms with the verb *bâda* (historically a future tense form of 'be'). The future tense can be formed in one of two ways: with the present tense forms of the verb *sâm* 'be' or with forms of the verb *bâda*. Thus the sentences in (10a) and (10b) are equivalent. As we saw, the inferential construction with the verb *sâm* has present time reference. If the verb *bâda* is used with the inferential construction, however, the time reference tends to be a future one (10c):

(10) a. Toj šte e na teatâr utre.
        he PRT be.PRS.3SG to theatre tomorrow
        'He will go to the theatre tomorrow.'

   b. Toj šte bâde na teatâr utre.
      he PRT be.PRS.3SG to theatre tomorrow
      'He will go to the theatre tomorrow.'

   c. Toj šte da bâde na teatâr utre.
      he PRT PRT be.PRS.3SG to theatre tomorrow
      'He must be going to the theatre tomorrow.'

   d. ??Toj šte da e na teatâr utre.
      he PRT PRT be.PRS.3SG to theatre tomorrow
      (intended) 'He must be going to the theatre tomorrow.'

Despite the nearly formal equivalence of the future tense and the inferential construction, the two need to have a distinct featural content in order to account for their different behaviour (for example in terms of negation). The features associated with these two constructions are important not simply in terms of the meaning they may be assigned but also in terms of their morphological and syntactic properties.

This section and the previous one outlined some problems that a bottom-up constructional approach may run into with respect to the assignment of morphosyntactic features to periphrastic constructions. Realizational approaches, which assume that, similarly to synthetic forms, features can be associated directly with a construction, seem better suited to an analysis of periphrasis. The next section will outline the principles that underlie realizational approaches to periphrastic constructions. The emphasis will be on approaches within the framework of Paradigm Function Morphology (PFM) (Stump 2001). For more details on the difficulties faced by syntactic approaches to periphrasis see Sadler and Spencer (2001), Spencer (2003), Ackerman and Stump (2004), and Ackerman et al. (forthcoming). Before analyses of periphrastic constructions are outlined, however, the next section will introduce briefly the main principles of PFM.

7.5 Paradigm Function Morphology

In PFM the features associated with lexemes are not contributed by the components of the word forms of these lexemes. Instead, the grammar associates each lexeme with a set of morphosyntactic properties which are appropriate for it and which define its paradigm. The sets of morphosyntactic properties that get associated with a lexeme (and define its paradigm) are subject to certain restrictions, the first of which is language universal: a set can contain only one of the permissible values for each feature, so if a set contains a specification NUMBER: *plural* it cannot also contain the specification NUMBER: *singular*. The well-formed sets of morphosyntactic properties are also subject to the so-called *property co-occurrence restrictions* (see Stump 2001: 41). These are language specific and can take the shape for example of the stipulation that, if a well-formed set of morphosyntactic properties contains the specification MOOD: *imperative*, then it also contains the specification PERSON: 2.

A central notion of PFM is that of a paradigm. A paradigm is defined as a set of cells where each cell is a pairing $\langle Y, \sigma \rangle$ of an inflected form Y of a given lexeme and a complete set of morphosyntactic properties σ appropriate for this cell of the lexeme's paradigm.

The inflected forms in a language are determined by the paradigm function of that language. The paradigm function takes as input the root of a lexeme L and a set of morphosyntactic properties appropriate for L, and returns the inflected form occupying the appropriate cell in the paradigm of L, and the set of morphosyntactic properties.

Formally this is shown in (11):

(11) $PF(\langle X, \sigma \rangle) = \langle Y, \sigma \rangle$

where X is the root of a lexeme L, Y is an inflected form occupying a cell in the paradigm of L, and σ is a complete set of morphosyntactic properties appropriate for this cell of the paradigm of L.

A paradigm function is defined further as a series of realization rules. A realization rule is also a function, which takes as input a form paired with a set of morphosyntactic properties, and returns a form paired with a set of morphosyntactic properties. Unlike in the case of the paradigm function, the input to a realization rule is not necessarily a root, and the output is not necessarily a word. Realization rules are ordered into blocks, such that the rules in each block are in competition, and the order of the blocks determines the order of application of the realization rules. Each rule is indexed with a set of morphosyntactic properties which this rule realizes and which is a subset of the complete set of morphosyntactic properties σ above. The formal expression of this can be seen in (12):

(12) $RR_{n,\tau,C}(\langle X, \sigma \rangle) =_{def} \langle Y', \sigma \rangle$
where n is an index showing which block a realization rule belongs to, the class index C specifies which class of lexemes this rule can apply to, and τ is a well-formed set of morphosyntactic properties which this rule realizes.

In the setup of PFM, if there is no applicable rule in a given block given a certain property set, then the so-called *identity function default* (IFD) applies. As can be deduced from the name, this rule maps a form onto itself in the absence of any applicable rules. The identity function default looks as in (13):[4]

(13) $RR_{n,\{\},U}(\langle X, \sigma \rangle) =_{def} \langle X, \sigma \rangle$
with respect to a language *l* the index n is a variable which ranges over the indices of all rule blocks in *l*, {} is the empty set of morphosyntactic properties, and U designates the class of all lexemes in the language *l*.

The rules in each of the blocks are in competition. This competition is resolved through the notion of *narrowness* – the most narrow applicable rule applies (or, in other words, the rules are subject to Pāṇini's principle). Roughly, a rule R_n is narrower than another rule R_m if the set of properties realized by R_n is a superset of the set of properties realized by R_m. Alternatively, a rule R_n is narrower than a rule R_m if it applies to a smaller class of morphemes.

The IFD is formulated in such a way that it is the most general rule of all – it realizes the empty set and applies to all classes of lexemes. Therefore, even if there is no other applicable rule, the IFD will always apply. On the other hand, if there is a narrower applicable rule in a block, it will prevent the IFD from applying.

---

[4] A more precise formulation of the IFD (see Stump 2001: 143) prevents it from applying in the case of rule blocks of the portmanteau type, but since this is not of concern here, I use the preliminary formulation in Stump (2001: 53) in the interests of expositional simplicity.

7.6 Some realizational proposals

There are a number of recent works which represent a departure from a bottom-up approach to periphrastic constructions (for example, Börjars et al. 1997, Sadler and Spencer 2001, Ackerman and Stump 2004, Ackerman et al. forthcoming).

Generally in such proposals periphrastic constructions are conceived of not as products of productive syntactic processes but as morphological realizations of lexemes. In other words, in such approaches the perfect tense form *mislila sâm* 'I have thought' is a form of the lexeme MISLJA 'think' just as much as the aorist form *mislix* 'I thought'.

A conception of periphrastic constructions as forms of lexemes means that they are part of the paradigm space of a lexeme and arise as a result of the association between the root of a lexeme (or in some versions of PFM the lexeme itself) and a complete set of morphosyntactic properties appropriate for that lexeme. Periphrastic constructions are obviously not inflected forms composed of affixes, so the paradigm function (or the series of realization rules it is composed of) must make sure that in these cases the realization is a syntactic structure.

In Ackerman and Stump (2004), for example, non-compositional periphrases are integrated in the system of realization rules. Realization rules which are responsible for periphrastic constructions appear in blocks together with the realization rules that are responsible for inflected forms and may look like the rule in (14) (original notation has been modified):

(14) $RR_{n,\tau,C}(\langle X, \sigma \rangle) = [Y Z]$
where X is the root of a lexeme L, τ is the set of properties realized by this realization rule, σ is a complete set of morphosyntactic properties appropriate for this cell of the paradigm of L, and Y and Z are words which may head syntactic phrases.

In other words, a realization rule may apply to a pairing of a root X and a property set σ and return a structure [Y Z] where Y and Z are words which can head syntactic phrases.

The rule in (14) is less explicit about the morphosyntactic properties associated with the elements of the syntactic structure that are in the range of this realization rule. Some indication of this is contained in a rule of periphrastic syntax (see Ackerman and Stump 2004: 136). Essentially, if a rule has specified that a syntactic structure is the exponent of some property of a lexeme L of category X for a pairing of a root and the full set of morphosyntactic properties σ, then this syntactic structure will project a phrase XP with the properties σ.

In other proposals this relationship between the features of the overall construction and the features of the elements that compose it is somewhat different. Sadler and Spencer (2001) make a distinction between syntactic features (*s*-features) and morphological features (*m*-features). S-features are 'visible' to syntax, whereas *m*-features are not. Generally, the features associated with the overall construction are *s*-features. The features associated with the elements of the construction are generally *m*-features, though Spencer (2003) seems to allow for the possibility that they are *s*-features as well.

However, in all approaches the features associated with the construction as a whole (*s*-features, or content paradigm features in Ackerman et al. forthcoming) are a complete and well-formed set of morphosyntactic features appropriate for a cell C in the paradigm of a lexeme L.

This, however, may prove problematic for some periphrases like the ones found in Bulgarian. These will be discussed in the next section with the focus being on agreement.

7.7 Agreement in periphrastic constructions

Since PFM-like approaches treat periphrastic constructions as forms of lexemes, there is a condition on the set of features associated with the overall construction (these are the features that are realized by the paradigm function) that it is complete and that it contains no incompatible values (Stump 2001: 41ff.). Since Bulgarian verbs, including those in periphrases, are usually specified for person and number (and participial forms have gender), agreement features are an important part of this set. In most cases there are no mismatches between the agreement values of the overall construction and the agreement values of the components:

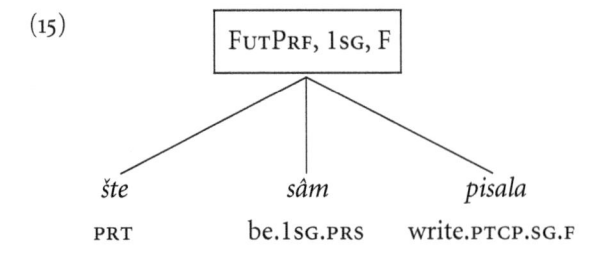

(15)

FutPrf, 1sg, F

šte — sâm — pisala
PRT — be.1sg.prs — write.ptcp.sg.f

The agreement features of the overall construction may be expressed by more than one of the components:

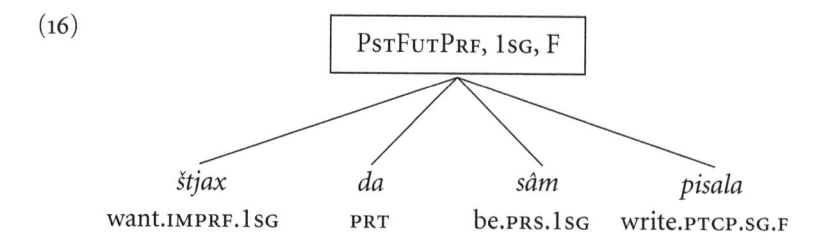

(16)

```
                    PstFutPrf, 1sg, F
              ╱          │        │         ╲
           štjax         da      sâm        pisala
        want.IMPRF.1SG   PRT   be.PRS.1SG   write.PTCP.SG.F
```

There are some cases, however, where the patterns of agreement are quite complex. This is illustrated in (17) with the pluperfect tense construction.

(17) Vie   ste   bila   xodila   v   Berlin   predi.
      you.PL be.PRS.2PL   be.PTCP.SG.F go.PTCP.SG.F in   Berlin   before
      'You have been to Berlin before.'

The pluperfect tense construction illustrated in (17) is similar to constructions like the future or the perfect tense. It fills a cell in the tense paradigm of the lexeme *xodja* 'walk'. The pluperfect tense construction is composed of an inflected present tense form of the verb *sâm* 'be', a participial form of the verb *sâm* 'be', and a participial form of the main verb. As a form of the lexeme *xodja*, the construction should be associated with a complete set of morphosyntactic features appropriate for a verb. The construction should therefore be associated with some values of the features PERSON and NUMBER. It is not clear what these could be, however, given the requirement within approaches like PFM that the same cell in a paradigm cannot be associated with incompatible values for the same feature. The inflected verb 'be' in the construction shown in (17) appears in its 2PL form, whereas the *l*-participles of the verb 'be' and of the verb *xodja* 'walk' appear in a singular form. This raises the question of whether the construction as a whole should be singular or plural.

There is no clear answer to this problem. The incompatibility of values arises from a complex pattern of agreement available to polite forms. The inflectional properties of the auxiliary 'be' are determined by the subject, whereas those of the participles are determined by the addressee (this sentence could be addressed appropriately to a woman given the feminine gender of the participles). Similar patterns of agreement in Czech are illustrated in Corbett (2006: 86–87) and Corbett (this volume). The problem of mismatches in agreement patterns which might be syntactic (determined by the formal properties of a controller) and semantic (determined by the semantic properties of a controller) are discussed also in Corbett (2006: 155–160ff.). There is a discussion of agreement phenomena which focuses specifically on auxiliary verb constructions in Anderson (2006: 18ff.).

Constructions like the ones in (17) seem to be a problem for realizational approaches to periphrastic constructions. Even though there is a need to associate the construction as a whole with some grammatical features (in this case at least the feature TENSE: *pluperfect*), the elements of the construction behave like independent syntactic elements with respect to other features (like the features of agreement).

The next section will indicate that data like that in (17) can be accommodated in a realizational approach to periphrasis without major modifications to the formalism.

7.8 A realizational approach to periphrastic constructions

As already mentioned, a realizational approach to periphrastic constructions has the advantage of being able to associate the whole construction with a set of features independently of the formal composition of the construction. This means that the features of the construction could potentially be different from the features associated with its elements, or that the construction can have features associated with it which it does not share with any of the elements that comprise it. Conversely, it should be theoretically possible that there are features associated with the elements of the construction which are not present in the set associated with the construction as a whole.

For example, with respect to the data presented in (17) we want to say that there are features which are realized by the construction as a whole. This construction fills the cell in the paradigm of the lexeme which is associated with the properties VOICE: *active*, MOOD: *indicative*, TENSE: *pluperfect*.

In a realizational approach this can be done fairly simply, by introducing a realization rule within a paradigm function which looks like (18) (see also 14):

(18) $RR_{n,\ \{tense:pluperfect\},C}(\langle\ X,\ \sigma\ \rangle) = [WYZ]$
where X is the root of a lexeme L, {tense: pluperfect} is the property realized by this realization rule, σ is a complete set of morphosyntactic properties appropriate for this cell of the paradigm of L, W is a present tense inflected form of the verb *sâm* 'be', Y is a participial form of *sâm* 'be', and Z is a participial form of X.

This realization rule will ensure that a lexeme which is associated with a property set which contains the feature–value combination TENSE: *pluperfect* is realized as a construction consisting of word forms.

This rule might be part of a series which will define the paradigm function for Bulgarian. The rule itself however does not solve the issue of the conflicting agreement data presented in (17). The problem here lies in the property set σ. PFM requires that the paradigm function (and the realization rules) apply to a pairing of a lexeme L (or the lexeme's root) and a complete set of properties appropriate for this lexeme. A complete set of properties appropriate for the synthetic verbal forms in Bulgarian, however, must contain the features NUMBER and PERSON. These features can have only one value each.

I propose that for periphrastic constructions the set σ may be different than the set associated with synthetic forms. More specifically, for the Bulgarian data at issue here, the set σ referred to in the rule in (18) does not contain agreement features. In other words, the construction which fills the pluperfect cell in the paradigm of Bulgarian verbal lexemes is not associated with agreement features.

Note that this does not mean that the parts of the pluperfect construction are not themselves associated with agreement features. The pluperfect construction is composed of elements which themselves are inflected synthetic forms and as such will themselves be associated with complete sets of properties appropriate for them.

There is a way of ensuring that periphrastic constructions in Bulgarian are not associated with agreement features without modifying the definition of the paradigm function or the definition of the set σ. To achieve this, it is sufficient to make the right stipulations in the language-specific property co-occurrence restrictions which help define the paradigm space of lexemes. For Bulgarian, one would need to include a condition that whenever a set of morphosyntactic properties appropriate for verbs includes the feature value combination TENSE: *pluperfect*, it **must not** include the features NUMBER and PERSON. This will ensure that the construction as a whole is not associated with any agreement features.

Including this condition in the grammar will presuppose greater independency between the features associated with a construction as a whole and the features associated with its parts. It may also mean that the syntax will interact directly not just with the features associated with the construction but also with the features associated with its parts. The exact shape of the interaction between the morphology and the syntax, however, is outside of the scope of this chapter.

7.9 Conclusion

In this chapter I have been looking at features in periphrastic constructions, focusing on data from Bulgarian. I have tried to show that in some respects periphrastic constructions are more amenable to a top-down realizational account, where the construction is a result of the association of some lexeme with some morphosyntactic properties. Indeed, this approach has been adopted in a number of recent accounts of periphrastic constructions. The account of periphrastic constructions, however, cannot be made completely parallel to accounts of non-periphrastic inflectional morphology. The crucial problematic data in Bulgarian come from agreement. Elements in periphrastic constructions have to be allowed to have morphosyntactic features which are determined not within the construction but, for example, by general mechanisms of agreement.

8

A Minimalist theory of feature structure

David Adger

8.1 Introduction[1]

This chapter has two intertwined aims. One is to outline, within a broadly Minimalist framework, a fairly explicit proposal for a theory of feature structures, that is, the structure of features and the syntax of how features combine to form lexical items; the other is to explore the consequences of the idea that structure embedding in human language is only ever syntactic (that is, that there is a single engine for the generation of structure and that engine is the syntax – see Marantz 1997, Borer 2005; also compare the ideas in Hauser, Chomsky, and Fitch 2002, Fitch, Hauser, and Chomsky 2005). The two aims are connected, since if structure embedding is only syntactic, then the feature structures that are the basic atoms of syntax (i.e. lexical items) cannot involve embedding of one feature inside another. This approach contrasts rather starkly with work in other approaches which take lexical items to have rich featural structure, such as HPSG, LFG, or FUG. My intention is not to relate the system developed here to these other frameworks, nor to provide a formalization of (an implementation of) the Minimalist framework. It is rather to be explicit enough that a practitioner of a unification-based framework can get an idea about what the theoretical issues are considered to be in Minimalism. A more conceptual discussion of related issues can be found in Adger and Svenonius (2009).

---

[1] Many thanks to Ash Asudeh, Pavel Caha, Annabel Cormack, Gabi Danon, Justin Fitzpatrick, Daniel Harbour, Terje Lohndal, Michal Starke, Peter Svenonius, the editors of this volume (Anna Kibort and Grev Corbett), the participants of the Features Workshop, the Tromsø Thursday Seminar, and two anonymous OUP referees for extremely helpful discussion and comments. The research reported here was funded by a Leverhulme Trust Major Research Fellowship.

Before launching in on features, a few words about what a grammar in Minimalism looks like. Much like Categorial Grammars, Minimalist grammars can be seen as lexically driven combinatory systems, involving the repeated application of very basic operations to lexical items and to the operators' own outputs (e.g. Stabler 1997; Stabler 1998; Frampton and Gutmann 1999; Retoré and Stabler 2004). Unlike Categorial Grammars, the operations build and alter structure, so that the grammar can be used to define legitimate syntactic objects (rather like TAGs; Kroch and Joshi 1987, Frank 2002). The core operation is Merge, which essentially defines what legitimate (non-atomic) syntactic objects are. I give the version of Merge defined in Chomsky (1995: 243) here, but we will change this directly:

(1) a. Lexical items are syntactic objects.
    b. If A is a syntactic object and B is a syntactic object, then Merge of A and B, K = {C, {A, B}}, is a syntactic object.

C in K is known as the *label* of K. Chomsky argues that the label is always identical to one of the two arguments of Merge; thus (1) can be reformulated as:

(2) a. Lexical items are syntactic objects.
    b. If A is a syntactic object and B is a syntactic object, then Merge of A and B, K = {A, {A, B}}, is a syntactic object.

We return to the issue of which of the two subconstituents of the output of Merge is chosen as the label in Section 8.3.1.1. K is more usually represented as a labelled bracketing or tree (although such a representation imposes an order which the sets do not have):

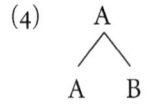

(3) [$_A$ A B]

(4)   A
       / \
      A   B

A generalized version of this operation (usually called Move, Remerge, or Internal Merge) allows Merge of an element that has already been Merged:

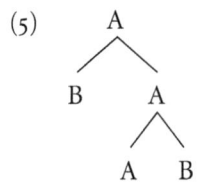

(5)   A
        / \
       B   A
          / \
         A   B

A Minimalist theory of features

This can be thought of in two ways: either the higher B is type-identical to the lower B, or it is token-identical. Both approaches have been pursued in the literature (under the 'copy' theory, Chomsky 1993; or the 'remerge' theory of Move, e.g. Gärtner 2002).

These structures are built by the syntax and are then interpreted by the interfaces that map the structures to sounds and meanings. Minimalism assumes a number of interface constraints that dictate how the structures are so mapped. For example, on the sound side, some statement needs to be made about the linearization of the structures, while on the meaning side, something needs to be said about how each part of the structure's interpretation relates to the interpretation of the other parts of the structure. These interface constraints are maximally general (for example, a constraint will require that only one of the two Bs in (5) be pronounced – see, for example, Nunes 1995, Bobaljik 1995, while a similar constraint will require only one to be semantically interpreted – e.g. the Theta Criterion essentially has the effect; see also Adger and Ramchand's 2005 Interpret Once Under Agree condition).

8.2 Types of feature system

In Adger (2006), in response to Asudeh and Toivonen (2006a), I noted that feature systems could be thought of as increasing in complexity given the kinds of rules required to generate lexical items in the system (see Gazdar, Pullum, Carpenter, Klein, Hukari, and Levine 1988 for a more formal discussion which defines categories via a recursive definition on sets). In the remainder of this section I extend this line of thinking, running through various types of feature system, from privative to category recursive, evaluating each in turn.

A simple privative system can be given by two statements which define features and lexical items as follows:

(6) a. An atomic symbol drawn from the set F = {A, B, C, D, E, ...} is a feature
b. A Lexical Item (LI) is a set of features, for example LI_i = {A, C, E}

I take the word privative here to characterize systems where atomic features may be present or absent, but have no other properties. We are interested in only syntactic features here, rather than in the features which distinguish lexical items phonologically and semantically. One could therefore think of LI in (6) as being close to the traditional notion of a syntactic category as a bundle of features. Note that since LI is defined as a set, the same feature cannot appear twice. Examples of LIs in such a system might be:

(7) a. {T, past, plural}
    b. {D, definite, accusative, plural}

However, a system like this suffers from the problem of how to state syntactic dependency relations. Since the features have no properties, there is no obvious way of encoding that two lexical items must have the same specification for a certain feature in a syntactic structure, a core explanandum of natural language, reducing to the fact that syntactic dependencies exist. To state such dependencies with purely atomic, unstructured, features, one would need a separate system of rules that explicitly state the relevant constraint:

(8) If a subject has the feature [plural] then the verb which it is a subject of must also have this feature.

It is unclear, within the Minimalist framework, where one could state such a constraint, since the framework allows only lexical items, syntactic operations, and interface constraints relating syntax to interpretation. One could perhaps hypothesize an interface constraint requiring the interpretation of the number feature on the subject and the interpretation of the number feature on the verb to be identical (e.g. the semantic theories of agreement defended by, for example, Dowty and Jacobson 1988), but that does not obviously capture the syntactic nature of the dependency. Moreover, it is difficult to see how one might extend such a system to, for example, structural case matching between adjectives and nouns (see Svenonius 2007a for discussion of this point). In any event, a system where features have no properties requires some syntax external theory of syntactic dependency formation, which seems rather problematic.

We can sidestep this problem by introducing some minimal complexity into our theory of privative features, allowing them to have exactly one property which will ensure that there is a matching feature elsewhere in the syntactic structure. This is the intuition behind the notion of uninterpretability introduced by Chomsky (1995). We add a statement to our theory specifying the form each $F_i \in F$ takes, giving (9) as our new feature theory:

(9) a. An atomic symbol drawn from the set $F = \{A, B, C, D, E, \ldots\}$ is a feature
    b. An atomic symbol drawn from the set F and prefixed by u is a feature
    c. A Lexical Item (LI) is a set of features, for example $LI_i = \{A, uC, E\}$

With this definition in place, we can now make our syntactic structure building rules sensitive to the presence of the *u* prefix, ensuring that, when a feature bears such a prefix, there must be another feature in the structure which is exactly the same but lacks the prefix. This implements Chomsky's notion of *checking*. We can now ensure that a subject will agree with its verb by endowing the verb with a set of features which bear the *u* prefix. Unless the subject bears exactly the same set of features unprefixed, a general constraint stipulating that all *u*-prefixed features must be checked will rule the structure out:

(10) {D, definite, plural} ... {T, past, *u*plural}

(11) *{D, definite, singular} ... {T, past, *u*plural}

Note that the prefix is doing purely formal work in this system. Chomsky proposed that the uninterpretability property of features not only implemented syntactic dependency in the way just outlined, but furthermore could be connected to the interpretation of the elements on which the features were specified. The idea is that a feature like [plural] only has an interpretation when specified on a category which can be potentially interpreted as plural (e.g. on a noun), otherwise an instance of this feature will be uninterpretable: interpretability is detectable from a feature's syntactic/semantic context. The formal property of features (the *u* prefix) which enables them to enter into dependency relations is thus linked to the interpretation of features by the (semantic) interface (see the discussion of Full Interpretation in Section 8.3.1.1 below).

This kind of system, where features have just one property (the 'match me' property of uninterpretability) appears to be the minimal system that is needed to capture the notion of syntactic dependency. The syntactic operations are sensitive to this property and will generate structures that satisfy its needs.[2]

However, one issue with this kind of privative theory is that it makes capturing morphological and semantic commonalities between features difficult. For example, there is no formal connection between the features [singular] and [plural] in such a privative system, yet there is a clear semantic connection between them and in many languages a clear morphological connection (for example, the corresponding morphemes are in complementary distribution).

One might think that this problem could be sidestepped by taking the semantic and morphological interpretation of absence of the feature [plural] to be whatever the semantics and morphology of singularity is. That is, the

---

[2] One can imagine other ways of implementing the 'match me' property, but they are no less complex than the system just described.

interface rules would take absence of a [plural] feature to be equivalent to an explicit statement of a [singular] feature. This would then connect the semantic and morphological notions of plurality and singularity with a single syntactic feature's presence or absence, thus solving the problem. However, this will not do.

To see this, take the following examples:

(12) a. The owl hoots.
     b. The owls hoot.

Under the analysis just sketched, we take the feature [plural] to have the following interpretations in English on a noun and on T (ignoring pronominal subjects and using capitals to signify whatever the relevant semantics is – see below for a more serious suggestion):

(13) a. PLURAL ← {N, plural} → -/z/
     b. SINGULAR ← {N} → -/0/
     c. PRESENT ← {T, present, *u*plural} → -/0/
     d. PRESENT ← {T, present} → -/z/

However, under such a system, nothing prevents the combination of (a) and (d):

(14) ...{N, plural}...{T, present}

Neither item bears a feature with the 'match me' property of uninterpretability. The semantics works out correctly, but the predicted morphology is wrong. We predict -/z/ on both the N and on T, giving:

(15) *The owls hoots.

The problem here is that agreement is obligatory, but, given the assumptions that the features are atomic and privative, and that the semantics of singularity follows from the absence of [plural], there is just no way of encoding the obligatoriness of agreement. Under this system of assumptions, to avoid generating (15), we are forced to posit a [singular] feature in the syntax:

(16) a. PLURAL ← {N, plural} → -/z/
     b. SINGULAR ← {N, singular} → -/0/
     c. PRESENT ← {T, present, *u*plural} → -/0/
     d. PRESENT ← {T, present, *u*singular} → -/z/

This will now capture what we want to be captured, but suffers from the problem that the two features [singular] and [plural] are completely independent. I take this conclusion to be incorrect.

For these reasons, one may wish to enrich the system so as to allow such a link to be made. The simplest way of doing this is to allow features to have values. We can then arrange the theory so that an unvalued feature on T gets its value from the subject.

There are many kinds of feature systems where features have values. We can rank them according to richness depending on what vocabulary the values are drawn from. One simple system is a binary system, where the values are drawn from the vocabulary {+, −}. Richer systems allow an expansion of the value vocabulary to other atomic symbols, to features, to lexical items, and to complex syntactic objects. I will discuss these in turn.[3]

For a binary system, we change our specification of the form of features thus:

(17) a. a feature is an ordered pair ⟨Att, Val⟩ where
 b. Att is drawn from the set of attributes, {A, B, C, D, E, ...}
 c. and Val is drawn from the set of values, {+, −}

Following linguistic tradition, we write the ordered pair ⟨A, +⟩ as either [A:+] or [+A]. This definition of course gives us a finite set of LIs (categories) on the assumption that there is a finite set of features. Our previous examples might now look as follows:

(18) a. {T:+, past:+, plural:+}
 b. {D:+, definite:+, plural:+}

This approach has an advantage over the privative approach in that it immediately allows one to capture the fact that the entities that plural marked elements denote are the complement set of those denoted by singular marked elements. It simplifies the interface to interpretation since the form of the feature does the work of establishing the semantic and morphological connection rather than the syntax external systems. Since features have values, we can encode the 'match me' property via a special value rather than via the

---

[3] Although I begin here with binary systems, there is actually a simpler system, which allows only one value (say +), with an unvalued feature being interpreted as − by the interfaces. This will capture the obligatoriness of agreement since T can bear an unvalued [plural] feature which will be valued by the [+plural] feature on the noun, so capturing the agreement pattern. An unvalued plural feature will then be interpreted by the morphology and semantics as singular. However, for features such as structural case, this is obviously not sufficient since standard analyses take case features to require valuation rather than to be spelled out with a default. There are clearly alternative theories of case one might pursue were one to take this general direction, and it may make some sense of the fact that languages often do have default case mechanisms. One advantage of such a 'one-value' system is that syntax does not seem to care overly about minus values: there do not seem to be processes that, for example, move all non-wh phrases to a specific position, and, in a binary system, this is a fairly easy thing to state. See Kiparsky (2001) for one way of instantiating this option. Thanks to Peter Svenonius and Daniel Harbour for discussion on this point.

diacritic *u*. A simple way of doing this is to allow the empty set to be the value in such cases: ⟨A: ∅⟩. We can now rewrite our checking situation as follows:

(19) {T:+, past:+, plural: ∅} ... {D:+, definite:+, plural:+}

Rather than checking, we define a valuing operation that ensures that the values of the singular feaures are the same (see Section 8.3.1.2), where the empty set value is replaced by a 'true' binary value. Lack of value, then, does the same work as the presence of the *u* prefix did in the privative system described above:

(20) {T:+, past:+, plural:+} ... {D:+, definite:+, plural:+}

This binary perspective also leads to a fracturing of the set of features. For example, I just noted that the system entails that the denotation of plural NPs is the complement set of the denotation of singular NPs. But of course there are languages with dual number too, where this statement would appear to be false. Since our features are binary, for a language with three number categories, we need to introduce another feature. This will predict, apparently wrongly, that we should have four numbers rather than three.

Is this a disadvantage of the system? It depends on the actual interpretations we give to the features. For example, if we assume a semantics where we have a set of individuals {a, b, c, ...} and a set of plural individuals { {a, b}, {b, c}, {a, {b, c}}, ... } etc. (where each plural individual is a structured set (or lattice: see Link 1983)) and we take D (the domain of all individuals) to be the union of these (minus the empty set), then we can define number features as follows (cf. Noyer 1992; Schlenker 2003; and especially Harbour 2007):

(21) a. [+atomic] partitions D into atomic and non-atomic members
      b. $\lambda f: \forall x \in f, atom(x).f$

(22) a. [+augmented] partitions D into a set whose elements have proper subsets, and one that does not.
      b. $\lambda f: \forall x \in f, \exists y, y \subset x.f$

In (22), the nature of the proper subsets is further determined by the other features in the LI.

This will now elegantly capture the three numbers we find phenomenologically (see again Noyer 1992 and Harbour 2007 for detailed discussion).

(23) a. [+atomic, +augmented]: this will require the relevant NP to be found in the domain of atomic individuals which have proper subsets. However, as atomic individuals cannot, by definition, have subsets, this feature specification will be contradictory.

b. [+atomic, −augmented]: this will require the relevant NP to be found in the domain of atomic individuals which do not have proper subsets, thus straightforwardly giving us the set of singulars.
c. [−atomic, +augmented]: this will require the relevant NP to be found in the domain of non-atomic individuals which have non-atomic proper subsets; this entails only non-atomic individuals with a cardinality greater than or equal to 3.
d. [−atomic, −augmented]: this will require the relevant NP to be found in the domain of non-atomic individuals which do not have non-atomic proper subsets (i.e. which have only atomic proper subsets). This is of course simply the set of duals.

A further nice consequence of such a system is that it captures certain natural classes in a way that is familiar from binary features in phonology. If we look at the feature specifications of a language with a dual number, we have the following:

(24)

	[±singular]	[±augmented]
1	+	−
2	−	−
≥3	−	+

Note that there is a way of referring to the class of singulars and duals together ([−augmented]) and of duals and plurals together ([−singular]), but no way of referring to the class of singulars and plurals to the exclusion of duals. This is the correct result: languages with duals do not treat singular and plural as a natural class to the exclusion of dual. To capture these kinds of effects in a privative system, it is necessary to organize the privative features into a geometry (see, for example, Harley and Ritter 2002). In a binary system, the geometry emerges as an epiphenomenon of the possible compositions of the meanings of the features (see, especially, Harbour 2007).

A further enrichment of the system would be to allow a larger set of values, giving a multi-valent feature theory (e.g. the system in Adger 2003, essentially the same as the view espoused in *Aspects*, Chomsky 1965: 171):

(25) a. a feature is an ordered pair ⟨Att, Val⟩ where
b. Att is drawn from the set of attributes, {A, B, C, D, E, ...}
c. and Val is drawn from the set of values, {+, −, a, b, c, ...}

Our example LIs now might look as follows, with a mix of binary and multi-valent features of other sorts, some of which are lexically valued while others are not:

(26) a. {T:+, tense:past, case:nom, number: Ø}
    b. {D:+, definite:+, case: Ø, number:pl}

This is similar to a privative system in that there is no notion of binary opposition built in, but similar to the binary system in that syntactic commonalities are expressed in the syntactic feature system, so that, for example, the notion of 'number' is syntactically represented.

One use that has been made of such a system is the analysis of English auxiliary inflection outlined in Adger (2003). I proposed there that each auxiliary bore a feature [Infl] which could take as its value elements from the set {past, present, perf, prog, pass}. Each auxiliary bears a valued Infl feature specifying its category, and an unvalued one. The unvalued feature receives its value from a higher Infl feature. To see how such an analysis works, take a sentence like:

(27) He had eaten.

The syntactic features bundled together to make the relevant lexical items are:

(28) {D, pro:+, case:nom, num:sing, pers:3, gender:masc}, {T, Infl:past, ... }, {Infl:Perf, Infl: Ø ... }, {v, Infl: Ø ... }, {V}

Simplifying somewhat, the structure is built up by Merge of the verb *eat* and the category v, followed by Move (Internal Merge) of *eat* to the left of v. Then the auxiliary bearing the feature [Infl:Perf] is Merged, and the unvalued Infl feature on v receives Perf as its value. When T is then Merged, the unvalued Infl feature on the auxiliary receives past as its value, giving the final output (after the subject is Merged) in (29) (see Adger 2003 for further details – this derivation is somewhat simplified, lacking a vP internal subject trace, and having the V in the specifier of v rather than adjoined, although see Matushansky 2006 for the latter):

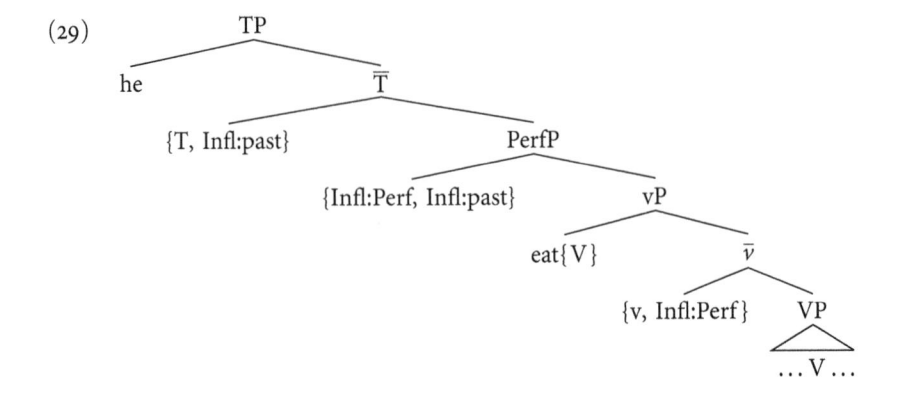

(29)
```
           TP
          /  \
        he    T̄
             /  \
      {T, Infl:past}  PerfP
                     /    \
          {Infl:Perf, Infl:past}  vP
                                 /  \
                              eat{V}  v̄
                                     /  \
                            {v, Infl:Perf}  VP
                                            △
                                          ...V...
```

The LI {v, Infl:Perf} is pronounced as -*en*, while the auxiliary {Infl:Perf, Infl: past...} is the past form of the perfect auxiliary, and is hence pronounced as *had*. The subject pronoun is pronounced as *he*, and the verb as *eat*. Putting all of these together we get *He had eat-en*. This analysis essentially treats affix-hopping as a feature-valuation phenomenon rather than as a post-syntactic lowering rule. Whether this is the correct analysis or not, it requires a complexity of feature values that goes beyond simple binary values.

However, such a multivalent attribute value system will also, for natural languages, require some kind of typing, to ensure that only appropriate values are given for the relevant attributes. For example, we do not want *past* to be a possible value of *number*, nor do we want *singular* to be a value of *mood*. There are two possibilities here: we can appeal to the interface and suppose that no interpretation is available for these features, or we can rule out these feature–value pairs within the specification of the feature system itself. For example, we can specify the syntax of Val in our definition of feature in something like the following way:

(30) a. Val → **e** / **a**:_
 b. Val → **f** / **a**:_
 c. Val → **f** / **c**:_
 d. Val → **g** / **d**:_

This set of rules constrains the possible values of **a** to be just **e** and **f**. The set of LIs (i.e. syntactic categories/permissible syntactic feature structures) is once again finite. Of course, such constraints are not necessary if the values are only {+,−} and if all features have just these as values.[4]

A richer system yet would allow attributes to themselves be the value of another attribute, introducing recursion into the feature structures, as is common in Functional Unification Grammar, LFG, HPSG, etc. We could do this by having the rule for Val expand as follows:

(31) Val → SynObj

This has the effect of allowing an entire category to be a possible value of another attribute, giving feature structures like those familiar from GPSG (Gazdar, Klein, Pullum, and Sag 1985). For example, it is now possible to have

---

[4] Annabel Cormack points out to me that this is essentially an issue about the learnability of the lexicon, since the child will determine the range of values on the basis of features of the input. This is the tack I took in Adger (2006) in response to criticism from Asudeh and Toivonen (2006a). (30) would then just be an abbreviation of knowledge rather than anything more insightful.

a GPSG-style category-valued [SLASH] feature which can be used to encode long distance dependencies:

(32)   {cat:V, tense:past, SLASH:{N, bar:2, case:acc, number:plural}}

An alternative allows values to expand directly as features, giving the Attribute Value Matrices (AVMs) familiar from work in HPSG, LFG, and FUG:

(33)   Val → F (or F → Att F)

(34)   [a:[b:[c:[d:z]]]]

(35)   [a:[^b_c]]

As I noted in Adger (2006), it is not possible to implement feature typing by simple context-sensitive rules now, since non-adjacent information is required: Val expands as F, and then F as [Att:Val], so there is no possible context-sensitive rule which allows us to say that an attribute that is a value of a higher attribute can be keyed to the category of that higher attribute, as the higher attribute is never its sister (mutatis mutandis for the alternative expansion given above). Typing must then be specifically stated separately from the mechanism that specifies what a possible feature structure can look like. Again, see Gazdar, Pullum, Carpenter, Klein, Hukari, and Levine (1988) for discussion. In a system like this, there is the possibility of an infinite number of syntactic categories with a single root feature unless there are additional constraints that prohibit recursion of a particular category within its own value. Not only would we need such constraints to rule out feature structures like A:A, but also, more problematically A:B:....:A (see Shieber 1986: 20). This is not true in non-embedding feature systems: the number of lexical items with different specifications is finite on the assumption that the number of features is finite.

We have seen a range of theories allowing different levels of complexity of feature structures, from simple atomic features to rich AVM structures. We have not been concerned with the theory of feature content, only of structure. In the next section I argue that a general constraint that follows from the architecture of Minimalism puts an upper bound on the complexity of the feature structures that constitute lexical items, disallowing feature embedding.

8.3 A Minimalist feature system

In the remainder of this chapter, I will explore the impact on feature structures of a basic Minimalist idea, that the only source of embedding in language is Merge (Hauser, Chomsky, and Fitch 2002; Fitch, Hauser, and Chomsky 2005). Since feature structures are substructures of lexical items, and lexical items are the input to Merge, it follows that feature structures cannot involve the kind of complexity that comes from embedding one structure inside another. Hence we have:

(36) No Complex Values Hypothesis: features cannot embed other features in a lexical item.

This hypothesis leads to a 'flat' structure for categories: they are simply sets of ordered pairs, as in (25). Adhering to the hypothesis means that the richest theory we can adopt is the multivalent theory. Note that this places an upper bound on the complexity of LIs, not a lower bound. It may, in fact, be the case that the 'one-value' system outlined in footnote 3 is sufficient, and is, in fact, the lower bound. I will not address this question in the remainder of the chapter, but simply assume that multivalent structures are available, as I did in Adger (2003). The fact that there is so little richness of structure in lexical entries gives the theory its particular flavour: the structure required by the phenomena of human languages ends up being a syntactic rather than lexical structure. In a sense, then, Minimalism is unlike other 'lexicalist' theories in that almost all the interesting structure is syntactic, although the information which leads to the building of that structure is entirely lexical.[5]

We have said nothing as yet about the distribution of featural information in a larger syntactic structure. That is, when two items Merge, is there some constraint on what they can/must be? Empirically, we clearly want to say that there is, to distinguish, for example, *the many men* from **many the men*, so the question is how this kind of distributional constraint is modelled theoretically.

This brings us to the topic of category features, and specifically functional categories. In Adger (2003), following Grimshaw (1991) and much subsequent work, the latter are seen as loci for the instantiation of features and are assumed to be ordered in a number of (universal) scopal hierarchies (the Hierarchies of Projection (HoPs), also known as Extended Projections, Grimshaw 1991, or Functional Sequences, Starke 2001). Each hierarchy is rooted in a specific kind of category (what we traditionally think of as the lexical categories N, V, A, P, etc.) and can terminate in a specific functional category (D, C, Deg, etc.). The hierarchies directly specify the distribution of featural information in the clause, noun phrase, etc. The motivation for these hierarchies is primarily empirical (see, for example, Cinque 1999, Julien 2002, or the papers in Cinque and Kayne 2005). This architecture now gives us two types of feature:

---

[5] One of the few recent works which takes providing a restrictive theory of lexical items as a major aim is Emonds (2000) (especially Chapters 2 and 8). Emonds proposes formal limits on the internal structure of lexical items. This theory, although it posits structures somewhat richer than the view I will defend here, shares the same programmatic goals.

(37) a. Category features (C, T, V, N, D, ...)
b. Morphosyntactic (MS) features (case, number, person, finiteness, definiteness, ...)

From this perspective, the HoPs organize the category features into syntactic hierarchies, while the distribution of the morphosyntactic (MS-)features is not so constrained. The general programme outlined here has some latitude, however, in that it would be consistent with the leading ideas of Minimalism to simply have one type of feature, with the HoPs specifying the distribution of all features. This leads us to the 'nano-syntactic' research programme pursued by Michal Starke and some of his colleagues (Caha 2007). I will argue here for a more conservative position that distinguishes between categorial features, organized into hierarchies by the HoPs, and MS-features which essentially sub-classify the categories.

This theoretical move requires us to expand our rule for lexical items. Rather than (25), we have:

(38) a. A lexical item is a set $\{K, F_1, \ldots, F_n\}$,
  (i) K is an ordered pair ⟨Cat, N⟩
  (ii) Cat is drawn from the set {C, D, T, Num, Asp, ... }–Ø, and N is drawn from the set of natural numbers above 0
b. F_i is a pair ⟨Att, Val⟩, where Att is drawn from a finite set of MS-features and Val from a finite set of values
c. Hierarchies of Projections: these are sequences of Ks whose second member is ordered by the relation <.

Two such hierarchies are offered in Adger (2003), essentially defining 'extended projections' (Grimshaw 1991):

(39) a. ⟨V, 1⟩ < ⟨v, 2⟩ < ⟨Pass(ive), 3⟩ < ⟨Prog, 4⟩ < ⟨Perf, 5⟩ < ⟨Mod(al), 6⟩ < ⟨Neg, 7⟩ < ⟨T, 8⟩ < ⟨Fin, 9⟩ < ⟨C, 10⟩
b. ⟨N, 1⟩ < ⟨n, 2⟩ < ⟨Poss, 3⟩ < ⟨Num, 4⟩ < ⟨D, 5⟩ < ⟨Q, 6⟩

For example, we will have the following items:

(40) a. {T:8, tense:past, num:sing, case:nom}
b. {D:5, num:sing, case:acc, def:+}

We can now answer the question of how HoPs constrain the building of structure. We define a well-formed structure as follows (assume an LI is a trivial syntactic object):

(41) If α and β are syntactic objects and
$\exists g \in \alpha \land \exists g' \in L(\beta)$
such that $g, g' \in K_H$ (Categorial Features in hierarchy H)
$\land \ val(g) > val(g')$
then {α, {α, β}} is a syntactic object.

L here is a function which returns the label of β.[6] (41) can be seen as incorporating an interface condition that allows only structures respecting HoPs, since only such structures are scopally interpretable. It is a variant of Merge in that it builds structure. Let us call it HoP-Merge. The function *val* returns the value of a feature (i.e. the second element of the pair). We will take the ordering relation > to be undefined if the value returned by *val* is the empty set (by assuming that the relation > does not order sets but rather numbers). HoP-Merge is then only possible between elements that bear valued categorial features.

To see how this works, take our previous example of *the many men* and concentrate just on categorial features:

(42) a. F(men) = {⟨N, 1⟩}
      b. F(many) = {⟨Num, 4⟩}
      c. F(the) = {⟨D, 5⟩}

HoP-Merge licenses a structure that looks as follows, since *many* bears a feature (Num) whose value is higher than the feature that *men* bears:

(43) {{⟨Num, 4⟩}, {{⟨Num, 4⟩}{⟨N, 1⟩}}}

To derive (43), we take α to be *many* and β to be *men*. Our definition of HoP-Merge requires that there be some feature $g \in \alpha$ and some feature $g' \in L(\beta)$ such that they are both in the same hierarchy. In this case $g \in \alpha = $ ⟨Num, 4⟩ and $g' \in L(\beta) = $ ⟨N, 1⟩, which are both part of the same HoP, as defined above. The next condition is that the values be strictly ordered, which is true since $4 > 1$. This licenses us to build a new syntactic object which is a set whose elements are α and the set {α, β}. We also allow *the men*, in a similar fashion:

(44) {{⟨D, 5⟩}, {{⟨D, 5⟩}{⟨N, 1⟩}}}

and *the many men*:

(45) {{⟨D, 5⟩}, {{⟨D, 5⟩}, {{⟨Num, 4⟩}, {{⟨Num, 4⟩} {⟨N, 1⟩}}}}}

---

[6] If we take a system where labels are eliminated (as in Collins 2002) then we need to ensure that g' is in the head of β, however that is defined in such a system.

Given the relevant HoP, *many the men* is ruled out: since the value of Num is not higher than the value of D, no structure is licensed which is labelled by Num but contains D:[7]

(46) *[{⟨Num, 4⟩}{⟨Num, 4⟩}[{⟨D, 5⟩}{⟨D, 5⟩}{⟨N, 1⟩}]]

From this operation on syntactic structures, it also follows that each LI must have a valued categorial feature, or else it cannot be ordered by HoP; given this, it is possible to remove the requirement in the specification of lexical items that they must contain a valued categorial feature, but I will leave this redundancy in place in the definition of LI for explicitness' sake.

The system outlined here raises a conceptual issue: the order of the scopal hierarchies is captured by associating categories with elements of the set of natural numbers which, themselves, follow a sequence. Ideally, one would want the ordering of the elements in a HoP to follow from semantic properties of the categories, rather than to be simply stipulated, as I have done here (see, for example, Nilsen 2003). However, I will stick with this technology here, as, once again, it allows us to be explicit.

8.3.1 Features driving syntax

8.3.1.1 Triggering Merge In the system outlined here, features drive the various syntactic operations. We can think about this in an essentially Fregean way: the features have some property that needs to be satisfied. The property is satisfied by being in certain structural configurations (which are all basically extensions of sisterhood). So satisfying this property of a feature forces syntactic operations to apply so as to achieve the requisite configurations.

With this much in place, we now turn to Merge. In Adger (2003) I suggested that one variety of Merge is licensed by a matching of categorial features on the selector and the selectee (see also Collins 2002 and, more recently, Pesetsky and Torrego 2007). We can implement this by taking the feature on the selector to be unvalued (i.e. having the empty set as its value). For example, take the verb *devour* and a simple pronominal object *it*:

(47) devour[V:1, D:∅] it [D:5]

We want to define the operation so as to ensure that *devour* will Merge with *it*, or with any other syntactic object bearing a valued D-feature. We also want to ensure that the operation will not allow *devour* to combine with a syntactic object that does not bear an appropriate category feature:

---

[7] I substitute labelled square brackets here for set brackets to aid readability. For the proper functioning of HoP-Merge, the labelled square bracket notation needs to be interpreted as the appropriate set brackets.

(48) *devour[V:1, D:Ø] [that[C] he was there]

Finally, we want the selectional feature, once it has done its job, to no longer be accessible to syntactic operations.

Let us call this variant of Merge Sel(ect)-Merge. We can define the triggering context for Sel-Merge as follows to achieve this:

(49) If α and β are syntactic objects and
  a. $\exists g \in \alpha \wedge \exists g' \in L(\beta)$
  b. such that $Cat(g) = Cat(g')$
  c. $\wedge\; val(g) = \emptyset \wedge val(g') \neq \emptyset$

The various parts of this definition have specific terminology in Minimalism: (a) specifies the *Probe* and the *Goal* of the operation; (b) ensures that the appropriate features *Match*; (c) is one version of what is usually termed the *Activity Condition*, requiring at least one of the relevant syntactic objects to bear an unvalued feature.[8]

Our definition of HoP-Merge involved a triggering context and an output, but we have not yet specified an output for Sel-Merge. Following a suggestion by Ash Asudeh (personal communication), we can take the valuing operation to be unification of values (Shieber 1986), where the empty set will unify with any other value, but no two other values can unify. That is, we specify token identity of feature value in a structure which is the output of Merge. More concretely:

(50) a. If $val(g) = \emptyset$ and $val(g') = +$, then $val(g) \sqcup val(g') = +$
   b. If $val(g) = \emptyset$ and $val(g') = -$, then $val(g) \sqcup val(g') = -$
   c. If $val(g) = \emptyset$ and $val(g') = \emptyset$, then $val(g) \sqcup val(g') = \emptyset$

Similar proposals within Minimalism have been made by Frampton and Gutmann (2002), Pesetsky and Torrego (2004), and Bhatt (2005) among others.[9] I will present some evidence that this interpretation of valuation is correct in Section 8.3.1.2. We then complete (50) as follows:

---

[8] (c) does not actually encompass the full range of effects of the Activity Condition, which specifies that both the probe and goal categories bear an unvalued feature. This version just requires the probe to bear one. The other half of the condition, which is essentially a version of the GB Case Filter, specifies that the goal category (i.e. β) should have an unvalued feature if it is to enter into a syntactic operation. An alternative, compatible with the implementation offered here, might be to take case to be the morphological realization of a tense or aspect feature (e.g. Pesetsky and Torrego 2001; Svenonius 2002). Other possibilities are mentioned in the literature (Řezáč 2004).

[9] If this is the right interpretation of valuation, then we may be able to remove the Activity Condition entirely, since the only pairs of matching features which will be able to unify their values will be those pairs of matching features (at least one of) which will have an empty-set value. However,

(51) If α and β are syntactic objects and
   a. $\exists g \in \alpha \wedge \exists g' \in L(\beta)$
   b. such that $Cat(g) = Cat(g')$
   c. $\wedge\ val(g) = \emptyset \wedge val(g') \neq \emptyset$
   d. then $\{\alpha - g, \{\alpha - g, \beta\}\}$ is a syntactic object where $val(g)$ and $val(g')$ are replaced by $val(g) \sqcup val(g')$[10]

Taking our example with *devour* and *it*, we have the LI $\{\langle V, 1\rangle, \langle D, \emptyset\rangle\}$ for the former and $\{\langle D, 5\rangle\}$ for the latter, so it is true that there are features g and g' where $Cat(g) = Cat(g')$, and where one of these is valued and the other unvalued. We are therefore licensed to apply Merge, resulting in the following representation (I again use labelled square brackets in place of set brackets for readability):

(52) $[_{\{\langle V, 1\rangle\}}\{\langle V, 1\rangle, \langle D, 5\rangle\}\{\langle D, 5\rangle\}]$

The label on the new object lacks the selectional D-feature of its head, partly capturing the Fregean intuition that this feature is satisfied. This ensures that this valued feature cannot serve as the goal for any higher operation. We could simplify the theory here by taking the label and the head to be identical (as in Brody's 2000 Mirror Theory). I return to this issue in the discussion of Agree below.

It is not possible to generate the example where we attempt to create a syntactic object by Merging *devour* and a CP, since Sel-Merge will not license this as a legitimate syntactic object (and nor will HoP-Merge). We now need to return to our definition of lexical item and revise it. We previously stated the following:

(53) a. A lexical item is a set $\{K, F_1, \ldots, F_n\}$,
   (i) K is an ordered pair $\langle Cat, N\rangle$
   (ii) Cat is drawn from the set $\{C, D, T, Num, Asp, \ldots\} - \emptyset$, and N is drawn from the set of natural numbers above 0
   b. F_i is a pair $\langle Att, Val\rangle$, where Att is drawn from a finite set of MS-features and Val from a finite set of values

---

this will entail that valued features will be able to be 'linked' by the Agree operation, and it is not at all clear that this only has beneficial effects.

[10] It might seem odd that the values of g and g' are unified and then the whole feature g is removed from the structure, but the definition does no harm here, and allows maximal uniformity when we come to other syntactic operations.

Given the theory of selection we have just espoused, we now need to allow a lexical item to also contain unvalued categorial features, which we notate as S (for selectional features):

(54) a. A lexical item is a set $\{K, S, F_1, \ldots, F_n\}$,
     (i)   K is an ordered pair $\langle Cat, N \rangle$
     (ii) S is an ordered pair $\langle Cat, \emptyset \rangle$
     (iii) Cat is drawn from the set $\{C, D, T, Num, Asp, \ldots\} - \emptyset$, and N is drawn from the set of natural numbers above 0
  b. F_i is a pair $\langle Att, Val \rangle$, where Att is drawn from a finite set of MS-features and Val from a finite set of values

We noted above that there was a certain redundancy between HoP-Merge and our definition of lexical item: to build a structure using HoP-Merge, any lexical item will have to have a valued categorial feature, or else it cannot be 'placed' in the structure. Sel-Merge as defined immediately above is a second way in which elements come to be in structure. It requires an unvalued categorial feature on one of the two syntactic objects. Note that the selectional feature is not obligatory, unlike the categorial feature, since the categorial feature is necessary and sufficient to allow the lexical item to enter the syntactic computation, while the selectional feature need not play any role. Selectional features are therefore not obligatory. A further question is whether we allow more than one (see, for example, Stabler 1997 who has no limit on the number of selectional features). We will simply stipulate in our definition of what makes a well-formed lexical item that at most one categorial feature and one selectional feature is possible.[11]

With this definition in place we have a typology of lexical items:

(55) a. $\{K, S, F_1, \ldots, F_n\}$ an item with both selectional and MS-features
  b. $\{K, F_1, \ldots, F_n\}$ an item bearing no selectional features, only MS-features
  c. $\{K, S\}$ an item bearing no MS-features, only an S-feature
  d. *$\{S, F_1, \ldots, F_n\}$ impossible, no valued categorial feature
  e. *$\{F_1, \ldots, F_n\}$ impossible, no valued categorial feature
  f. *$\{S\}$ impossible, no valued categorial feature
  g. $\{K\}$ an item bearing only a categorial feature

---

[11] I see no obvious way of deriving this stipulation at the moment. The intuition that motivates it is as follows: since hierarchy is given in HoP, we would like to avoid it in the lexical entries, but with two selectional features it seems we need it. Two selectional features will require some order on their checking, but no order is available inside a set. This redundancy is avoided if only one selectional feature is permitted on a lexical item.

This typology, together with the two kinds of Merge, partly gives us a reconstruction of the intuitive difference between functional and non-functional lexical items. Lexical items like (b) are what we usually term functional categories – they cannot select their complements and so can never project in a Sel-Merge operation, only in a HoP-Merge one. Lexical items lacking a valued categorial feature (d, e, f) are impossible since they can never be entered into a HoP. Both functional and non-functional lexical items can bear selectional features, although only non-functional ones can select their complements, while functional ones can only select their specifiers, so (a), (c), and (g) can be either lexical or functional.[12]

The final thing to note about both HoP-Merge and Sel-Merge is that they both create local tree structures on the basis of matching categorial features: there is a deep commonality between them. One could abstract out a general operation (Merge) as follows:

(56) If α and β are syntactic objects and
    a. $\exists g \in \alpha \wedge \exists g' \in \beta$
    b. such that $R(g, g')$,
    c. then $\{\alpha, \{\alpha, \beta\}\}$ is a syntactic object

The two different types of Merge would then depend on the nature of some featural relation R between the two syntactic objects concerned: if the projecting object bears a lexical category feature (N, V, A), then it needs to have a selectional feature that matches the categorial feature of its complement; if it is a functional category, then its complement must occur lower in the relevant HoP. This, in turn, is related to the fact that the lexical categories are the lowest elements of the HoPs and so can never Merge with a complement via HoP-Merge.

There are various alternative ways of expanding or eliminating R, leading to related but different versions of the approach. For example, one might assume that each category in a HoP selects its sister via an unvalued feature, reducing HoP-Merge to Sel-Merge (e.g. Abney 1987). Alternatively, one might deny the existence of syntactic selectional features and require all Merge to be via HoP-Merge (e.g. Borer 2005). One could eliminate the requirement that there is some R, and assume that all constraints on Merge reduce to semantic (interface) constraints, so that the syntactic system allows anything to Merge with

---

[12] A recent trend in Minimalism (Marantz 1997; Borer 2005) has been to take the lowest level of HoPs to bear no features at all, denying any syntactic selectional properties to lexical items.

anything. We leave these alternatives aside here in favour of the HoP-Merge/Sel-Merge distinction.

If we take Merge to be triggered, as I have suggested here, then we need some way of ensuring that it actually takes place. For example, nothing we have said so far disallows (57):

(57) *Anson hit.

The verb *hit* is specified as {V:1, D:Ø} and by virtue of its valued categorial feature can be the lowest item in the 'verbal' HoP. It follows that we can build further structure above it, introducing the subject and the inflectional material. However, we have so far said nothing which forces the selectional feature it bears to be 'satisfied'; that is, we have not yet quite made good on the intuition we began with that features could have a Fregean property, that they somehow need to be satisfied. The way we do this is by specifying an interface constraint that ensures that all features have a value at the interface to interpretation. This constraint is usually called Full Interpretation, and here is the version I will adopt:[13]

(58) Structures containing unvalued features are marked as deviant at the interfaces.

On the usual derivational interpretation of Minimalism, we can further constrain this by specifying that the output of Merge is submitted to the interface at certain points in the derivation. The most stringent requirement would be that each output is immediately submitted to the interface (giving a directly compositional interpretation of Minimalism); a weaker constraint is that chunks of the derivation are submitted to the interfaces at specified points (perhaps at certain points within each HoP, or at the end of a HoP), giving what Chomsky calls 'derivation by phase' (Chomsky 2001).

Chomsky suggests that phases are propositional-like units of structure: verb phrases which have all of their arguments (vPs) and clauses. Alternative suggestions abound: Svenonius (2004) proposes that phases are simply chunks of the derivation which have no unvalued features. Adger (2003) suggested that CPs, PPs, and DPs are phases, essentially making the notion of phase identical to that of a full HoP.

---

[13] See Frampton and Gutmann (2004) for discussion of a system where syntax is 'crash-proof' and so filters on derivations like Full Interpretation are automatically met by the system.

8.3.1.2 Triggering agreement
We have seen how selection proceeds: Merge, triggered by the need to satisfy unvalued categorial features, builds structures where two elements bearing the relevant features become sisters, with the whole structure bearing the same features as the 'selector', minus the selectional feature itself. We can also use the unvaluedness property to tackle agreement and (case-)government effects. Again, lack of value for a feature triggers a syntactic operation, although this is not in this instance a structure-building operation; it merely alters properties of matching features. The operation is called Agree and we define it as follows:

(59) In a structure $\{\alpha, \{\alpha, \beta\}\}$,
If $\exists g \in \alpha \wedge \exists g' \in \bigcup \Delta(\beta)$
such that $att(g) = att(g')$
$\wedge\ val(g) = \emptyset \wedge val(g') \neq \emptyset$
then $\{\alpha - g, \{\alpha - g, \beta\}\}$ is a syntactic object where $val(g)$ and $val(g')$ are replaced by $val(g) \sqcup val(g')$

Here Δ is a function which returns the set of terms strictly dominated by its argument (it is basically the inverse of L, which returns the labels – see Chomsky 1995: 247), so $\bigcup \Delta(\beta)$ is simply the union of all the subsets of β that have sets as members. The function att is analogous (possibly identical) to *Cat*, returning the attribute of a MS-feature. C-command is built into the triggering configuration via Δ.

A further property of Agree, shared with HoP-Merge, is that the unvalued feature is always 'higher' in the structure. This immediately precludes analyses like the Adger (2003) account of English verbal inflection outlined above. See Section 8.3.1.3 for discussion.

The decision to remove the feature g from the head has an implication for morphology. If g is not present when morphological interpretation of the syntax takes place, then we expect that the morphology is not sensitive to g, contrary to what is usually the case. The literature contains a number of ways of tackling this issue: Chomsky (1995) suggests a distinction between deletion of the feature and erasure, where a deleted feature is not available for further syntactic computation but is available to the morphology, while Chomsky (2008) suggests that the valuing operation (i.e. Agree in (59)) takes place as part of the transfer of information to the morphological component, so that the feature g is visible to the morphology but not visible to further syntactic computation. For concreteness here, I will simply assume that a morphological interface rule takes as its input the information $\{\alpha - g\}$, so g is available to condition the application of the rule, while as far as the syntax is concerned, $\{\alpha - g\}$ is actually computed, so g is no longer available in the syntactic derivation. For example, take a sentence like (60):

(60) *We asks you.

Under this system, *asks* (or rather the tense node associated with it) bears the unvalued features [number: Ø, person: Ø], while the pronoun bears [number: plural, person:first]. Assuming that *asks* c-commands *we* at some stage of the derivation, the structural relation required by Agree holds. This will unify the values, so that the features on (the T associated with) *ask* are also specified as [number:plural, person:first]. The morphological interface simply has no way of spelling out such a feature bundle as *asks* in Standard English, and so (60) is never generated. Full Interpretation requires that the features on the verb receive a value before the morphological interpretation of these features takes place.

Some evidence that agreement requires unification comes from Hindi long distance agreement. Bhatt (2005) shows that, in Hindi, a higher verb can agree with the object of a lower verb, as in (61):

(61) Firoz-ne   rotii   khaa-nii   chaah-ii
     Firoz-ERG   bread.F   eat-INF.F   want-PFV.3.FSG
     'Firoz wanted to eat bread.'

Here we see that the infinitive in the embedded clause agrees with its object, and that, in such a case, the higher selecting verb also agrees with the object. The higher verb exhibits this kind of agreement when its own subject is ergatively marked. Such agreement is optional (with some pragmatic effects):

(62) Firoz-ne   rotii   khaa-naa   chaah-aa
     Firoz-ERG   bread.F   eat-INF.M   want-PFV.3.MSG
     'Firoz wanted to eat bread.'

Bhatt also shows that the infinitival verb agrees with its object only if the matrix verb does, giving the following contrast:

(63) Shahrukh-ne   [ṭehnii   kaaṭ-nii]   chaah-ii   thii
     Shahrukh-ERG branch.F   cut-INF.F   want-PFV.3.FSG be.PST.FSG
     'Shahrukh had wanted to cut the branch.'

(64) *Shahrukh-ne [ṭehnii   kaaṭ-nii]   chaah-aa   thaa
     Shahrukh-ERG branch.F   cut-INF.F   want-PFV.3.FSG be.PST.MSG
     'Shahrukh had wanted to cut the branch.'

(64) shows infinitival agreement with no finite agreement, while (65) shows finite agreement with no infinitival agreement. Both are bad:

(65) *Shahrukh-ne [ṭehnii   kaaṭ-naa]   chaah-ii   thii
     Shahrukh-ERG branch.F   cut-INF.M   want-PFV.3.FSG be.PST.FSG
     'Shahrukh had wanted to cut the branch.'

One might assume from this that the agreement on the matrix verb is some sort of copy of the agreement on the embedded verb, and it is the latter that is the core phenomenon. However, Bhatt shows that this will not explain the following example:

(66) *Shahrukh [ṭehnii kaaṭ-nii] chaah-aa thaa
Shahrukh branch.F cut-INF.F want-PFV.3.MSG be.PST.MSG
'Shahrukh had wanted to cut the branch.'

Since *Shahrukh* is not ergative, and is masculine, the matrix verb should be able to agree with it. But, on the hypothesis that the long distance agreement on the matrix verb is parasitic on the independently occurring local agreement on the infinitive, (66) should be perfectly well formed. Bhatt, following, for example, Shieber (1986) and Frampton and Gutmann (2002), suggests a unification type account. The idea is that the infinitival agreement is blocked from happening in the lower clause for some reason.[14] However, the finite element creates an agreement relation between its features and the as yet unvalued features of the infinitive. Bhatt calls this co-valuation, and we can think of it as unification. I notate it with the index 1 in the derivation below. The finite verb then sets up an agreement relationship with the object, and this values the verb's features, as a side effect valuing the infinitive's gender feature:

(67) branch[fem:+, sg:+] cut[fem: ∅] want[fem: ∅, sg: ∅] →
branch[fem:+, sg:+] cut[fem:1] want[fem:1, sg: ∅] →
branch[fem:+, sg:+] cut[fem:+] want[fem:+, sg:+]

The definition of Agree here is very similar to the definition of Sel-Merge. Both set up a requirement that the two elements entering into the operation have matching features and both require unification of those features. Furthermore, the feature matching operation is defined in asymmetric terms, such that one of the features 'projects'. The difference is that Merge builds structure while Agree operates on pre-built structure. A further difference is that Merge is a local operation, looking at the immediate labels of the two Merged elements, while Agree looks into one of the structures via the Δ function. We will see in the next section that the operation of Move involves a cross-cutting of these properties.

---

[14] Bhatt suggests that this is because the features on the infinitive are not a 'full agreement' set, a suggestion which, following Chomsky (2001), adds a further condition to Agree such that only a full φ-feature set satisfies the case requirements of the lower DP; I am sceptical about this analysis of case, and so do not adopt this idea in the theory outlined here. There are other possibilities, such as the features not being in the appropriate c-command relationship.

8.3.1.3 *Triggering Movement* The final important property of features in the Minimalism is their role in triggering Movement. In Chomsky (1995) and Adger (2003) this is dealt with via the concept *strength* (notated by an asterisk after the feature [F:val*]). However, given the bifurcation between categorial and MS-features that we have introduced, we can rethink strength as simply being a notation for an unvalued categorial feature: that is, since categorial features can only be valued in a Merge configuration (as we have already seen), Movement takes place to ensure the appropriate Merge configuration for valuation of a selectional feature. We define Move, then, by cross-cutting our definitions of (Sel-)Merge and Agree:

(68) In a structure $\{\alpha, \{\alpha, \beta\}\}$,   Like Agree
If $\exists g \in \alpha \wedge \exists g' \in \cup \Delta(\beta)$ Like Agree
such that $Cat(g) = Cat(g')$ Like (Sel-)Merge
$\wedge val(g) = \emptyset \wedge val(g') \neq \emptyset$ Like both
then $\{\alpha - g, \{\tau(g'), \alpha - g\}\}$ is a syntactic object where
$val(g)$ and $val(g')$ are replaced by $val(g) \sqcup val(g')$ Like both

Here τ is a function which returns some constituent that dominates its argument. Note, just as in Sel-Merge, the new object created lacks the categorial feature that triggered the operation.

Note how this triggering configuration conflates aspects of the previous configurations for Merge and Agree. Like Agree, it operates on a pre-built structure; it searches into that structure. Like Merge, however, it operates on categorial rather than non-categorial features, and it triggers the creation of a new structure. Like both, it requires a probe–goal relation, matching of the feature, the unvaluedness of at least one of the features, and the unification of their values.

Let us see how the system runs with a simple sentence like *he kissed him*. I have not discussed case features in any great detail as yet, and I will simply assume here that they are unvalued on the assigner and valued on the assignee.[15]

(69) a. him = $\{\langle D, 5\rangle, \langle acc, +\rangle, \ldots\}$
b. kiss = $\{\langle V, 1\rangle, \langle D, \emptyset\rangle, \ldots\}$
c. Since both bear a categorial feature D, but D on the verb is unvalued, we Merge the two syntactic objects, projecting the

---

[15] This is a different analysis to that in Adger (2003) as the theory developed there allowed the unvalued feature to be either higher or lower than the valued one. The theory in the present chapter is stricter and closer to the primary literature, and rules out such an analysis.

verb (minus its selectional feature), and we value the verb's D-feature

(70)

$$\text{kiss}\{\langle V, 1\rangle\}$$
$$\diagup\quad\diagdown$$
$$\text{kiss}\qquad\text{him}\{\langle D, 5\rangle, \langle \text{case}, \emptyset\rangle\}$$

We then take another lexical item, v:

(71) $v = \{\langle v, 2\rangle, \langle D, \emptyset\rangle, \langle \text{acc}, \emptyset\rangle\}$

(72) a. Since the value of the categorial feature of v is higher than that of V, we can HoP-Merge these projecting the former.
b. In the resulting structure, we have a trigger for Agree, since the case feature on v matches that on *him*. We therefore value the former.
c. The projection of v is now: $\{\langle v, 2\rangle, \langle D, \emptyset\rangle, \langle \text{acc}, +\rangle\}$

(73) a. $he = \{\langle D, 5\rangle, \langle \text{nom}, +\rangle\}$
b. Since the attributes D are the same on *he* and on v, but D on the v is unvalued, we Merge the two, projecting v.

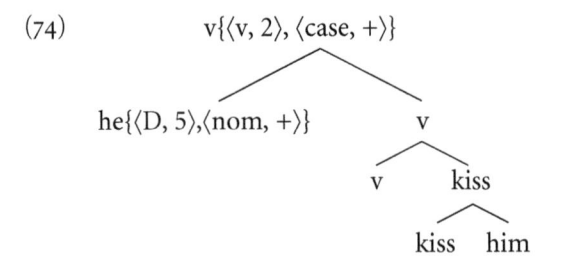

(74)

$$v\{\langle v, 2\rangle, \langle \text{case}, +\rangle\}$$
$$\diagup\qquad\diagdown$$
$$he\{\langle D, 5\rangle,\langle \text{nom}, +\rangle\}\qquad v$$
$$\diagup\quad\diagdown$$
$$v\qquad \text{kiss}$$
$$\diagup\quad\diagdown$$
$$\text{kiss}\quad\text{him}$$

The next step for this simple sentence is to Merge T:

(75) $LI = \{\langle T, 8\rangle, \langle D, \emptyset\rangle, \langle \text{nom}, \emptyset\rangle, \langle \text{tense, past}\rangle\}$

(76) Since the value of the Cat attribute of (75) is higher than that of v, we Merge (74) with (75) projecting T.

(77)   T{⟨T, 8⟩, ⟨D, ∅⟩, ⟨nom, +⟩, ⟨tense, past⟩}

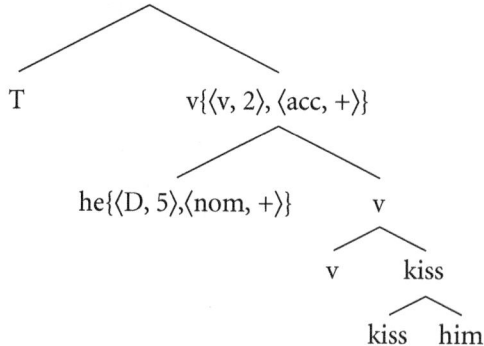

```
              T
             / \
            T   v{⟨v, 2⟩, ⟨acc, +⟩}
                / \
   he{⟨D, 5⟩,⟨nom, +⟩}   v
                        / \
                       v   kiss
                          / \
                        kiss him
```

(78) a. The resulting structure is a trigger for Agree, and values the nominative case feature analogously to the valuing of the accusative one lower down.

   b. This structure is also a trigger for Internal Merge, since the D feature on T is unvalued. It matches with the interpretable D feature of the subject pronoun, and licenses an application of Merge of a term containing the D-feature of the subject pronoun with T. In this case we take the subject pronoun itself.

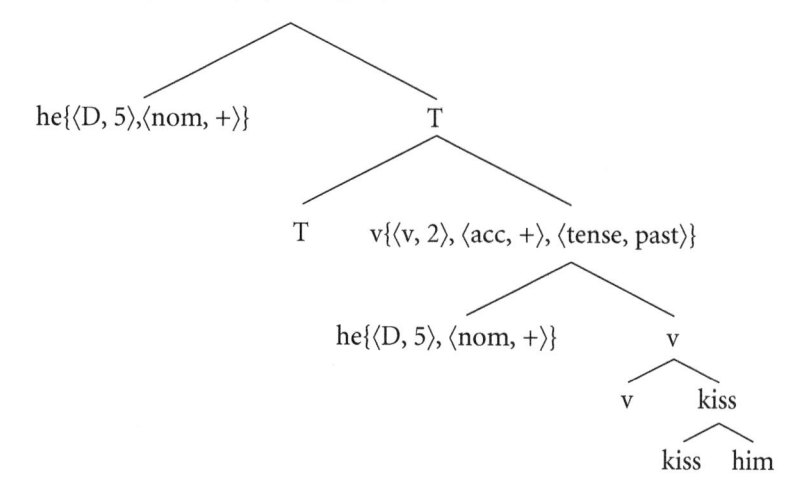

(79)   T{⟨T, 8⟩, ⟨nom, +⟩, ⟨tense, past⟩}

```
                    / \
   he{⟨D, 5⟩,⟨nom, +⟩}   T
                        / \
                       T   v{⟨v, 2⟩, ⟨acc, +⟩, ⟨tense, past⟩}
                           / \
              he{⟨D, 5⟩, ⟨nom, +⟩}   v
                                    / \
                                   v   kiss
                                      / \
                                    kiss him
```

In this final structure all of the unvalued features have now been valued via Agree or Merge. I have neglected to move the verb to the left of v in this tree. In Adger (2003), I took inflectional morphology to be dealt with via (head) movement. I am now more inclined to take it to be read off the functional spine of the clause, as in Mirror Theory (Brody 2000; see Adger, Harbour, and Watkins 2009 for argument). The idea is that the morphology simply mirrors the functional spine of the clause, so that the verb is just the pronunciation of V+v+T with the relevant features. This will account for the morphological position of the past tense on the verb.

Two major questions have not been answered yet: why does the function τ choose the pronoun to move rather than some higher term? And why does T's D feature match with that of the subject rather than the object?

The answer to the second question is the so-called *Minimal Link Condition*. This is a condition on closeness which is added into the triggering configurations for Merge and Agree. It essentially ensures that the two features in a matching relation have no other matching feature 'between' them. It is relevant only for Agree and Internal Merge (as for External Merge the features can never, by definition, have any other feature between them). We can specify the MLC as a constraint on all syntactic operations. It is redundant for External Merge. I give the revised versions of the configurations for Agree and Internal Merge:

(80) In a structure $\{\alpha, \{\alpha, \beta\}\}$,

If $\exists g \in \alpha \wedge \exists g' \in \bigcup \Delta(\beta)$	Probe-Goal
$\wedge \neg \exists g'' \in \gamma, \beta \in \Delta(\gamma)$	MLC
such that $att(g) = att(g') = att(g'')$	Match
$\wedge\ val(g) = \emptyset \wedge val(g') \neq \emptyset$	Activity Condition
then $\{\alpha, \{\alpha, \beta\}\}$ is a syntactic object where	
$val(g)$ and $val(g')$ are replaced by $val(g) \sqcup val(g')$	Value

(81) In a structure $\{\alpha, \{\alpha, \beta\}\}$,

If $\exists g \in \alpha \wedge \exists g' \in \bigcup \Delta(\beta)$	Probe-Goal
$\wedge \neg \exists g'' \in \gamma, \beta \in \Delta(\gamma)$	MLC
such that $Cat(g) = Cat(g') = Cat(g'')$	Match
$\wedge\ val(g) = \emptyset \wedge val(g') \neq \emptyset$	Activity Condition
then $\{\alpha - g, \{\tau(g'), \alpha\}\}$, is a syntactic object where	
$val(g)$ and $val(g')$ are replaced by $val(g) \sqcup val(g')$	Merge and Value

The question of which constituent τ picks out is more vexed, and is basically the question of pied-piping. For the case we have here, it is straightforward to simply define τ to return the largest constituent that contains all instances of the feature that is τ's argument. However, it is well known that there are important problems with this type of solution when we come to wh-movement. The theory developed here basically predicts that what is pied-piped will always be a projection of the element which introduces the relevant feature, since the definition of Merge involves the projection of the features of the head. For the classic Ross examples, such as (82), this is obviously problematic:

(82) a. Letters, which I specified the height of, were on the cover of the report.
b. Letters, [the height of which] I specified, were on the cover of the report.

Which is selected by the preposition *of*. The categorial feature [Wh] is Merged in the projection of the DP, presumably below the highest functional projection in DP (which I will assume is D). In any event, this feature is certainly no higher than D, so the representation of the (a) example is (83), where the D is null:

(83) Letters, [Wh which] I specified the height of [D ⟨[Wh which]⟩], were on the cover of the report.

However, the (b) example is potentially problematic, since the Wh-feature is embedded in the structure that is moved. One possibility here is that the categorial feature which drives the movement can be Merged higher in the DP projection, some distance from its apparent morphological locus. For example, in (84), if the feature triggering Internal Merge is g, then some α containing g must be able to Merge at various levels in the higher HoP. The Wh-feature would then be checked under Agree rather than being the trigger for Move:

(84) Letters, [C[g: Ø] I specified [α[f: Ø, g:8] the height of which[f:+]], were on the cover of the report. →
Letters, [α[f:+, g:8] the height of which[f:+]] [C[g:8] I specified, were on the cover of the report.

See Cable (2007) for a theory of pied-piping with these characteristics.

One final issue is that in the definitions of Agree and Internal Merge here I have taken the unvalued feature to be the higher one. This is standard (see, for example, Chomsky 2001). However, in Adger (2003), I proposed a number of analyses that relied on the lower feature being unvalued. If these analyses turn out to be on the right lines then the activation condition must be specified as a disjunction, allowing either or both features to lack a value.

8.4 No Complex Values revisited

A recurrent issue in feature systems which allow embedded feature structures is that nothing disallows a selectional feature having as a value a category which itself bears a selectional feature. For example, in HPSG, without further constraints, it is possible to write such structures as the following:

(85)　V[SUBCAT⟨N[SUBCAT ⟨P⟩]⟩]

This kind of specification will allow a lexical entry for a verb which subcategorizes for a noun with a PP complement. However, natural languages do not seem to work like this: they allow only one level of subcategorization (see Sag's chapter in this volume for extensive discussion).

The feature system developed above does not allow complex values, so a feature specification like (85) is impossible. There is no legitimate LI that looks as follows:

(86)　*[V:1, N:P: Ø]

The nearest we can get is to specify a selectional feature on the verb for both an N and a P:

(87)　[V:1, N: Ø, P: Ø]

This will allow us to Merge with a noun but it also requires us to Merge with a P. However, this merely specifies a V that selects an N and a P, not one that selects an N that selects a P. Moreover, the specification of lexical item we gave above blocks multiple selectional features, so even (87) is not a well-formed lexical item.

Rich feature structures also allow us to specify properties of the complement. For example, in a system that allows complex categories, without further stipulation, it is possible to write a lexical item which looks as follows:

(88)　V[SUBCAT⟨S[DAUGHTER [CAT N] animate]⟩]

This would be a verb which subcategorizes for a clausal complement which has an animate nominal daughter. It is impossible to write such a lexical item in the system developed above, as there simply is not enough structure to the features. The impossibility of (88) follows from the theory of feature structures itself. However, this restriction might get us into trouble. Although it is true that we do not seem to have verbs which look as follows:

(89)　*V where V selects CP containing an animate DP

(90) *V where V selects CP containing a perfect auxiliary

we also now predict that we cannot have verbs which specify a PRO subject:

(91) *V where V selects CP containing a PRO subject

There is simply no way to write a lexical item in our feature theory which will directly have this effect:

(92) try [V:1, C[PRO: Ø]: Ø]

However, we do seem to have such verbs, as the following contrast shows:

(93) a. *I tried him to be there.
 b. I tried to be there.
 c. *I tried that you are here.

One approach to this problem would be to appeal to semantic selection. That is, we specify the verb *try* as [C: Ø], so that both (b) and (c) in (93) are syntactically impeccable (as in Grimshaw 1979, Stowell 1983). The problem with (c) is that a finite clause with indicative mood and the complementizer *that* is semantically incompatible with *try*.

The ungrammaticality of the (a) example would then follow if *try* selects C, but the null C in English cannot license an accusative. This analysis receives support from the fact that it is possible to have an overt subject in the complement of *try*, but it requires the accusative licensing complementizer *for*:

(94) ?I tried (very very hard) for him to be there.

The only other parse available for the (a) example above is that *him to be there* is a TP, but this will of course mean that the [C: Ø] feature on *try* is not valued.

An alternative approach to this is to say that there must be a category distinction rather than a featural distinction at play here (e.g. Rizzi's 1997 suggestion that the C layer includes a Fin(iteness)P, distinct from the top of the relevant HoP). We could then have *try* select for that category, while *that* would realize another category, ruling out (93c):

(95) {V:1, Fin: Ø}

Under this analysis, both the zero element that licenses PRO and *for* would be versions of Fin. For an argument that the apparent case licensing correlations between finiteness and overt subject should be distinguished from the semantic category of finiteness, see Adger (2007). A related issue arises for verbs which select TP rather than CP (such as raising and ECM class verbs). There is a strong generalization that such verbal complements in English cannot be finite:[16]

(96) a. *He seems is here.
b. He seems to be here.

(97) a. *I took him/he is a priest.
b. I took him to be a priest.

(98) Generalization: selected TP is never finite (raising, ECM).

This generalization is a surprise if a complex value like [V:1, T[finite:−]:∅] or its equivalent is possible. There is no reason not to write a lexical item which will license such structures.

To capture the generalization, I argued in Adger (2003) that finite T bears a clause-type feature which has to be valued by C (this is the feature that is responsible for T-to-C movement in questions as opposed to declaratives). This unvalued feature needs to be valued, but in the absence of C there is no element bearing a matching feature which is local enough (the T of the higher clause, in this analysis, does not enter the derivation in time and the structure is interpreted with an unvalued clause-type feature; I suggested a different route to the generalization in Adger 2003, one which is not open to us under the unification interpretation of valuation).

A further issue which raises similar questions comes from the apparently very detailed selectional requirements of prepositions. For example, the verb *depend* seems to require the preposition *on*:

(99) I depend on/*in/*to/*under ... cocaine.

Other verbs seem to require classes of prepositions:

(100) I put the book on, in, under, ..., *to the table.

In a system where we can specify complex values, this is easy to capture:

(101) depend {V:1, P[on]:∅}

(102) put {V:1, P[location:+]:∅}

Under the theory developed in this chapter, these are not possible LIs. I think that the solution to this problem is that there is no category P. Rather P is a

---

[16] I am assuming that cases like *I believe he is here* involve at least Fin, if not a full CP. I use the example of the ECM verb *take* here as it does not allow a corresponding finite complement, even with an overt *that*.

cover term for a whole range of category labels involving semantic notions like location, path, direction, etc. (see Svenonius 2007b). (102) is really just:

(103)   put {V:1, Loc:Ø}

Of course it now follows that the feature [Loc] is a category feature (since it enters into selection); since it is not an MS-feature, it should not enter into long distance in situ agreement, which seems correct. It should also be possible to single out locative prepositions for movement, arguably what happens in locative inversion.

The idiosyncratic P-selection of verbs like *depend* is a little trickier, but note that *depend* also allows *upon*. It may very well be the case that {*on*, *upon*} form a category, but I leave this for future work.

A yet harder problem is *tough*-constructions, where certain adjectives really do seem to select for a complement which contains a trace:

(104)   Anson is easy/*possible to please.

It is straightforward to analyse these in a system which allows complex features, for example by specifying that the complement contain a gap, perhaps via a GPSG-style SLASH feature:

(105)   easy {A:1, C[SLASH:NP]:Ø}

However, the system we have developed above makes such an analysis unstateable. One option would be to propose a category which is interpreted as a function from propositions to predicates (a certain kind of a relative clause), and to have the adjective select for that category.

A complex values system would also allow us to state generalizations like the following:

(106)   Plural DPs move to Spec TP.

However, on the assumption that plural is not a categorial feature (an assumption motivated by the fact that it enters into the Agree relation), such a generalization cannot be easily captured in the system outlined here. Merge, whether Internal or External, operates only on categorial features rather than on MS-features. Given this, we cannot write a lexical item for T which will embody the generalization in (106):

(107)   *[T:8, D[plural]:Ø]

The closest we can get is:

(108)   [T:8, D:Ø, plural:Ø]

But this will not do the job for us: there is no dependency between the value of the number feature [plural] and the selectional feature [D], and so no way to ensure that only plural DPs move to the specifier of T. The only way to capture such a generalization would be to show that [plural] is a categorial feature rather than an MS-feature. However, that would entail that [plural] was a feature that could be selected for, and that it should not enter into agreement. Neither of these claims is true. The way we have set up the system, movement and selection should always correlate.

The No Complex Values Hypothesis restricts the theory of selection in an interesting way, blocking certain analyses of phenomena, and, at the same time, ensuring locality of selectional properties. Given the way we have defined Merge, Move, and Agree, so that they are sensitive to the categorial/MS-feature distinction, we also make predictions about correlations in languages between what is selectable, what is moveable, and what enters into long-distance agreement. These various predictions need to be worked out on a case-by-case basis, but the prospects look interesting, to say the least.

8.5 Conclusion

In this chapter I have attempted to develop a fairly explicit proposal for what a feature theory in Minimalism might look like, which attempts to resolve the inevitable tension that arises between the simplicity of theories and their restrictiveness. I have argued that one can maintain a fairly simple theory of features by adhering to the No Complex Values Hypothesis, and have shown how that leads to a certain restrictiveness in the theories of selection and movement.

I should stress that the theory is certainly not as 'minimal' as one might like: I have made stipulations about the structure of lexical items (for example, the stipulation that any lexical item can contain at most one categorial and one selectional feature), which one would hope to derive from more fundamental properties of the system; I have allowed a multivalent feature system, which is probably too rich, and whose semantics is not as transparent as a simple binary system; I have stipulated a version of the activation condition, although it seems almost derivable if we take feature valuation to be unification; I have stipulated the deletion (subtraction) of triggering features in the projection line, something which should probably follow from an interface condition (Brody 1997; Adger and Ramchand 2005). Still, I hope that the explicitness of the proposals outlined here will be helpful in the further development of feature theory within Minimalism, and will also be useful to those who come from different perspectives.

Part III

Formal Perspectives

9

Features and computational semantics

Ann Copestake and Dan Flickinger

9.1 Introduction

The purpose of this chapter is to discuss some aspects of the methodology of computational semantics and how this affects representation decisions made in computational grammars, concentrating in particular on how features derived from morphology and syntax integrate with semantics. We first give an introduction to the use of semantics in broad-coverage computational linguistics and outline some collaborative work on multilingual grammar development in HPSG that forms the background to this chapter. In Section 9.2 we introduce some general principles of semantic representation in large-scale computational grammar engineering and then go on in Section 9.3 to discuss feature representation in the DELPH-IN grammars specifically. In Section 9.4 we discuss English morphological plurals and use this to illustrate some of the issues in translating between grammar representations and conventional formal semantic accounts.

9.1.1 *The role of semantics in modern computational linguistics*

Much of the discussion in this chapter follows from a series of assumptions about the relevance of compositional semantics to modern computational linguistics. We shall try and spell these out here: these assumptions are not shared by all computational linguists (many of whom ignore compositional semantics entirely or use a very simple representation that essentially just links verbs to their syntactic arguments and adjuncts), but we think they are probably shared by most people who are interested in deriving detailed semantic representations from computational grammars (whether hand-constructed or automatically derived).

In the 1980s, the paradigm example of an application of natural language processing was the natural language interface. The idea was that a user could communicate with a system by typing text rather than entering a formal command language. For instance, natural language interfaces were built that could access databases in order to answer queries such as:

(1) Who had the highest sales figures in June 1982?
(2) Is there a doctor on board the Vincennes?

Although several of the later systems used a general purpose core grammar, the approach relied on the use of domain-specific lexicons and on exploiting constraints that came from the underlying database to resolve ambiguity. For instance, in (1), the term *sales figures* would have been directly encoded in the lexicon, and would map directly or indirectly to a database concept. Such systems thus had precise notions of denotation with respect to a database and it was viable to exploit various forms of limited inference. Much of the most important early work on computational compositional semantics was done in the context of such applications (e.g. Woods et al. 1972; Bronnenberg et al. 1980; Grosz 1983).

Although some of these systems were used commercially, they had a number of limitations and, in most cases, graphical user interfaces were preferred when they became available. In some environments, there is a role for spoken language interfaces, but the problems of imperfect speech recognition were difficult to overcome with this architecture. Even the most recent spoken dialogue systems assume that the user input is very simple compared with some of the earlier text-based systems.[1]

Most researchers in computational linguistics are now more interested in applications that involve broad-coverage text processing. Most of these applications are designed for information management: typically they aid users in getting information out of some large collection of text. At one extreme, web search is the modern form of information retrieval, returning full documents (though initially displayed as snippets with query terms highlighted) and typically involving little language processing. On the other hand, information extraction (IE) operates on relatively unrestricted text to acquire specific types of information (e.g. company takeovers, terrorist incidents) that can be used to instantiate fixed templates. Most commercial IE systems are based on hand-coded extraction rules operating on text that has undergone shallow processing (part-of-speech tagging, named entity recognition,

---

[1] More precisely, they assume that the portion of the user input that corresponds to a query is relatively simple. Any parts of the input that cannot be translated into the database will generally be ignored, whereas in many of the earlier systems, this situation would be likely to cause failure.

phrase chunking) but not deeper parsing with full grammars. Question answering (QA), like IE, is designed to provide the user with targeted information, but the classes of questions are not known in advance. QA involves matching the query with pieces of text in a document collection (possibly the web) and returning short text snippets or precise answers. Machine translation and summarization can also best be seen as facilitating information-gathering operations of various types: their quality is too poor to replace human translations or summaries but they are useful adjuncts in situations where these cannot be obtained.

Until relatively recently, there was little attempt to use compositional semantics in broad-coverage applications. However, this is changing, for a number of reasons:

1. It has become possible to parse large quantities of text with relatively deep parsers that can support forms of semantic composition.
2. Statistical techniques for parse ranking are effective on deep grammars and can be used to disambiguate even when there are millions of analyses.[2]
3. A number of practical applications can be thought of as relying on (robust) entailment.
4. The increasing availability of ontologies and description logics allows linkages between terms in the natural language and representations of the concepts, especially in scientific and medical applications.
5. Many users now require more targeted/precise results than conventional search can provide.

In particular, some of the most successful QA systems use semantic representations (e.g. Narayanan and Harabagiu 2004). While some researchers are using automatically extracted semantic representations with theorem provers (e.g. Bos and Markert 2005), others treat semantics as a way of providing a better level of abstraction for forms of matching operations to support IE and QA.

There are a number of implications of this trend towards working with broad-coverage/large-scale text processing which relate to the subsequent discussion:

1. Semantic processing is relatively shallow. We cannot rely on any sort of underlying knowledge base for disambiguation (although we want to allow for domain constraints to come into play if they are available).

---

[2] However, it is important to note here that these techniques work well only for syntactically different structures: distinctions such as lexical ambiguity within an open-class syntactic category cannot generally be resolved with such techniques because of lack of sufficient training data.

2. Semantic processing cannot require detailed lexical information. The most we can realistically assume is reasonable coverage of irregular morphology and of syntactic subcategorization for the more frequent word senses. For lexical semantics, WordNet is broad-coverage but limited in what it provides. There are no generally available broad-coverage lexicons with good information about multiword expressions, aspectual classes of verbs, nouns which are likely to appear as mass terms, nouns which appear in pseudo-partitive constructions (such as *loads of*) and so on.
3. Allowing for inter-sentential anaphora and text structure is essential. Although support for anaphor resolution is not a requirement for formal semantic representation in general, the only alternative in a computational approach is for anaphor resolution to work off the syntactic representation. This is unattractive, especially since in many cases some inference is required to select between antecedents or to construct possible antecedents from conjuncts.
4. Multiplication of readings must be avoided as far as possible. This leads to devices for representing underspecified information, discussed in more detail below.

It was to some extent viable to adopt a strictly Montagovian approach for the earlier work on natural language interfaces, such that the logical form itself was seen as merely a convenience for getting at the underlying denotation in terms of the database (although interpreting questions under this assumption involved some fudging). This is clearly not true of the broad-coverage work, where the semantic representation itself is important and has to be suitable for supporting tasks such as matching and anaphor resolution. In particular, in underspecified semantic representations, the models are often seen as fully scoped logical form.

9.1.2 *DELPH-IN*

The context of this chapter is work on large-scale grammars using HPSG, developed within a semi-formal collaboration known as DELPH-IN (http://www.delph-in.net/). However we believe most of what is discussed here is relevant to other frameworks. Most of the examples in this chapter are taken from the LinGO English Resource Grammar (ERG) primarily developed by Dan Flickinger (Flickinger 2002).[3] There are also substantial grammars for a number of other languages. The DELPH-IN grammars utilize the Minimal

---

[3] Examples are from the ERG version of 17 March 2007.

Features and computational semantics 225

$$\begin{bmatrix} \text{mrs} \\ \text{HOOK} \begin{bmatrix} \text{hook} \\ \text{INDEX } \boxed{0} \text{ E} \begin{bmatrix} \text{event} \\ \text{past\_tam} \\ \text{TENSE past} \\ \text{MOOD indicative} \\ \text{SF prop} \\ \text{ASPECT} \begin{bmatrix} \text{no\_aspect} \\ \text{PROG -} \\ \text{PERF -} \end{bmatrix} \end{bmatrix} \\ \text{LTOP } \boxed{1} \text{ handle} \end{bmatrix} \\ \text{RELS} < \begin{bmatrix} \text{\_every\_q\_rel} \\ \text{LBL } \boxed{2} \\ \text{ARG0 } \boxed{3} \begin{bmatrix} \text{ref-ind} \\ \text{PNG} \begin{bmatrix} \text{nonconj\_refind} \\ \text{PN 3s} \\ \text{GEN real\_gender} \end{bmatrix} \end{bmatrix} \\ \text{RSTR } \boxed{4} \text{ handle} \\ \text{BODY handle} \end{bmatrix}, \begin{bmatrix} \text{\_dog\_n\_rel} \\ \text{LBL } \boxed{6} \\ \text{ARG0 } \boxed{3} \end{bmatrix}, \begin{bmatrix} \text{\_probable\_a\_rel} \\ \text{LBL } \boxed{7} \\ \text{ARG1 } \boxed{8} \end{bmatrix}, \begin{bmatrix} \text{\_sleep\_v\_rel} \\ \text{LBL } \boxed{9} \\ \text{ARG0 } \boxed{0} \\ \text{ARG1 } \boxed{3} \end{bmatrix} > \\ \text{HCONS} < \begin{bmatrix} \text{qeq} \\ \text{HARG } \boxed{4} \\ \text{LARG } \boxed{6} \end{bmatrix}, \begin{bmatrix} \text{qeq} \\ \text{HARG } \boxed{8} \\ \text{LARG } \boxed{9} \end{bmatrix} > \end{bmatrix}$$

```
[LTOP: h1
 INDEX: e0 [e TENSE: PAST MOOD: INDICATIVE PROG: - PERF: - SF: PROP]
 RELS: <
   [_every_q_rel
    LBL: h2
    ARG0: x3 [x PERS: 3 NUM: SG ]
    RSTR: h4
    BODY: h5]
   [_dog_n_rel
    LBL: h6
    ARG0: x3]
   [_probable_a_rel
    LBL: h7
    ARG1: h8]
   [_sleep_v_rel
    LBL: h9
    ARG0: e0
    ARG1: x3 ] >
 HCONS: <h4 qeq h6, h8 qeq h9 >
Resolved structures:
_every_q(x3, _dog_n(x3), _probable_a(_sleep_v(e0,x3)))
_probable_a(_every_q(x3, _dog_n(x3), _sleep_v(e0,x3)))
```

FIGURE 9.1 MRS in feature structures and in the 'external' representation

Recursion Semantics (MRS, Copestake et al. 2005) approach to semantic representation. A very simple example from the ERG is shown in Figure 9.1.[4]

---

[4] The details of MRS are not important here. What is important is the features which are associated with the indices in the MRS, but these are not discussed by Copestake et al. (2005) which simply states that the approach is standard within HPSG. This is technically true, but as will be seen below, this is something of an oversimplification when it comes to discussing the way the features are used in the grammars.

The Grammar Matrix (http://www.delph-in.net/matrix/) is a framework for the development of grammars for diverse languages: this can be used as a starter kit for development of new grammars (cf. the LFG ParGram project, Butt et al. 1999). The DELPH-IN grammars have been used in a range of applications, including IE and QA as well as Machine Translation, e-mail response, and ontology extraction.

9.2 Semantic principles in grammar engineering

In the MRS paper (Copestake et al. 2005), we gave the following criteria for computational semantic representation languages:

Expressive adequacy the framework must allow linguistic meanings to be expressed correctly.
Grammatical compatibility Semantic representations must be linked cleanly to other kinds of grammatical information (most notably syntax).
Computational tractability It must be possible to process meanings and to check semantic equivalence efficiently and to express relationships between semantic representations straightforwardly.
Underspecifiability Semantic representations should allow underspecification, in such a way as to allow flexible, monotonic resolution of such partial semantic representations.

These criteria for the representation language go together with some informal principles for semantic representation in computational grammars, at least of the sort which we work with in HPSG. These are: (i) avoiding unresolvable ambiguity; (ii) cross-linguistic adequacy; (iii) providing a well-defined interface for applications; and (iv) supporting alternative formal interpretations. These are discussed in more detail in the next sections.

Avoiding unresolvable ambiguity We assume that there should be a one-to-one relationship between syntax and semantics. Since HPSG is a monostratal framework, this follows from the basic architecture to some extent. But there is nothing in HPSG which prevents a grammar developer from constructing multiple lexical entries or constructions simply in order to represent meaning differences. However, this increases the number of ambiguous structures (which is in any case vast) and, more importantly, the statistical techniques for selection between syntactic analyses do not work well for semantic differences.

The principle we strive to adhere to is that semantic representations which are output from parsing should capture all and only the information that is available from the syntax and morphology.[5] In the LinGO ERG, we even ignore cases of clear lexical ambiguity which do not give rise to syntactic differences. For instance, there is a single analysis for (3):

(3) Kim approached the bank.

One reason for this, as discussed in Section 9.1.1, is that there are still no detailed broad-coverage lexicons, and there is no agreed inventory of senses. WordNet sense distinctions are commonly used for experiments in English, but are often quite fine-grained, and to incorporate them into parsing would lead to an ambiguity explosion. Furthermore, it is not at all clear that there is any notion of word sense which is useful across applications. Approaches to word sense disambiguation which rely on encoding hard constraints in a grammar can work to some extent for limited domains and limited lexicons, but do not work for broad-coverage processing. We thus assume that word senses are to some extent resolved in a post-parsing phase, with the job of the grammar being only to make the distinctions that are syntactically or morphologically marked. Data-driven approaches to word sense disambiguation can be applied to semantic representations after syntactic parsing.

Techniques for underspecification of quantifier scope avoid one systematic source of semantic structure duplication, but there are many others (e.g. distributivity, kind/individual readings). Going along with the principle of avoiding the multiplication of unresolvable readings is the principle that there should be no semantically irrelevant ambiguity arising from the syntax. Unfortunately, this is not always possible to avoid. For instance, (4) has two syntactically different analyses (adverb attaching before or after the auxiliary) which are semantically identical on our analysis.

(4) Kim had approached the bank reluctantly.

However, such isolated examples of spurious ambiguity are not a serious practical issue.

Cross-linguistic adequacy Most of the DELPH-IN grammars are based on the Grammar Matrix, a hierarchy of language-independent type definitions which establish the core architecture of the linguistic framework, and in particular the basic mechanisms for semantic composition. As a result, these grammars produce semantic representations in MRS which reflect strong hypotheses about cross-linguistic commonality for core linguistic phenomena such as quantification, modification, control, negation,

---

[5] In fact, in current practice we ignore much information that could be obtained from derivational morphology.

coordination, etc. One central motivating force within DELPH-IN is the continuous negotiation of improved language-independent encoding for the semantics of parallel phenomena across these grammars, balancing expressive adequacy and notational parsimony. The Matrix itself continues to develop even as the grammars based on it steadily expand coverage, and negotiated hypotheses about MRS representation choices are then worked into succeeding versions, and ideally accommodated in each of the grammars. These cross-linguistic harmonization efforts can be broadly grouped into three kinds: (i) establishing a uniform definition for a common semantic relation such as the conditional which might be realized very differently syntactically (in English with the 'if-then' construction, but with inverted word order in Norwegian); (ii) agreeing on the best encoding in MRS for a common syntactic phenomenon such as nominal modification by a relative clause, or apposition involving two noun phrases, or noun–noun compounding; (iii) standardizing the semantic reflexes of language-specific morphosyntactic distinctions such as tense/aspect, or number, which will be discussed below. Ideally, the MRS representations for translationally equivalent sentences in two languages should exhibit significant commonality even though they will of course employ distinct lexically introduced predicate names; yet these representations must also be free to reflect real differences in which semantic properties a language chooses to encode.

Providing a well-defined interface for applications For a linguistically deep grammar to be useful as a component of a larger system, whether for linguistic research or for NLP applications, it must present a relatively uniform and stable external semantic interface which masks idiosyncracy. Figure 9.1 shows an example of an external MRS. The external MRS contains explicit variables with unique identifiers corresponding to the coindexation in the feature structure (indicated by boxed integers). The feature structure associated with the individual variables is rearranged for the external interface, as discussed further below.

A range of properties which appear on the semantic component of the feature structure are not exported to the external semantic interface and are treated as grammar-internal. Some of these properties correspond to genuine syntactic quirks of the language, such as the ordering of certain prenominal modified adjective phrases in English as in *too tall a building* (**a too tall building*), while others concern the morphosyntactic conflation of semantically distinct features, as happens with person and number in English verb inflection. Such language specific idiosyncracies, while a continuing source of interest to grammarians, need not and should not be visible in the semantic representations that the grammar presents externally. What the grammar does need to make public is the full inventory of available elementary predications which can appear in any valid semantics for an expression of the language the grammar encodes. Each definition in this inventory consist of the name of the predicate, the names of its arguments, and any constraints on the types and properties of those arguments, including which if any must be realized overtly. As an example, here is the specification for the predication introduced by the English verb *put*:

```
"_put_v_1_rel" : ARG0 e, ARG1 x, ARG2 x, ARG3 h.
```

This communicates that *put* introduces a three-place relation (plus the inherent event argument, ARG0), where all three arguments must be overtly realized, with the first two constrained to be referential indices introduced by noun phrases, and the third constrained to be a hole for the proposition expressing the resultant state for the ARG2 individual. Most elementary predications are introduced lexically, but some, like the two-place relation for noun–noun compounds in English, are introduced by a syntactic or lexical rule. The full inventory of lexical and grammar predicates comprises the Semantic Interface (SEM-I) for a grammar, establishing a kind of contract for the use of the grammar as a component of a larger system. Any changes in the grammar which affect the semantics can then be communicated in precise terms to external users in terms of changes to specific elements of the SEM-I. For the ERG, the SEM-I has been used (and refined) within the LOGON machine translation demonstrator (Flickinger et al. 2005).

Most relevant for the present discussion is the inclusion in the SEM-I of constraints on semantic properties of the arguments in these elementary predications. This aspect of the English SEM-I has only been partially developed to date, but includes count-mass distinctions for nominal relations, e.g. constraining the EP introduced by *information* to be non-individuated; and a few constraints on event properties, as for the EP introduced by the verb *used to*, which must be [TENSE past].

Supporting alternative formal interpretations MRS is intended to be interpreted further. For instance, it is possible to define an MRS to DRS translation procedure, although this involves multiplying out structures. To exemplify this, the issue of interpreting the account of plurality implemented in the ERG is explored in Section 9.4 below.

9.3 Semantic features in DELPH-IN grammars

A considerable amount of experimentation has been involved in working on feature sets for DELPH-IN grammars and this work continues. So the discussion here should be taken as an attempt to explain the issues rather than as a definitive account of the features. In our current approach, we distinguish between grammar-internal feature configurations and the standardized features which appear on the output semantics. The reason for this is that feature configurations which make sense as a way of most economically capturing the inflectional morphology of an individual language do not apply cross-linguistically and are not always straightforward to interpret. For instance, internally the ERG bundles PERSON, NUMBER, and GENDER into the PNG feature, which has subfeatures PN and GEN (see the feature structure in Figure 9.1). PN takes values which correspond to a lattice of the possibilities for person and number, with values such as **3s** and −**3s**. The 'intermediate' values in the lattice are not needed in the external semantic interface and the values are 'spelled out' as more conventional feature–value pairs. For example, in Figure 9.1, the following feature structure is associated with a nominal index:[6]

$$\begin{bmatrix} \textbf{ref-ind} \\ \text{PNG} \begin{bmatrix} \textbf{nonconj\_refind} \\ \text{PN } \textbf{3s} \\ \text{GEN } \textbf{real\_gender} \end{bmatrix} \end{bmatrix}$$

This corresponds to a variable in the external MRS which is displayed as:

```
x3 [ x PERS: 3 NUM: SG ]
```

However, although such external MRS structures have proven utility in a range of computational applications, this does not mean that their interpretation is entirely straightforward when it comes to the feature–value pairs. For instance, there is no direct, uniform formal semantic interpretation of 'NUM: SG'. In fact, we believe that it is not currently feasible to construct a broad-coverage computational grammar which has simple compositionally derived features which have a uniform semantic interpretation in terms of plurality.

9.4 English plural marking and computational semantics

The purpose of this section is to illustrate some of the issues which arise when trying to link a morphologically derived feature with a formal account. For generality, we will assume a simple sg/pl feature distinction at the level of the grammar.

---

[6] In fact, the ERG has some additional features, but these are excluded here for simplicity since they are not relevant to the core argument.

Within formal semantics, the most influential proposal for the treatment of plurals is that of Link (1983). Link assumes a closure operator: if *apple* denotes the set of all elements in the lattice that correspond to single apple, *apple also includes all combinations of apples constructed by the lattice join operation. The proper plural operator includes only the non-atomic elements from the closure. The notion of plurality here is thus non-atomicity with respect to a predicate. More concretely, for computational purposes, we will assume that there is a notion of semantic plurality which corresponds to the question *Is there more than one X?* which we want to be able to derive from an utterance. This may seem so trivial as to be not worth stating, but the relevance should become clear in what follows.

There is an immediate issue in translating an account with features on indices (such as the MRS account in the ERG) since the closure and plural operators apply to predicates. Link's account, in effect, allows for a situation where entities are not inherently singular or plural but rather are counted with respect to a particular predicate (Krifka 1987 makes this more explicit by introducing a classifier-like predicate for counting). So equality could be stated between an entity which is described as *a bikini* and *two items of clothing*, between *clothing*, *clothes* and *garments*, and so on. The following example should illustrate that this is not a purely hypothetical issue:

(5) In England, a Scots Magistrate at Bow Street ordered that bagpipes were a noisy instrument and unsuitable to be played in Regent Street. (BNC)

If semantic plurality is marked on indices, as in the ERG, entities referred to by different indices cannot be equated if there is a sg/pl difference between the indices. In fact, in the ERG, no construction results in nouns having the same index, so the feature system does not lead to direct clashes. In the case of the example above, there are separate indices associated with *bagpipes* and *instrument* which are related by a predicate corresponding to *be*. But the problem with interpreting such features directly in the semantics arises when we wish to allow inference. For instance, it would be reasonable for bagpipes to be classified as a type of instrument, but any inference of the form:

$$\forall(x)[\text{bagpipes}'(x) \rightarrow \text{instrument}'(x)]$$

is problematic if x is identified as being inherently single or multiple. Thus, if we want a formal account which supports inference, we cannot associate semantic plurality (in the 'more than one' sense) directly with indices and a translation into a Link-style account is desirable. Note, however, that the plurality feature associated with indices is still necessary to allow for anaphor resolution.

We could provide an initial account of the interpretation of the NUM feature in the external MRS representation by treating all cases where a nominal MRS predication has a characteristic variable with a 'pl' value of NUM as corresponding to a Link predicate with a proper plural operator. Informally, we can think of the characteristic variable of a nominal relation as the one that the noun 'introduces' – it would distract from the point of this chapter to go into details, but it is a property of an MRS that each nominal variable it contains is the characteristic variable of a single nominal predication. These characteristic variables can be uniquely identified since they are always values of the ARG0 slot. Along these lines, a NUM value of 'sg' on an ARG0 variable would correspond to a Link predicate with no operator and an underspecified value of NUM to a predicate with the closure operator. However, there are a number of problems with Link's account, which have been noted by a number of authors (e.g. Ojeda 1993). We will briefly list here some of the issues which affect grammaticality and coverage and which mean that the simple interpretation cannot work in general.

Link's closure operator only includes whole objects, which means the account must be extended to deal with fractions: e.g. *apple* only includes entities which correspond to whole numbers of apples and thus we cannot obtain an interpretation for *two and a half apples*.

Morphologically plural nominals do not necessarily correspond to situations where the proper plural operator is appropriate:

(6) There are too many Conservative MPs in Scotland.

could be taken to be true even if there was only one Conservative MP in Scotland.

Plural morphology is used with *no* and with decimals:

(7) The average family owns 1.0 dogs.

(8) Kim saw no dogs.

Examples (7) and (8) demonstrate that we cannot assume that a variable marked with 'pl' corresponds to more than one entity. There are also dependent plurals (see, for example, Kamp and Reyle 1993):

(9) The students all got their graduation certificates from the principal.

In this example, it is unlikely that a student received more than one certificate so we have to avoid the semantics entailing this.

What does this imply for computational semantics? The ERG treats all of the examples above as having a plural nominal index but they do not correspond to Link proper plurals. It should have become apparent from the earlier discussion that it is not viable in a broad-coverage computational grammar to have multiple constructions, ambiguity between 'real' plurals and plurals of agreement, or any other solution that leads to systematic multiplication of analyses.

These examples might suggest that the plural be treated as the semantically unmarked case, and that we could just use the closure operator instead of the proper plural operator, but we do have to make a distinction between pairs such as (10) and (11) such that (11) is interpreted as involving more than one entity.

(10) The dog barked.
(11) The dogs barked.

The argument might be made that this follows from general pragmatic principles (i.e. that a speaker would use (10) if there were only one dog), but a system that implements such principles for general language interpretation is a very distant prospect. Thus, as computational linguists, we are still left with the issue of how we ought to encode this in practice.

A further issue arises with the range of idiosyncratic English plurals, including the pair nouns (see Corbett 2000 for a much less parochial discussion of defective nouns). Pair nouns in English generally denote objects which are bipartite (i.e. bilaterally symmetrical, normally with a single, relatively small middle part joining two halves). They mostly fall into three semantic subclasses: trouser-like, binocular-like, pincer-like. There are a few examples which do not fit quite so neatly, such as *scales, handcuffs, castanets*, and *bellows*. Objects referred to by trade names may (will?) be pair nouns if they are used to refer to something in the three main subclasses: *Levis, Jockeys*. Thus pair nouns must be treated as a productive class. But it is not fully predictable on the basis of denotation: *scales* may be used as a pair noun (in British English at least) even when it refers to bathroom scales, which are not bipartite structures.

Objects that can be described by pair nouns are generally referred to by plural agreement pronouns. This is often the case even if there is no antecedent in the discourse; for example, it would be normal to say *who owns those?* pointing to a pair of binoculars. It has thus been argued that the object really is semantically plural in some sense. However, it is also clear that it is not counted as 'more than one' with respect to all predicates. We thus require a distinction between notions of plurality here. A 'pl' feature associated with a pair noun in an example such as (12) should allow for reference by plural pronouns (and perhaps also for singular pronouns) but should not entail that there is more than one object. Thus, Link's proper plural operator is inappropriate, but the general closure operator underspecifies the distinction, which is desirable here.

(12) The scissors are on the table.

Given the discussion at the beginning of the chapter, it should come as no surprise that there is no complete list of pair nouns in English available to a computational grammar. In fact, if the behaviour of trade names is taken to indicate productivity, it might be impossible to treat this as a closed class in principle. A solution acceptable in a computational setting is one that allows us to take advantage of knowledge that something belongs to a special class if we have it, but does not require complete knowledge of all such nouns in order to treat the normal cases. Thus, if we have an example such as 'The Xs are on the table' where X is an unknown word, a computational grammar should support the inference that there is more than one X. This will be incorrect if X is a pair noun, but it is preferable to make mistakes in such cases than to have incorrect behaviour in the much more likely situation that X is a non-defective noun.

To sum up the discussion so far: although there are complications with converting a 'sg'/'pl' feature into an operator associated with a predicate, this is technically possible. Thus, as far as the formalism goes, the output from the DELPH-IN grammars could be interpreted to support a Link/Ojeda account of plurality. However, this cannot be a uniform mapping, since the plural feature marking does not indicate semantic plurality in the 'more than one' sense. An alternative proposal, more in line with our general approach of avoiding overcommitment, is to leave predicates generally underspecified for the single/multiple entity distinction (e.g. via Link's closure operator) and to only make the direct connection between the feature and this aspect of the semantics specifically in contexts where the feature is the only source of information. For instance, the mapping is required in contexts such as (13) and (14) but is not required in (15) or (16).

(13) Kim saw the dog.
(14) I see Kim walking her dogs every day.
(15) Kim saw a dog.
(16) Kim owns three dogs.

Such an account makes examples such as (7) irrelevant: singular and plural are both unmarked, in some sense. In such an approach, all nominal predicates are treated as corresponding uniformly to $^*P$ (e.g. both _dog_n_rel(x_{sg}) and _dog_n_rel(x_{pl}) map to *dog_n$'(x)$). Most determiners and modifiers specify quantities and the 'sg'/'pl' feature distinction only maps onto a distinction in the formal semantics in the context of *the*, *her*, etc. However, note that, as mentioned above, the feature marking on indices is relevant for anaphor resolution.

9.5 Conclusion

One conclusion that could be drawn from the discussion in this chapter is that we cannot do 'proper' semantics within broad-coverage computational grammars. However, we think that the restrictions that arise from broad-coverage grammars force us to think more clearly about the relative contribution of morphology, syntax, the lexicon, and real world constraints. The general programme underlying this idea of computational semantics is an approach to formally interpreting structures which are relatively 'surfacy' in nature and which are in one-to-one correspondence with syntax. Although this approach is required because of the demands of computational linguistics, we would argue that the idea of keeping semantics 'natural' has some more general theoretical interest.

10

Feature geometry and predictions of locality

Ivan A. Sag

10.1 Introduction[1]

This chapter deals with a number of issues having to do with locality in natural language. *Locality of selection* is the problem of delimiting what syntactic and semantic information lexical items select. Related issues include the proper analysis of idiomatic expressions, control of overt pronominals, and cross-linguistic variation in lexical sensitivity to filler–gap dependencies. Closely related to selectional locality is the issue of *locality of construction* – the problem of delimiting the syntactic and semantic information accessible to grammar rules. These issues have considerable history in the field, though matters of locality are sometimes left implicit in theoretical discussions.

After providing some necessary background, I will propose a version of grammatical theory that embodies a particular hypothesis about locality. In the general theory I outline, the feature geometry serves to delimit the grammatical information accessible for lexical selection or constructional constraints.

---

[1] For valuable discussions about locality, I would like to thank Emily Bender, Ann Copestake, Grev Corbett, Bill Croft, Bruno Estigarribia, Charles Fillmore, Dan Flickinger, Adele Goldberg, Andreas Kathol, Paul Kay, Bob Levine, Detmar Meurers, Laura Michaelis, Carl Pollard, Jan Strunk, and Tom Wasow. I am particularly grateful to Detmar Meurers and Stefan Müller for detailed comments on an earlier draft of this chapter and to Grev Corbett and Anna Kibort for excellent editorial advice. This work was supported in part by grant BCS-0094638 from the National Science Foundation to Stanford University and in part by the Research Collaboration between NTT Communication Science Laboratories, Nippon Telegraph and Telephone Corporation, and CSLI, Stanford University.

10.2 Background

The locality of selection is one of the theoretical issues that were hotly debated during the 1960s. For example, Chomsky (1965, Chapter 2) proposed that the lexical entries of verbs and other lexical 'formatives' include 'strict subcategorization restrictions' like those shown in (1):[2]

(1) a. prove, V, [+ __ NP]
      b. run, V, [+ __ DIR]

Context-sensitive lexical insertion transformations (which involved the substitution of a lexical formative for a dummy symbol 'Δ') were subject to a 'matching condition' that required the subcategorization restrictions to match the local context in the deep structure phrase marker. Chomsky proposed that the matching condition obeyed a principle of 'strict locality', which stipulated that strict subcategorization restrictions such as those illustrated in (1) could only make reference to (could only be matched against) elements that are dominated by the VP directly dominating the V in deep structure subtrees like (2a, b):

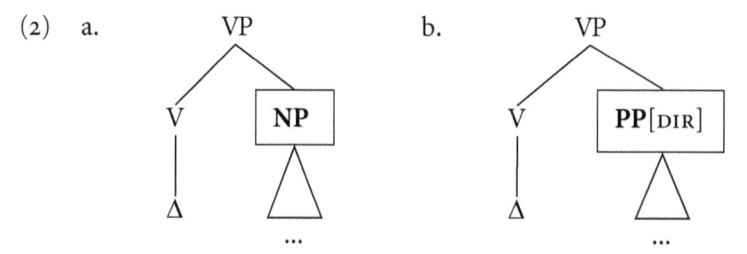

(2) a.

Strict locality imposed an upper bound on the domain of subcategorization, but not a lower bound. That is, an element referred to by a subcategorization restriction did not have to be a sister of the V; it could be an element embedded within a sister of the V, as in (3):

---

[2] The field has fallen into an oddly mutated use of the verb *subcategorize*. One frequently finds in the literature expressions like 'This verb subcategorizes for X' or 'This verb is subcategorized for X'. Here and throughout, I will maintain what I believe is the original way of describing the dependencies in question, e.g. 'This verb is subcategorized by X'. That is, the particular syntactic environment X is used to classify the verb in question into the given subcategory.

(3) a. believe, V, [+ __ that S]

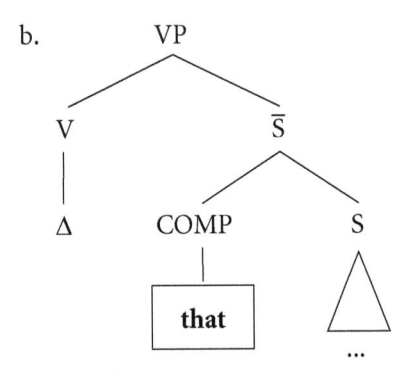

b.
```
        VP
       /  \
      V    S̄
      |   / \
      Δ  COMP  S
         |    /\
        that  ...
```

But strict locality sharply distinguished subcategorization restrictions from selectional restrictions, the similar device introduced by Chomsky to analyse semantic cooccurrence restrictions. The selectional restrictions of a verb, for example, were permitted to access properties of the subject NP, but the strict subcategorization restrictions were not.

This matter was taken up anew by Kajita (1968), who argued that Chomsky's notion of strict locality was both too strong and too weak. In particular, Kajita (1968: 96) argued, on the basis of contrasts like (4a, b), that subcategorizational domains should be extended to include a verb's subject:[3]

(4) a. That Kim was right bothered me.
    b. *That Kim was right loved me.

Although contrasts like this might be explained away as semantic (selectional) in nature, there are other minimal pairs that perhaps make Kajita's point more convincingly:

(5) a. The question of whether Kim was right perplexed me.
    b. *?Whether Kim was right perplexed me.

In any case, it is now well established that many languages have verbs that select a subject with idiosyncratic case properties (e.g. Icelandic verbs requiring a 'quirky' dative, accusative, or genitive subject; see Thráinsson 1979). Hence, given that case information is (at least partly) syntactic in nature,

---

[3] This argument, of course, turns on the assumption that English has hierarchical clause structure, and not the flat structure assumed, for example, in a number of proposals for German, Japanese, and other languages with considerable word order freedom. Assuming the flat structure for clauses, the subject is accessible to a verb without modifying Chomsky's theory of strict subcategorization.

permitting the syntactic selection of subjects, as Kajita suggested, provides the most straightforward account of quirky subject case and related phenomena.

Chomsky's strict locality proposal was too weak, Kajita argued, because it allowed subcategorization restrictions to access elements deeply embedded within a verb's complement. For example, under Chomsky's definition of strict locality, an object within a clause would be locally accessible to a verb that selected that clause as a complement, as in Figure 10.1:

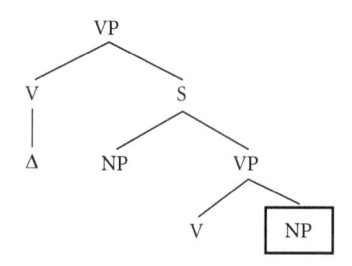

FIGURE 10.1 An illicit selection of an embedded NP

The objection runs as follows: although we commonly find verbs like *prove*, which require a direct object NP (and disallow a PP complement), there are no languages (as far as we know) where we find a verb like *prove* that imposed the same requirement on the complementation pattern realized within its sentential complement. That is we would not expect to find a verb *evorp* whose selectional properties produced contrasts like the following:

(6) a. Lee **evorped** that someone bought the car.
 b. *Lee **evorped** that someone died __.
 c. *Lee **evorped** that someone ran into the room.

Kajita is to my knowledge the first to point out the theoretical importance of characterizing the lower bound on subcategorization restrictions.

Kajita also considered examples like the following, arguing that the verb *serve* requires an infinitival VP complement (an S, in his system) that contains a direct object NP:

(7) a. The ice served to chill the beer.
 b. *The ice served to melt.

To accommodate this contrast and other data he considered, Kajita (1968: 105) proposed that the upper bound of a verb's subcategorization domain be the minimal S node that dominates it and that the lower bound be determined by a constraint requiring that the path from the upper bound to the selected constituent contain at most one S node.[4] Kajita's theory must be understood in terms of the particular theory of deep structure that he was assuming, which countenanced deep phrase markers like the one shown in Figure 10.2 as the analytic basis for sentences like *John thinks that Mary is certainly smart.*

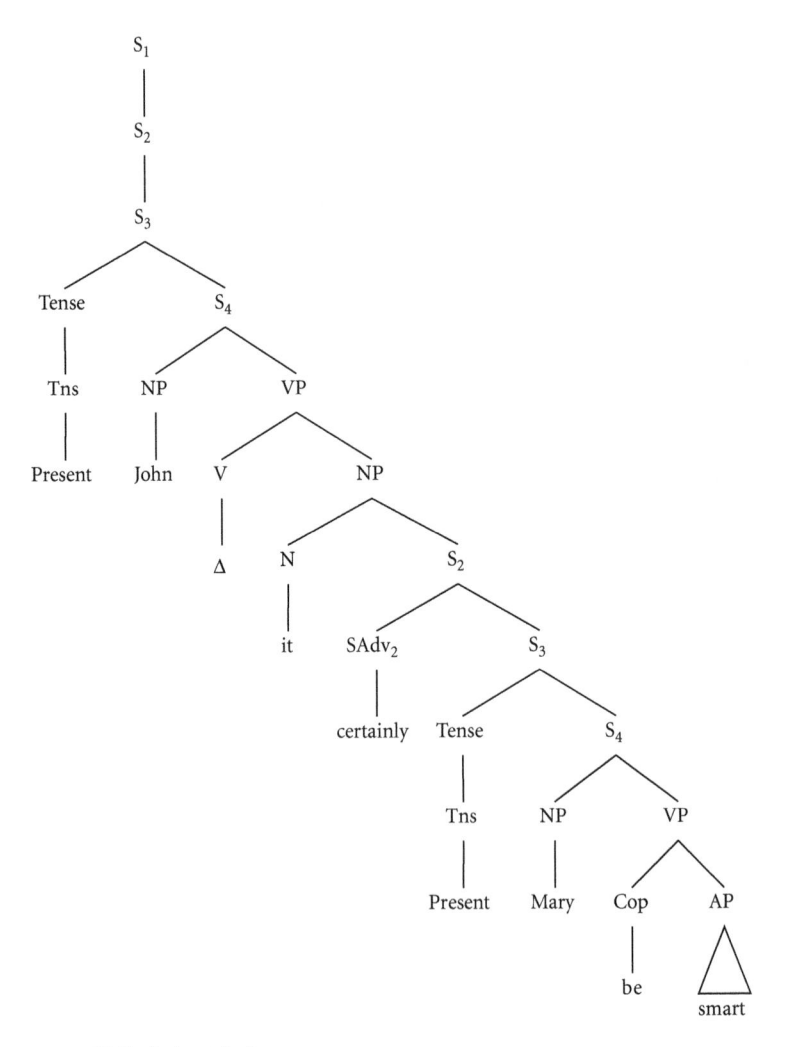

FIGURE 10.2 Kajita's (1968) clause structure

---

[4] I am loosely paraphrasing Kajita's theory, replacing his distinction 'width' and 'depth' of the subcategorization by 'upper bound' and 'lower bound'.

The intent here was to rule out the possibility of a verb substituted for Δ whose lexical entry contained a subcategorization restriction that made reference to, say, the Present Tense of the embedded clause or the AP within that clause's VP. However, Kajita treated subjunctive selection, for example in *He demanded that everyone take the examination next Monday*, in terms of selection for future tense, as illustrated in Figure 10.3 (Kajita's deep structure for sentences like *He suggested that everyone take the exam next Monday*). Thus, under his assumptions about clausal structure (which were justified in considerable detail), it was crucial that subcategorizatonal domains be allowed to cross exactly one sentential node.

Kajita's conclusions about the verb *serve* were reassessed by Higgins (1979: 173, fn. 5), who argued that the correct generalization is a semantic requirement: the unexpressed subject of the VP complement of the verb *serve* must be interpretable as an instrument. Shieber supported this conclusion by observing (personal

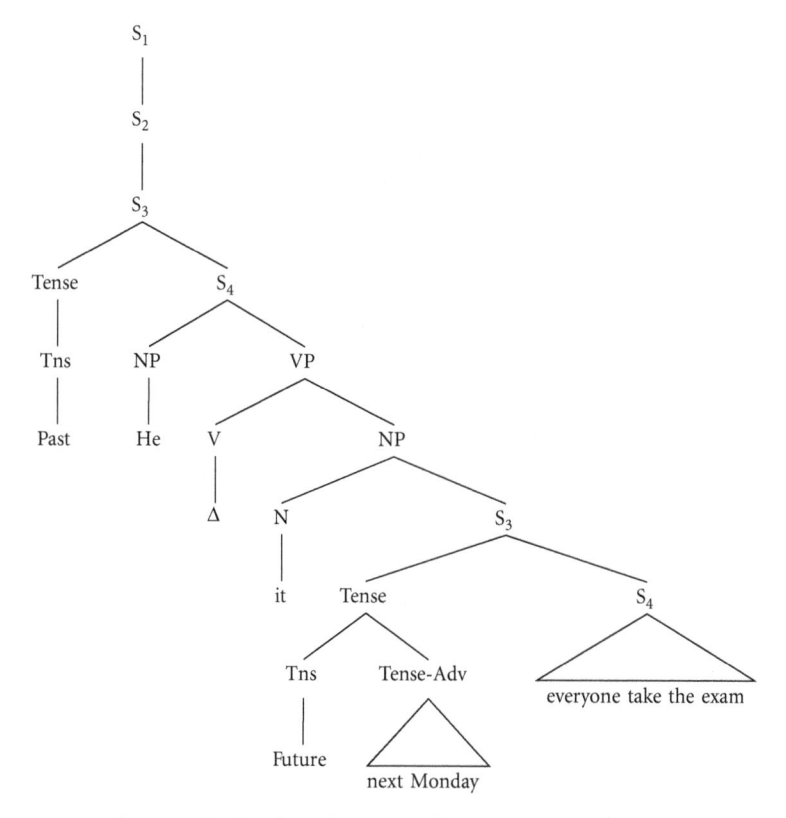

FIGURE 10.3 Subcategorization by subjunctive clause (Kajita)

communication reported in Pollard and Sag 1987: 145) that examples like the following follow Higgins' constraint, but not Kajita's:

(8)   *Kim served to break the window with a hammer.

The verb *serve* thus imposes semantic constraints on the unexpressed subject of its VP complement, but makes no direct reference to the internal syntactic properties (e.g. the presence of an object NP) within that VP.

I am not aware of transformational studies that have sought to refine or update Kajita's conclusions. Indeed, the question of locality of subcategorization seems to have fallen by the wayside within the mainstream of transformational grammar. It is important to realize, however, that '$\overline{X}$ Theory', as developed by Chomsky (1970) (but cf. Harris 1946), bears on this question. A verb that is subcategorized by an NP complement (that is, a transitive verb) really selects a phrase with a nominal head. And $\overline{X}$ Theory, which relies on the reformulation of syntactic categories as feature structures, provides a way of projecting the category information of the lexical head 'up' to its maximal projection (e.g. the maximal NP headed by a given noun, the maximal AP headed by a given adjective, etc.). $\overline{X}$ Theory thus plays a crucial role in considerations of locality – a verb can refer to the category features of the phrases it combines with, i.e. the phrases (NP, AP, etc.) that are sisters of the verb, and $\overline{X}$ Theory will ensure that those phrases will be headed by a word of the appropriate category.

These ramifications of $\overline{X}$ Theory played an important analytic role in Generalized Phrase Structure Grammar (GPSG). Gazdar (1981, 1982) and Gazdar et al. (1985) argued that $\overline{X}$ Theory, with a slightly enriched inventory of syntactic features, provides the basis for a wholesale revision of linguistic theory, one that eliminates transformational operations altogether. GPSG researchers proposed that the 'HEAD' features, those whose specifications were passed up from head daughter to mother in a headed structure, included not only N and V, which (following Chomsky) were used to (coarsely) distinguish grammatical categories, but also all the features illustrated in Figure 10.4.

With this feature inventory, the explanatory domain of $\overline{X}$ Theory is expanded to include not only the locality of category selection but also the locality of case assignment, verb form government, selection of expletives, preposition selection, auxiliary selection, and the selection of phrases containing gaps of a particular kind (e.g. by *tough*-adjectives in English). Assuming that specifications for these features are 'percolated up' from lexical heads to the phrases they project (by the Head Feature Principle (HFP), an uncontroversial principle of $\overline{X}$ Theory), the information required for the analysis of all these phenomena becomes locally accessible to the lexical elements that select those phrasal projections as complements. In other words, once $\overline{X}$ Theory and

CASE (values in {*nom, acc*}, specified for all NPs, but distinguishing among pronouns, e.g. *she* vs. *her*);

VFORM (values in {*fin, base, inf, prp, psp, ger*}, distinguishing the various inflected forms of the V that heads a VP or S);

NFORM (values in {*norm, it, there*}, distinguishing referential nominals from dummies);

PFORM (values in {*to, of, loc, dir*}, distinguishing the various kinds of prepositions (and PPs) that can be involved in subcategorization);

PRED (values in {+, −}, distinguishing the predicative Xs (and XPs) from their non-predicative counterparts);

AUX (values in {+, −}, distinguishing the auxiliary verbs (and VPs) from their non-auxiliary counterparts);

SLASH (values in sets or lists of categories, distinguishing 'saturated' phrases from those that contain one or more unbound gaps of a particular kind).

FIGURE 10.4 HEAD features in GPSG

an expanded inventory of HEAD features were adopted, proponents of GPSG were able to reformulate grammar rules as shown in Figure 10.5, where verbs are subcategorized only by properties of their sister constituents:[5]

$$VP \to H[1], \text{ where } V[1] \text{ is in } \{walk, die, laugh, \ldots\}$$
$$VP \to H[2], NP[acc], \text{ where } V[2] \text{ is in } \{prove, clarify, reveal, \ldots\}$$
$$VP \to H[3], VP[base], \text{ where } V[3] \text{ is in } \{can, should, may, \ldots\}$$
$$AP \to A[27], VP[inf]/NP[acc], \text{ where } A[27] \text{ is in } \{tough, easy, \ldots\}$$
$$\ldots$$

FIGURE 10.5 Lexical ID rules in GPSG

---

[5] Note that here the following abbreviations are used:

$$\text{VF} = \text{VFORM}$$

$$V[i] = [\text{SUBCAT } i] \qquad NP[acc] = \begin{bmatrix} N & + \\ V & - \\ \text{CASE} & acc \\ \text{BAR} & 2 \end{bmatrix}$$

$$VP[base] = \begin{bmatrix} N & - \\ V & + \\ \text{VFORM} & base \\ \text{SUBJ} & - \end{bmatrix} \qquad VP[inf]/NP = \begin{bmatrix} N & - \\ V & + \\ \text{VFORM} & inf \\ \text{SUBJ} & - \\ \text{SLASH} & NP[acc] \end{bmatrix}$$

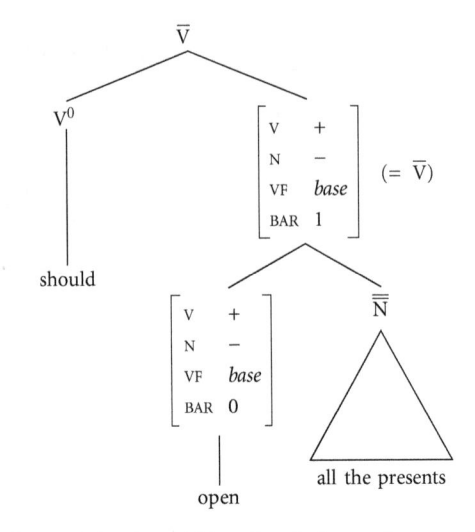

FIGURE 10.6 Head feature identity within a headed complement (GPSG)

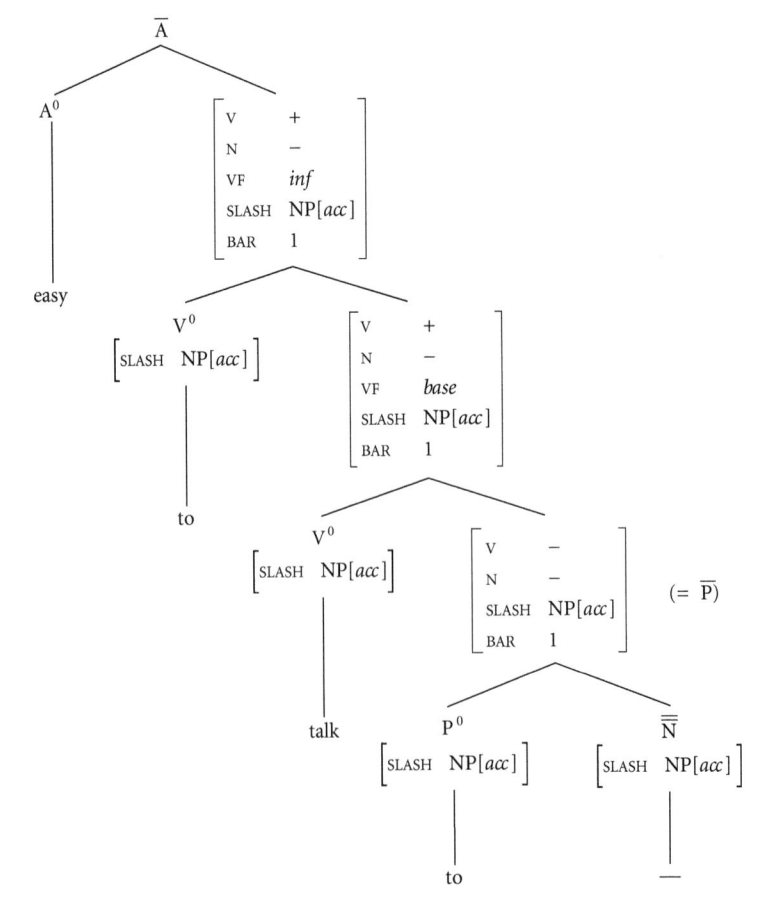

FIGURE 10.7 Head and foot feature identity within a VP complement (GPSG)

This 'context-free' theory of subcategorization relies on the HFP and other general principles (e.g. the Foot Feature Principle) to define the domain in which subcategorization restrictions hold, e.g. in structures like those in Figures 10.6 and 10.7. In fact, given the possibility of modification and the unbounded expansion of 'slashed' constituents, the domain over which subcategorization is allowed in a GPSG/HPSG approach is in principle unbounded, as it should be, given across-the-board effects in coordination, and unbounded effects in modification, extraposition, and other structures, as illustrated for VFORM selection in (9):

(9) a. Kim will [**leave**/***leaving**/***left** home].
 b. Kim will [[**leave** home] and [**get** famous]].
 c. Kim will [apparently [never [**leave** home]]].
 d. Kim will [[[**drink** [so much]] [at the party]] [that we'll be embarrassed]].

To put it somewhat differently, GPSG did not deny that there were long distance dependency phenomena of the sort just illustrated. Rather, the claim made by GPSG (and also by the HPSG approach to be discussed below) is that non-local dependency phenomena are a consequence of strictly local constraints (e.g. lexical specifications involving the category, meaning, case, etc. of a word's selected dependents) and their interaction with independent principles of grammar, such as the HFP.

GPSG accommodated subcategorization by subjects in terms of another HEAD feature AGR, which allowed a verb to 'pass up' information (again, via the HFP) to its VP projection, whose AGR value had to be identified with the subject NP, by a separate principle (the Control Agreement Principle):

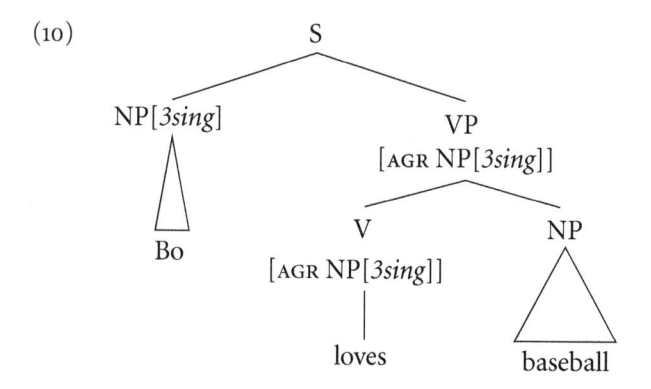

(10)
```
              S
           /     \
     NP[3sing]    VP
        /\      [AGR NP[3sing]]
       /  \       /        \
      Bo   V                NP
           [AGR NP[3sing]]  /\
           |              /  \
         loves         baseball
```

Note also that the difference between subjunctive verbs ([VFORM *base*]) and indicative verbs ([VFORM *fin*]) is projected by the HFP, and thus provides an account of Kajita's example in Figure 10.3 above in terms of context-free subcategorization: *believe* is subcategorized by an S[*fin*] complement; *demand* is subcategorized by an S[*base*]. Without a doubt, GPSG achieved a theory of subcategorization that embodied a notion of locality quite similar to the one proposed by Kajita. The GPSG theory is not about deep structure phrase markers, of course; GPSG embraced the ambitious goal of generating surface syntactic structures directly. And in the GPSG theory, Kajita's domain stipulation, as well as the exceptions to it that must be countenanced in a surface-based subcategorization theory, actually follows as a theorem from the nature of the subcategorization mechanism and its interaction with independently motivated grammatical principles – a welcome result.

GPSG's approach to subcategorization was based on local trees and the decomposition of categories via syntactic features. The best known tree-based approach to subcategorization, however, is probably Tree-Adjoining Grammar (TAG; first proposed by Joshi et al. 1975), which differs from GPSG in grounding sentence generation not in local trees but rather in elementary trees that can be viewed as approximating Kajita's local domains:

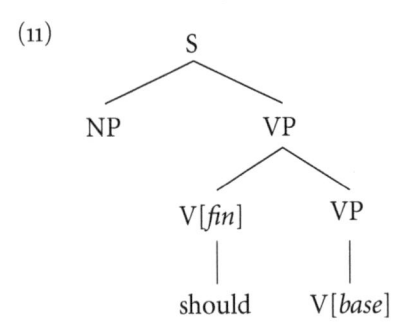

(11)
```
        S
       / \
      NP  VP
          / \
       V[fin] VP
         |    |
       should V[base]
```

In TAGs, lexically anchored elementary trees like this can undergo two kinds of operations: a tree structure can be substituted for either of the unexpanded nodes in (11) (the NP or the V[*base*]) or else an auxiliary tree can be grafted into the middle of (11) by the adjunction operation. In this set-up, the question of locality is in essence the question of how deep elementary trees can be. One might attempt to retain $\overline{X}$ Theory within TAG, for example, and replace (11) with a more shallow tree like (12), possibly providing a tighter theory of locality:

(12)
```
         S
        / \
       NP  VP
           / \
        V[fin] VP[base]
          |
        should
```

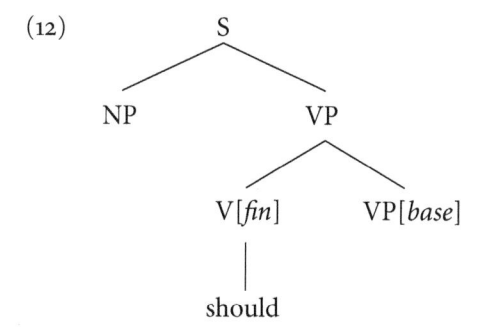

A lexically anchored tree in TAG corresponds to a lexical entry in other frameworks. In Categorial Grammar (CG) and Head-Driven Phrase Structure Grammar (HPSG), for instance, a notion of locality is built into the structure of lexical categories. The GPSG grammar rules in Figure 10.5 above correspond to lexical entries such as the following, where NP, S, and AP are abbreviations for feature structure categories similar to those illustrated above:[6]

(13) a. S\NP: {walk, die, laugh, ...}
 b. (S\NP)/NP[acc]: {prove, clarify, reveal, ...}
 c. (S\NP)/(S[base]\NP): {can, should, may, must, ...}
 d. (AP)/((S\NP)/NP[acc]): {tough, easy, ...}
 ...

Hence, assuming a simple regime of function application for the construction of basic sentences, as illustrated in (14), these lexical representations provide an extended locality domain for subcategorization that is, again, quite like Kajita's:

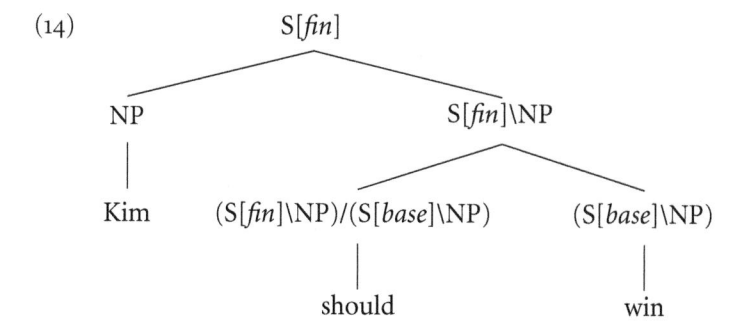

(14)
```
           S[fin]
          /      \
         NP       S[fin]\NP
         |        /        \
        Kim  (S[fin]\NP)/(S[base]\NP)  (S[base]\NP)
                  |                        |
               should                     win
```

---

[6] A note on notation in this style of CG: In the most basic combinatoric mode, (1) if α is an expression of type X/Y, and β is an expression of type Y, then αβ is an expression of type X and (2) if α is an expression of type X\Y, and β is an expression of type Y, then βα is an expression of type X.

Here too, because of modification and the composition employed, e.g. in Steedman's (1996, 2000) analysis of filler–gap phenomena, subcategorization dependencies are extended over an unbounded domain in predictable ways.

In sum, I assume that grammatical theory must include some hypothesis about the domain in which subcategorization dependencies hold. Any such hypothesis involves basic lexical subcategorization restrictions which function within narrowly specified domains and which interact with other grammatical principles to account for the fact that local subcategorization domains are extended in precisely characterizable ways to allow extensions of local constraints in coordinate structures, modification structures, and so forth. The mechanisms for handling basic subcategorization dependencies vary from theory to theory, ranging from the pristine lexical categories of CG to the arcane theory of lexical insertion presented by Chomsky (1965), which is formulated in terms of pre-terminal phrase markers, lexical substitution transformations, and a matching condition. The mechanisms for extending local subcategorization domains also differ from theory to theory: the work is done variously by transformations (Chomsky/Kajita's model), adjunction (TAGs), composition and modification (CG), and general principles of feature inheritance (GPSG). HPSG analyses (e.g. that of Pollard and Sag 1994) have attempted to integrate the basic lexical subcategorization mechanism of CG (reformulated slightly in terms of valence lists) with the general principles of feature inheritance that were pioneered within GPSG.

As we will see, the locality of basic subcategorization restrictions, and with it the locality of agreement, case assignment, and government, raises a variety of issues. In essence, the fundamental locality of these phenomena follows from the nature of the arguments on valence lists, as in CG. I will refine this idea in the proposal that now follows.

10.3 Locality of construction

Since the inception of work in HPSG, it has been assumed that there are two kinds of signs – words and phrases, with the feature DAUGHTERS (DTRS) being appropriate only for the type *phrase*. Grammar schemata were introduced in Pollard and Sag (1994) as the HPSG analogue of grammar rules. These schemata specified an inventory of phrase types, where phrases had the geometry shown in Figure 10.8. Since (1) phrases contained daughter structures of arbitrary depth and (2) schemata imposed constraints directly on phrases, there was nothing in this set-up that imposed any notion of locality. Putting this in more familiar terms, in this 'standard' version of HPSG, one could write grammar rules like those in (15), where the right-hand side of the

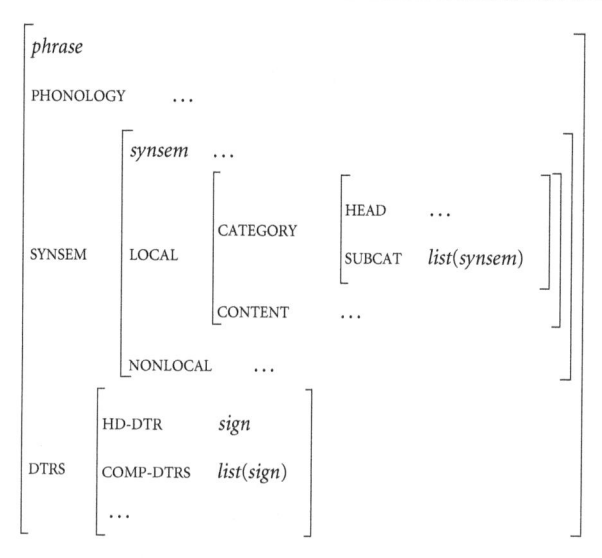

$$\begin{bmatrix} \textit{phrase} \\ \text{PHONOLOGY} \quad \ldots \\ \text{SYNSEM} \begin{bmatrix} \textit{synsem} \quad \ldots \\ \text{LOCAL} \begin{bmatrix} \text{CATEGORY} \begin{bmatrix} \text{HEAD} \quad \ldots \\ \text{SUBCAT} \quad \textit{list(synsem)} \end{bmatrix} \\ \text{CONTENT} \quad \ldots \end{bmatrix} \\ \text{NONLOCAL} \quad \ldots \end{bmatrix} \\ \text{DTRS} \begin{bmatrix} \text{HD-DTR} \quad \textit{sign} \\ \text{COMP-DTRS} \quad \textit{list(sign)} \\ \ldots \end{bmatrix} \end{bmatrix}$$

FIGURE 10.8 Feature geometry of Pollard and Sag (1994)

rule need not be confined to a sequence of categories (as in CFG), but could in fact be a structure of arbitrary complexity:

(15) a. VP → V [$_S$ NP$_{sing}$ VP]
    b. VP → V [$_{NP}$ Det Adj N]
    c. S → NP [$_{VP}$ V [$_S$ [$_{NP}$ NP Conj NP] VP]]

Nothing but an unspoken 'gentleman's agreement' prevented the HPSG grammarian from writing a schema that directly referenced a daughter's daughters, or in fact elements that appear at any arbitrary depth of embedding.

HPSG had thus evolved far from its GPSG (CFG) roots, an evolutionary path that did not go unnoticed. For example, Copestake (1992) observed that:

[...] it is unclear that the HPSG account of phrasal signs as feature structures which incorporate their daughters is the best one to adopt. Constraint resolution can be used to perform operations which cannot be straightforwardly mimicked by more conventional grammar rules. [...] However, it is not clear to me whether HPSG currently takes advantage of this possibility in any very significant way. There have to be good reasons to adopt an approach which makes most known parsing technology inapplicable.

Copestake's observation still has force today, though of course there is now considerable work developing analyses based on linearization theory,[7] which

---

[7] See, for example, Reape (1994, 1996), Kathol (2000), and Daniels and Meurers (2004).

uses a DOMAIN feature to allow 'liberation' of embedded elements, making them locally accessible at 'higher' levels of tectogrammatical derivation.[8] Apart from this line of research, there are to my knowledge no HPSG analyses that propose a grammatical schema making direct reference to embedded structure. The practice of the HPSG community seems to adhere to the notion of locality that is inherent in CFGs.

English tag questions pose an interesting challenge to constructional locality, since they involve agreement between the main clause subject and the subject pronoun realized within the tag:

(16) a. He is going to get into trouble, isn't he/*she/*it?
 b. *He is going to get into trouble, aren't they/you/we?

Bender and Flickinger (1999) assume that there is uniform agreement between verbs and subjects in tag constructions, and hence that the two verbs and the two subjects in any tag question must all agree. This view, however, is inconsistent with well-known data like (17), which argues that the agreement in question is semantic rather than syntactic:[9]

(17) a. Sears is open, aren't they?
 b. At least one of us is sure to win, aren't we?

But however the agreement in question is to be analysed, the agreement relation between the two subjects is non-local, i.e. it involves agreement between the two boxed NP constituents shown in Figure 10.9.

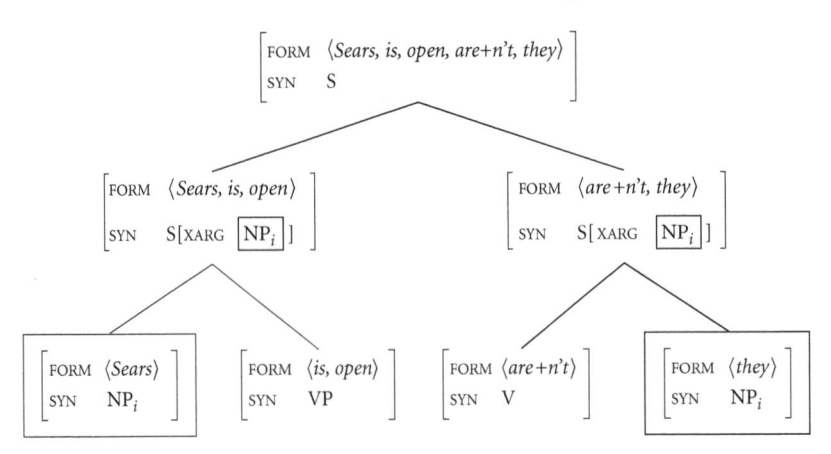

FIGURE 10.9 A tag-question

---

[8] For critical discussion of this approach, see Müller (2004, 2005).
[9] See Kay (2002) and the references cited there.

As Bender and Flickinger argue, the English tag-question construction is evidence not for an analysis in terms of non-local constraints but rather for a treatment in terms of a feature that 'passes up' information about the subject NP to the clausal level, indicated here via the boxed values of the feature XARG, discussed further below. Under such an analysis it is possible to treat the agreement in tag questions locally, i.e. via a local constraint requiring the relevant identity (coindexing) between the XARG value of the main clause and that of the tag clause (the two daughters of the root S in Figure 10.9).

10.4 Sign-Based Construction Grammar

Here I sketch a version of grammatical theory, building on the modelling assumptions developed within the HPSG research community, that incorporates a strong version of locality. To this end, phrases are distinguished from the structures associated with them. Phrases, like words, are signs and hence specify values for the features PHONOLOGY, FORM, SYNTAX, SEMANTICS, and CONTEXT, but, crucially, not DAUGHTERS (and herein lies the key departure from previous work in HPSG). A construction, like a schema in Pollard and Sag (1994), is a constraint licensing a local pattern of sign combination. That is, a construction places restrictions on what properties signs must have if they are to directly combine with one another (or, to use Minimalist terminology, to 'externally merge'). A construction may in addition place constraints on the sign that results from such a combination. On this conception of grammar, a construction is a CFG-like grammar rule that provides a particular set of constraints on the form, syntactic category, meaning, and use conditions of the mother sign, stated in terms of the properties of its daughters. The objects defined by constructions are thus configurations of signs: a set of daughter signs and one more sign that is the mother of those daughters. Let us call each such configuration a 'construct'.

Once this distinction is recognized, it becomes possible to adopt a simpler feature geometry like the one proposed in Pollard and Sag (1987), eliminating the feature SYNSEM. In fact, I will eliminate (following Sag 2010) a number of other features that have appeared in HPSG analyses, including LOCAL, NON-LOCAL, and HEAD. The resulting feature geometry I assume here is sketched in Figure 10.10. In addition, constructs will be modelled as feature structures, as shown in Figure 10.11.[10] This last move is easily achieved by the type declarations sketched in Figure 10.12.

---

[10] For expositional purposes, I will sometimes represent constructs in tree notation and will use SYNTAX and SEMANTICS values, as in Figure 10.11.

$$\begin{bmatrix} \text{sign} \\ \text{PHONOLOGY} & \text{phon-object} \\ \text{FORM} & \text{morph-object} \\ \text{SYNTAX} & \text{syn-object} \\ \text{SEMANTICS} & \text{sem-object} \\ \text{CONTEXT} & \text{ctxt-object} \end{bmatrix}$$

FIGURE 10.10 The sign in SBCG

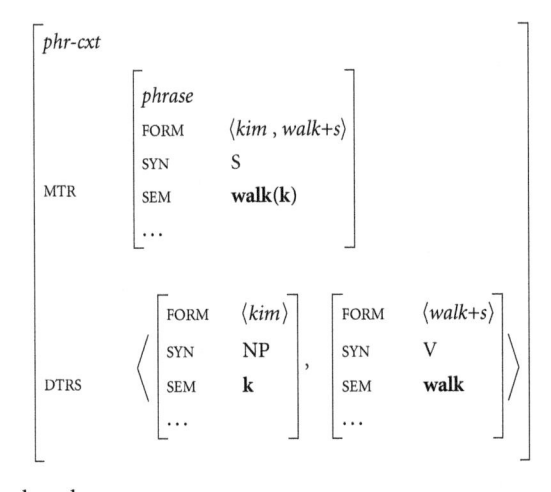

$$\begin{bmatrix} \textit{phr-cxt} \\ \text{MTR} & \begin{bmatrix} \textit{phrase} \\ \text{FORM} & \langle \textit{kim}, \textit{walk+s} \rangle \\ \text{SYN} & S \\ \text{SEM} & \textbf{walk(k)} \\ \ldots \end{bmatrix} \\ \text{DTRS} & \left\langle \begin{bmatrix} \text{FORM} & \langle \textit{kim} \rangle \\ \text{SYN} & \text{NP} \\ \text{SEM} & \textbf{k} \\ \ldots \end{bmatrix}, \begin{bmatrix} \text{FORM} & \langle \textit{walk+s} \rangle \\ \text{SYN} & \text{V} \\ \text{SEM} & \textbf{walk} \\ \ldots \end{bmatrix} \right\rangle \end{bmatrix}$$

FIGURE 10.11 A clausal construct

$$\textit{cxt}: \begin{bmatrix} \text{MOTHER} & \textit{sign} \\ \text{DTRS} & \textit{list}\,(\textit{sign}) \end{bmatrix}$$

$$\textit{ph-cxt}: \begin{bmatrix} \text{MOTHER} & \textit{phrase} \end{bmatrix}$$

$$\textit{hd-cxt}: \begin{bmatrix} \text{HD-DTR} & \textit{sign} \end{bmatrix}$$

$$\textit{sign}: \begin{bmatrix} \text{PHON} & \textit{phon-object} \\ \text{FORM} & \textit{morph-object} \\ \text{SYNTAX} & \textit{syn-object} \\ \text{SEMANTICS} & \textit{sem-object} \\ \text{CONTEXT} & \textit{ctxt-object} \end{bmatrix}$$

FIGURE 10.12 Type declarations

A few words of explanation for readers not familiar with these notions and notations: I assume a grammar contains a 'signature' (like the key and time signatures in a piece of music) that spells out the general nature of the objects in the language model, assumed here to be a collection of feature structures each of which is either an atom (e.g. *accusative*, +) or a function (e.g. the phrasal construct sketched in Figure 10.11). This work is done in terms of a set of types and a 'declaration' (for each of the non-atomic types) specifying which features are appropriate for feature structures of that type and what kind of value each of those features is mapped to. Thus, the last specification in Figure 10.12 declares (1) that there is a type of feature structure called *sign*, (2) that the domain of functions of this type includes the features PHONOLOGY, FORM, SYNTAX, SEMANTICS, and CONTEXT, and (3) that any value assigned to each of these features must be of the indicated type. *morph-object* indicates (that any value assigned to the feature FORM must be) a *morphological-object*, represented here as a list of orthographic forms.

The diagram in Figure 10.13 specifies a hierarchical classification of the types which interacts with the type declarations in Figure 10.12. A feature structure assigned to a type *T* also exhibits the properties that the signature prescribes for the supertypes of *T*. Thus, words have properties of their own, but they also exhibit the properties of signs; headed constructs must also obey the general properties of both phrasal constructs and constructs in general, and so forth.

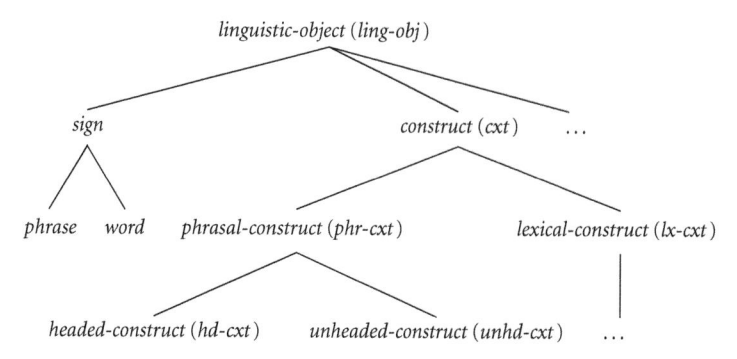

FIGURE 10.13 An SBCG type hierarchy

An SBCG defines complex expressions including a principle like (18), which allows recursive application of constructions:

(18) **The Sign Principle:**
Every sign must be lexically or constructionally licensed, where: a sign is lexically licensed only if it satisfies some lexical entry and a sign is constructionally licensed only if it is the mother of some construct.

This framework has come to be known as Sign-Based Construction Grammar (SBCG),[11] though of course it is still a kind of HPSG, given that it embodies signs, linguistically motivated types, type constraints, and a hierarchically organized lexicon, inter alia.

It follows from SBCG, as a matter of principle, that a construction cannot have direct access to properties of a mother and its granddaughters. If we observe that there is some such dependency, then we must provide an analysis in terms of some property of the granddaughter that is systematically encoded on the daughter, and hence rendered locally accessible at the higher level. This has the virtue of making explicit exactly where non-locality resides in grammatical structures. It also fosters the development of general principles constraining the distribution of feature specifications across constructs. In fact, the fundamental principles of Pollard and Sag (1994) are now recast as constraints on constructs, as shown in (19):[12]

(19) a. **Head Feature Principle:**

$$hd\text{-}cxt \Rightarrow \begin{bmatrix} \text{MTR} & \begin{bmatrix} \text{SYN} | \text{CAT} & \boxed{1} \end{bmatrix} \\ \text{HD-DTR} & \begin{bmatrix} \text{SYN} | \text{CAT} & \boxed{1} \end{bmatrix} \end{bmatrix}$$

b. **Subcategorization Principle:**

$$hd\text{-}cxt \Rightarrow \begin{bmatrix} \text{MTR} & \begin{bmatrix} \text{SYN} | \text{VAL} & \boxed{A} \end{bmatrix} \\ \text{DTRS} & \boxed{B} \bigcirc \langle \boxed{1} \rangle \\ \text{HD-DTR} & \boxed{1}\begin{bmatrix} \text{SYN} | \text{VAL} & \boxed{A} \oplus \boxed{B} \end{bmatrix} \end{bmatrix}$$

---

[11] For an early formulation, see Chapter 16 of Sag, Wasow, and Bender (2003), which develops ideas first presented in Sag (2001). For a more detailed exposition, see Sag (2010).

[12] Note that the feature SUBCAT is replaced by VALENCE (VAL). '○' is Reape's domain union operator: $\boxed{A} \bigcirc \boxed{B}$ is satisfied by any list containing exactly the elements of $\boxed{A}$ and $\boxed{B}$, as long as any α which precedes some β in $\boxed{A}$ or in $\boxed{B}$ also precedes β in $\boxed{A} \bigcirc \boxed{B}$. '○' is thus a 'shuffle' operator.

The effect is the same as in Pollard and Sag (1994): the head daughter projects certain featural information (the HEAD feature specifications) to its mother and the VALENCE list of the head daughter is matched against the other daughters, with the remaining members of that list being passed up to be the mother's VALENCE list.

Finally, SBCG also provides a precise way of formulating lexical rules, i.e. by treating them as varieties of lexical construction.[13] We may posit three subtypes of lexical construct: *inflectional-construct*, *derivational-construct*, and *post-inflectional-construct*, each with its own properties. Following in the main Sag et al. (2003, see especially Chapter 16), we may assume that lexical entries in general describe feature structures of type *lexeme* (rather than *word*). Hence derivational constructions involve constructs (of type *deriv-cxt*) whose mother is of type *lexeme*; inflectional constructions involve unary constructs (of type *infl-cxt*) whose mother is of type *word* and whose daughter is of type *lexeme*; and post-inflectional constructions involve unary constructs (of type *post-infl-cxt*) where both mother and daughter are of type *word*. This proposal thus provides a unified approach to the construction of words and phrases, allowing for hierarchical generalizations of varying grain, without the need for ancillary devices.

10.5 Predictions of locality

The syntactic objects of SBCG (modelled as feature structures of type *syn-obj*) are the values of the feature SYN. These feature structures include specifications for category and valence information, as illustrated in (20):

(20) $\begin{bmatrix} sign \\ \text{SYN} \begin{bmatrix} syn\text{-}object \\ \text{CAT} \quad category \\ \text{VAL} \quad list(sign) \\ \ldots \end{bmatrix} \end{bmatrix}$

Category and valence information are within the sign and lexical subcategorization obeys the Subcategorization Principle in (19b) above, which identifies the head's VAL specifications with the signs (not the constituent structure) of

---

[13] See Copestake (1992) and Meurers (1999).

the selected elements. It therefore follows that a complement's category and valence information is accessible to a subcategorizing head, and that information associated only with elements used to construct that complement is not. This circumscription of information is quite like CFG, where a rule like (21) has no access to information about which of the rules in (22) will be used to expand the complement $\overline{\overline{N}}$:

(21) $\overline{V} \rightarrow V^0 \overline{\overline{N}}$

(22) $\overline{\overline{N}} \rightarrow \text{Det}\, \overline{N}$
$\overline{\overline{N}} \rightarrow \overline{\overline{N}}^+ C \overline{\overline{N}}$
$\overline{\overline{N}} \rightarrow \overline{\overline{N}}\, \overline{\overline{P}}$
...

SBCG thus embodies a strong theory of the locality of category selection in the normal sense of that term. The predictions of course rely crucially on the HFP as well, in much the same way as earlier work in GPSG and HPSG. That is, among SBCG's HEAD features are CASE, VFORM, PFORM, PRED, and AUX, and a phrase's HEAD value must be the same as that of its head daughter in order for the HFP to be satisfied. For example, verbs like *depend* or *rely* require that the prepositional head within their PP complement be *on* or *upon* and this is ensured by a lexical specification like the one in (23):

(23) $\begin{bmatrix} \text{FORM} & \langle rely \rangle \\ \text{SYN} & \begin{bmatrix} \text{VAL} & \langle \text{NP}, \text{PP}[\text{PFORM}\ on] \rangle \end{bmatrix} \end{bmatrix}$

Similarly, the modal verbs select for a VP complement whose verbal head is specified as [VF *base*]. This will have the intended effect on the VP's head daughter, as sketched in Figure 10.14. Note in addition that since a verb's VAL list includes reference to its subject (the first valent), the domain of locality is automatically extended to include subjects without the introduction of the AGR feature discussed earlier in connection with GPSG.

To see how this set-up also imposes locality on agreement, consider the following well-attested agreement patterns:

(24) a. Verb–subject agreement
b. Verb–object agreement
c. Noun–possessor agreement

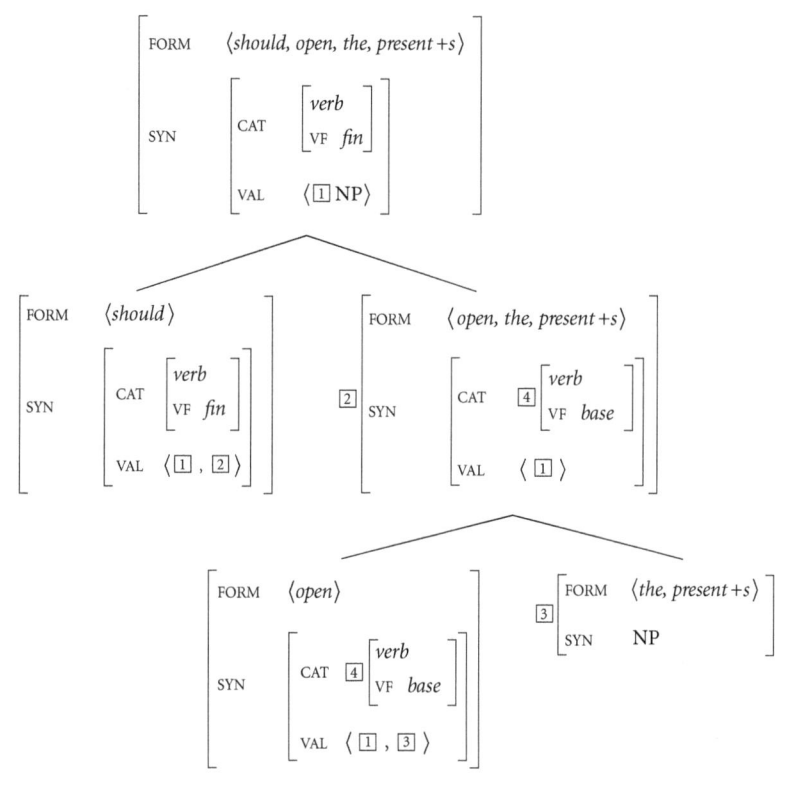

$$\begin{bmatrix} \text{FORM} & \langle \text{should, open, the, present +s} \rangle \\ \text{SYN} & \begin{bmatrix} \text{CAT} & \begin{bmatrix} \text{verb} \\ \text{VF } \textit{fin} \end{bmatrix} \\ \text{VAL} & \langle \boxed{1}\, \text{NP} \rangle \end{bmatrix} \end{bmatrix}$$

$$\begin{bmatrix} \text{FORM} & \langle \text{should} \rangle \\ \text{SYN} & \begin{bmatrix} \text{CAT} & \begin{bmatrix} \text{verb} \\ \text{VF } \textit{fin} \end{bmatrix} \\ \text{VAL} & \langle \boxed{1}, \boxed{2} \rangle \end{bmatrix} \end{bmatrix} \quad \boxed{2}\begin{bmatrix} \text{FORM} & \langle \text{open, the, present +s} \rangle \\ \text{SYN} & \begin{bmatrix} \text{CAT} & \boxed{4}\begin{bmatrix} \text{verb} \\ \text{VF } \textit{base} \end{bmatrix} \\ \text{VAL} & \langle \boxed{1} \rangle \end{bmatrix} \end{bmatrix}$$

$$\begin{bmatrix} \text{FORM} & \langle \text{open} \rangle \\ \text{SYN} & \begin{bmatrix} \text{CAT} & \boxed{4}\begin{bmatrix} \text{verb} \\ \text{VF } \textit{base} \end{bmatrix} \\ \text{VAL} & \langle \boxed{1}, \boxed{3} \rangle \end{bmatrix} \end{bmatrix} \quad \boxed{3}\begin{bmatrix} \text{FORM} & \langle \text{the, present +s} \rangle \\ \text{SYN} & \text{NP} \end{bmatrix}$$

FIGURE 10.14 Interaction of the Subcategorization and Head Feature Principles

d. Determiner–noun agreement
e. Modifier–modified agreement

Following the long-term practice of the constraint-based grammar community, including LFG, GPSG/HPSG, TAG, and CCG, among others, all these phenomena have been analysed in terms of feature compatibility. In the GPSG/HPSG tradition, the particular method of analysis has involved features of selection (AGR, SUBCAT, VAL, MOD, SPEC, SELECT, etc., depending on the particular proposal). In all such analyses, the selecting sign specifies a value for one of these features that is identified with the relevant part of the selected element. For example, a third singular verb (e.g. *runs*) is specified as in (25) and the Subcategorization Principle requires that the VAL value of *runs* be identified with the sign of its subject:

(25) $\begin{bmatrix} \text{FORM} & \langle run+s \rangle \\ \text{SYN} & \begin{bmatrix} \text{VAL} & \langle \text{NP}[3rd, sing] \rangle \end{bmatrix} \end{bmatrix}$

Subject–verb agreement is thus treated by the very same mechanisms as case government and category selection – that is via simple specifications in the lexical entries of agreeing elements, governors, or modifiers, as described above. No special 'agreement theory' needs to be introduced for verb–subject agreement, verb–object agreement, or indeed agreement between a head and any of its valents.

Notice that this analysis also embodies a clear notion of directionality. The subject NP (in English) bears certain feature specifications 'inherently', while a verb that agrees with the subject NP specifies its requirements in terms of the 'selection' feature VAL. This parallels the intuitive directionality of government: a verb that requires a quirky subject or object case uses VAL to specify those requirements, while the governed valent bears its case specification inherently.

Let us now turn to other kinds of agreement. I follow the economical and insightful analysis of Van Eynde, who employs the non-valence feature SELECT.[14] SELECT is used to let an expression select what it can modify or combine with as a 'marker'. The SELECT value of a modifier, a specifier, or a marker is a sign and this value must be identified with the head daughter in a 'head-functor' construct. Given this analysis, agreement is again accounted for in terms of lexical entries for the agreeing elements that use SELECT to restrict the range of the elements to be modified, specified, or simply 'marked', as illustrated in (26):[15]

---

[14] Following Van Eynde (1998), who builds directly on Allegranza (1998), the features MOD and SPR of Pollard and Sag (1994) are replaced by the single feature SELECT (SEL). See also Van Eynde (2006, 2007) and Allegranza (2007).

[15] Pullum and Zwicky (1988) suggest that the *a/an* alternation should not be analysed via a condition that is part of the determiner's lexical entry. They suggest that such a condition should be impossible because it would refer to the following syntactic context. Instead, they offer a condition on shape that overrides the lexical entry for the indefinite article and stipulates that another shape is called for.

However, Pullum and Zwicky offer no argument against a lexical *a/an* analysis such as the one presented here, which provides a straightforward account of the relevant data, including such contrasts as *an interesting suggestion* vs. *a clever idea* (since the SELECT value corresponds to the entire CNP that the determiner combines with syntactically). Moreover, the lexical analysis proposed here avoids any appeal to competition among alternative forms, 'overriding', or other non-monotonic devices.

(26) a. French feminine plural adjective:
$$\begin{bmatrix} \text{FORM} & \langle grand+e+s \rangle \\ \text{SYN} & \begin{bmatrix} \text{CAT} & \begin{bmatrix} \text{SELECT} & N[\textit{fem, pl}] \end{bmatrix} \end{bmatrix} \end{bmatrix}$$

b. English marker:
$$\begin{bmatrix} \text{FORM} & \langle that \rangle \\ \text{SYN} & \begin{bmatrix} \text{CAT} & \begin{bmatrix} \text{SELECT} & S[\textit{fin}] \end{bmatrix} \end{bmatrix} \end{bmatrix}$$

c. English determiner:
$$\begin{bmatrix} \text{FORM} & \langle a \rangle \\ \text{SYN} & \begin{bmatrix} \text{CAT} & \begin{bmatrix} \text{SELECT} & \begin{bmatrix} \text{PHON} & [\text{FIRST } \textit{consonant}] \\ \text{SYN} & \begin{bmatrix} \text{CAT} & \begin{bmatrix} \textit{noun} \\ \text{MRKG } \textit{unmkd} \end{bmatrix} \end{bmatrix} \end{bmatrix} \end{bmatrix} \end{bmatrix} \end{bmatrix}$$

Assuming that agreement information is specified in terms of category features such as PERS, NUM, and GEND, all such agreement is localized through the interaction of the Subcategorization Principle and the Head Feature Principle.[16] Crucially, however, this means that agreement phenomena, like government and category selection, are local in their basic case, but are extended within complex structures by other, independently motivated grammatical principles to induce indirect, long distance agreement. Notable among such examples is the long distance agreement of reflexive pronouns that is mediated by the theories of binding, control, and subcategorization in examples like (27):

(27) $\left\{\begin{matrix} \text{They} \\ \text{*She} \\ \text{*He} \end{matrix}\right\}$ may want to consider trying to get **themselves** on the ballot.

Finally, let us consider the issue of semantic selection, which intuitively exhibits a locality constraint as well. For example, intuition tells us that there is no verb in any human language that requires its second argument to be a proposition built up from a relation whose second argument is itself a proposition. That is, we assume that no human language could be just like

---

[16] If, on the other hand, some agreement information is encoded via semantic indices (as proposed by Pollard and Sag 1994), then something more needs to be said to ensure locality of agreement. See below.

English except for the inclusion of a verb *hink* whose selection properties give rise to semantic contrasts such as the following:

(28) a. Kim hinks that Sandy believes that the earth is flat.
b. #Kim hinks that Sandy died.
c. #Kim hinks that Sandy loves Pat.

And it seems equally unlikely that there could be an English-like language that included a verb *fask* which, though similar to *ask*, would require its second argument to be an animate *wh*-question, determining semantic contrasts like the following:

(29) a. Bo fasked who left.
b. #Bo fasked whether Carrie had left.
c. #Bo fasked what Carrie had left.

Though we should not lose sight of the fact that these are only intuitions, the intuitions are nonetheless quite robust. And if semantic composition proceeded entirely in terms of the unstructured senses of the immediate constituents of an expression (as in Montague Grammar and its various descendants), then SBCG would indeed predict that semantic selection obeyed the same locality constraints as the phenomena just discussed. However, if compositionally derived meanings are more structured, as is often assumed in order to solve the problem of individuating propositions at a sufficiently fine grain, then the meanings of the constituents of an expression might well be visible (albeit hard to identify) to a selecting element.[17] Structured meanings thus have the potential to vitiate the predictions of SBCG with respect to the locality of semantic selection. I regret being able to do no more at present than to flag this issue, hoping that it will be clarified by future research.

10.6 Some analytic challenges

The theory of SBCG is attractive for its simplicity, precision, and predictive power, yet there are various empirical phenomena that, at least in their outward appearance, appear to defy the localism embodied in SBCG. In the

---

[17] Within the framework of Minimal Recursion Semantics (MRS – see Copestake et al. 2001, and Copestake et al. 2005), all the semantic predications of an embedded phrase are present on its RELATIONS list, and hence are 'locally visible', just as they are in earlier approaches to semantics within HPSG. Particular levels of embedding would be quite difficult to identify within MRS, where the order of elements on the RELATIONS list has no semantic significance. Hence one might argue that MRS provides sufficient prediction in this domain.

remainder of this chapter, I will examine a number of such phenomena, showing that an attractive localist analysis within SBCG is readily available.

10.6.1 Non-local case assignment in English

English *for/to* clauses present an interesting analytic challenge for the locality of case assignment. In order to analyse contrasts like the one in (30), it is necessary that an accusative case constraint be imposed somehow:

(30) a. *I prefer [for [they to be happy]].
 b. I prefer [for [them to be happy]].

But given the standardly assumed structure in (30), the subject NP of the infinitive is not locally accessible to the complementizer *for*, which selects for the infinitival S either as a head (via VAL) or as a marker (via SPEC). Nor can the infinitive marker *to* assign accusative case to its subject, as in examples like (31); that subject must be compatible with nominative case:

(31) [He/*Him seems [to be happy]].

Sag (1997) argues that the standard structure for *for/to* clauses should be replaced by the flat head-complement structure in Figure 10.15.[18] Assuming this structure, rather than the one in (30), the lexical entry for the complementizer *for* can

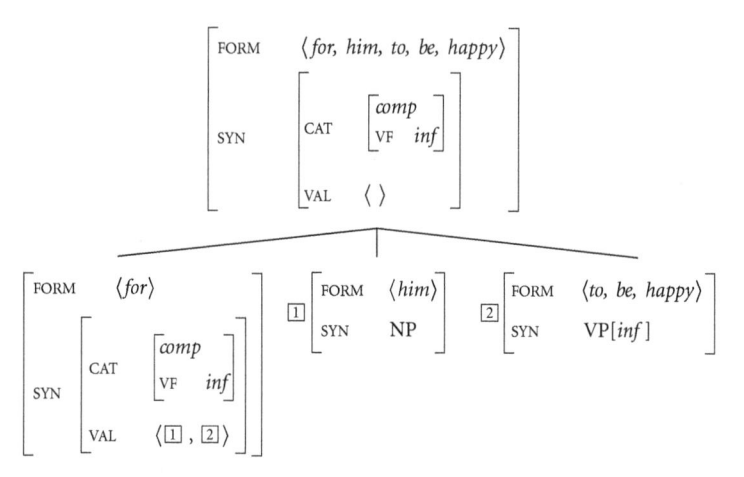

$$\begin{bmatrix} \text{FORM} & \langle \textit{for, him, to, be, happy} \rangle \\ \text{SYN} & \begin{bmatrix} \text{CAT} & \begin{bmatrix} \textit{comp} \\ \text{VF} & \textit{inf} \end{bmatrix} \\ \text{VAL} & \langle \, \rangle \end{bmatrix} \end{bmatrix}$$

$$\begin{bmatrix} \text{FORM} & \langle \textit{for} \rangle \\ \text{SYN} & \begin{bmatrix} \text{CAT} & \begin{bmatrix} \textit{comp} \\ \text{VF} & \textit{inf} \end{bmatrix} \\ \text{VAL} & \langle \boxed{1}, \boxed{2} \rangle \end{bmatrix} \end{bmatrix} \quad \boxed{1} \begin{bmatrix} \text{FORM} & \langle \textit{him} \rangle \\ \text{SYN} & \text{NP} \end{bmatrix} \quad \boxed{2} \begin{bmatrix} \text{FORM} & \langle \textit{to, be, happy} \rangle \\ \text{SYN} & \text{VP}[\textit{inf}] \end{bmatrix}$$

FIGURE 10.15 A *for/to* clause

---

[18] Here and throughout this section, I have regularized valence features and the attendant feature geometry to conform with the preceding discussion.

simply require that its first VALENCE element be an accusative NP. The problematic NP is now locally accessible.

Moreover, the structure in Figure 10.15 is independently motivated, for it provides an immediate account of contrasts like the following, first noted by Emonds (1976):

(32) a. Mary asked me [if, in St. Louis, [John could rent a house cheap]].
 b. He doesn't intend [that, in these circumstances, [we be rehired]].
 c. *Mary arranged for, *in St. Louis*, John to rent a house cheap.
 d. *He doesn't intend for, *in these circumstances*, us to be rehired.

Assuming that only finite CPs have the traditional structure indicated in (32a, b), there is no constituent for the italicized modifiers to modify in (32c, d). The deviance of these examples follows from the same constraints that disallow the indicated modifiers in (33a, b), whose structure is analogous to the new *for/to*-clausal structure:

(33) a. *Kim persuaded *in St. Louis* Sandy to rent a house cheap.
 b. *Lee believed *in these circumstances* Sandy to be in the right.

10.6.2 *The local registration of filler–gap dependencies*

Over the last thirty years, it has been shown that numerous languages exhibit phenomena that are sensitive to the presence or absence of an extraction path – the part of the grammatical structure connecting the filler and the 'gap' in a filler–gap dependency. These phenomena include:

(34) Irish complementizer selection (McCloskey 1979, 1990)
 French 'stylistic' inversion (Kayne and Pollock 1978)
 Spanish 'stylistic' inversion (Torrego 1984)
 Kikuyu downstep suppression (Clements 1984; Zaenen 1983)
 Chamorro verb agreement (Chung 1982, 1998[19])
 Yiddish verb–subject inversion (Diesing 1990)
 Icelandic expletive constructions (Zaenen 1983)
 Adyghe '*wh*-agreement' (Caponigro and Polinsky 2008)

It has often been pointed out (see Zaenen 1983, Hukari and Levine 1995, Bouma et al. 2001, and Levine and Hukari 2006), that constraint-based accounts of extraction provide a straightforward account of phenomena sensitive to extraction paths without the introduction of otherwise unmotivated intermediate

---

[19] But see Donohue (2003) and the references cited there for a critical assessment of Chung's analysis.

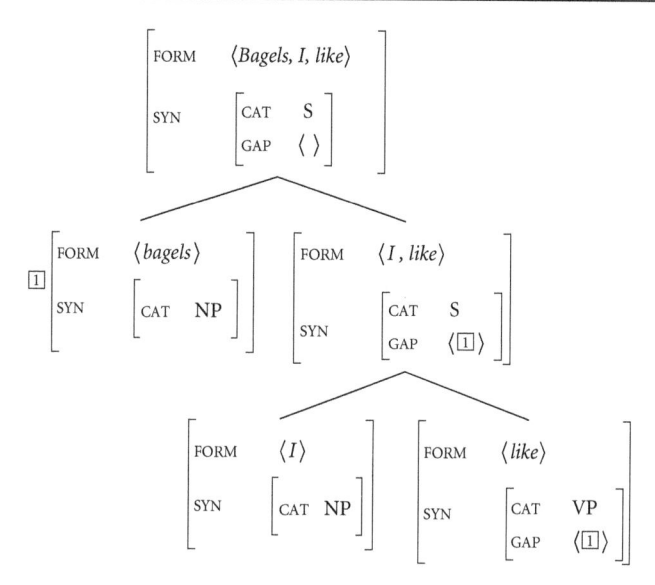

$$\begin{bmatrix} \text{FORM} & \langle \textit{Bagels, I, like} \rangle \\ \text{SYN} & \begin{bmatrix} \text{CAT} & \text{S} \\ \text{GAP} & \langle \, \rangle \end{bmatrix} \end{bmatrix}$$

$$\boxed{1}\begin{bmatrix} \text{FORM} & \langle \textit{bagels} \rangle \\ \text{SYN} & \begin{bmatrix} \text{CAT} & \text{NP} \end{bmatrix} \end{bmatrix} \quad \begin{bmatrix} \text{FORM} & \langle \textit{I, like} \rangle \\ \text{SYN} & \begin{bmatrix} \text{CAT} & \text{S} \\ \text{GAP} & \langle \boxed{1} \rangle \end{bmatrix} \end{bmatrix}$$

$$\begin{bmatrix} \text{FORM} & \langle \textit{I} \rangle \\ \text{SYN} & \begin{bmatrix} \text{CAT} & \text{NP} \end{bmatrix} \end{bmatrix} \quad \begin{bmatrix} \text{FORM} & \langle \textit{like} \rangle \\ \text{SYN} & \begin{bmatrix} \text{CAT} & \text{VP} \\ \text{GAP} & \langle \boxed{1} \rangle \end{bmatrix} \end{bmatrix}$$

FIGURE 10.16 A filler–gap dependency in SBCG

traces. For example, in GPSG/HPSG/SBCG analyses, the information about a FG dependency is locally encoded along the extraction path, as shown in Figure 10.16.[20] This provides a set of local syntactic distinctions that are suitable for analysing the critical effect of extraction path domains on lexical choice and constructional options.

Under these assumptions, the Irish complementizers are distinguished in terms of sentential complements – S[GAP ⟨X⟩] vs. S[GAP ⟨ ⟩], for example. And a lexical entry for a gap-binding predicate like English *easy* can be formulated that requires its complement to contain a NP-type gap, i.e. to be specified as [GAP ⟨NP⟩]. Note, however, that it is not possible to write a lexical entry that requires a gap appearing at some fixed level of embedding. That is, the 'localist' analysis of filler–gap dependencies that has emerged from the GPSG/HPSG tradition comes close to predicting (correctly, to the best of my knowledge) that no grammar for a natural language can impose an arbitrary depth on a filler–gap dependency. The positions in which the gap

---

[20] This figure illustrates a traceless analysis of English topicalization. Analyses that include *wh*-traces, e.g. those of Pollard and Sag (1994) or Levine and Hukari (2006), are also wholly consistent with SBCG.

can appear are always determined by general constraints on the 'inheritance' of GAP (or SLASH) specifications.[21]

10.6.3 Case-stacking languages

One of the best known examples of apparent non-local case assignment is the phenomenon of case 'stacking', as in the following examples from Martuthunira, a Pama-Nyungan language:[22]

(35) Ngayu   nhuwa-lalha   tharnta-a   kupuyu-marta-a
     1SG.NOM   spear-PST   euro-ACC   little-PROP-ACC
     thara-ngka-marta-a.
     pouch-LOC-PROP-ACC
     'I speared a euro with a little one in its pouch.'
     (Dench and Evans 1988)

(36) Ngunhu   wartirra   puni-lha   ngurnu-ngara-mulyarra
     the   woman   go-PST   that-PL-ALL
     kanyara-ngara-mulyarra   kapunmarnu-marta-ngara-mulyarra
     man-PL-ALL   shirt-PROP-PL-ALL
     jirli-wirra-marta-ngara-mulyarra.
     arm-PRIV-PROP-PL-ALL
     'That woman went towards those men with shirts without sleeves.'
     (Andrews 1996)

The operant generalization about these examples is that nominals within NPs are inflected not only in accordance with their local grammatical function but also so as to reflect the function of the NPs that contain them. The unbounded case dependency phenomenon illustrated in (35)–(36) seems to pose a serious challenge for any locality hypothesis, including the one entailed by the interaction of the Subcategorization Principle and the HFP.

However, an elegant analysis of this phenomenon in terms of purely local constraints has been developed by Malouf (2000). Malouf proposes that in case-stacking languages the value of the feature CASE is not an atomic case but rather a list of such atoms. Assuming that nouns select for their NP dependents, the lexical entry for the noun *tharnt* 'euro' looks like (37):

---

[21] This should be compared with a different approach that could also be incorporated within HPSG, namely the use of regular expressions to characterize the relation between fillers and gaps. Under this alternative (cf. its deployment within LFG under the rubric of 'functional uncertainty'), no such prediction is made, as one could write a lexical entry that forced that gap to appear at some fixed depth within the infinitival complement of *hard*.

[22] A euro is a kind of marsupial distinct from kangaroos, wallabies, pademelons, and potoroos.

(37) $\begin{bmatrix} \text{FORM} & \langle \textit{tharnt-} \rangle \\ \text{SYN} & \begin{bmatrix} \text{CAT} & \begin{bmatrix} \textit{noun} \\ \text{CASE} & \boxed{B} \end{bmatrix} \\ \text{VAL} & \langle \text{NP[CASE } \langle \textit{prop} \rangle \oplus \boxed{B} \text{]} \rangle \end{bmatrix} \end{bmatrix}$

The key thing to see here is that every word formed from this stem will bear a particular case specification that is then passed on to the NP on that word's VAL list.

Malouf's treatment of nouns interacts with the analysis of verbs, which is sketched in (38):

(38) $\begin{bmatrix} \text{FORM} & \langle \textit{nhuwalalha} \rangle \\ \text{SYN} & \begin{bmatrix} \text{CAT} & \begin{bmatrix} \textit{verb} \\ \text{CASE} & \boxed{B}\langle\rangle \end{bmatrix} \\ \text{VAL} & \langle \text{NP[}\langle\textit{nom}\rangle \oplus \boxed{B}\text{]}, \text{NP[}\langle\textit{acc}\rangle \oplus \boxed{B}\text{]} \rangle \end{bmatrix} \end{bmatrix}$

Finite verbs bear an empty CASE specification. However, (38) is formulated so as to illustrate the general principle that lexical heads add their own CASE value to that of their dependents. As a result of this case addition, CASE values become longer with embedding, as shown in Figure 10.17.

Long distance case stacking is thus a consequence of CASE specifications that pass the case properties of a superordinate context down into a subordinate

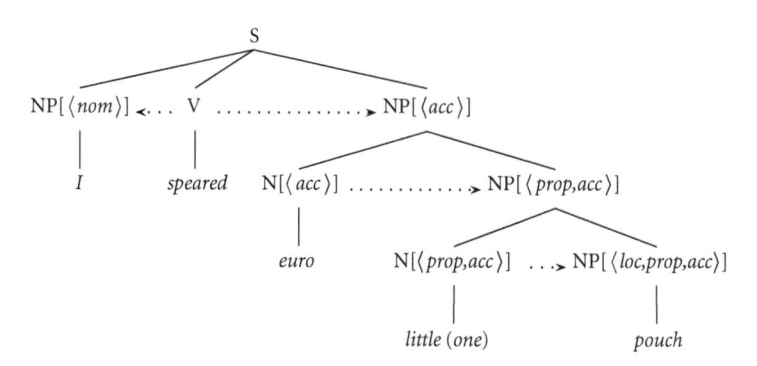

FIGURE 10.17 Case government in Martuthunira

one, adding only the case information that reflects the local grammatical function of a given head-dependent combination. The morphological case inflections are based on local CASE specifications, just as they are in languages that lack case stacking. But when multiple case affixes are present (e.g. on *pouch* in Figure 10.17), it follows that the CASE specification of the noun is non-singleton. This in turn entails that the immediately embedding syntactic context (e.g. little (one)) must introduce an appropriate case specification. Otherwise, the maximal NP in Figure 10.17 would fail to meet the VALENCE requirements of the verb *speared*. The local constraints of lexical items and general grammatical principles thus interact to guarantee a long distance case dependency that is bounded only by the complexity of the embedding environment.

10.6.4 *The role of subjects*

Earlier, I mentioned the presumed locality of semantic role assignment. However, as a number of researchers have recently argued, there are phenomena in a variety of languages whose analysis requires, for example, that a verb selecting a sentential complement must be able to place constraints on the subject realized within that complement. One of these is English 'copy raising' (Rogers 1974; Potsdam and Runner 2001; Asudeh 2002), illustrated in (39):

(39) There looks like there's going to be a storm/*it's going to rain/*Kim's going to win.

Also relevant are controlled pronominal subjects in Serbo-Croatian (Zec 1987), Halkomelem Salish (Gerdts and Hukari 2001), and other languages, where a control verb requires that the subject pronoun realized within its clausal complement be coindexed with one of the verb's other arguments (its subject (*promise*-type) or its object (*persuade*-type)), as shown in (40):

(40) a. NP_i promise [Comp he_i VP]
      b. NP persuade NP_i [Comp he_i VP]

The problems of raising across Polish prepositions (Przepiórkowski 1999; Dickinson 2004), and complementizer agreement in Eastern Dutch dialects (Höhle 1997) are similar: a particular argument realized within a given expression must be 'visible' to an external entity that combines with that expression. Moreover, as is well known, there are many English idioms that require referential and agreement identity between a subject and a possessor within an object NP, or which assign a semantic role to the object's possessor. These are illustrated in (41):

(41) a. He$_i$ lost [his$_i$/*her$_j$ marbles].
   b. They$_i$ kept/lost [their$_i$/*our$_j$ cool].

A principled solution to all of these problems, suggested independently by a number of these researchers, is the introduction of a feature (distinct from VAL) that passes up to a given phrase information about one of the daughters used to construct that phrase. Kiss (1995) proposed such a feature for the subject of non-finite verbal clauses in German, calling it SUBJECT, and this feature has been used by Meurers (1999, 2001) and others to make subjects accessible at higher levels of structure.[23] However, it would be desirable to use the same feature to make genitive pronouns realized within a given NP available for selection by elements outside that NP. In addition, the Polish preposition raising phenomenon discussed by Przepiórkowski (1999) and Dickinson (2004) motivates an analysis where the object of certain prepositions is available for selection by elements external to the PP that the preposition projects. In sum, there is some variation as to which element within a phrase is externally accessible. Since 'subject' is too narrow a notion empirically, SUBJECT is an inappropriate name for the feature in question. I have previously proposed instead to name the relevant feature EXTERNAL ARGUMENT (XARG).[24] Because XARG is a category feature, it percolates information about a designated phrasal constituent, as illustrated in Figure 10.18:

$$\begin{bmatrix} \text{FORM} & \langle \textit{Kim's, book} \rangle \\ \text{SYN} & \begin{bmatrix} \text{CAT} & \begin{bmatrix} \textit{noun} \\ \text{XARG} & \boxed{1} \end{bmatrix} \\ \text{GEN} & - \\ \text{VAL} & \langle \, \rangle \end{bmatrix} \end{bmatrix}$$

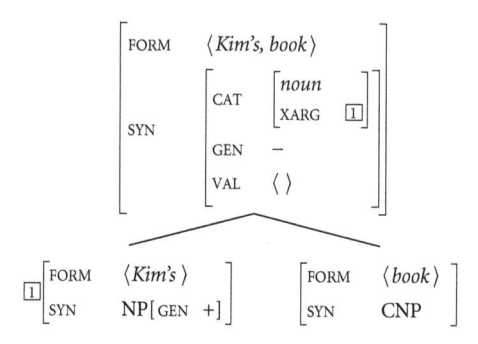

$\boxed{1} \begin{bmatrix} \text{FORM} & \langle \textit{Kim's} \rangle \\ \text{SYN} & \text{NP[GEN +]} \end{bmatrix}$ $\begin{bmatrix} \text{FORM} & \langle \textit{book} \rangle \\ \text{SYN} & \text{CNP} \end{bmatrix}$

FIGURE 10.18 XARG analysis of genitive-embedding NP

---

[23] Kiss's proposal is an extension of earlier proposals that have been made within GPSG/HPSG, e.g. the AGR feature used by Gazdar et al. (1985) and Pollard's (1994) ERG feature.

[24] Sag and Pollard (1991) proposed a semantic feature EXTERNAL-ARGUMENT (XARG), which made only the index of the subject argument available at the clausal level. This analysis has been incorporated into Minimal Recursion Semantics (and the English Resource Grammar) by Flickinger and Bender (2003).

Assuming, following Pollard and Sag (1994), that there are three subtypes of the type *index* (*ref* (*referential-index*), *it* (*expletive-it-index*), and *there* (*expletive-there-index*)), the copy raising examples mentioned in (39) above can be treated simply by associating the relevant lexical entry for *looks* (*like*) with the VAL list in (42):

(42) $\begin{bmatrix} \text{VAL} & \langle \text{NP}_i, \begin{bmatrix} \text{S} \\ \text{XARG NP}[pro]_i \end{bmatrix} \rangle \end{bmatrix}$

And if an object NP includes information about its (prenominal) possessor in its XARG value, then an idiomatic verb like *lose* can be specified as in (43):

(43) $\begin{bmatrix} \text{FORM} & \langle lose \rangle \\ \text{SYN} & \begin{bmatrix} \text{CAT} & \text{verb} \\ \text{VAL} & \langle \text{NP}_i, \begin{bmatrix} \text{NP} \\ \text{XARG NP}[pro]_i \end{bmatrix} \rangle \end{bmatrix} \end{bmatrix}$

Similarly, an idiomatic verb like *tickle* can assign a semantic role to its object's possessor. In both cases, all that is required is that the NP's XARG value be identified with the NP's possessor, as sketched in Figure 10.19:

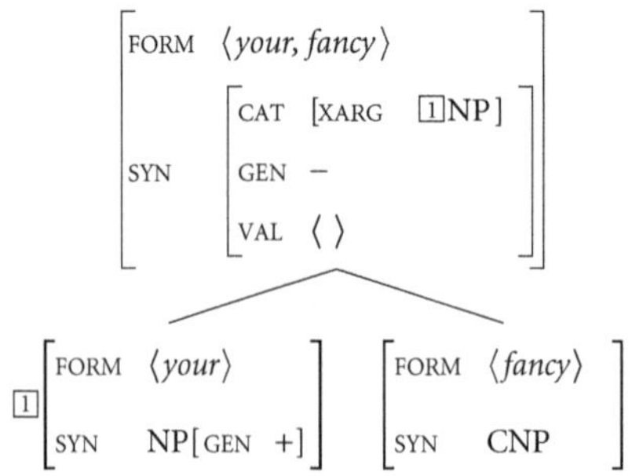

$\begin{bmatrix} \text{FORM} & \langle your, fancy \rangle \\ \text{SYN} & \begin{bmatrix} \text{CAT} & [\text{XARG} \quad \boxed{1}\text{NP}] \\ \text{GEN} & - \\ \text{VAL} & \langle \rangle \end{bmatrix} \end{bmatrix}$

$\boxed{1}\begin{bmatrix} \text{FORM} & \langle your \rangle \\ \text{SYN} & \text{NP}[\text{GEN} \ +] \end{bmatrix}$ $\begin{bmatrix} \text{FORM} & \langle fancy \rangle \\ \text{SYN} & \text{CNP} \end{bmatrix}$

FIGURE 10.19 XARG analysis of *your fancy*

All of the phenomena just enumerated, in addition to the English tag-question construction discussed earlier, provide motivation for XARG specifications as part of the CAT value of sentential and NP signs. Note that the XARG value (either a sign or the distinguished atom *none*) differs from the VAL value (a list of signs) in that only the latter undergoes 'cancellation' in the construction of phrasal signs.

10.6.5 Idiomatic expressions

Idioms also pose a potential problem for the strong locality claims made by SBCG, as I have outlined here. It is well known that certain idiomatic interpretations arise only when the particular pieces of the idiom are in construction with one another. The proper characterization of the notion of 'in construction with', however, remains controversial. Since Nunberg et al. (1994), it has generally been agreed that syntactic flexibility is related to semantic decomposability. Thus, a particularly decomposable idiom like *pull strings*, occurs flexibly in a variety of configurations, as illustrated in (44):

(44) a. Sandy *pulled strings* to get Kim the job.
  b. *Strings* were *pulled* to get Kim the job.
  c. The *strings* that seem likely to have been *pulled* to get Kim the job were an offence to man and nature.
  d. We objected to the *strings* that Sandy had to *pull* to get Kim the job.
  e. Sandy *pulled* the *strings* that got Kim the job.
  f. The *strings* that Sandy *pulled*, nobody else could have *pulled*.

Idioms vary considerably in terms of their syntactic flexibility and it is perhaps unclear where to draw the line between an idiomatic sentence that should be allowed by the grammar and an extension of the grammar (or 'language play'). However, it is reasonably clear that copredication is a necessary condition for idiomaticity. That is, in order for *pull strings* to receive its idiomatic interpretation, the second semantic argument of *pull* must also have *strings* predicated of it, however the grammar allows for that to happen.[25]

My proposal uses the persistent defaults of Lascarides and Copestake (1999) to write lexical entries like those in (45) (LID is the feature LEXICAL-IDENTIFI-ER, originally proposed by Fillmore and Kay in unpublished work, and explained more fully in Sag 2010):

---

[25] Sailer (2000) proposes a treatment of flexible idioms in terms of lexical constraints (called 'conditions on lexical licensing' (COLL)) that can access arbitrarily distant elements within a given phrasal structure. Sailer argues that the domain of COLL constraints should be the entire sentence (a sentential sign) in which the idiomatic word occurs. This is necessary, he claims, in order to describe what he takes to be purely syntactic restrictions on particular idiom 'chunks'. I will not comment further on Sailer's proposals here, or on the subsequent attempts to improve upon them by Soehn (2004, 2006). My approach differs from both of these in treating each idiom in terms of a single local constraint that interacts with other independently motivated aspects of the grammar.

(45)
$$\begin{bmatrix} \text{FORM} & \langle \textit{strings} \rangle \\ \text{SYN} & \begin{bmatrix} \text{CAT} & \begin{bmatrix} \textit{noun} \\ \text{LID} & \boxed{0}[\textit{strings\_rel} \,/_p \, \textit{l\_strings\_rel}\,] \end{bmatrix} \\ \text{VAL} & \langle\,\rangle \end{bmatrix} \\ \text{SEM} & \begin{bmatrix} \text{INDEX} & i \\ \text{RELS} & \langle h_0 : \boxed{0}(i) \rangle \end{bmatrix} \end{bmatrix}$$

Assuming that literal and idiomatic relations are hierarchically organized, as shown in Figure 10.20, then the noun *strings* will default to its literal interpretation except when its LID value is resolved to the idiomatic relation *i_strings_rel* by the idiomatic verb *pull*, whose lexical entry is sketched in (46):

(46)
$$\begin{bmatrix} \text{FORM} & \langle \textit{pull} \rangle \\ \text{SYN} & \begin{bmatrix} \text{VAL} & \left\langle \begin{bmatrix} \text{SYN} & \text{NP}_i \end{bmatrix}, \begin{bmatrix} \text{LID} & \textit{i\_strings\_rel} \\ \text{SYN} & \text{NP}_j \end{bmatrix} \right\rangle \end{bmatrix} \\ \text{SEM} & \begin{bmatrix} \text{RELS} & \langle h_0 : \textit{i\_pull\_rel}(i,j) \rangle \end{bmatrix} \end{bmatrix}$$

Making the reasonable assumption that the LID of a gap and its filler are identified in a filler–gap construction, it follows that the idiomatic resolution can take place in examples (44d–f), as well as (44a–c), thus solving what Nunberg et al. (1994) refer to as 'McCawley's Paradox'. This account of syntactically flexible, semantically decomposable idioms is fully compatible with the localist perspective of SBCG.

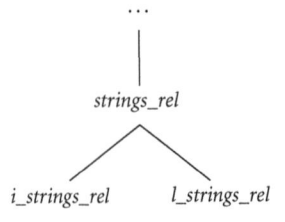

FIGURE 10.20 Literal and idiomatic strings relations

10.7 Conclusion

In this chapter, I have surveyed the issues of *locality of selection* and *locality of construction*, placing these matters in both theoretical and historical perspective. I have also sketched the basics of a particular blend of HPSG and Construction Grammar, called *Sign-Based Construction Grammar*, which draws a fundamental distinction between signs and constructs. The two basic principles of SBCG, the Subcategorization Principle and the Head Feature Principle are fundamental to the results presented here. These principles interact with appropriate lexical specifications and a particular inventory of features, including GAP, XARG, and LID, to make predictions of locality – a principled circumscription of the domains in which lexical selection and constructional constraints apply.

In addition, I have examined a number of problems involving non-local grammatical dependencies and have offered localist solutions to them. In the process, I have argued that SBCG offers numerous advantages, including:

- a unified approach to the apparent non-local dependencies involving embedded subjects and possessors (through the feature XARG);
- a principled account of the locality of lexical selection;
- a proper treatment of the syntactic flexibility of semantically decomposable idioms, including a resolution of 'McCawley's Paradox';
- a simplification of the Subcategorization Principle (by eliminating the need for relational constraints);
- a simplification of grammar rules (phrasal constructions) that precludes non-local constraints as a matter of principle.

11

Inessential features and expressive power of descriptive metalanguages

Geoffrey K. Pullum and Hans-Jörg Tiede

11.1 Introduction

It is natural enough for linguists to think that the features they posit in descriptions of natural languages are genuine, not spurious – that they reflect aspects of the subject matter rather than aspects of the machinery invoked in devising the description or the linguistic theory.

Having seen features like CASE, GENDER, NUMBER, PERSON, and TENSE used repeatedly in describing hundreds of languages, linguists tend to feel that such features have some inherent connection with the way human languages work, rather than with the way human linguists work. And anyone who has attempted to describe English syntax would probably feel that features like AUX (distinguishing the verbs that can be clause-initial in closed interrogative independent clauses) or WH (distinguishing the relative and interrogative pronouns from other pronouns) also draw real rather than artefactual distinctions.

But linguists do not always feel this way about all of the rich array of features posited in current or past work on syntax. Few feel the same way about devices such as the DOOM feature, used by Postal (1970) to mark noun phrases targeted for erasure later in the derivation, or the '[±F]' annotations that have often been used to draw ad hoc distinctions among constituents with differing behaviours.

What is the basis of the feeling that we can tell a spurious feature from a genuine one? Generalized Phrase Structure Grammar (GPSG) and Head-driven Phrase Structure Grammar (HPSG), for example, posit features such as SLASH, marking constituents containing 'gaps'; BAR, indicating the 'bar level' of phrasal constituents; SUBCAT, coding the subcategorization of lexical heads according to the complements they select; and so on. These do not necessarily strike linguists as having the same kind of status as more traditional features.

Inessential features and expressive power 273

Why (to put it rather flippantly) does one feel so confident that the Cambridge Textbooks in Linguistics devoted to particular features – Corbett (1991) on *Gender*, Blake (1994) on *Case*, Corbett (2000) on *Number*, and so on – will never be joined by future books in the series called *Slash*, or *Bar*, or *Doom*?

Linguists are so used to focusing on microproblems and ignoring irrelevant surrounding complexities that they seldom try to pull together even a partial list of the syntactic or morphosyntactic features that they are likely to need to recognize in, say, an analysis of Standard English. But we can get a rough idea by reviewing the (non-semantic) feature distinctions implicitly or explicitly appealed to by a comprehensive grammar of the language such as Huddleston et al. (2002) (henceforth *CGEL*). Some of these are shown in Table 11.1. (Here and from now on we give feature names in small caps.)

The terminology for features in Table 11.1 is either traditional (as with CASE or GENDER), or fairly transparent (PHRASAL, INFLECTABLE), or used in works such as Gazdar et al. (1985) (PFORM, VFORM), or adapted from the informal presentation in *CGEL* (CLAUSETYPE, HOLLOW). Examples of constituents that would bear particular values for the features are given in parentheses in the right-hand column. None of these features seems likely to be dispensable in any fully explicit grammar of English. But are they all genuine properties of natural language constituents, or are some of them just artefacts of choices made in theory construction? This is the question we ultimately address in this chapter.

For our purposes, we can ignore the fact that Table 11.1 takes features to be n-ary, for various $n \geq 2$. It should be obvious to any formally sophisticated linguist that issues about the arity of features are extremely unlikely to be interpretable as having empirical implications. Given any description using a feature with x values (for $x \geq 3$), an exactly equivalent description could be achieved using x unary (privative) features, or a set of n-ary features for any choice of n (provided $2 \leq n \leq x$), possibly with some feature co-occurrence restrictions. (To be exact, the minimum number of n-ary features needed to keep x distinct subcategories apart is the smallest integer equal to or greater than $\log_n(x)$.)

Take CLAUSETYPE, which we can take to have the values Declar (declarative), Imper (imperative), ClosInt (closed interrogative), OpenInt (open interrogative), and Exclam (exclamative). We could recode it in terms of binary features, possibly in a way that had some kind of intuitive semantic rationale: [±INTERROG] to separate interrogatives from the rest, with [±OPEN] (limited to [+INTERROG] clauses) subclassifying question-expressing clauses as having open or closed answer sets; [±ASSERTIVE] to separate the proposition-expressing declaratives and exclamatives from the imperatives; and [±EMOTIVE] (limited to [+ASSERTIVE]) to separate exclamatives off from declaratives.

TABLE 11.1 Some features used in English syntax

Feature name	Value range (with examples)
ADJ-FUNC	Normal, AttribOnly, NeverAttrib, PostPosOnly
AUX	+ (*may*), − (*make*)
AUXINIT	+ (*May I go*), − (*I may go*)
CASE	Nom (*I*), Acc (*me*), DepGen (*my*), IndGen (*mine*)
CATEGORY	Noun, Verb, Adj, Adv, P, D, Sbr, Cdr, Intj
CLAUSESTRUC	Main, Content, Relative, Comparative, Verbless, ...
CLAUSETYPE	Declar, Imper, ClosInt, OpenInt, Exclam
COUNT	+ (*cup*), − (*crockery*)
DEFINITE	+ (*the*), − (*some*)
EVER	+ (*whoever*), − (*who*)
FINITENESS	+ (*that it go*), − (*for it to go*)
DET-HEAD	+ (*this*), − (*the*)
GENDER	Masc (*he*), Fem (*she*), Neut (*it*)
GRADE	Plain, Compar, Superl
HOLLOW	+ (*to look at* ___), − (*to look at it*)
HUMAN	+ (*who*), − (*which*)
INFLECTABLE	+ (*big*), − (*enormous*)
NEGATIVE	+ (*no*), − (*all*)
NFORM	Ordinary, Pron, Dummy-*it*, Dummy-*there*
NUMBER	Sing (*woman*), Plur (*women*)
NUMTYPE	Cardinal (*two*), Ordinal (*second*)
PERSON	1st (*we*), 2nd (*you*), 3rd (*they*)
PFORM	By, To, Of, On, ...
PHRASAL	+ (*see it*), − (*see*)
PROPER	+ (*Microsoft*), − (*microscope*)
VFORM	Pret, 3sgPres, Pres, Plain, Psp, Ger
WH	+ (*who*), − (*he*)
WH-TYPE	Wh-Interrogative, Wh-Relative

And there would of course be many other ways to do it, some involving only three features (since three binary features that cross-classify fully yield $2^3 = 8$ definable subsets of constituents).

Ruminations on which set of features to use, and whether they should be binary, were common in the era of generative phonology. Halle (1957: 67) treats the proposition that all phonetic features are binary as a scientific hypothesis, and seeks to support it on the grounds that (i) it does not impair coverage, (ii) it permits some simplifications, and (iii) it permits an 'evaluation procedure' to be devised. But it is logically impossible for reducing n-ary features to binary ones to impair coverage of any set of facts; and it is notoriously difficult to bring claims about descriptive simplicity or evaluation metrics to bear on comparison of theories couched in different theoretical metalanguages. It seems quite implausible that anything factual could be discovered about languages that would settle a question about whether there exists a syntactic feature having more than two values.

We note in passing a point about cross-linguistic identification of features (discussed in Section 2.3.2 of Corbett, this volume, as 'the correspondence problem'). Since features are structurally defined – it is the system of contrasts between values that defines them, not their names – they are most unlikely to be cross-linguistically identifiable, except in the rather loose and approximate semantically based way discussed in *CGEL*, pp. 31–33. For example, we cannot determine that some particular feature in a formal grammar of French is to be equated with some particular feature in a formal grammar of German. Even if they have the same arity, we do not have a formally precise way of determining which one to equate with which using formal criteria. And they may not have the same arity even when they are intuitively similar in semantic terms.

Thus, we have no grounds for formally equating the notion of 'feminine' gender in French with what we call 'feminine' in German: in French the feature we call gender is binary (*le* ~ *la*) and in German it is ternary (*der* ~ *die* ~ *das*). At a detailed level, meaning fails to clarify anything: the French translation of 'the table' is *la table*, the same gender as *la personne* 'the person' and *la jeune fille* 'the girl'; but the German translation of 'the table' is *der Tisch*, a different value from *die Person* 'the person', and different again from *das Mädchen* 'the girl'. So is it *der*, *die*, or *das* that corresponds to French *la*, and why, exactly?

The best we can do is to say that the class of French nouns co-occurring with the *la* form of the French definite article includes a large number of the core nouns denoting female humans (as well as thousands of other referents), and the same is true of the class of German nouns co-occurring with the *die* form of the definite article, and in that sense there is a common-sense semantic rationale for calling both the French *la* class and the German *die* class 'feminine nouns' (see Huddleston et al. 2002: 31–33, for some related remarks).

But there is no hope of rigorous necessary and sufficient conditions being given for calling some feature value the 'feminine' value for an arbitrary language. And there is no hope of answering questions about whether some feature in a Minimalist account is to be equated with a feature employed in an HPSG grammar, or even whether a certain feature in one Minimalist grammarian's analysis is the same one as some other Minimalist is employing.

The specific thesis of this chapter is that distinguishing between the 'real' features and the spurious, artefactual, or superfluous features is even more difficult than might have been thought. We argue that notions like 'spurious feature distinction' or 'artefact of the descriptive machinery' are not really well defined. This means that linguists' feelings of distaste or acceptance for particular features may be based in nothing more solid than personal prejudice.

Our main point is a mathematical one. In making it we shall employ the methods of what is becoming known as model-theoretic syntax.

11.2 Model-theoretic syntax

Model-theoretic syntax, henceforth MTS, is represented by several different theoretical frameworks, but only a small minority of theoreticians. The Arc Pair Grammar of Johnson and Postal (1980) was the first full presentation of the MTS idea within linguistics. HPSG in its recent versions is another fairly clear example.

The leading idea is that linguistic expressions – syllables, words, phrases, etc. – should be represented for theoretical purposes as *structures* in the sense familiar from model theory. A structure is simply a set with various relations and functions defined on it and certain individual constants identified within it. And an MTS grammar is simply a finite set of statements, formulated in a logical metalanguage adapted to the statement of descriptions of natural language structural properties.

Model theory is typically familiar to linguists only through its application in semantics, but the application we are talking about here is very different. In semantics, model-theoretic structures are used to make sentence meaning precise in terms of denotation in a model: the meaning of an expression is explicated in terms of the set of structures (e.g. possible worlds, or situations) that are its models. In effect, we fix a particular natural language sentence in some semantic representational form and consider which structures satisfy it. The way structures are used in MTS is in a sense the opposite of this: instead of fixing a sentence and giving it a meaning by specifying what models it has, we *fix a certain structure and consider what statements it satisfies* – the relevant statements, of course, being the metalanguage statements that make up (or are entailed by) the grammar.

To be more specific, we use a logical metalanguage interpreted on structures of a certain sort. These structures are taken to be idealized representations of syntactic form for particular expressions. For any such structure we can ask whether all of the statements in the grammar are true in it – i.e. whether it is a model of the grammar. We define a structure as well formed in the natural language being described iff it satisfies all the statements that make up the grammar.

Notice that there is no single MTS framework. MTS is an approach to formalization. It is possible, in fact, to take a generative grammatical framework and re-formalize its claims in MTS terms. The insights that can be gained from such re-formalization are explored in such works as Blackburn and Gardent (1995) (on LFG), Blackburn et al. (1993) and Rogers (1997) (on GPSG), Rogers (1998) (on GB), etc. Certain wider theoretical consequences of the MTS approach are discussed by Pullum and Scholz (2001) and Pullum and Scholz (2005). Here, however, we are not attempting to compare or relate MTS to generative frameworks. We merely use certain techniques that have emerged within MTS to make explicit a point that holds for all theories of syntax of whatever kind.

The structures we use below will be of the very simple type known as relational structures. In these there are no functions or individual constants. A relational structure is simply a set of points (the domain) with certain relations defined on it. Properties are just the special case of unary (one-place) relations.

Strings, trees, and graphs of all sorts clearly fall under this definition. Strings represent a very simple special case. A single word like *aardvark* in its ordinary spelling could be represented as a relational structure with the domain $\{1,2,3,4,5,6,7,8\}$ (the eight positions in the string of letters), with six relations defined on it. There are five unary relations (properties) that we can write with **a**, **d**, **k**, **r**, and **v**, each intuitively corresponding to the property of being (a position labelled with) a certain letter. In addition there is one binary relation intuitively corresponding to the arithmetical successor relation on the integers in the domain. Writing such a structure down in the usual way can be seen as compressing the information it contains in two ways: the actual elements of the domain are represented by the unary relation letters, and the successor relation is represented by immediate right-adjacency on the page.

To say that a grammar Γ defines a certain structure $\mathcal{A}$ as well formed is just to say that $\mathcal{A}$ *satisfies* Γ (or *is a model of* Γ), notated $\mathcal{A} \vDash \Gamma$. The structure which represents *aardvark*, for instance, satisfies the first-order formula $\exists x \exists y [\mathbf{a}(x) \land \mathbf{a}(y) \land x \prec y]$, meaning 'there is an *a* that has an *a* immediately following it'. It does not satisfy $\forall x [\mathbf{a}(x) \Rightarrow \exists y [\mathbf{r}(y) \land x \prec y]]$, meaning 'every *a* has an *r* immediately following it' (position 1, for instance, is a counterexample to this).

However, most of the interest within model-theoretic syntax has centered on the study of logics interpreted on relational structures much more complex than strings. Logics interpreted on strings can be remarkably weak in expressive power. For example, the example just cited used a first-order metalanguage with a predicate interpreted by 'immediately precedes', and this is an extremely weak formalism. It cannot even describe all the regular (finite-state) sets of strings. It can describe only the 'locally threshold testable' stringsets (Straubing 1994: 46–49), a proper subclass of the star-free or 'counter-free' stringsets studied by McNaughton and Papert (1971), which are in turn a proper subclass of the finite-state. Even if we switch to the most powerful kind of logic that has played a major role in model-theoretic syntax, namely the logics known as weak monadic second-order (wMSO) on string models, we get no more than the regular stringsets, so our descriptions are limited to the descriptive power of finite-state machines. (A wMSO logic is like a first-order language with an extra set of variables for quantifying over finite sets of nodes. See Straubing 1994 or Libkin 2004 for detailed exposition of results on first-order and wMSO logics on strings.)

The most important structures employed in natural language syntax are labelled constituent-structure trees. Our next task is to present a brief introduction to the study of logics on trees because it will be crucial for our main argument.

11.2.1 *Logics on trees*

To illustrate how trees can be represented mathematically, we consider the phrase structure tree in (1).

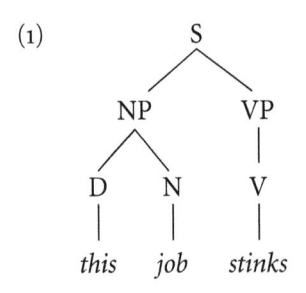

(1)
```
              S
             / \
           NP   VP
          /  \   |
         D    N  V
         |    |  |
       this  job stinks
```

This tree has nine nodes. These will be the elements of the domain of the structure. It does not really matter what we take them to be – it is the system of relations defined on them that is crucial – but it is convenient to take them to be not just atomic elements like integers but rather *addresses of nodes* – descriptions of positions relative to the root. These addresses can be represented by strings of integers. Starting from the root, which has the empty string (ϵ) as its address, we add '0' for the left child of the root and '1' for the right child, and we go on down: '01' for the right child of the left child of the root, '010' for the left child of that, and so on, thus:

(2)
```
          ε
         / \
        0   1
       / \  |
      00 01 10
      |  |  |
     000 010 100
```

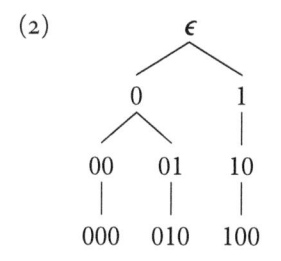

This means we can identify each node in a binary branching tree with a string over {0, 1}; and since no string ever appears at more than one node – each string over {0, 1} corresponds to a unique address – we can equate trees with sets of such strings.

Not every set of strings over {0, 1} represents a tree; but the two conditions we need to impose to guarantee that such a set does correspond to a tree are remarkably simple. Simplifying by assuming (with much recent literature) that all branching is binary (see Rogers 1998: 19 for a more general statement, which also is very simple), the conditions defining binary tree domains are these:

(3) A *binary tree domain* is a set $T \subseteq \{0, 1\}^*$, such that (where x and y are strings over $\{0, 1\}$),

    (a) if xy is in T, then so is x, and
    (b) if $x1$ is in T, then so is $x0$.

Part (a) of this definition requires any node to have all of its ancestors in the domain (because prefixes of digit strings correspond to addresses higher up on the path to the root), and part (b) requires all right branches to have left siblings (because ending in 1 corresponds to being a leaf on a right branch, and for every right branch there has to be a left branch).

This defines binary tree domains in terms quite independent of both the diagrams with which we depict trees and the generative grammars that linguists often assume for generating them, though thus far the result looks a bit unfamiliar.

We now define a *binary tree structure* as a triple $\langle T, R_\downarrow, R_\rightarrow \rangle$, where T is a binary tree domain, $R_\downarrow$ is the child-of relation (we use androgynous kinship terminology for relations between nodes: 'parent', 'child', and 'sibling'); i.e. $(n, m) \in R_\downarrow$ iff $m = n0$ or $m = n1$, and $R_\rightarrow$ is the left-sibling-of relation, i.e. $(m, n) \in R_\rightarrow$ iff $m = s0$ and $n = s1$ for some s.

So the tree in (2) would be formalized as a tree structure, $(T, R_\downarrow, R_\rightarrow)$, where T is the set {ε, 0, 1, 00, 01, 10, 000, 010, 100} and, for example, the pair (10, 100) stands in the $R_\downarrow$ relation and the pair (00, 01) stands in the $R_\rightarrow$ relation.

Writing such a structure down in the way linguists usually do can be seen as compressing the information in three ways: writing the appropriate unary relation letters for the elements of the domain; representing the parent relation by sloping downward lines connecting parents to children; and representing precedence by left-right orientation of siblings on the page.

11.2.2 *Modal logic metalanguages*

To talk about trees in this chapter we will use *propositional modal logics*. This choice may need some explanation, though the idea of using modal logics to describe trees goes back at least as far as Gazdar et al. (1988) (see Blackburn et al. 1993 for a more thoroughgoing development of the idea, and Moss and Tiede 2007 for a detailed and up-to-date survey). Modal logics provide a very tightly restricted way of describing the structure of trees, and their relationships with and translations into other formalisms are beginning to be very well understood. Though they originate in philosophical efforts to understand the notions of necessity and possibility, they are best seen much more generally, as languages for describing relational structures (such as trees) from a local and internal perspective. Blackburn, de Rijke, and Venema (2001: xii) observe that 'the reader who pictures a modal formula as a little automaton standing at some state in a relational structure, and only permitted to explore the structure by making journeys to neighbouring states, will have grasped one of the key intuitions of modal model theory.' The linguist can read 'state' as 'node' and (here, at least) 'relational structure' as 'tree'.

The key idea is to represent the labels attached to nodes in trees by atomic propositional formulas of the logic. In other interpretations of modal logic these would be propositions true at particular worlds in a set of worlds under an accessibility relation; here they simply represent labellings present at certain points in the model.

Before we formalize labelled trees in these terms, we need to fix the syntax of the logics that we will be considering. We can use a very simple and basic kind of modal logic $\mathcal{L}_B$ as a reference point. $\mathcal{L}_B$ has a set of atomic formulas corresponding to syntactic categories (we can assume this is finite), and just two modalities, $\langle\rightarrow\rangle$ and $\langle\downarrow\rangle$.

The semantics is such that a formula $\langle\downarrow\rangle\phi$ is true at a node v iff ϕ is true at a child of v (so it means 'v has a ϕ-labelled child') and $\langle\rightarrow\rangle\phi$ is true at a node v iff ϕ is true at a right sibling of v.

$\mathcal{L}_B$ can be used to say many of the things about trees that could be guaranteed by a context-free grammar. Consider the two formulas in (4):

(4) a. **PP** $\Rightarrow \langle \downarrow \rangle$**P**
 b. $\langle \downarrow \rangle$**during** $\Rightarrow$ (**P** $\wedge \langle \rightarrow \rangle$**NP**)

We use '$\Rightarrow$' for material implication, defined by $\phi \Rightarrow \psi \equiv \neg(\phi \wedge \neg(\psi))$. So what (4a) says is that a node where **PP** is true has a child where **P** is true; that is, it expresses the claim of X-bar theory that every PP node must immediately dominate a Preposition node. And what (4b) says is that a node that has a child labelled **during** is labelled P and has a right sibling labelled NP – a subcategorization statement for the preposition *during*.

However, in general $\mathcal{L}_B$ is too weak to permit much interesting progress toward the description of human languages – it is far weaker than context-free grammars, for example. We need to consider stronger logics.

Three modal logics of increasing expressive strength have been a particular focus of attention in the context of model-theoretic syntax. They are known as $\mathcal{L}_{core}$, $\mathcal{L}_{cp}$, and PDL$_{tree}$ respectively. All of them are less expressive than wMSO.

For our purposes here, it will be sufficient to concentrate on $\mathcal{L}_{core}$ and $\mathcal{L}_{cp}$. (For a detailed discussion of PDL$_{tree}$, which is increasingly important for reasons relating to the rise of XML as a data representation language, see Afanasiev et al. 2005.) The syntax of formulas for the $\mathcal{L}_{core}$ and $\mathcal{L}_{cp}$ languages is defined as follows:

(5) Basic syntax for $\mathcal{L}_{core}$ and $\mathcal{L}_{cp}$

 a. any atomic proposition is a formula;
 b. $\neg(\phi)$ is a formula if ϕ is;
 c. $\phi \wedge \psi$ is a formula if ϕ and ψ are;
 d. a formula prefixed by a modal operator is a formula.

In addition we will use $\top$ for a dummy proposition that is always true (it could be defined as $\neg(\mathbf{a} \wedge \neg(\mathbf{a}))$ or in some similar way; its utility will become clear below).

The logics $\mathcal{L}_{core}$ and $\mathcal{L}_{cp}$ differ only with respect to the modal operators they employ. These operators are logically akin to the diamond operators that represent possibility in the alethic modal logics familiar from formal semantics. Each is written in the form $\langle \pi \rangle$ (the angle brackets are intended to convey a visual suggestion of the diamond $\diamond$). The 'box' modalities are used as well, and as usual they are defined in terms of the diamond ones: $[\pi]\phi$ (with the square brackets visually suggesting the box $\square$) abbreviates $\neg\langle\pi\rangle\neg\phi$.

$\mathcal{L}_{core}$ is a logic with eight modal operators, the two in $\mathcal{L}_B$ plus their inverses, and operators corresponding to the ancestrals of all four:

(6) $\mathcal{L}_{core}$ modal operators: $\rightarrow$ $\leftarrow$ $\uparrow$ $\downarrow$ $\rightarrow^*$ $\leftarrow^*$ $\uparrow^*$ $\downarrow^*$

$\mathcal{L}_{core}$ permits not only statements like $\langle \downarrow \rangle \phi$, meaning that at one dominance step down there is a node where ϕ holds, but also $\langle \downarrow^* \rangle \phi$, which corresponds to the ancestral of the relation that $\downarrow$ corresponds to: it means that there is some finite number k such that at k dominance steps down there is a node where ϕ holds. Thus, $\langle \downarrow^* \rangle \phi$ means that either ϕ holds ($k=0$), or $\langle \downarrow \rangle \phi$ holds ($k=1$), or $\langle \downarrow \rangle \langle \downarrow \rangle \phi$ holds ($k=2$), and so on for all $k \geq 0$.

The logic $\mathcal{L}_{cp}$ has an infinite set of modalities. They are defined recursively. All modalities from $\mathcal{L}_{core}$ are available in $\mathcal{L}_{cp}$, but it has additional modalities that cannot be defined using those modalities. The following four simple operators are included (as in $\mathcal{L}_{core}$):

(7) $\mathcal{L}_{cp}$ basic modal operators: $\rightarrow$ $\leftarrow$ $\uparrow$ $\downarrow$

But in addition, for any modal operator π and any formula ϕ, the following are both modal operators in $\mathcal{L}_{cp}$:

(8) Recursively defined modal operators of $\mathcal{L}_{cp}$:

  π^* for each modal operator π
  $\pi; \phi?$ for each modal operator π and formula ϕ

As in the case of the $\langle \downarrow^* \rangle \phi$ modality of $\mathcal{L}_{core}$, the π^* operators afford access to the ancestral of the accessibility relation for π: the formula $\langle \pi^* \rangle \phi$ is satisfied at a node u iff ϕ holds at a node v that you can get to from u via a sequence of zero or more steps mediated by the R_π relation.

The interpretation of $\langle \pi; \phi? \rangle$ needs a little more explanation. Intuitively, evaluating $\langle \pi; \phi? \rangle \psi$ involves checking that ψ holds at a node that we can get to using π and at which ϕ holds. The two examples in (9) will help.

(9) a. $\langle \downarrow; \phi? \rangle \psi$
     b. $\langle (\downarrow; \phi?)^* \rangle \psi$

Formula (9a) can be read as 'at some child of this node where ϕ is true, ψ is true'. This is equivalent to $\langle \downarrow \rangle (\phi \wedge \psi)$, and thus would also be expressible in $\mathcal{L}_{core}$. But the same is not true of (9b). For (9b) to be satisfied at a node u, there has to be a node v, dominated by u, at which ψ is true, and additionally ϕ has to be true at all nodes on the path from u to v. Notice that the asterisk is on '$(\downarrow; \phi?)$', so what is repeated is both the step down from parent to child and the check on whether ϕ holds. There has to be a parent–child chain in which at every node the check to see if ϕ holds is successful, and it has to lead down to a node where ψ holds. This relation is inexpressible in $\mathcal{L}_{core}$.

Notice the potential applications of a formula like (9b) in describing syntactic facts in human languages. It has been suggested for various syntactic phenomena that they are permitted only within the region between the top and bottom of an unbounded dependency (see Zaenen 1983). Such phenomena could be described with a statement using $\langle(\downarrow;\phi?)^*\rangle\psi$, where ψ is the property of being a trace and ϕ, holding at all the nodes on the spine leading down to the node where ψ holds, is the property that determines the relevant phenomena.

11.2.3 Trees as models for modal logics

We can identify a labelled tree with a tree model in the following sense. A *binary tree model* is a pair $\mathcal{M} = \langle T, \text{Val} \rangle$ where T is a tree structure and Val is a *valuation function* – a function from formulas to node sets which assigns to each atomic formula the set of all and only those nodes in the tree at which it holds.

So, to complete our example, assume that we have atomic formulas **S, NP, VP, D,**..., and thus the binary tree model corresponding to the example in (1) would contain a valuation Val such that Val(**NP**) = {0}, Val(**V**) = {10}, etc.

The remaining thing we need is a definition of the satisfaction relation. We write '$\mathcal{M}, v \vDash \phi$' for 'the model $\mathcal{M}$, at the node v, *satisfies* (or, *is a model of*) the formula ϕ.' We define the relation ⊨ in the following standard way.

(10) For a model $\mathcal{M}$, a node v of $\mathcal{M}$, and a formula ϕ:

    a. $\mathcal{M}, v \vDash p \Leftrightarrow v \in \text{Val}(p)$
       (v satisfies atomic formula p iff v is in the set Val assigns to p)
    b. $\mathcal{M}, v \vDash \phi \wedge \psi \Leftrightarrow \mathcal{M}, v \vDash \phi \wedge \mathcal{M}, v \vDash \psi$
       (v satisfies a conjunction iff it satisfies both conjuncts)
    c. $\mathcal{M}, v \vDash \neg\phi \Leftrightarrow \mathcal{M}, v \nvDash \phi$
       (v satisfies the negation of any formula that it does not satisfy)

As is familiar from alethic modal logic, evaluating a formula containing a modality always involves an accessibility relation that defines permitted access from one state or node to another in the model. Given that both $\mathcal{L}_{core}$ and $\mathcal{L}_{cp}$ have multiple modalities, each modality $\langle\pi\rangle$ will have a corresponding accessibility relation R_π:

(11) $\mathcal{M}, v \vDash \langle\pi\rangle\phi \Leftrightarrow \exists u[(v,u) \in R_\pi \wedge \mathcal{M}, u \vDash \phi]$
      (v satisfies $\langle\pi\rangle\phi$ iff it bears the π relation to a node u that satisfies ϕ)

Given our discussion of $R_\downarrow$ and $R_\rightarrow$ in Section 11.2.1 above, it is fairly straightforward to get a sense of the accessibility relations for the modalities in $\mathcal{L}_{core}$. The accessibility relations for the modalities in $\mathcal{L}_{cp}$ are more complex, and will be omitted here (but the details are in Moss and Tiede 2007).

11.2.4 *Definability*

In order to relate the model-theoretic approach to the generative approach, we need a model-theoretic notion that corresponds to the set of derived structures in the former approach. We will restrict the set of atomic formulas, denoted by F, to be finite. Atomic formulas will be used to represent features. We will denote the set of trees that are labelled only with the features from the set F by $\mathcal{T}^F$, and for the set of formulas in the logic $\mathcal{L}$ that only use the atomic formulas from the set F we will write $\mathcal{L}^F$.

We say that a subset of $\mathcal{T}^F$ is *definable* in $\mathcal{L}$ if there is a formula in $\mathcal{L}^F$ such that the subset in question is exactly the set of all those trees which at their root nodes satisfy the formula. What it means to say that some set $\mathcal{T} \subseteq \mathcal{T}^F$ is definable in $\mathcal{L}$ is simply that there is some $\phi \in \mathcal{L}$ such that $\mathcal{T} = \{\tau \mid \tau, \varepsilon \models \phi\}$ (that is, $\mathcal{T}$ is the set of all and only those trees which at the root node satisfy ϕ).

As an example of how grammars of certain specific types can be formalized in certain specific logics, it is worth noting – with an informally sketched proof – that despite its very limited expressive power, $\mathcal{L}_{core}$ is capable of defining the set of all the parse trees obtainable from an arbitrary context-free phrase structure grammar (CF-PSG).

(12) **Theorem** For any context-free phrase structure grammar G there is a formula ϕ_G in $\mathcal{L}_{core}$ that defines the set of all parse trees of G.

Proof Let the terminals, non-terminals, rules, and start symbol of G be respectively V_T, V_N, P, and S. Since we are only considering binary branching trees (it is not hard to generalize the result to n-ary branching), every rule in P is of the form $A \rightarrow BC$ or $A \rightarrow a$, with $A, B, C \in V_N$ and $a \in V_T$. The effects of such rules can be encoded directly in $\mathcal{L}_{core}$ as follows.

The set of formulas covering the binary branching rules contains for each symbol A appearing on the left-hand side of a branching rule a statement '$A \Rightarrow \Psi$', where Ψ is a disjunction that for each rule $A \rightarrow BC$ contains a disjunct of this for

(13) $\langle\downarrow\rangle(\mathbf{B} \wedge \langle\rightarrow\rangle\mathbf{C})$

So if the only rules with VP on the left of the arrow were (i) VP $\rightarrow$ V$_1$, (ii) VP $\rightarrow$ V$_2$ NP, and (iii) VP $\rightarrow$ V$_3$ Clause, the corresponding logical statement would contain a statement that in effect says this: 'If **VP** holds at a node then either (i) $\mathbf{V_1}$ holds at a child node that has no right sibling, or (ii) $\mathbf{V_2}$ holds at a child node that has a right sibling where **NP** holds, or (iii) $\mathbf{V_3}$ holds at a child node that has a right sibling where **Clause** holds.'

To this we add, for each A that appears on the left-hand side of a unary rule, a statement $\mathbf{A} \Rightarrow \Psi$, where Ψ is a disjunction with disjuncts of the form $\langle\downarrow\rangle\mathbf{a}$, one for each a such that $A \to a$.

This much ensures that the models of ϕ_G comply with the restrictions that the rules impose on parse trees of G. The rest of what we need to do is to ensure that *only* parse trees of G are models of ϕ_G (from what has been said so far, there could be other models of ϕ_G with all sorts of labellings about which the rules say nothing, and they could vacuously satisfy the statements summarized above). This we accomplish by adding four further statements.

First, we affirm that node labels are unique – at each node exactly one propositional symbol is true – by stating that at every node some proposition holds:

(14) $\quad [\downarrow^*](\mathbf{A_1} \vee \mathbf{A_2} \vee \ldots \vee \mathbf{A_n})\quad$ where $V_T \cup V_N = \{A_1, A_2, \ldots, A_n\}$

and we state that for all pairs of distinct propositions the negation of one of them holds:

(15) $\quad [\downarrow^*](\phi_1 \wedge \phi_2 \wedge \ldots \phi_k)\quad$ where $\phi_1, \ldots, \phi_k$ is the list of all statements of the form '$(\neg(\alpha) \vee \neg(\beta))$', for $\alpha, \beta \in V_T \cup V_N$ and $\alpha \neq \beta$

Second, we assert that the start symbol S is true at the root – that is, **S** must hold at any node where not even the dummy tautology $\top$ holds at the immediately dominating node:

(16) $\quad [\uparrow]\neg(\top) \Rightarrow \mathbf{S}$

Third, we stipulate that the terminal symbols are true only at leaves – that wherever a terminal symbol holds, not even the dummy tautology holds at any immediately dominated node thereof (which means there cannot be one):

(17) $\quad [\downarrow^*]\Phi$, where Φ is the conjunction
$\quad\quad (\mathbf{a_1} \Rightarrow \neg\langle\downarrow\rangle\top) \wedge (\mathbf{a_2} \Rightarrow \neg\langle\downarrow\rangle\top) \wedge \ldots \wedge (\mathbf{a_k} \Rightarrow \neg\langle\downarrow\rangle\top)$ for all $a_i \in V_T$.

Fourth, we assert that non-terminal symbols are true only at internal nodes – that wherever a non-terminal holds, the dummy tautology holds at the immediately dominated node (which means there must be one).

(18) $[\downarrow^*]\Phi$, where Φ is the conjunction
$(\mathbf{A}_1 \Rightarrow \langle\downarrow\rangle\top) \wedge (\mathbf{A}_2 \Rightarrow \langle\downarrow\rangle\top) \wedge \ldots \wedge (\mathbf{A}_k \Rightarrow \langle\downarrow\rangle\top)$
for all $A_i \in V_N$.

This guarantees that any model of the complex formula we have constructed will be a parse tree of G, which completes the proof.

11.3 Features

The trees considered so far are labelled with atomic category labels, represented in the description logic as atomic formulas with the property that each node satisfies exactly one of them. If we want to label trees with features, we have to extend the approach presented above. One easy way to include features is to allow each node to satisfy *multiple* atomic formulas. That way, each atomic formula corresponds to a binary valued feature: if some feature F holds at a node, that node is [+F], and if it is false, the node is [−F].

We can use the approach to represent non-binary features too, as long as it is combined with some formulas limiting their co-occurrence. Thus we could represent the BAR feature in a two-bar system by means of three features, call them BAR0, BAR1, and BAR2. It is easy to assert what the GPSG literature calls a feature co-occurrence restriction – a statement of the type exemplified in (15) – saying that one and only one of these features is true at each node ('**bar0** $\Rightarrow$ ($\neg$**bar1** $\wedge$ $\neg$**bar2**)', and so on).

To give an example of the use of $\mathcal{L}_{cp}$, consider the following formalization of projection from heads, based on Palm (1999). We first introduce an abbreviation meaning 'the feature F belongs to a node that is a head', where (for this purpose) we treat being a head as simply a matter of bearing an atomic feature, corresponding to the atomic proposition **head**, with the statement $H\phi \equiv \phi \wedge$ **head**.

Then we define what it is for a feature ϕ to be projected from a leaf:

(19) Proj $\phi \equiv \langle(\downarrow; (H\phi))^*\rangle(H\phi \wedge$ **lexical**)

Here **lexical** is just an abbreviation for '$\langle\downarrow\rangle\neg(\langle\downarrow\rangle\top)$'.

Finally, we can require every node to be a projection: given a finite set of lexical features Lex, we assert $[\downarrow^*]\Phi$, where Φ is the disjunction of all the statements Proj ϕ such that ϕ is in Lex.

The feature indicating that a node is the head would be needed in cases where two siblings shared the same lexical feature. Furthermore, there are certain regularities that this head feature has to observe, such as that (if we set aside the multiple-heads treatment of coordination argued for in some GPSG work) no two siblings may both be heads, a condition that we could state thus:

(20) [↓*](**head** ⇒ ¬(⟨←⟩**head** ∨ ⟨→⟩**head**))

11.3.1 Eliminable features

The clearest sense in which a feature can be considered intuitively superfluous is when one can eliminate it from the grammar without any loss to the description. Given a tree $\tau \in \mathcal{T}^F$ and a subset of features $G \subseteq F$, there is a corresponding tree $\tau' \in \mathcal{T}^G$ that is the result of removing the features in $F - G$ from τ. We will denote the corresponding function by $\hat{\pi}$; thus $\hat{\pi}(\tau) = \tau'$, and define $\hat{\pi}(\mathcal{T})$ as $\{\hat{\pi}(\tau) \mid \tau \in \mathcal{T}\}$.

The notion of a feature being superfluous, in the sense that it can be eliminated without loss to the description, can now be formalized by means of the following definition:

(21) Let F be a finite set of features, $G \subseteq F$, $\mathcal{T} \subseteq \mathcal{T}^F$, and $\mathcal{L}$ a logic. Suppose that $\mathcal{T}$ is definable in $\mathcal{L}^F$. We say that G is *eliminable in $\mathcal{L}$ for $\mathcal{T}$* iff $\hat{\pi}(\mathcal{T})$ is definable in $\mathcal{L}^{F-G}$.

Notice that this notion of eliminability is relative to a given logic: the features in G are eliminable in some language $\mathcal{L}$ with respect to some set of trees $\mathcal{T}$ if and only if the function that gets rid of the G features is definable in $\mathcal{L}$ without using any G features. This might hold for some particular $\mathcal{L}$ but not in another metalanguage. In other words, questions of whether some feature is truly needed cannot be addressed in isolation but only in the context of a particular descriptive metalanguage in which the feature is used. This observation is made more precise in the following theorem:

(22) **Theorem** (Tiede 2008) Any tree language that is not definable in $\mathcal{L}_{core}$ but is definable in $\mathcal{L}_{cp}$ can be defined with additional features in $\mathcal{L}_{core}$ that are not eliminable in $\mathcal{L}_{core}$.

This theorem could actually be strengthened, as its proof (for which see Tiede 2008) does not depend on any of the logics in particular. It applies to any case of two different formal ways of defining sets of trees, each capable of defining all local sets (those that a CF-PSG can define), and one defining a proper subset of the tree-sets definable by the other, provided they are not more powerful than wMSO. For any set $\mathcal{T}$ of trees definable in the more powerful formalism but not in the less powerful one, $\mathcal{T}$ will be definable in the less powerful formalism if we are permitted to decorate its nodes with additional features.

These results can be read in two different ways. First, they state that any language that cannot be defined in a weaker formalism but can in a stronger one can be defined in the weaker one if additional features are added. Conversely, they state that the only difference between the different formalisms mentioned above, as well as a variety of other formalisms, is which features are required to define languages: the more expressive the formalism, the fewer features are required for defining languages.

When we move to the most powerful of the logics commonly used in model theoretic syntax, wMSO, a single feature suffices. This follows from the fact that wMSO characterizes the tree-sets that are recognizable by finite-state tree automata (Doner 1970). These tree-sets are known as the *regular* tree-sets (or 'regular tree languages'). The set of all regular tree-sets is known to be closed under linear tree homomorphisms, which means that any systematic symbol-for-symbol relabelling of all the nodes in all the trees of a regular tree-set will always yield a regular tree-set.

To make this clearer, imagine a finite-state tree automaton that recognizes some set of trees with all nodes labelled by either A or B. Suppose we wanted to relabel the B nodes as A nodes without losing track of which were the original A nodes. We can simply modify the automaton so it has two different states for admitting A nodes: one in effect corresponding to 'original A node', and the other to 'relabelled B node'. Since *any* finite-state tree automaton is equivalent to a wMSO logical description (Doner 1970), there is a wMSO theory that corresponds to the new automaton.

So consider in this light the question of whether the SLASH feature of GPSG and HPSG is a genuine substantive element of the grammars of human languages. A node dominated by a category α is marked with a feature specification [SLASH:β] in GPSG in order to identify it as containing a β extraction site. This eliminates any need for movement transformations in the description of unbounded dependencies (Gazdar 1981), as seen in (23), where we simplify visually by notating α[SLASH:β] in the form α/β.

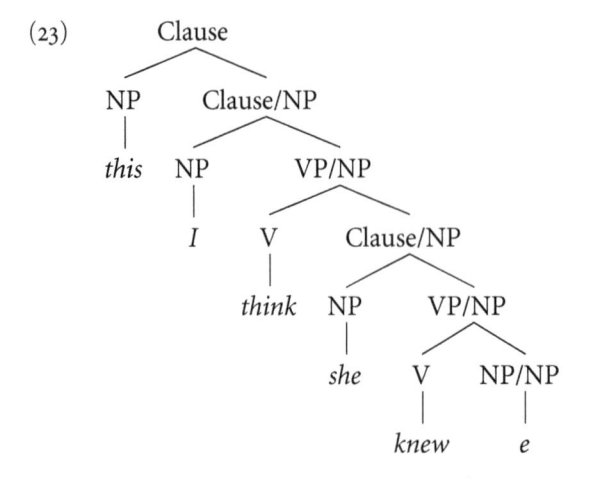

(23)
```
              Clause
             /      \
           NP      Clause/NP
           |       /       \
         this    NP       VP/NP
                 |        /    \
                 I       V    Clause/NP
                         |     /       \
                       think  NP     VP/NP
                              |      /    \
                             she    V    NP/NP
                                    |      |
                                  knew     e
```

It might be charged that this simply substitutes another formal device for the formal device of movement: instead of the NP *this* being moved from an NP position to another NP position as sibling of a Clause node, it is a sister of a Clause/NP node that dominates a chain of α/NP nodes that leads to an NP/NP node at what would have been the pre-movement location. The chain of slash categories marks the path from the root of the landing-site constituent down to the extraction site. So is the feature SLASH artefactual, rather than corresponding to a genuine syntactic property of constituents?

Our thesis is that the answer is neither yes nor no. The question is a pseudo-question, insufficiently well defined to receive an answer.

11.3.2 *Inessential features*

Given that the question whether a feature is eliminable depends on the formalism employed, it is only natural to try to give a purely structural definition of uselessness applying to features. Marcus Kracht (1997) has proposed such a definition. Kracht called a feature *inessential* 'if its distribution is fixed by the other features', and he proposed the following formal definition.

(24) Let *F* be a finite set of features; let *G* be a subset of *F*; and let *T* be a set of trees labelled with the features in *F*. The features in *G* are **inessential for** *T* if the function that eliminates the features in *G* is one-to-one.

The reason for identifying superfluous features with those that can be eliminated by a one-to-one (injective) function is that no two trees can be distinguished only with these features. If they could, the function that eliminates them would map them to the same tree, hence it would not be one-to-one.

The features referred to in the theorem in (22) are inessential in exactly Kracht's sense. And this might seem to conform to the intuition that when a feature is added solely to make a non-definable set of structures definable, it has an ad hoc nature. When there is a distinction in tree structure that we are unable to capture using a given logic, and we add a special feature to certain nodes in certain trees just to enable the distinction to be captured using that logic, erasing the feature we added would just give us back our original trees. They would not be identical with any other trees in the set because, if they were, we would not have needed to add the feature annotations in the first place.

An example due to Thatcher and used by Rogers (1998: 60) will be useful in making the point. Consider the set of all finite binary trees in which all nodes are labelled *A* except that in each tree exactly one node is labelled *B*. This set of trees is not definable in $\mathcal{L}_{core}$, or by any CF-PSG. But we can make it describable if we add a feature. We will assume that its presence or absence can be explicitly referenced at any node, and we will indicate its presence by '˅'. We annotate a tree like (25a) as shown in (25b).

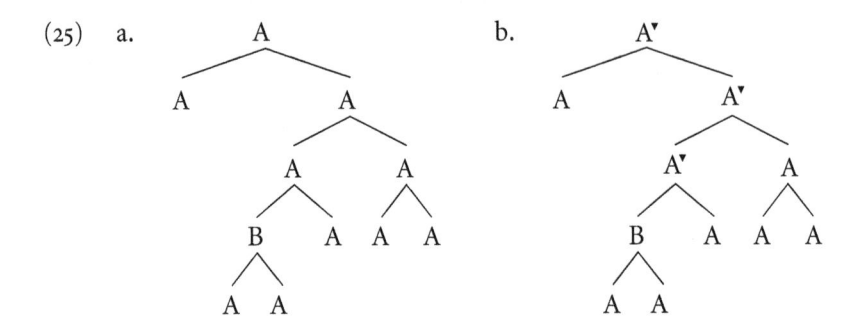

(25) a. [tree with root A, internal nodes A, leaves including B dominating A A] b. [tree with root A˅, with A˅ nodes dominating B]

The '˅' feature is attached to every A node that dominates the unique B, and to no other node. This allows us to describe the set with a CF-PSG, using $A^˅$ as the start symbol:

(26) $A^˅ \rightarrow AA^˅$ $\quad A^˅ \rightarrow AB$ $\quad A \rightarrow AA$
 $A^˅ \rightarrow A^˅A$ $\quad A^˅ \rightarrow BA$ $\quad B \rightarrow AA$

By the theorem in (12) we know that the set of trees this grammar generates is describable in $\mathcal{L}_{core}$. However, if we erase the ˅ feature from every tree, we will get exactly the set mentioned above: in every tree there will be one B and all other nodes will be labelled A. Yet no two distinct trees will ever be collapsed into one under this ˅-erasure operation. Therefore the ˅ feature is inessential in Kracht's technical sense.

Both the SLASH feature of GSPG and the BAR feature familiar from X-bar syntax are inessential in exactly the same way. The feature SLASH works in a way almost exactly analogous to '˅' above: a constituent containing a gap is marked by placing a specification of a value for SLASH on the root of the constituent and on each node in the continuous sequence of nodes from the root downwards, that dominate the gap.

The BAR feature is also (as Kracht notes) inessential. To see this intuitively, imagine being presented with a tree from, say, Jackendoff (1977), with all of the bar-level indications removed. It would be easy to put them all back without error, given the content of the X-bar principles that Kornai and Pullum (1990) call Lexicality, Uniformity, Succession, and Weak Maximality, plus the observation that Jackendoff simplifies his diagrams in certain respects (specifically, a branch of the form X‴—X″—X′—X—σ will be shown as X‴—σ). Stripping the primes from Jackendoff's trees never collapses a legal tree into the prime-stripped version of another legal tree. (This might not be true for every version of X-bar theory.)

It would be most desirable if the notion 'inessential' were diagnostic for features that are spurious in the sense of being linguists' artefacts. Unfortunately, things do not work out this way. Many features that linguists probably would not want to eliminate are inessential under this definition, and many features of which they would be suspicious are not inessential.

Take the feature CASE in a language with a simple Nom vs. Acc contrast, for example. In many such languages no two trees will be distinguished on the basis of this feature distinction, as its distribution will be fixed by other aspects of the trees: an NP functioning as Subject in a tensed Clause will take the Nom value and an NP functioning as Object will take Acc, and so on. In such a case the morphosyntactic feature CASE will be inessential.

At first, it might seem that any feature appearing on lexical category labels would be inessential in Kracht's sense, but this is not so. Counter-intuitively, features are essential when they are *optional* on a node. Consider AUX in English. Any 'subject-aux inversion' clause will predictably have AUX on the initial verb. So will any tree with a verb form ending in the suffix *n't*. But take a dialect where both *We haven't enough milk* and *We don't have enough milk* are grammatical. In such dialects, possession **have** is optionally [+AUX]. So all three of these trees should be well formed (the V in the third is [−AUX]):

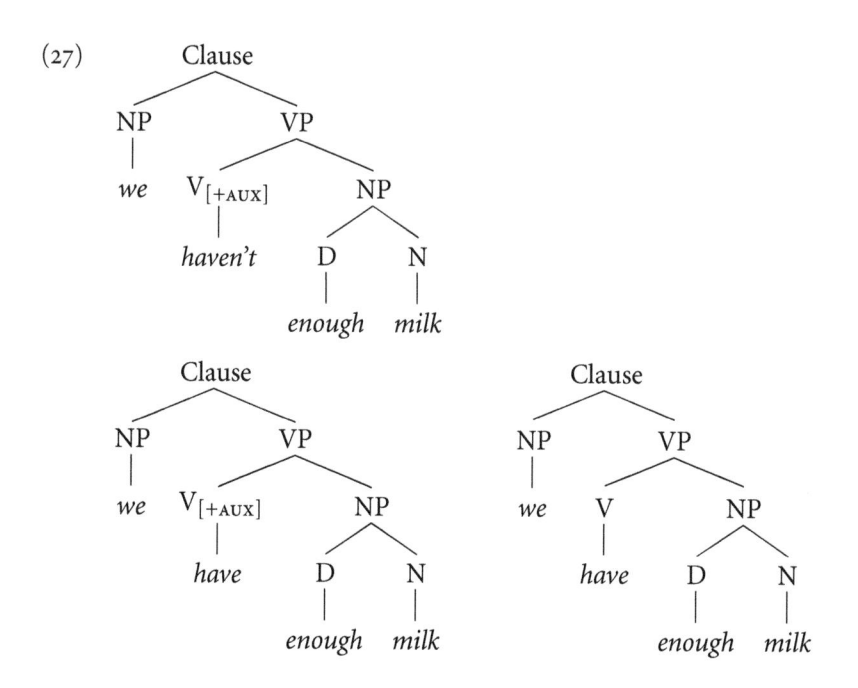

(27)

```
        Clause
       /      \
      NP      VP
      |      /  \
      we   V[+AUX]  NP
             |     /  \
          haven't  D   N
                  |   |
                enough milk
```

```
        Clause                    Clause
       /      \                  /      \
      NP      VP                NP      VP
      |      /  \               |      /  \
      we   V[+AUX]  NP          we    V    NP
             |     /  \               |   /  \
           have   D   N              have D   N
                  |   |                   |   |
                enough milk             enough milk
```

The second and third of these trees will be collapsed if the [±AUX] markings are erased. Solely because of this, AUX counts as an essential feature. Yet of course, on the second and third of the trees in (27) its presence is intuitively quite unimportant: because the verb is not in one of the auxiliary-only *n't* forms, and is not before the subject, it simply does not matter whether it bears the marking [+AUX] or not. Though essential in the technical sense, it is entirely superfluous in the intuitive descriptive sense.

In short, Kracht's notion of being essential – the contrary of being inessential – does not correspond at all to the descriptive linguist's notion of being an essential or significant component of a description.

11.4 Conclusions

We have argued that it is highly unlikely that any formal reconstruction can be given of the intuitive notion of a feature that is a technical artefact rather than a genuine element of natural language structure that we should expect to turn up in some guise in any reasonable description. There is a crucial trade-off between eliminability of features and expressive power of the descriptive metalanguage; the two issues cannot be separated.

Thus, just like the question of when a feature used in the description of one language should be equated with a feature used in the description of another, the issue of when a feature is a technical trick and when it is a properly motivated distinguishing property of linguistic expressions will not, we suspect, be reducible to any formal criterion. It may perhaps be approached informally through an understanding of what natural languages are typically like, but it will not submit to an authoritative mathematical adjudication.

Philosophy of linguistics, like any other branch of the philosophy of science, is just not going to be that easy.

References

Abney, Steven P. (1987). *The English Noun Phrase in Its Sentential Aspect*. PhD thesis, MIT, Cambridge, MA.

Ackerman, Farrell and Gregory Stump (2004). 'Paradigms and periphrastic expressions', in Louisa Sadler and Andrew Spencer (eds) *Projecting Morphology* (Stanford Studies in Morphology and the Lexicon). Stanford, CA: CSLI Publications, 111–157.

—— —— and Gert Webelhuth (forthcoming). 'Lexicalism, periphrasis and implicative morphology', in Bob Borsley and Kersti Börjars (eds) *Nontransformational Syntax: A Guide to Current Models*. Oxford: Blackwell.

Adger, David (2003). *Core Syntax*. Oxford: Oxford University Press.

—— (2006). 'Remarks on Minimalist feature theory and Move', *Journal of Linguistics* 42: 663–673.

—— (2007). 'Three domains of finiteness: a Minimalist perspective', in Irina Nikolaeva (ed.) *Finiteness. Theoretical and Empirical Foundations*. Oxford: Oxford University Press, 23–58.

—— and Daniel Harbour (2007). 'The syntax and syncretisms of the person case constraint', *Syntax* 10(1): 2–37.

—— —— and Laurel Watkins (2009). *Mirrors and Microparameters: Phrase Structure beyond Free Word Order*. Cambridge: Cambridge University Press.

—— and Gillian Ramchand (2005). 'Move and Merge: *wh*-dependencies revisited', *Linguistic Inquiry* 36: 161–194.

—— and Peter Svenonius (2009). 'Features in Minimalist syntax', ms available as lingBuzz/000825. To appear in Cedric Boeckx (ed.) *The Oxford Handbook of Linguistic Minimalism*. Oxford: Oxford University Press.

Afanasiev, Loredana, Patrick Blackburn, Ioanna Dimitriou, Bertrand Gaiffe, Evan Goris, Maarten Marx, and Maarten de Rijke (2005). 'PDL for ordered trees', *Journal of Applied Non-Classical Logic* 15(2): 115–135.

Aikhenvald, Alexandra (2006). 'Serial verb constructions in typological perspective', in Alexandra Aikhenvald and Robert M. W. Dixon (eds) *Serial Verb Constructions: A Cross-Linguistic Typology*. Oxford: Oxford University Press, 1–68.

Alexiadou, Artemis (2005). 'Possessors and (in)definiteness', *Lingua* 115(6): 787–819.

Allegranza, Valerio (1998). 'Determiners as functors: NP structure in Italian', in Sergio Balari and Luca Dini (eds) *Romance in Head-Driven Phrase Structure Grammar*. Stanford, CA: CSLI Publications, 55–108.

—— (2007). *The Signs of Determination*. Frankfurt am Main: Peter Lang.

Anderson, Gregory D. S. (2006). *Auxiliary Verb Constructions*. Oxford: Oxford University Press.

Anderson, Stephen R. (1992). *A-Morphous Morphology*. Cambridge: Cambridge University Press.

Andrews, Avery D. (1996). 'Semantic case-stacking and inside-out unification', *Australian Journal of Linguistics* 16(1): 1–54.

Archangeli, Diana (1984). *Underspecification in Yawelmani Phonology and Morphology*. PhD thesis, MIT, Cambridge, MA.

Aristar Dry, Helen (2002). 'E-MELD: overview and update'. Paper presented at the International Workshop on Resources and Tools in Field Linguistics, Las Palmas, 26–27 May 2002. Available at: http://linguistlist.org/emeld/documents/index.cfm.

Aronoff, Mark (1994). *Morphology by Itself: Stems and Inflectional Classes*. Cambridge, MA: MIT Press.

Aronson, Howard I. (1968). *Bulgarian Inflectional Morphophonology*. The Hague: Mouton.

Asudeh, Ash (2002). 'Richard III', in Mary Andronis, Erin Debenport, Anne Pycha, and Keiko Yoshimura (eds) *CLS 38: Papers from the 38th Regional Meeting of the Chicago Linguistic Society*. Chicago, IL: Chicago Linguistic Society. 18 pp.

—— and Ida Toivonen (2006a). 'Symptomatic imperfections', *Journal of Linguistics* 42: 395–422.

—— —— (2006b). 'Response to David Adger's "Remarks on Minimalist feature theory and Move"', *Journal of Linguistics* 42: 675–686.

Avery, Peter and William J. Idsardi (2001). 'Laryngeal dimensions, completion and enhancement', in T. Alan Hall (ed.) *Distinctive Feature Theory*. Berlin: Mouton de Gruyter, 41–70.

Avgustinova, Tania (1994). 'On Bulgarian verbal clitics', *Journal of Slavic Linguistics* 2: 29–47.

Baerman, Matthew, Dunstan Brown, and Greville G. Corbett (2005). *The Syntax–Morphology Interface: A Study of Syncretism*. Cambridge: Cambridge University Press.

Baker, Brett and Mark Harvey (2010). 'Complex predicate formation', in Menigstu Amberber, Brett Baker, and Mark Harvey (eds) *Complex Predicates: Cross-Linguistic Perspectives on Event Structure*. Cambridge: Cambridge University Press.

Barlow, Michael (1992). *A Situated Theory of Agreement*. New York: Garland. [Published version of (1988) PhD thesis, Stanford University.]

Barwise, Jon and Robin Cooper (1981). 'Generalized quantifiers and natural language', *Linguistics and Philosophy* 4: 159–219.

Béjar, Susana (2003). *Phi-Syntax: A Theory of Agreement*. PhD thesis, University of Toronto.

Bender, Emily and Dan Flickinger (1999). 'Peripheral constructions and core phenomena: agreement in tag questions', in Gert Webelhuth, Jean-Pierre Koenig, and Andreas Kathol (eds) *Lexical and Constructional Aspects of Linguistic Explanation*. Stanford, CA: CSLI Publications, 199–214.

Berman, Ruth (1985). 'The acquisition of Hebrew', in Dan I. Slobin (ed.) *The Crosslinguistic Study of Language Acquisition*. Hillsdale, NJ: Lawrence Erlbaum, 255–371.

Bhatt, Rajesh (2005). 'Long distance agreement in Hindi-Urdu', *Natural Language and Linguistic Theory* 23(4): 757–807.

Blackburn, Patrick and Claire Gardent (1995). 'A specification language for lexical functional grammars', in *Seventh Conference of the European Chapter of the Association for Computational Linguistics: Proceedings of the Conference*. Morristown, NJ: European Association for Computational Linguistics, 39–44.

—— —— and Wilfried Meyer-Viol (1993). 'Talking about trees', in *Sixth Conference of the European Chapter of the Association for Computational Linguistics: Proceedings of the Conference*. Morristown, NJ: European Association for Computational Linguistics, 21–29.

—— Maarten de Rijke, and Yde Venema (2001). *Modal Logic*. Cambridge: Cambridge University Press.

Blake, Barry (1994). *Case*. Cambridge: Cambridge University Press.

Blevins, James (2006). 'Features and feature structures', in Keith Brown (ed.) *Encyclopedia of Language and Linguistics. Second Edition. Volume 12*. Oxford: Elsevier, 390–393.

—— (forthcoming). 'Periphrasis as syntactic exponence', in Farrell Ackerman, James Blevins, and Gregory Stump (eds) *Paradigms and Periphrasis*. Stanford, CA: CSLI Publications.

Bobaljik, Jonathan (1995). *Morphosyntax: On the Syntax of Verbal Inflection*. PhD thesis, MIT, Cambridge, MA.

Booij, Geert (1994). 'Against split morphology', in Geert Booij and Jaap van Marle (eds) *Yearbook of Morphology 1993*. Dordrecht: Kluwer Academic Publishers, 27–49.

—— (1996). 'Inherent versus contextual inflection and the split morphology hypothesis', in Geert Booij and Jaap van Marle (eds) *Yearbook of Morphology 1995*. Dordrecht: Kluwer Academic Publishers, 1–15.

Borer, Hagit (1999). 'Deconstructing the construct', in Kyle Johnson and Ian Roberts (eds) *Beyond Principles and Parameters*. Dordrecht: Kluwer Academic Publishers, 43–89.

—— (2005). *Structuring Sense*. Oxford: Oxford University Press.

—— (2009). 'Afro-Asiatic, Semitic: Hebrew [compounds]', in Rochelle Lieber and Pavol Stekauer (eds) *The Oxford Handbook of Compounding*. Oxford: Oxford University Press, 491–511.

Börjars, Kersti, Nigel Vincent, and Carol Chapman (1997). 'Paradigms, periphrases and pronominal inflection', in Geert Booij and Jaap van Marle (eds) *Yearbook of Morphology 1996*. Dordrecht: Kluwer Academic Publishers, 155–180.

Bos, Johan and Katja Markert (2005). 'Recognising textual entailment with logical inference techniques', in *Proceedings of Human Language Technology Conference and Conference on Empirical Methods in Natural Language Processing (HLT/EMNLP 2005)*, Vancouver, Canada, 6–8 October 2005. Association for Computational Linguistics, 628–635.

Bošković, Željko (2001). *On the Nature of the Syntax–Phonology Interface: Cliticization and Related Phenomena*. Amsterdam: Elsevier.

Bouma, Gosse, Rob Malouf, and Ivan A. Sag (2001). 'Satisfying constraints on extraction and adjunction', *Natural Language and Linguistic Theory* 19: 1–65.

Brody, Michael (1997). 'Perfect chains', in Liliane Haegeman (ed.) *Elements of Grammar: Handbook of Generative Syntax*. Dordrecht: Kluwer Academic Publishers, 139–167.

—— (2000). 'Mirror theory: syntactic representation in perfect syntax', *Linguistic Inquiry* 31(1): 29–56.

Broe, Michael B. (1993). *Specification Theory: The Treatment of Redundancy in Generative Phonology*. PhD thesis, University of Edinburgh.

Bronnenberg, Wim, Harry Bunt, Jan Landsbergen, Remko Scha, Wijnand Schoenmakers, and Eric van Utteren (1980). 'The question-answering system PHLIQA1', in Leonard Bolc (ed.) *Natural Language Question Answering Systems*. Munich and Vienna: Hanser; London: Macmillan, 217–305.

Brown, Dunstan (1998). 'Defining "subgender": virile and devirilized nouns in Polish', *Lingua* 104: 187–233.

—— (2007). 'Peripheral functions and overdifferentiation: the Russian second locative', *Russian Linguistics* 31(1): 61–76.

Butt, Miriam, Tracy Holloway King, María-Eugenia Niño, and Frédérique Segond (1999). *A Grammar Writer's Cookbook*. Stanford, CA: CSLI Publications.

Bybee, Joan (1985). *Morphology: A Study of the Relation between Meaning and Form*. Amsterdam: John Benjamins.

—— (2002). 'Word frequency and context of use in the lexical diffusion of phonetically conditioned sound change', *Language Variation and Change* 14: 261–290.

Cable, Seth (2007). 'Q-particles and the nature of wh-fronting', ms, MIT, Cambridge, MA.

Caha, Pavel (2007). 'The shape of paradigms'. Paper presented at GLOW XXX, Tromsø, 11–14 April 2007.

Caponigro, Ivano and Maria Polinsky (2008). 'Relatively speaking (in Circassian)', in Natasha Abner and Jason Bishop (eds) *Proceedings of the 27th West Coast Conference on Formal Linguistics (WCCFL 27)*. Somerville, MA: Cascadilla Proceedings Project, 81–89.

Carpenter, Bob (1992). *The Logic of Typed Feature Structures: With Applications to Unification Grammars, Logic Programs and Constraint Resolution*. Cambridge: Cambridge University Press.

—— (2002). 'Constraint-based processing', in Lynn Nadel (ed.) *Encyclopedia of Cognitive Science I*. London: Nature Publishing Group, 800–804.

Carstairs-McCarthy, Andrew (1999). 'Category and feature', in Geert Booij, Christian Lehmann, and Joachim Mugdan (eds) *Morphology: An International Handbook on Inflection and Word-Formation*. Berlin: Walter de Gruyter, 264–272.

Chomsky, Noam (1965). *Aspects of the Theory of Syntax*. Cambridge, MA: MIT Press.

—— (1970). 'Remarks on nominalization', in Roderick A. Jacobs and Peter S. Rosenbaum (eds) *Readings in English Transformational Grammar*. Waltham, MA: Ginn and Co., 184–221.

—— (1993). 'A minimalist program for linguistic theory', in Kenneth Hale and Samuel Jay Keyser (eds) *The View from Building 20*. Cambridge, MA: MIT Press, 1–52.

—— (1995). *The Minimalist Program*. Cambridge, MA: MIT Press.

—— (2000). 'Minimalist inquiries: the framework', in Roger Martin, David Michaels, and Juan Uriagereka (eds) *Step by Step: Essays in Minimalist Syntax in Honor of Howard Lasnik*. Cambridge, MA: MIT Press, 89–155.

—— (2001). 'Derivation by phase', in Michael Kenstowicz (ed.) *Ken Hale: A Life in Language*. Cambridge, MA: MIT Press, 1–52.

—— (2008). 'On phases', in Robert Freidin, Carlos P. Otero, and Maria Luisa Zubizarreta (eds) *Foundational Issues in Linguistic Theory*. Cambridge, MA: MIT Press, 133–166.

—— and Morris Halle (1968). *The Sound Pattern of English*. New York, NY: Harper and Row.

Chumakina, Marina, Dunstan Brown, Harley Quilliam, and Greville G. Corbett (2007). *Slovar' arčinskogo jazyka (arčinsko-anglo-russkij)* [A dictionary of Archi: Archi-Russian-English]. Makhachkala: Delovoj Mir. Also available at: http://www.smg.surrey.ac.uk/.

—— Anna Kibort, and Greville G. Corbett (2007). 'Determining a language's feature inventory: person in Archi', in Peter K. Austin and Andrew Simpson (eds) *Endangered Languages* (Linguistische Berichte, Sonderheft 14). Hamburg: Helmut Buske, 143–172.

Chung, Sandra (1982). 'Unbounded dependencies in Chamorro grammar', *Linguistic Inquiry* 13: 39–77.

—— (1998). *The Design of Agreement: Evidence from Chamorro*. Chicago, IL: University of Chicago Press.

Chvany, Catherine V. (1986). 'Jakobson's fourth and fifth dimensions: on reconciling the cube model of case meanings with the two-dimensional matrices for case forms', in Richard D. Brecht and James Levine (eds) *Case in Slavic*. Columbus, OH: Slavica, 107–129.

Cinque, Guglielmo (1999). *The Syntax of Adverbs*. Oxford: Oxford University Press.

—— and Richard Kayne (2005). *The Oxford Handbook of Comparative Syntax*. Oxford: Oxford University Press.

Clark, Eve V. (1993). *The Lexicon in Acquisition*. Cambridge: Cambridge University Press.

Clements, George N. (1984). 'Binding domains in Kikuyu', *Studies in the Linguistic Sciences* 14: 37–56.

—— (1985). 'The geometry of phonological features', *Phonology Yearbook* 2: 225–252.

—— and Elizabeth V. Hume (1995). 'The internal organization of speech sounds', in John A. Goldsmith (ed.) *Handbook of Phonology*. Oxford: Blackwell, 245–306.

Collins, Chris (2002). 'Eliminating labels', in Samuel D. Epstein and T. Daniel Seely (eds) *Derivation and Explanation in the Minimalist Program*. Oxford: Blackwell, 42–64.

Colmerauer, Alain (1970). 'Les systèmes-q ou un formalisme pour analyser et *synthétiser* des phrases sur ordinateur'. Internal publication 43, Département d'informatique de l'Université de Montréal, September 1970.

Comrie, Bernard (1986). 'On delimiting cases', in Richard D. Brecht and James S. Levine (eds) *Case in Slavic*. Columbus, OH: Slavica, 86–106.

—— Martin Haspelmath, and Balthasar Bickel (2004). 'The Leipzig Glossing Rules'. Available at: http://www.eva.mpg.de/lingua/resources/glossing-rules.php [Revised 2008].

Copestake, Ann (1992). 'The representation of lexical semantic information', PhD thesis, University of Sussex. Published (1993) as *Cognitive Science Research Paper* 280, University of Sussex.

—— (1995). 'The representation of group denoting nouns in a lexical knowledge database', in Patrick Saint-Dizier and Evelyne Viegas (eds) *Computational Lexical Semantics*. Cambridge: Cambridge University Press, 207–230.

—— (2002). *Implementing Typed Feature Structure Grammars* (CSLI Lecture Notes 110). Stanford, CA: CSLI Publications.

—— Dan Flickinger, Ivan A. Sag, and Carl Pollard (2005). 'Minimal Recursion Semantics: an introduction', *Journal of Research on Language and Computation* 3(2–3): 281–332.

—— Alex Lascarides, and Dan Flickinger (2001). 'An algebra for semantic construction in constraint-based grammars', in *Proceedings of the 39th Annual Meeting of the Association for Computational Linguistics (ACL 2001), Toulouse, France*. University of Pennsylvania, Philadelphia, PA: Association for Computational Linguistics. 8 pp.

Corbett, Greville G. (1979). 'The agreement hierarchy', *Journal of Linguistics* 15: 203–224. Reprinted (2003) in Francis X. Katamba (ed.) *Morphology: Critical Concepts in Linguistics. IV: Morphology and Syntax*. London: Routledge, 48–70.

—— (1987). 'The morphology/syntax interface: evidence from possessive adjectives in Slavonic', *Language* 63: 299–345.

—— (1991). *Gender*. Cambridge: Cambridge University Press.

—— (2000). *Number*. Cambridge: Cambridge University Press.

—— (2006). *Agreement*. Cambridge: Cambridge University Press.

—— (2007). 'Canonical typology, suppletion and possible words', *Language* 83: 8–42.

—— (2008). 'Determining morphosyntactic feature values: the case of case', in Greville G. Corbett and Michael Noonan (eds) *Case and Grammatical Relations: Papers in Honor of Bernard Comrie* (Typological Studies in Language 81). Amsterdam: John Benjamins, 1–34.

—— and Matthew Baerman (2006). 'Prolegomena to a typology of morphological features', *Morphology* 16: 231–246.

—— and Richard J. Hayward (1987). 'Gender and number in Bayso', *Lingua* 73: 1–28.

Craig, Colette (ed.) (1986). *Noun Classes and Categorization*. Amsterdam: John Benjamins.

Crowley, Terry (1978). *The Middle Clarence Dialects of Banjalang*. Canberra: Australian Institute of Aboriginal Studies.

—— (2002). *Serial Verbs in Oceanic: A Descriptive Typology*. Oxford: Oxford University Press.

Dalrymple, Mary and Ronald M. Kaplan (2000). 'Feature indeterminacy and feature resolution', *Language* 76: 759–798.

Daniels, Mike and Detmar Meurers (2004). 'GIDLP: a grammar format for linearization-based HPSG', in Stefan Müller (ed.) *Proceedings of the HPSG-2004 Conference, Center for Computational Linguistics, Katholieke Universiteit Leuven*. Stanford, CA: CSLI Publications, 93–111.

Danon, Gabi (2001). 'Syntactic definiteness in the grammar of Modern Hebrew', *Linguistics* 39(6): 1071–1116.
—— (2002). 'The Hebrew object marker and semantic type', in Yehuda Falk (ed.) *Proceedings of IATL 17*. The Hebrew University of Jerusalem: The Israel Association for Theoretical Linguistics. 19 pp.
—— (2006). 'Caseless nominals and the projection of DP', *Natural Language and Linguistic Theory* 24(4): 977–1008.
—— (2008). 'Definiteness spreading in the Hebrew construct state', *Lingua* 118(7): 872–906.
Deen, Kamil Ud (2005). *The Acquisition of Swahili*. Amsterdam: John Benjamins.
—— (2006). 'Object agreement and specificity in early Swahili', *Journal of Child Language* 33: 223–246.
DeLoache, Judy S. (1995). 'Early understanding and use of symbols', *Current Directions in Psychological Science* 4: 109–113.
Demuth, Katherine (1988). 'Noun classes and agreement in Sesotho acquisition', in Michael Barlow and Charles Ferguson (eds) *Agreement in Natural Languages: Approaches, Theories and Descriptions*. Stanford, CA: CSLI Publications, 305–321.
—— (1992). 'Acquisition of Sesotho', in Dan I. Slobin (ed.) *The Crosslinguistic Study of Language Acquisition. Volume 3*. Hillsdale, NJ: Lawrence Erlbaum, 557–638.
—— (2000). 'Bantu noun class systems: loan word and acquisition evidence of semantic productivity', in Günter Senft (ed.) *Classification Systems*. Cambridge: Cambridge University Press, 270–292.
—— (2003). 'The acquisition of Bantu languages', in Derek Nurse and Gerald Phillipson (eds) *The Bantu Languages*. Surrey: Curzon Press, 209–222.
Dench, Alan and Nicholas Evans (1988). 'Multiple case-marking in Australian languages', *Australian Journal of Linguistics* 8(1): 1–47.
Dickinson, Markus (2004). 'Polish numeral phrases and predicative modification', ms. To appear in *The Ohio State University Working Papers in Linguistics (OSUWPL)*, Columbus, OH. 22 pp.
Diesing, Molly (1990). 'Verb movement and the subject position in Yiddish', *Natural Language and Linguistic Theory* 8: 41–79.
Dixon, Robert M. W. (1972). *The Dyirbal Language of North Queensland*. Cambridge: Cambridge University Press.
—— (1977). *A Grammar of Yidiny*. Cambridge: Cambridge University Press.
—— (1980). *The Languages of Australia*. Cambridge: Cambridge University Press.
—— (1982a). 'Problems in Dyirbal dialectology', in John Anderson (ed.) *Language Form and Linguistic Variation: Papers Dedicated to Angus McIntosh* (Current Issues in Linguistics 15). Amsterdam: John Benjamins, 43–74.
—— (1982b). *Where Have All the Adjectives Gone? and Other Essays in Semantics and Syntax*. Berlin: Mouton de Gruyter.
—— (1984). *Searching for Aboriginal Languages*. St. Lucia: University of Queensland Press.
—— (1989). 'The Dyirbal kinship system', *Oceania* 59: 245–268.
—— (1990). 'Compensating phonological changes: an example from the northern dialects of Dyirbal', *Lingua* 80: 1–34.

Dixon, Robert M. W. and Grace Koch (1996). *Dyirbal Song Poetry: The Oral Literature of an Australian Rainforest People*. St. Lucia: University of Queensland Press.

Dobrovie-Sorin, Carmen (2000). '(In)definiteness spread: from Romanian genitives to Hebrew construct state nominals', in Virginia Motapanyane (ed.) *Comparative Studies in Romanian Syntax*. Oxford: Elsevier, 177–226.

—— (2003). 'From DPs to NPs: a bare phrase structure account of genitives', in Martine Coene and Yves D'hulst (eds) *From NP to DP. Volume 2: The Expression of Possession in Noun Phrases*. Amsterdam: John Benjamins, 75–120.

Doner, John (1970). 'Tree acceptors and some of their applications', *Journal of Computer and System Sciences* 4: 406–451.

Donohue, Mark (2003). 'Review of *The Design of Agreement: Evidence from Chamorro* by Sandra Chung', *Linguistic Typology* 7: 285–292.

Dorais, Louis-Jacques (2003). *Inuit Uqausiqatigiit: Inuit Languages and Dialects* (second, revised edition). Iqaluit: Nunavut Arctic College.

Dorian, Nancy (1980). *Language Death: The Life Cycle of a Scottish Gaelic Dialect*. Philadelphia, PA: University of Pennsylvania Press.

Dowty, David and Pauline Jacobson (1988). 'Agreement as a semantic phenomenon', in Joyce Powers and Kenneth de Jong (eds) *Proceedings of the Fifth Eastern States Conference on Linguistics (ESCOL), University of Pennsylvania, Philadelphia, PA, September 30–October 2, 1988*. Columbus, OH: Ohio State University, 95–101.

Dresher, B. Elan (2009). *The Contrastive Hierarchy in Phonology*. Cambridge: Cambridge University Press.

—— and Keren Rice (2007). *Markedness and the Contrastive Hierarchy in Phonology*. Project description available at http://www.chass.utoronto.ca/~contrast/.

—— and Xi Zhang (2005). 'Contrast and phonological activity in Manchu vowel systems', *Canadian Journal of Linguistics/Revue canadienne de linguistique* 50: 45–82.

Dziwirek, Katarzyna (1990). 'Default agreement in Polish', in Katarzyna Dziwirek, Patrick Farrell and Errapel Mejías-Bikandi (eds) *Grammatical Relations: A Cross-Theoretical Perspective*. Stanford, CA: CSLI Publications, 147–161.

Efere, Emmanuel Efereala (2001). 'The pitch system of the Bumo dialect of Izon', *University of British Columbia Working Papers in Linguistics* (Current Research on African Languages and Linguistics) 4: 115–259.

Emonds, Joseph E. (1976). *A Transformational Approach to English Syntax: Root, Structure-Preserving, and Local Transformations*. New York, NY: Academic Press.

—— (2000). *Lexicon and Grammar: The English Syntacticon*. Berlin: Mouton de Gruyter.

Engelhardt, Miriam (2000). 'The projection of argument-taking nominals', *Natural Language and Linguistic Theory* 18(1): 41–88.

Evans, Nicholas (1995). *A Grammar of Kayardild, with Historical-Comparative Notes on Tangkic*. Berlin: Mouton de Gruyter.

—— (1997). 'Head classes and agreement classes in the Mayali dialect chain', in Mark Harvey and Nicholas Reid (eds) *Nominal Classification in Aboriginal Australia* (Studies in Language Companion Series 37). Amsterdam: John Benjamins, 105–46.

—— (2003). 'Typologies of agreement: some problems from Kayardild', in Dunstan Brown, Greville G. Corbett, and Carole Tiberius (eds) *Agreement: A Typological Perspective*. Special issue of the *Transactions of the Philological Society* 101(2). Oxford: Blackwell, 203–234.

—— (2007). 'Insubordination and its uses', in Irina Nikolaeva (ed.) *Finiteness: Theoretical and Empirical Foundations*. Oxford: Oxford University Press, 366–431.

Falk, Yehuda (2006). 'Constituent structure and grammatical functions in the Hebrew action nominal', in Jane Grimshaw, Joan Maling, Chris Manning, Jane Simpson, and Annie Zaenen (eds) *Architectures, Rules, and Preferences: A Festschrift for Joan Bresnan*. Stanford, CA: CSLI Publications, 185–207.

Farrar, Scott and D. Terence Langendoen (2003). 'A linguistic ontology for the Semantic Web', *GLOT International* 7(3): 97–100.

Fassi Fehri, Abdelkader (1993). *Issues in the Structure of Arabic Clauses and Words*. Dordrecht: Kluwer Academic Publishers.

—— (1999). 'Arabic modifying adjectives and DP structures', *Studia Linguistica* 53(2): 105–154.

Faßke, Helmut (1981). *Grammatik der obersorbischen Schriftsprache der Gegenwart: Morphologie*. Bautzen: Domowina Verlag.

Fitch, W. Tecumseh, Marc D. Hauser, and Noam Chomsky (2005). 'The evolution of the language faculty: clarifications and implications', *Cognition* 97(2): 179–210.

Flemming, Edward (2004). 'Contrast and perceptual distinctiveness', in Bruce Hayes, Robert Kirchner, and Donca Steriade (eds) *Phonetically-Based Phonology*. Cambridge: Cambridge University Press, 232–276.

Flickinger, Dan (2002). 'On building a more efficient grammar by exploiting types', in Stephan Oepen, Dan Flickinger, Jun-ichi Tsujii, and Hans Uszkoreit (eds) *Collaborative Language Engineering*. Stanford, CA: CSLI Publications, 1–17.

—— and Emily M. Bender (2003). 'Compositional semantics in a multilingual grammar resource', in Emily M. Bender, Dan Flickinger, Frederik Fouvry, and Melanie Siegel (eds) *Proceedings of the Workshop on Ideas and Strategies for Multilingual Grammar Development, ESSLLI 2003, Vienna, Austria, 18–29 August 2003*. 33–42.

—— Jan Tore Lønning, Helge Dyvik, Stephan Oepen, Francis Bond (2005). 'SEM-I rational MT – enriching deep grammars with a semantic interface for scalable Machine Translation', in *Proceedings of Machine Translation Summit X, Phuket, Thailand*, 165–172.

Frampton, John and Samuel Gutmann (1999). 'Cyclic computation, a computationally efficient minimalist syntax', *Syntax* 2: 1–27.

—— —— (2002). 'How sentences grow in the mind', ms, Northwestern University. Published as Frampton and Gutmann (2006).

—— —— (2004). 'Crash-proof syntax', in Samuel D. Epstein and T. Daniel Seely (eds) *Derivation and Explanation in the Minimalist Program*. Oxford: Blackwell, 90–105.

—— —— (2006). 'How sentences grow in the mind: agreement and selection in an efficient minimalist syntax', in Cedric Boeckx (ed.) *Agreement Systems*. Amsterdam: John Benjamins, 121–157.

Frank, Robert (2002). *Phrase Structure Composition and Syntactic Dependencies.* Cambridge, MA: MIT Press.

Franks, Steven (1995). *Parameters of Slavic Morphosyntax* (Oxford Studies in Comparative Syntax). New York, NY: Oxford University Press.

—— and Tracy Holloway King (2000). *A Handbook of Slavic Clitics.* New York and Oxford: Oxford University Press.

Fraser, Norman M. and Greville G. Corbett (1997). 'Defaults in Arapesh', *Lingua* 103: 25–57.

Frisch, Stefan (1996). *Similarity and Frequency in Phonology.* PhD thesis, Northwestern University.

—— Janet Pierrehumbert, and Michael B. Broe (2004). 'Similarity avoidance and the OCP', *Natural Language and Linguistic Theory* 22: 179–228.

Gallistel, Charles R. (1990). *The Organization of Learning.* Cambridge, MA: MIT Press.

Gärtner, Hans-Martin (2002). *Generalized Transformations and Beyond: Reflections on Minimalist Syntax.* Berlin: Akademie-Verlag.

Gazdar, Gerald (1981). 'Unbounded dependencies and coordinate structure', *Linguistic Inquiry* 12: 155–84.

—— (1982). 'Phrase structure grammar', in Pauline I. Jacobson and Geoffrey K. Pullum (eds), *The Nature of Syntactic Representation.* Dordrecht: Reidel, 131–186.

—— Ewan Klein, Geoffrey K. Pullum, and Ivan A. Sag (1985). *Generalized Phrase Structure Grammar.* Oxford: Blackwell.

—— and Chris Mellish (1989). *Natural Language Processing in Prolog: An Introduction to Computational Linguistics.* Wokingham: Addison-Wesley.

—— Geoffrey K. Pullum, Bob Carpenter, Ewan Klein, Thomas E. Hukari, and Robert D. Levine (1988). 'Category structures', *Computational Linguistics* 14(1): 1–19.

Gelman, Susan A. (2000). 'The role of essentialism in children's concepts', in Harvey Reese (ed.) *Advances in Child Development and Behavior. Volume 27.* San Diego, CA: Academic Press, 55–98.

—— (2003). *The Essential Child: Origins of Essentialism in Everyday Thought.* New York, NY: Oxford University Press.

—— and Paul Bloom (2000). 'Young children are sensitive to how an object was created when deciding what to name it', *Cognition* 76: 91–103.

Gentner, Deidre and Laura Namy (1999). 'Comparison in the development of categories', *Cognitive Development* 14: 487–513.

Gerdts, Donna B. and Thomas E. Hukari (2001). 'A-subjects and control in Halkomelem', in Dan Flickinger and Andreas Kathol (eds) *Proceedings of the 7th International Conference on Head-Driven Phrase Structure Grammar.* Stanford, CA: CSLI Publications, 100–123.

Gerken, LouAnn, Rachel Wilson, and William Lewis (2005). 'Infants can use distributional cues to form syntactic categories', *Journal of Child Language* 32: 249–268.

Ginzburg, Jonathan and Ivan A. Sag (2000). *Interrogative Investigations: The Form, Meaning, and Use of English Interrogatives.* Stanford, CA: CSLI Publications.

Givón, Talmy (2001). *Syntax: An Introduction. Volume I.* Amsterdam: John Benjamins.

Greenberg, Joseph H. (1963). 'Some universals of grammar with particular reference to the order of meaningful elements', in Joseph H. Greenberg (ed.) *Universals of Language*. Cambridge, MA: MIT Press, 73–113. [Paperback edition published (1966); page references to this edition.]

Grimshaw, Jane (1979). 'Complement selection and the lexicon', *Linguistic Inquiry* 10: 279–326.

—— (1991). 'Extended projections', ms, Brandeis University.

Grosz, Barbara J. (1983). 'TEAM: a Transportable Natural-Language Interface System', in *Proceedings of the 1st Conference on Applied Natural Language Processing, Santa Monica, CA*, 39–45.

Gvozdev, Aleksandr N. (1961). *Voprosy izučenija detskoj reči*. Moscow: Izdatelstvo Akademii Pedagogičeskix Nauk RSFRS.

Hale, Ken (1973). 'Deep-surface canonical disparities in relation to analysis and change: an Australian example', in Thomas A. Sebeok (ed.) *Current Trends in Linguistics 8: Linguistics in Oceania*. The Hague: Mouton, 401–458.

—— (1998). 'On endangered languages and the importance of linguistic diversity', in Lenore A. Grenoble and Lindsay J. Whaley (eds) *Endangered Languages: Language Loss and Community Response*. Cambridge: Cambridge University Press, 192–216.

Hall, Daniel Currie (2007). *The Role and Representation of Contrast in Phonological Theory*. PhD thesis, University of Toronto.

—— (2008). 'Prophylactic features and implicit contrast', in Peter Avery, B. Elan Dresher, and Keren Rice (eds) *Contrast in Phonology: Theory, Perception, Acquisition*. Berlin: Mouton de Gruyter, 35–54.

Halle, Morris (1957). 'In defence of the number two', in Ernst Pulgram (ed.) *Studies Presented to Joshua Whatmough on His Sixtieth Birthday*. The Hague: Mouton, 65–72.

—— (1959). *The Sound Pattern of Russian: A Linguistic and Acoustical Investigation*. The Hague: Mouton. Second printing (1971).

Hansson, Gunnar Ólafur (2001). *Theoretical and Typological Issues in Consonant Harmony*. PhD thesis, University of California, Berkeley.

Harbour, Daniel (2007). *Morphosemantic Number*. Dordrecht: Kluwer Academic Publishers.

Harley, Heidi and Elizabeth Ritter (2002). 'Person and number in pronouns: a feature-geometric analysis', *Language* 78(3): 482–526.

Harman, Gilbert (1963). 'Generative grammars without transformational rules: a defense of phrase structure', *Language* 39: 597–616.

Harris, Zellig S. (1946). 'From morpheme to utterance', *Language* 22(3): 161–183.

Harvey, Mark (1997). 'Nominal classification and gender in Aboriginal Australia', in Mark Harvey and Nicholas Reid (eds) *Nominal Classification and Gender in Aboriginal Australia*. Amsterdam: John Benjamins, 17–62.

Haspelmath, Martin (2006). 'Against markedness (and what to replace it with)', *Journal of Linguistics* 42: 25–70.

Hauser, Marc D., Noam Chomsky, and W. Tecumseh Fitch (2002). 'The faculty of language: what is it, who has it, and how did it evolve?' *Science* 298: 1569–1579.

Hazout, Ilan (1991). *Verbal Nouns: Theta Theoretic Studies in Hebrew and Arabic*. PhD thesis, University of Massachusetts.
—— (2000). 'Adjectival genitive constructions in Modern Hebrew: a case study in coanalysis', *The Linguistic Review* 17(1): 29–52.
Heller, Daphna (2002). 'Possession as a lexical relation: evidence from the Hebrew construct state', in Line Mikkelsen and Christopher Potts (eds) *Proceedings of WCCFL 21*. Somerville, MA: Cascadilla Press, 127–140.
Herd, Jonathon (2005). 'Loanword adaptation and the evaluation of similarity', *Toronto Working Papers in Linguistics* (Special Issue on *Similarity in Phonology*) 24: 65–116.
Higgins, Francis R. (1979). *The Pseudo-Cleft Construction in English*. New York, NY: Garland.
Hockett, Charles F. (1958). *A Course in Modern Linguistics*. New York, NY: Macmillan.
Höhle, Tilman N. (1997). 'Vorangestellte Verben und Komplementierer sind eine Naturliche Klasse', in Christa Dürscheid, Karl-Heinz Ramers, and Monika Schwarz (eds) *Sprache im Fokus: Festschrift für Heinz Vater zum 65. Geburtstag*. Tübingen: Max Niemeyer, 107–120.
Huddleston, Rodney, Geoffrey K. Pullum, et al. (2002). *The Cambridge Grammar of the English Language*. Cambridge: Cambridge University Press.
Hudson Kam, Carla and Elissa Newport (2005). 'Regularizing unpredictable variation: the roles of adult and child learners in language formation and change', *Language Learning and Development* 1: 151–195.
Hukari, Thomas E. and Robert D. Levine (1995). 'Adjunct extraction', *Journal of Linguistics* 31: 195–226.
Idiata, Daniel F. (2005). *What Bantu Child Speech Data Tells Us about the Controversial Semantics of Bantu Noun Class Systems* (LINCOM Studies in African Linguistics 67). Munich: LINCOM.
Jackendoff, Ray S. (1977). *X-Bar Syntax: A Study of Phrase Structure*. Cambridge, MA: MIT Press.
Jakobson, Roman (1958). 'Morfologičeskie nabljudenija nad slavjanskim skloneniem (sostav russkix padežnyx form)', in *American Contributions to the Fourth International Congress of Slavists, Moscow, September 1958*. The Hague: Mouton, 127–156. Reprinted in Roman Jakobson (1971) *Selected Writings II*. The Hague: Mouton, 154–183. Translated (1984) as 'Morphological observations on Slavic declension (the structure of Russian case forms)', in Linda R. Waugh and Morris Halle (eds) *Roman Jakobson. Russian and Slavic Grammar: Studies 1931–1981*. Berlin: Mouton de Gruyter, 105–133.
—— C. Gunnar Fant, and Morris Halle (1952). *Preliminaries to Speech Analysis: The Distinctive Features and Their Correlates*. Cambridge, MA: MIT Press.
—— and Morris Halle (1956). *Fundamentals of Language*. The Hague: Mouton.
—— and John Lotz (1949). 'Notes on the French phonemic pattern', *Word* 5: 151–158.
Ji, Yonghai, Zhizhong Zhao, and Liyuan Bai (1989). *Xiandai Manyu Babaiju* [*Eight Hundred Sentences of the Modern Manchu*]. Beijing: Zhongyang Minzu Xueyuan Chubanshe.

Johnson, David E. and Paul M. Postal (1980). *Arc Pair Grammar*. Princeton, NJ: Princeton University Press.

Joshi, Aravind, Leon Levy, and Masako Takahashi (1975). 'Tree adjunct grammars', *Journal of Computer and System Sciences* 10(1): 136–163.

Julien, Marit (2002). *Syntactic Heads and Word Formation*. New York, NY: Oxford University Press.

Jusczyk, Peter W., Angela Friederici, Joachim Wessels, Viktor Y. Svenkerud, and Anne M. Jusczyk (1993). 'Infants' sensitivity to the sound patterns of native language words', *Journal of Memory and Language* 32: 402–420.

—— Paul A. Luce, and Jan Charles-Luce (1994). 'Infants' sensitivity to phonotactic patterns in native language', *Journal of Memory and Language* 33: 630–645.

Kajita, Masaru (1968). *A Generative-Transformational Study of Semi-Auxiliaries in Present-Day American English*. Tokyo: Sanseido.

Kamp, Hans and Uwe Reyle (1993). *From Discourse to Logic*. Dordrecht: Kluwer Academic Publishers.

Kapust, Waltraud (1998). *Universality in Noun Classification*. MA thesis, San Jose State Unversity.

Karmiloff-Smith, Annette (1979). *A Functional Approach to Child Language: A Study of Determiners and Reference*. Cambridge: Cambridge University Press.

Katamba, Francis (2003). 'Bantu nominal morphology', in Derek Nurse and Gérard Philippson (eds) *The Bantu Languages*. New York, NY: Routledge, 103–120.

Kathol, Andreas (2000). *Linear Syntax*. New York and Oxford: Oxford University Press.

Katz, Jerrold J. and Jerry A. Fodor (1963). 'The structure of a semantic theory', *Language* 39: 170–210.

—— and Paul M. Postal (1964). *An Integrated Theory of Linguistic Descriptions*. Cambridge, MA: MIT Press.

Kaun, Abigail Rhoades (1995). *The Typology of Rounding Harmony: An Optimality Theoretic Approach*. PhD thesis, University of California, Los Angeles.

Kay, Martin (1979). 'Functional grammar', in Christine Chiarello, John Kingston, Eve E. Sweetser, James Collins, Haruko Kawasaki, John Manley-Buser, Dorothy W. Marschak, Catherine O'Connor, David Shaul, Marta Tobey, Henry Thompson, and Katherine Turner (eds) *BLS 5: Proceedings of the Fifth Annual Meeting of the Berkeley Linguistics Society*. Berkeley, CA: Berkeley Linguistics Society, 142–158.

Kay, Paul (2002). 'English subjectless tagged sentences', *Language* 78: 453–481.

Kayne, Richard and Jean-Yves Pollock (1978). 'Stylistic inversion, successive cyclicity, and Move NP in French', *Linguistic Inquiry* 12: 93–133.

Kean, Mary-Louise (1980). *The Theory of Markedness in Generative Grammar*. PhD thesis, MIT, Cambridge, MA. Reproduced by the Indiana University Linguistics Club, Bloomington, IN.

Keenan, Edward L. (1987). 'A semantic definition of indefinite NP', in Eric J. Reuland and Alice G. B. ter Meulen (eds) *The Representation of (In)definiteness*. Cambridge, MA: MIT Press, 286–317.

Kellman, Philip and Martha E. Arterberry (1998). *The Cradle of Knowledge: Development of Perception in Infancy*. Cambridge, MA: MIT Press.

Kempe, Vera and Patricia Brooks (2001). 'The role of diminutives in Russian gender learning: can child-directed speech facilitate the acquisition of inflectional morphology?' *Language Learning* 51: 145–151.

—— —— Natalija Mironova, and Olga Fedorova (2003). 'Diminutivization supports gender acquisition in Russian children', *Journal of Child Language* 30: 471–485.

Kiparsky, Paul (1982). 'From cyclic to lexical phonology', in Harry van der Hulst and Norval Smith (eds) *The Structure of Phonological Representations. Part I*. Foris: Dordrecht, 131–176.

—— (1985). 'Some consequences of Lexical Phonology', *Phonology Yearbook* 2: 85–138.

—— (2001). 'Structural case in Finnish', *Lingua* 111: 315–376.

Kiss, Tibor (1995). *Infinite Komplementation*. Tübingen: Max Niemeyer.

Klokeid, Terry (1976). *Topics in Lardil Grammar*. PhD thesis, MIT, Cambridge, MA.

Korn, David (1969). 'Types of labial vowel harmony in the Turkic languages', *Anthropological Linguistics* 11: 98–106.

Kornai, András and Geoffrey K. Pullum (1990). 'The X-bar theory of phrase structure', *Language* 66: 24–50.

Kracht, Marcus (1997). 'Inessential features', in Christian Retoré (ed.) *Logical Aspects of Computational Linguistics: First International Conference, LACL '96, Selected Papers* (Lecture Notes in Artificial Intelligence 1328). Berlin: Springer, 43–62.

Krifka, Manfred (1987). 'Nominal reference and temporal constitution: towards a semantics of quantity', *FNS-Bericht 17, Forschungsstelle für natürlich-sprachliche Systeme*, Tübingen. Also in J. Groenendijk et al. (eds) *Proceedings of the 6th Amsterdam Colloquium, ITALI*, University of Amsterdam, 153–173. And in R. Bartsch, J. van Benthem, and P. van Emde Boas (eds) (1989) *Semantics and Contextual Expression*. Dordrecht: Foris, 75–115.

Kroch, Anthony and Aravind Joshi (1987). 'Analyzing extraposition in a tree adjoining grammar', in Geoffrey Huck and Almerindo Ojeda (eds) *Discontinuous Constituency* (*Syntax and Semantics* 20). New York, NY: Academic Press, 107–149.

Kuhn, Jonas and Louisa Sadler (2007). 'Single conjunct agreement and the formal treatment of coordination in LFG', in Miriam Butt and Tracy Holloway King (eds) *Proceedings of the LFG07 Conference, Stanford University*. Stanford, CA: CSLI Publications. 302–322.

Kunene, Euphrasia C. L. (1979). *The Acquisition of Siswati as a First Language: Morphological Study with Special Reference to Noun Classes and Some Agreement Markers*. PhD thesis, University of California, Los Angeles.

Kuroda, Sige-Yuki (1967). *Yawelmani Phonology* (Research Monograph 43). Cambridge, MA: MIT Press.

Laidig, Wyn D. and Carol J. Laidig (1990). 'Larike pronouns: duals and trials in a Central Moluccan language', *Oceanic Linguistics* 29: 87–109.

Lakoff, George (1972). 'Foreword' in *Where the Rules Fail: A Student's Guide: An Unauthorized Appendix to M. K. Burt's 'From Deep to Surface Structure'*, prepared by Susan Andres et al., rewritten and edited by Ann Borkin with the assistance of David Peterson. Bloomington, IN: Indiana University Linguistics Club, ii–v.

—— (1987). *Women, Fire, and Dangerous Things*. Chicago, IL: University of Chicago Press.

Lascarides, Alex and Ann Copestake (1999). 'Default representation in constraint-based frameworks', *Computational Linguistics* 25: 55–105.

Leech, Geoffrey and Andrew Wilson (main authors) (1996). *EAGLES: Recommendations for the Morphosyntactic Annotation of Corpora (EAGLES Document EAG–TCWG–MAC/R)*. Available online.

Lenček, Rado L. (1972). 'O zaznamovanosti in nevtralizaciji slovnične kategorije spola v slovenskem knjižnem jeziku', *Slavistična revija* 20: 55–63.

Levin, Magnus (2001). *Agreement with Collective Nouns in English* (Lund Studies in English 103). Stockholm: Almqvist & Wiksell.

Levine, Robert D. and Thomas E. Hukari (2006). *The Unity of Unbounded Dependency Constructions*. Stanford, CA: CSLI Publications.

Levy, Yonata (1983). 'It's frogs all the way down', *Cognition* 15: 75–93.

Libkin, Leonid (2004). *Elements of Finite Model Theory* (Texts in Theoretical Computer Science). New York, NY: Springer.

Liljencrants, Johan and Björn Lindblom (1972). 'Numerical simulation of vowel quality systems: the role of perceptual contrast', *Language* 48: 839–862.

Link, Godehard (1983). 'The logical analysis of plurals and mass terms: a lattice-theoretical approach', in Rainer Bäuerle, Christoph Schwarze, and Arnim von Stechow (eds) *Meaning, Use and Interpretation of Language*. Berlin: Walter de Gruyter, 302–323.

Longobardi, Giuseppe (1996). *The Syntax of N-raising: A Minimalist Theory* (UiL OTS Working Papers). Utrecht: Research Institute for Language and Speech.

Lyster, Roy (2006). 'Predictability in French gender attribution: a corpus analysis', *French Language Studies* 16: 69–92.

Mackenzie, Sara (2005). 'Similarity and contrast in consonant harmony systems', *Toronto Working Papers in Linguistics* (Special Issue on *Similarity in Phonology*) 24: 169–182.

—— (2009). *Contrast and Similarity in Consonant Harmony Processes*. PhD thesis, University of Toronto.

Malouf, Robert (2000). 'A head-driven account of long-distance case assignment', in Ronnie Cann, Claire Grover, and Philip H. Miller (eds) *Grammatical Interfaces in HPSG*. Stanford, CA: CSLI Publications, 201–214.

Mandler, Jean (2004). *The Foundations of Mind: Origins of Conceptual Thought*. Oxford: Oxford University Press.

Marantz, Alec (1997). 'No escape from syntax: don't try morphological analysis in the privacy of your own lexicon', in Alexis Dimitriadis, Laura Siegel, Clarissa Surek-Clark, and Alexander Williams (eds) *University of Pennsylvania Working Papers in Linguistics* 4(2): 201–225.

Martinet, André (1964). *Elements of General Linguistics*. With a foreword by L. R. Palmer. Translated by Elisabeth Palmer. Chicago, IL: University of Chicago Press.

Maslov, Jurij Sergeevič (1982). *Gramatika na bâlgarskija ezik*. Sofia: Nauka i izkustvo.
Matthews, Peter H. (1965). 'The inflectional component of a word-and-paradigm grammar', *Journal of Linguistics* 1: 139–171.
—— (1972). *Inflectional Morphology: A Theoretical Study Based on Aspects of Latin Verb Conjugation*. Cambridge: Cambridge University Press.
—— (1991). *Morphology. Second Edition*. Cambridge: Cambridge University Press.
Matushansky, Ora (2006). 'Head movement in linguistic theory', *Linguistic Inquiry* 37(1): 69–109.
McCloskey, James (1979). *Transformational Syntax and Model Theoretic Semantics: A Case Study in Modern Irish*. Dordrecht: Reidel.
—— (1990). 'Resumptive pronouns, A'-binding, and levels of representation in Irish', in Randall Hendrick (ed.), *The Syntax of the Modern Celtic Languages* (*Syntax and Semantics* 23). New York, NY: Academic Press, 199–248.
McGinnis, Martha (2005). 'On markedness asymmetries in person and number', *Language* 81(3): 699–718.
McNaughton, Robert and Seymour Papert (1971). *Counter-Free Automata*. Cambridge, MA: MIT Press.
Mel'čuk, Igor (1993a). *Cours de morphologie générale. Volume I: Introduction et première partie: Le mot*. Montréal: Les Presses de l'Université de Montréal; Paris: CNRS Éditions.
—— (1993b). 'Agreement, government, congruence', *Lingvisticae Investigationes* 17: 307–372.
Meurers, W. Detmar (1999). *Lexical Generalizations in the Syntax of German Non-Finite Constructions*. PhD thesis, Universität Tübingen. Published (2000) as Volume 145 in *Arbeitspapiere des SFB 340*.
—— (2001). 'On expressing lexical generalizations in HPSG', *Nordic Journal of Linguistics* 24(2): 161–217.
Meyer, Peter (1994). 'Grammatical categories and the methodology of linguistics: Review article on W. Andries van Helden (1993) *Case and Gender: Concept Formation Between Morphology and Syntax*', *Russian Linguistics* 18: 341–377.
Mielke, Jeff (2008). *The Emergence of Distinctive Features*. Oxford: Oxford University Press.
Mills, Anne E. (1985). 'The acquisition of German', in Dan I. Slobin (ed.) *The Crosslinguistic Study of Language Acquisition. Volume 1: The Data*. Hillsdale, NJ: Lawrence Erlbaum, 383–415.
—— (1986). *The Acquisition of Gender: A Study of English and German*. New York, NY: Springer.
Moravcsik, Edith A. (1988). 'Agreement and markedness', in Michael Barlow and Charles A. Ferguson (eds) *Agreement in Natural Language: Approaches, Theories, Descriptions*. Stanford, CA: CSLI Publications. 89–106.
Moss, Lawrence S. and Hans-Jörg Tiede (2007). 'Applications of modal logic in linguistics', in Patrick Blackburn, Johan van Benthem, and Frank Wolter (eds) *Handbook of Modal Logic*. Amsterdam: Elsevier, 1031–1076.

Müller, Stefan (2004). 'Continuous or discontinuous constituents? A comparison between syntactic analyses for constituent order and their processing systems', *Research on Language and Computation* 2(2): 209–257. (Special Issue on *Linguistic Theory and Grammar Implementation*).
—— (2005). 'Zur Analyse der deutschen Satzstruktur', *Linguistische Berichte* 201: 3–39.
Mylne, Tom (1995). 'Grammatical category and world view: Western colonization of the Dyirbal language', *Cognitive Linguistics* 6: 379–404.
Namy, Laura and Deidre Gentner (2002). 'Making a silk purse out of two sows' ears: young children's use of comparison in category learning', *Journal of Experimental Psychology: General* 131: 5–15.
Narayanan, Srini and Sanda Harabagiu (2004). 'Question answering based on semantic structures', in *Proceedings of the 20th International Conference on Computational Linguistics (COLING), Geneva, Switzerland, 22–29 August 2004.* 10 pp.
Newman, Stanley (1944). *The Yokuts Language of California.* New York, NY: The Viking Fund Publications in Anthropology (No. 2).
Newport, Elissa and Richard Aslin (2000). 'Innately constrained learning: blending old and new approaches to language acquisition', *Proceedings of the 24th Annual Boston University Conference on Language Development.* Somerville, MA: Cascadilla Press.
—— —— (2004). 'Learning at a distance: I. Statistical learning of non-adjacent dependencies', *Cognitive Psychology* 48: 127–162.
Nilsen, Øystein (2003). *Eliminating Positions.* PhD thesis, LOT, Utrecht Institute of Linguistics OTS.
Noyer, Rolf (1992). *Features, Positions and Affixes in Autonomous Morphological Structure.* PhD thesis, MIT, Cambridge, MA.
Nunberg, Geoffrey, Ivan A. Sag, and Thomas Wasow (1994). 'Idioms', *Language* 70(3): 491–538.
Nunes, Jairo (1995). *The Copy Theory of Movement and Linearization of Chains in the Minimalist Program.* PhD thesis, University of Maryland.
O'Grady, Geoff N. (1998). 'Toward a Proto-Pama-Nyungan stem list, Part I: Sets J1–J25', *Oceanic Linguistics* 37: 209–233.
Ojeda, Almerindo (1993). *Linguistic Individuals* (CSLI Lecture notes 31). Stanford, CA: CSLI Publications.
Ortmann, Albert (2000). 'Where plural refuses to agree: feature unification and morphological economy', *Acta Linguistica Hungarica* 47: 249–288.
Palm, Adi (1999). 'Propositional tense logic for finite trees'. Paper presented at the *Sixth Meeting on Mathematics of Language*, University of Central Florida, Orlando, FL. Available at: http://www.phil.uni-passau.de/linguistik/palm/papers/mol99.pdf.
Pašov, Petâr (1966). *Bâlgarskijat glagol. Klasifikacija. Vidoobrazuvane. Slovoobrazuvane.* Volume 1. Sofia: Nauka i izkustvo.
—— (1994). *Praktičeska bâlgarska gramatika* (Second revised edition). Sofia: Prosveta.
Pensalfini, Robert (2003). *A Grammar of Jingulu: An Aboriginal Language of the Northern Territory* (Pacific Linguistics 536). Canberra: Pacific Linguistics.

Pesetsky, David and Esther Torrego (2001). 'T to C movement: causes and consequences', in Michael Kenstowicz (ed.) *Ken Hale: A Life in Language.* Cambridge, MA: MIT Press, 355–426.

—— —— (2004). 'Tense, case and the nature of syntactic categories', in Jacqueline Guéron and Jacqueline Lecarme (eds) *The Syntax of Time.* Cambridge, MA: MIT Press, 495–538.

—— —— (2007). 'The syntax of valuation and the interpretability of features', in Simin Karimi, Vida Samiian, and Wendy K. Wilkins (eds) *Phrasal and Clausal Architecture: Syntactic Derivation and Interpretation.* Amsterdam: John Benjamins, 262–294.

Plaster, Keith and Maria Polinsky (2007). 'Women are not dangerous things: gender and categorization', *Harvard Working Papers in Linguistics* 12. 44 pp.

Polinsky, Maria (2008). 'Gender under incomplete acquisition: heritage speakers' knowledge of noun categorization', *Heritage Language Journal* 6(1). 34 pp.

—— and Ezra van Everbroeck (2003). 'Development of gender classifications: modeling the historical change from Latin to French', *Language* 79: 356–390.

Pollard, Carl J. (1994). 'Toward a unified account of passive in German', in John Nerbonne, Klaus Netter, and Carl J. Pollard (eds) *German in Head-Driven Phrase Structure Grammar.* Stanford, CA: CSLI Publications, 273–296.

—— and Ivan A. Sag (1987). *Information-Based Syntax and Semantics, Volume 1.* Stanford, CA: CSLI Publications.

—— —— (1988). 'An information-based theory of agreement', in *CLS 24: Proceedings of the 24th Regional Meeting of the Chicago Linguistic Society. Parasession on Agreement.* Chicago, IL: Chicago Linguistic Society, 236–257.

—— —— (1994). *Head-Driven Phrase Structure Grammar.* Chicago, IL: University of Chicago Press.

Postal, Paul M. (1970). 'On coreferential complement subject deletion', *Linguistic Inquiry* 1: 439–500.

Potsdam, Eric and Jeffrey T. Runner (2001). 'Richard returns: copy raising and its implications', in *CLS 37: Proceedings of the 37th Regional Meeting of the Chicago Linguistic Society.* Chicago, IL: Chicago Linguistic Society, 453–468.

Preissler, Melissa and Susan Carey (2004). 'Do both pictures and words function as symbols for 18- and 24-month-old children?' *Journal of Cognition and Development* 5: 185–212.

Prince, Alan and Paul Smolensky (2004). *Optimality Theory: Constraint Interaction in Generative Grammar.* Oxford: Blackwell.

Przepiórkowski, Adam (1999). *Case Assignment and the Complement-Adjunct Dichotomy: A Non-Configurational Constraint-Based Approach.* PhD thesis, Universität Tübingen.

—— (2003). 'A hierarchy of Polish genders', in Piotr Bański and Adam Przepiórkowski (eds) *Generative Linguistics in Poland: Morphosyntactic Investigations.* Warsaw: Instytut Podstaw Informatyki PAN, 109–122.

—— (2004). *Korpus IPI PAN. Wersja wstępna/The IPI PAN Corpus: Preliminary Version.* Warsaw: Institute of Computer Science, Polish Academy of Sciences.

Pulleyblank, Douglas (1986). *Tone in Lexical Phonology.* Dordrecht: Reidel.

Pullum, Geoffrey K. and Barbara C. Scholz (2001). 'On the distinction between model-theoretic and generative-enumerative syntactic frameworks', in Philippe de Groote, Glyn Morrill, and Christian Retoré (eds) *Logical Aspects of Computational Linguistics: 4th International Conference* (Lecture Notes in Artificial Intelligence 2099). Berlin and New York: Springer, 17–43.

—— —— (2005). 'Contrasting applications of logic in natural language syntactic description', in Petr Hajek, Luis Valdés-Villanueva, and Dag Westerståhl (eds) *Proceedings of the 13th International Congress of Logic, Methodology and Philosophy of Science*. London: KCL Publications, 481–503.

—— and Arnold M. Zwicky (1988). 'The syntax–phonology interface', in Frederick J. Newmeyer (ed.) *Linguistics: The Cambridge Survey. Volume I, Linguistic Theory: Foundations*. Cambridge: Cambridge University Press, 255–280.

Reape, Mike (1994). 'Domain union and word order variation in German', in John Nerbonne, Klaus Netter, and Carl J. Pollard (eds) *German in Head-Driven Phrase Structure Grammar*. Stanford, CA: CSLI Publications, 151–197.

—— (1996). 'Getting things in order', in Harry C. Bunt and Arthur van Horck (eds) *Discontinuous Constituency*. Berlin and New York: Mouton de Gruyter, 209–253.

Retoré, Christian and Edward Stabler (2004). 'Generative grammars and resource logics', *Research on Language and Computation* 2: 3–25.

Řezáč, Milan (2004). *Elements of Cyclic Syntax: Agree and Merge*. PhD thesis, University of Toronto.

Rizzi, Luigi (1997). 'The fine structure of the left periphery', in Liliane Haegeman (ed.) *Elements of Grammar: Handbook of Generative Syntax*. Dordrecht: Kluwer Academic Publishers, 281–337.

Rogers, Andy (1974). 'A transderivational constraint on Richard?' in *CLS 10: Papers from the 10th Regional Meeting of the Chicago Linguistic Society*. Chicago, IL: Chicago Linguistic Society, 551–558.

Rogers, James (1997). '"Grammarless" phrase structure grammar', *Linguistics and Philosophy* 20: 721–746.

—— (1998). *A Descriptive Approach to Language-Theoretic Complexity*. Stanford, CA: CSLI Publications.

Rose, Sharon and Rachel Walker (2004). 'A typology of consonant agreement as correspondence', *Language* 80: 475–531.

Sadler, Louisa (2000). 'Noun phrase structure in Welsh', in Miriam Butt and Tracy Holloway King (eds) *Argument Realization*. Stanford, CA: CSLI Publications, 73–110.

—— and Andrew Spencer (2001). 'Syntax as an exponent of morphological features', in Geert Booij and Jaap van Marle (eds) *Yearbook of Morphology 2000*. Dordrecht: Kluwer Academic Publishers, 71–96.

Saffran, Jenny, Richard Aslin, and Elissa Newport (1996a). 'Statistical learning by 8-month-old infants', *Science* 274: 1926–1928.

Saffran, Jenny, Elissa Newport, and Richard Aslin (1996b). 'Word segmentation – the role of distributional cues', *Journal of Memory and Language* 35: 606–621.

Sag, Ivan A. (1997). 'English relative clause constructions', *Journal of Linguistics* 33(2): 431–484.

—— (2001). 'Dimensions of natural language locality'. Paper presented at the *8th Annual Conference on Head-Driven Phrase Structure Grammar*, NTNU, Trondheim, Norway.

—— (2007). 'Sign-Based Construction Grammar: an informal synopsis', ms, Stanford University.

—— and Carl J. Pollard (1991). 'An integrated theory of complement control', *Language* 67: 63–113.

—— Thomas Wasow, and Emily Bender (2003). *Syntactic Theory: A Formal Introduction*. Stanford, CA: CSLI Publications. [Second edition. First edition published as Sag and Wasow (1999).]

Sailer, Manfred (2000). *Combinatorial Semantics and Idiomatic Expressions in Head-Driven Phrase Structure Grammar*. PhD thesis, Universität Tübingen.

Sapir, Edward (1925). 'Sound patterns in language', *Language* 1: 37–51. Reprinted (1957) in Martin Joos (ed.) *Readings in Linguistics I*. Chicago, IL: University of Chicago Press, 19–25.

Sauerland, Uli, Jan Andersen, and Kazuko Yatsushiro (2005). 'The plural is semantically unmarked', in Stephan Kepser and Marga Reis (eds) *Linguistic Evidence*. Berlin: Mouton de Gruyter, 413–434.

Saussure, Ferdinand de (1916/1972). *Cours de linguistique générale*. Publié par Charles Bally et Albert Sechehaye; avec la collaboration d'Albert Riedlinger. Éd. critique préparée par Tullio de Mauro. Paris: Payot.

—— (1986). *Course in General Linguistics*. Translation of Saussure (1972) by Roy Harris. La Salle, IL: Open Court.

Scatton, Ernest A. (1984). *A Reference Grammar of Modern Bulgarian*. Columbus, OH: Slavica.

Schenker, Alexander M. (1955). 'Gender categories in Polish', *Language* 31(3): 402–408.

Schlenker, Philippe (2003). 'Indexicality, logophoricity, and plural pronouns', in Jacqueline Lecarme (ed.) *Research in Afroasiatic Grammar II (Selected Papers from the Fifth Conference on Afroasiatic Languages, Paris, 2000)* Amsterdam: John Benjamins, 409–428.

Schmidt, Annette (1985). *Young People's Dyirbal: An Example of Language Death from Australia*. Cambridge: Cambridge University Press.

Ševa, Nada, Vera Kempe, Patricia Brooks, Natalija Mironova, and Olga Fedorova (2007). 'Crosslinguistic evidence for the diminutive advantage: gender agreement in Russian and Serbian children', *Journal of Child Language* 34: 111–131.

Shieber, Stuart M. (1986). *An Introduction to Unification-Based Approaches to Grammar* (CSLI lecture notes 4). Stanford, CA: CSLI Publications.

Sichel, Ivy (2002). 'Phrasal movement in Hebrew adjectives and possessives', in Artemis Alexiadou, Elena Anagnostopoulou, Sjef Barbiers, and Hans-Martin

Gärtner (eds) *Dimensions of Movement: From Features to Remnants*. Amsterdam: John Benjamins, 297–339.
Siloni, Tal (2001). 'Construct states at the PF interface', in Pierre Pica and Johan Rooryck (eds) *Linguistic Variation Yearbook. Volume 1*. Amsterdam: John Benjamins, 229–266.
—— (2002). 'Adjectival constructs and inalienable constructions', in Jamal Ouhalla and Ur Shlonsky (eds) *Themes in Arabic and Hebrew Syntax*. Dordrecht: Kluwer Academic Publishers, 161–187.
—— (2003). 'Prosodic case checking domain: the case of constructs', in Jacqueline Lecarme (ed.) *Research in Afroasiatic Grammar II*. Amsterdam: John Benjamins, 481–510.
Slobin, Dan I. (1973). 'Cognitive prerequisites for the development of grammar', in Charles Ferguson and Dan I. Slobin (eds) *Studies of Child Language Development*. New York, NY: Holt, Rinehart and Winston, 175–208.
Smoczyńska, Magdalena (1985). 'The acquisition of Polish', in Dan I. Slobin (ed.) *The Crosslinguistic Study of Language Acquisition. Volume 1: The Data*. Hillsdale, NJ: Lawrence Erlbaum, 595–685.
Soehn, Jan-Philipp (2004). 'License to COLL', in Stefan Müller (ed.) *Proceedings of the HPSG-2004 Conference, Center for Computational Linguistics, Katholieke Universiteit Leuven*. Stanford, CA: CSLI Publications, 261–273.
—— (2006). 'On idiom parts and their contexts', *Linguistik online* 27(2): 11–28.
Spencer, Andrew (2003). 'Periphrastic paradigms in Bulgarian', in Uwe Junghanns and Luka Szucsich (eds) *Syntactic Structures and Morphological Information. Volume 7: Interface Explorations*. Berlin and New York: Mouton de Gruyter, 249–282.
Stabler, Edward (1997). 'Derivational minimalism', in *LACL '96: Selected Papers from the First International Conference on Logical Aspects of Computational Linguistics, London, UK*. New York, NY: Springer, 68–95.
—— (1998). 'Acquiring languages with movement', *Syntax* 2: 72–97.
Stankov, Valentin (1969). *Bâlgarskite glagolni vremena*. Sofia: Nauka i izkustvo.
Stanley, Richard (1967). 'Redundancy rules in phonology', *Language* 43: 393–436.
Starke, Michal (2001). *Move Dissolves into Merge*. PhD thesis, University of Geneva.
Steedman, Mark (1996). *Surface Structure and Interpretation*. Cambridge, MA: MIT Press.
—— (2000). *The Syntactic Process*. Cambridge, MA: MIT Press/Bradford Books.
Steriade, Donca (1987). 'Redundant values', in Anna Bosch, Barbara Need, and Eric Schiller (eds) *CLS 23: Papers from the 23rd Annual Regional Meeting of the Chicago Linguistic Society. Part II: Parasession on Autosegmental and Metrical Phonology*. Chicago, IL: Chicago Linguistic Society, 339–362.
Stockwell, Robert P., Paul Schachter, and Barbara Hall Partee (1973). *The Major Syntactic Structures of English*. New York: Holt, Rinehart and Winston.
Stowell, Tim (1983). 'Subjects across categories', *The Linguistic Review* 2: 285–312.
Straubing, Howard (1994). *Finite Automata, Formal Logic and Circuit Complexity*. Boston, MA: Birkhäuser.

Stump, Gregory T. (2001). *Inflectional Morphology: A Theory of Paradigm Structure*. Cambridge: Cambridge University Press.

—— (2005). 'Word-formation and inflectional morphology', in Pavol Štekauer and Rochelle Lieber (eds) *Handbook of Word-Formation* (Studies in Natural Language and Linguistic Theory 64). Dordrecht: Springer, 49–71.

—— and Ramawater Yadav (1988). 'Maithili verb agreement and the control agreement principle', in Diane Brentari, Gary N. Larson, and Lynn A. MacLeod (eds) *CLS 24: Papers from the 24th Annual Regional Meeting of the Chicago Linguistic Society. Part II: Parasession on Agreement in Grammatical Theory*. Chicago, IL: Chicago Linguistic Society, 304–321.

Suzman, Susan (1991). *Language Acquisition in Zulu*. PhD thesis, University of the Witwatersrand, Johannesburg.

—— (1996). 'Acquisition of noun class systems in related Bantu languages', in Carolyn E. Johnson and John Gilbert (eds) *Children's Language. Volume 9*. Hillsdale, NJ: Lawrence Erlbaum, 87–104.

Svantesson, Jan-Olaf (1985). 'Vowel harmony shift in Mongolian', *Lingua* 67: 283–327.

Svenonius, Peter (2002). 'Icelandic case and the structure of events', *Journal of Comparative Germanic Linguistics* 5: 197–225.

—— (2004). 'On the edge', in David Adger, Cécile de Cat, and George Tsoulas (eds) *Peripheries: Syntactic Edges and Their Effects*. Dordrecht: Kluwer Academic Publishers, 259–287.

—— (2007a). 'Interpreting uninterpretable features', *Linguistic Analysis* 33: 375–413.

—— (2007b). 'Projections of p', ms available as lingBuzz/000484.

Thráinsson, Höskuldur (1979). *On Complementation in Icelandic*. New York, NY: Garland.

Tiede, Hans-Jörg (2008). 'Inessential features, ineliminable features, and modal logics for model theoretic syntax', *Journal of Logic, Language and Information* 17(2): 217–227.

Tilkov, Dimitâr, Stojan Stojanov, and Konstantin Popov (eds) (1983). *Gramatika na sâvremennija bâlgarski knižoven ezik. Morfologija*. Sofia: Izdatelsto na Bâlgarskata Akademija na Naukite.

Tomasello, Michael (1992). *First Verbs: A Case Study of Early Grammatical Development*. Cambridge: Cambridge University Press.

Torrego, Esther (1984). 'On inversion in Spanish and some of its effects', *Linguistic Inquiry* 15: 103–129.

Trubetzkoy, Nikolai S. (1939). *Grundzüge der Phonologie*. Göttingen: Vandenhoek & Ruprecht. Translated by Christiane A. M. Baltaxe and published (1969) as *Principles of Phonology*. Berkeley, CA: University of California Press.

Tucker, G. Richard, Wallace Lambert, and André Rigault (1977). *The French Speaker's Skill with Grammatical Gender: An Example of Rule-Governed Behavior*. The Hague: Mouton.

Van Eynde, Frank (1998). 'The Immediate Dominance Schemata of HPSG. A deconstruction and a reconstruction', in Peter-Arno Coppen, Hans van Halteren, and Lisanne Teunissen (eds) *Computational Linguistics in the Netherlands 1997. Selected Papers from the Eighth CLIN Meeting.* Amsterdam and Atlanta: Rodopi, 119–133.

—— (2006). 'NP-internal agreement and the structure of the noun phrase', *Journal of Linguistics* 42(1): 139–186.

—— (2007). 'The big mess construction', in Stefan Müller (ed.) *The Proceedings of the 14th International Conference on Head-Driven Phrase Structure Grammar, Stanford University.* Stanford, CA: CSLI Publications, 415–433.

van Helden, W. Andries (1993). *Case and Gender: Concept Formation between Morphology and Syntax. Volumes 1–2.* (Studies in Slavic and General Linguistics 20). Amsterdam: Rodopi.

Walker, Rachel (2001). 'Round licensing, harmony, and bisyllabic triggers in Altaic', *Natural Language and Linguistic Theory* 19: 827–878.

Walsh, Michael (1993). 'Classifying the world in an Aboriginal language', in Michael Walsh and Colin Yallop (eds) *Language and Culture in Aboriginal Australia.* Canberra: Aboriginal Studies Press, 107–122.

Warner, Anthony R. (1988). 'Feature percolation, unary features, and the coordination of English NPs', *Natural Language and Linguistic Theory* 6: 39–54.

Wechsler, Stephen and Larisa Zlatić (2003). *The Many Faces of Agreement.* Stanford, CA: CSLI Publications.

Weiss, Daniel and Elissa Newport (2006). 'Mechanisms underlying language acquisition: benefits from a comparative approach', *Infancy* 9: 241–257.

Williamson, Kay (1965). *A Grammar of the Kolokuma Dialect of Ijo.* Cambridge: Cambridge University Press.

Winter, Yoad (2005). 'On some problems of (in)definiteness within flexible semantics', *Lingua* 115(6): 767–786.

Wintner, Shuly (2000). 'Definiteness in the Hebrew noun phrase', *Journal of Linguistics* 36: 319–363.

Woisetschlaeger, Erich (1983). 'On the question of definiteness in "an old man's book"', *Linguistic Inquiry* 14(1): 137–154.

Woods, William A., Ronald M. Kaplan, and Bonnie Nash-Webber (1972). *The Lunar Sciences Natural Language Information System: Final Report. BBN Report 2378.* Cambridge, MA: Bolt Beranek and Newman.

Wurzel, Wolfgang Ullrich (1984). *Flexionsmorphologie und Natürlichkeit.* (Studia grammatica 21). Berlin: Akademie-Verlag. English translation (1989) *Inflectional Morphology and Naturalness.* Dordrecht: Kluwer Academic Publishers.

Zaenen, Annie (1983). 'On syntactic binding', *Linguistic Inquiry* 14: 469–504.

Zaliznjak, Andrej A. (1964). 'K voprosu o grammatičeskix kategorijax roda i oduševlennosti v sovremennom russkom jazyke', *Voprosy jazykoznanija* 4: 25–40.

—— (1973). 'O ponimanii termina 'padež' v lingvističeskix opisanijax', in Andrej A. Zaliznjak (ed.) *Problemy grammatičeskogo modelirovanija.* Moscow: Nauka, 53–87.

Zec, Draga (1987). 'On obligatory control in clausal complements', in Masayo Iida, Stephen Wechsler, and Draga Zec (eds) *Working Papers in Grammatical Theory and Discourse Structure*. Stanford, CA: CSLI Publications, 139–168.

Zeijlstra, Hedde (2008). 'On the syntactic flexibility of formal features', in Theresa Biberauer (ed.) *The Limits of Syntactic Variation*. Amsterdam: John Benjamins, 143–173.

Zhang, Xi (1996). *Vowel Systems of the Manchu-Tungus Languages of China*. PhD thesis, University of Toronto.

—— and B. Elan Dresher (1996). 'Labial harmony in Written Manchu', *Saksaha: A Review of Manchu Studies* 1: 13–24.

Zhao, Jie (1989). *Xiandai Manyu Yanjiu* [*Studies on the Modern Manchu Language*]. Beijing: Minzu Chubanshe.

Zubin, David and Klaus-Michael Köpcke (1986). 'Gender and folk taxonomy: the indexal relation between grammatical and lexical categorization', in Colette Craig (ed.) *Noun Classes and Categorization*. Amsterdam: John Benjamins, 139–180.

Zwicky, Arnold M. (1985). 'How to describe inflection', in Mary Niepokuj, Mary Van Clay, Vassiliki Nikiforidou, and Deborah Feder (eds) *BLS 11: Proceedings of the Eleventh Annual Meeting of the Berkeley Linguistics Society*. Berkeley, CA: Berkeley Linguistics Society, 372–386.

—— (1986a). 'German adjective agreement in GPSG', *Linguistics* 24: 957–990.

—— (1986b). 'Imposed versus inherent feature specifications, and other multiple feature markings', in *The Indiana University Linguistics Club 20th Anniversary Volume*. Bloomington, IN: Indiana University Linguistics Club, 85–106.

—— (1992). 'Jottings on adpositions, case inflections, government and agreement', in Diane Brentari, Gary N. Larson, and Lynn A. MacLeod (eds) *The Joy of Grammar: A Festschrift in Honor of James D. McCawley*. Amsterdam: John Benjamins, 369–383.

—— (1996). 'Syntax and phonology', in Keith Brown and Jim Miller (eds) *Concise Encyclopedia of Syntactic Theories*. Oxford: Elsevier Science, 300–305.

Author index

Abney, Steven P. 204
Ackerman, Farrell 171, 177, 179, 180
Adger, David 3, 9–10, 28, 164, 185–218
Afanasiev, Loredana 281
Aikhenvald, Alexandra 84, 102
Alexiadou, Artemis 143, 145 n. 1, 147, 157, 160, 162–3, 164
Allegranza, Valerio 258 n. 14
Anderson, Gregory D. S. 182
Anderson, Stephen R. 3, 73, 169
Andrews, Avery D. 264
Archangeli, Diana 48, 57
Aristar Dry, Helen 35
Aronoff, Mark 169
Aronson, Howard I. 168
Arterberry, Martha E. 123
Aslin, Richard 116, 142
Asudeh, Ash 28, 187, 195 n. 4, 266
Avery, Peter 61
Avgustinova, Tania 170, 173

Baerman, Matthew 6, 17, 18, 19–20, 31, 82
Baker, Brett 102
Barlow, Michael 27
Barwise, Jon 163 n. 13
Béjar, Susana 164
Bender, Emily 27, 250–1, 254 n. 11, 267 n. 24
Berman, Ruth 142
Bhatt, Rajesh 201, 207–8
Bickel, Balthasar 34
Blackburn, Patrick 277, 280
Blake, Barry 273
Blevins, James 64, 171
Bloom, Paul 111
Bobaljik, Jonathan 187

Booij, Geert 2, 25, 73
Borer, Hagit 143, 145, 150, 154, 155, 158, 185, 204
Börjars, Kersti 171, 179
Bos, Johan 223
Bošković, Željko 170
Bouma, Gosse 262
Brody, Michael 160, 202, 212, 218
Broe, Michael 58
Bronnenberg, Wim 222
Brooks, Patricia 111
Brown, Dunstan 19–20, 31, 72, 73
Butt, Miriam 226
Bybee, Joan 66

Cable, Seth 213
Caha, Pavel 198
Caponigro, Ivano 262
Carey, Susan 111
Carpenter, Bob 26, 28 n. 7, 187, 196
Carstairs-McCarthy, Andrew 66
Chomsky, Noam 1, 3, 27, 48, 146, 149, 160, 185, 186, 187, 188, 193, 196, 205, 206, 208 n. 14, 209, 213, 237–9, 242, 248
Chumakina, Marina 72
Chung, Sandra 262
Chvany, Catherine 19 n. 3
Cinque, Guglielmo 197
Clark, Eve 111
Clements, George N. 48, 262
Collins, Chris 199 n. 6, 200
Colmerauer, Alain 28 n. 7
Comrie, Bernard 34, 72
Cooper, Robin 163 n. 13
Copestake, Ann 2, 10, 17, 26, 28, 221–35, 249, 255 n. 13, 260 n. 17, 269

Author index

Corbett, Greville G. 3, 4, 6, 17–36, 67, 68–9, 70, 72–3, 75, 76, 78–9, 82, 84, 87, 88, 92, 96, 101, 104, 109 n. 2, 110, 117, 119, 123, 142, 145, 146, 149, 153 n. 8, 181–2, 233, 273, 275
Cormack, Annabel 195 n. 4
Craig, Colette 110
Crowley, Terry 102, 119

Dalrymple, Mary 30
Daniels, Mike 249 n. 7
Danon, Gabi 2, 7–8, 143–65
Deen, Kamil Ud 110–11
DeLoache, Judy S. 111
Demuth, Katherine 110
Dench, Alan 264
De Rijke, Maarten 280
Dickinson, Markus 266, 267
Diesing, Molly 262
Dixon, Robert M.W. 7, 112–15, 117, 119, 120, 121–2, 124 n. 13, 125–6, 127, 131, 135–7, 138, 140
Dobrovie-Sorin, Carmen 143, 150 n. 6, 154, 156–8, 160
Doner, John 288
Donohue, Mark 262 n. 19
Dorais, Louis-Jacques 48
Dorian, Nancy 138
Dowty, David 188
Dresher, B. Elan 3, 4–5, 37–63
Dziwirek, Katarzyna 75, 104

Efere, Emmanuel Efereala 58–59
Emonds, Joseph E. 197 n. 5, 262
Engelhardt, Miriam 152–3
Evans, Nicholas 69 n. 5, 88–104, 264

Falk, Yehuda 145
Fant, C. Gunnar 1
Farrar, Scott 35
Fassi Fehri, Abdelkader 152, 156
Faßke, Helmut 25
Fitch, W. Tecumseh 185, 196

Flemming, Edward 38
Flickinger, Dan 2, 10, 17, 221–35, 250–1, 267 n. 24
Fodor, Jerry A. 1
Frampton, John 160, 186, 201, 205 n. 13, 208
Frank, Robert 186
Franks, Steven 19 n. 3, 170
Fraser, Norman M. 25
Frisch, Stefan 58

Gallistel, Charles R. 111
Gardent, Claire 277
Gärtner, Hans-Martin 187
Gazdar, Gerald 1, 17, 19 n. 3, 26, 27, 33, 187, 195, 196, 242, 267 n. 23, 273, 280, 288
Gelman, Susan A. 111
Gentner, Deidre 123
Gerdts, Donna B. 266
Gerken, LouAnn 111
Ginzburg, Jonathan 28
Givón, Talmy 69
Greenberg, Joseph H. 26
Grimshaw, Jane 197, 198, 215
Grosz, Barbara J. 222
Gutmann, Samuel 160, 186, 201, 205 n. 13, 208
Gvozdev, Aleksandr N. 110

Hajičová, Eva 30
Hale, Ken 94
Hall, Daniel Currie 57–8 n. 10
Halle, Morris 1, 18, 43–4, 47–8, 274
Hansson, Gunnar Ólafur 58, 60
Harabagiu, Sanda 223
Harbour, Daniel 164, 192–3, 212
Harley, Heidi 164, 193
Harman, Gilbert 1
Harris, Zellig S. 242
Harvey, Mark 102, 113, 116
Haspelmath, Martin 24, 34
Hauser, Marc D. 185, 196

Hayward, Richard J. 33
Hazout, Ilan 155, 156
Heller, Daphna 154
Herd, Jonathon 60–62
Higgins, Francis R. 241–2
Hockett, Charles F. 84
Höhle, Tilman N. 266
Huddleston, Rodney 273, 275
Hudson Kam, Carla 111, 116
Hukari, Thomas E. 187, 196, 262, 263 n. 20, 266
Hume, Elizabeth V. 48

Idiata, Daniel F. 110
Idsardi, William J. 61

Jackendoff, Ray S. 290–1
Jacobson, Pauline 188
Jakobson, Roman 1, 18, 19 n. 3, 41, 43–4, 47–8
Ji, Yonghai 54
Johnson, David E. 276
Joshi, Aravind 186, 246
Julien, Marit 197
Jusczyk, Peter W. 142

Kajita, Masaru 238–42, 246, 247, 248
Kamp, Hans 232
Kaplan, Ronald M. 28, 30
Kapust, Waltraud 110
Karmiloff-Smith, Annette 110–11, 142
Katamba, Francis 110
Kathol, Andreas 249 n. 7
Katz, Jerrold J. 1
Kaun, Abigail Rhoades 55, 56–8
Kay, Martin 28
Kay, Paul 1, 250 n. 9
Kayne, Richard 197, 262
Kean, Mary-Louise 48
Keenan, Edward L. 163 n. 13
Kellman, Philip 123
Kempe, Vera 110–11
Kibort, Anna 3, 5–6, 64–106, 145 n. 1, 149

King, Tracy Holloway 170
Kiparsky, Paul 48, 191 n. 3
Kiss, Tibor 267
Klein, Ewan 1, 26, 27, 187, 195, 196
Klokeid, Terry 94
Koch, Grace 117, 119 n. 7, 125
Korn, David 56
Kornai, András 290
Köpcke, Klaus-Michael 116
Kracht, Marcus 12, 289–92
Krifka, Manfred 231
Kroch, Anthony 186
Kuhn, Jonas 29 n. 9
Kunene, Euphrasia C.L. 110
Kuroda, Sige-Yuki 57

Laidig, Carol J. 20
Laidig, Wyn D. 20
Lakoff, George 7, 31, 113, 114 n. 6, 115–16, 120, 122–3, 124 n. 13, 127
Langendoen, D. Terence 35
Lascarides, Alex 269
Leech, Geoffrey 34
Lenček, Rado L. 30
Levin, Magnus 29
Levine, Robert D. 187, 196, 262, 263 n. 20
Levy, Yonata 142
Libkin, Leonid 278
Liljencrants, Johan 38
Lindblom, Björn 38
Link, Godehard 192, 231–4
Longobardi, Giuseppe 143, 156–7
Lotz, John 41
Lyster, Roy 119

Mackenzie, Sara 58–9
Malouf, Robert 264–5
Mandler, Jean 111, 123, 142
Marantz, Alec 185, 204 n. 12
Markert, Katja 223
Martinet, André 40
Maslov, Jurij S. 174
Matthews, Peter H. 1, 18, 64, 66, 169

Matushansky, Ora 194
McCloskey, James 262
McGinnis, Martha 164
McNaughton, Robert 278
Mel'čuk, Igor 66, 69 n. 4
Mellish, Chris 17
Meurers, W. Detmar 249 n. 7, 255 n. 13, 267
Meyer, Peter 32
Mielke, Jeff 45 n. 3
Mills, Anne E. 110
Moravcsik, Edith A. 67
Moss, Lawrence S. 280, 284
Müller, Stefan 250 n. 8
Mylne, Tom 113, 114 n. 4, 116, 120, 122–3, 124 n. 13

Namy, Laura 123
Narayanan, Srini 223
Newman, Stanley 57
Newport, Elissa 111, 116, 142
Nilsen, Øystein 200
Noyer, Rolf 192
Nunberg, Geoffrey 270
Nunes, Jairo 187

O'Grady, Geoff N. 119
Ojeda, Almerindo 232, 234
Ortmann, Albert 146

Palm, Adi 286
Panevová, Jarmila 30
Papert, Seymour 278
Partee, Barbara Hall 1
Pašov, Petâr 168, 174
Pensalfini, Robert 21, 22 n. 5
Pesetsky, David 160, 200, 201
Pierrehumbert, Janet 58
Plaster, Keith 2, 6–7, 109–42
Polinsky, Maria 2, 6–7, 109–42, 262
Pollard, Carl J. 10, 27, 69 n. 5, 242, 248, 251, 254–5, 258 n. 14, 259 n. 16, 263 n. 20, 267 n. 23

Pollock, Jean-Yves 262
Popova, Gergana 3, 8–9, 95, 166–84
Postal, Paul M. 1, 272, 276
Potsdam, Eric 266
Preissler, Melissa 111
Prince, Alan 49
Przepiórkowski, Adam 36, 73 n. 9, 266–7
Pulleyblank, Douglas 48
Pullum, Geoffrey K. 1, 2, 11–12, 18, 26, 27, 187, 195, 196, 258 n. 15, 272–92

Ramchand, Gillian 187, 218
Reape, Mike 249 n. 7
Retoré, Christian 186
Reyle, Uwe 232
Řezáč, Milan 201 n. 8
Ritter, Elizabeth 164, 193
Rizzi, Luigi 215
Rogers, Andy 266
Rogers, James 277, 279, 289
Rose, Sharon 58
Runner, Jeffrey T. 266

Sadler, Louisa 29 n. 9, 156, 171, 177, 179, 180
Saffran, Jenny 116, 142
Sag, Ivan A. 1, 3, 10, 11, 26–7, 28, 69 n. 5, 195, 214, 236–71
Sailer, Manfred 269 n. 25
Sapir, Edward 38–9
Sauerland, Uli 146
Saussure, Ferdinand de 33, 37–8
Scatton, Ernest A. 168
Schachter, Paul 1
Schenker, Alexander M. 72
Schlenker, Philippe 192
Schmidt, Annette 119 n. 7, 121 n. 10, 122 n. 12, 126, 136, 138–9
Scholz, Barbara C. 277
Ševa, Nada 111
Shieber, Stuart M. 28, 196, 201, 208, 241–2

Sichel, Ivy 145 n. 2
Siloni, Tal 147, 150, 152, 155, 157, 160, 162–3
Slobin, Dan I. 142
Smoczyńska, Magdalena 110 n. 3, 142
Smolensky, Paul 49
Soehn, Jan-Philipp 269 n. 25
Spencer, Andrew 171, 177, 179, 180
Stabler, Edward 186
Stankov, Valentin 168, 174
Stanley, Richard 25, 48
Starke, Michal 197–8
Steedman, Mark 248
Steriade, Donca 48
Stockwell, Robert P. 1
Stowell, Tim 215
Straubing, Howard 278
Stump, Gregory T. 18, 26, 66, 72, 75, 169, 171, 177, 178 n. 4, 179, 180
Suzman, Susan 110
Svantesson, Jan-Olaf 55
Svenonius, Peter 18, 185, 188, 201 n. 8, 217

Thráinsson, Höskuldur 238
Tiede, Hans-Jörg 2, 11–12, 272–92
Tilkov, Dimitâr 168
Toivonen, Ida 28, 187, 195 n. 4
Tomasello, Michael 111
Torrego, Esther 160, 200, 201, 262
Trubetzkoy, Nikolai S. 1, 46–7
Tucker, G. Richard 119

van Everbroeck, Ezra 119
Van Eynde, Frank 258
van Helden, W. Andries 32
Venema, Yde 280

Walker, Rachel 53, 58
Walsh, Michael 114 n. 5
Warner, Anthony R. 18 n. 2
Wasow, Thomas 27, 254 n. 11
Watkins, Laurel 212
Wechsler, Stephen 30
Weiss, Daniel 111
Williamson, Kay 48–9
Wilson, Andrew 34
Winter, Yoad 156
Wintner, Shuly 145
Woisetschlaeger, Erich 157 n. 11
Woods, William A. 222
Wurzel, Wolfgang Ullrich 66

Yadav, Ramawater 75

Zaenen, Annie 262, 283
Zaliznjak, Andrej A. 5, 19 n. 3, 32, 72
Zec, Draga 266
Zeijlstra, Hedde 149
Zhang, Xi 50–3, 55
Zhao, Jie 54
Zlatić, Larisa 30
Zubin, David 116
Zwicky, Arnold M. 3, 18, 25, 33, 66, 68, 73, 169, 258 n. 15

Language index

Language groupings named in the volume are given in italic. ISO codes have been provided where available.

Arabic (ara) 145, 149
Arawak (arw) 84
Archi (aqc) 24, 72
Austronesian (map) 75

Baniwa (bwi) 84
Banjalang (bdy) 119
Bantu (bnt) 84, 110, 122
Bayso (bsw) 33
Bininj Gun-wok (Mayali) (gup) 21
Bosnian (bos) 30
Bulgarian (bul) 8, 95, 167–77, 180–1, 183–4
Bumo Izon (ijc) 58–60
Burarra (bvr) 19

Central Moluccan 20
Chichewa (nya) 30
Croatian (hrv) 30
Czech (ces) 30, 181

Daghestanian 24, 72
Daly 88
Dogon (Tommo So: no ISO code to date) 19
Dutch (nld) 73
  eastern dialects 266
Dyirbal (dbl) 2, 7, 111–42
  Young People's Dyirbal 121, 126, 128, 136, 138–40, 141

English (eng) 24, 29, 32, 48, 60, 76, 77, 79, 124, 131, 143, 146, 148–9, 156–9, 166, 228–34, 238 n. 3, 242, 250, 263, 266–7, 273–4
Eskimo-Aleut 48

French (fra) 2, 17, 40–2, 102, 119, 141, 146, 275

Gaelic (gla) 138
German (deu) 19, 20, 26, 75, 102, 110, 116, 238 n. 3, 267, 275
  Bavarian German 75
Greek (ell) 145 n. 1, 157 n. 10

Halkomelem (hur) 266
Hawaiian (haw) 60–2
Hebrew (heb) 2, 7–8, 143–65
Hindi (hin) 207–8
Hungarian (hun) 146

Icelandic (isl) 238
Ijoid (ijo) 48, 58
Indo-European (ine) 23, 119, 122, 141
Indo-Iranian 75
Inuit 48
Irish (gle) 263

Japanese (jpn) 238 n. 3
Jingulu (jlg) 21–3

Kabyle (kab) 84
Kala Lagaw Ya (mwp) 130
Kayardild (gyd) 6, 65, 69, 88, 89–106
Khakass (Kachin dialect) (kjh) 56
Kolokuma Ijo (ijc) 48–9
Konkani (knn) 30
Kuku-Jalanji (gvn) 130

Lardil (lbz) 94
Larike (alo) 20–1

Language index

Latin (lat) 119, 141
Latvian (lav) 2

Maithili (mai) 75
Manchad (lae) 19
Manchu (mnc) 50–7
Maori (mri) 60, 61–2
Martuthunira (vma) 264–5
Mbabaram (vmb) 130
Mongolian (mon) 55–7
Mongolian (Khalkha dialect) (khk) 55
Muluridyi (vmu) 130
Muna (mnb) 75

Ngyangumarta (nna) 130
Niger-Congo 48
Northeast Caucasian 122
Northern Nyungar (nys) 130
Nyawaygi (nyt) 129

Oroqen (orh) 55

Paama (pma) 102
Pama-Nyungan 7, 111, 117, 119, 130, 264
  non-Pama-Nyungan 21
Polabian (pox) 47
Polish (pol) 30, 36, 67–8, 71, 73, 75, 77, 104, 266–7
Polynesian 60–1

Romanian (ron) 2, 33, 72–3, 156
Russian (rus) 19 n. 3, 27, 30, 32–3, 47, 77, 79, 102, 110–11, 166–7
  Heritage Russian 138

Semitic (sem) 143–4, 149, 152, 156
Serbian (srp) 30
Serbo-Croatian (hbs) 30, 266
Siglitun (ikt) 48–9
Slavic; Slavonic (sla) 8, 111, 167
Slovene (slv) 30

Tamazight (tzm) 84
Tamil (tam) 75
Tangkic 6, 89, 94
Tariana (tae) 84
Tashelhit (shi) 84
Tungusic 55, 56–7
Turkic 55–7
Turkish (tur) 56

Upper Sorbian (hsb) 25–6

Welsh (cym) 156

Xibe (sjo) 53, 55

Yidiny (yii) 118–19, 121
Yowlumne Yokuts (yok) 57

Subject index

accessibility relation 280, 282–3
acquisition:
 of gender system 7, 110–11, 141
 of phonology 43–4, 47
Activity Condition 201, 212
adjunction 246, 248
Advanced Tongue Root 50, 51–4
 see also height contrast
Agree operation 160, 187, 202, 206–13, 217–18
agreement 1, 4–6, 8–10, 21, 25, 64–105, 111–12, 122, 138, 144–67, 172, 180–4, 188–91, 206–8, 217–18, 233, 245, 248, 250–1, 256–9, 262, 266
 adjectival 26, 156
 canonical 22–3, 69, 79, 96, 100, 103
 controller of, see controller of agreement
 directionality of 88, 99–100, 102
 non-canonical 25
 semantic 30, 78–80, 153 n. 8, 250
 syntactic 30, 78–80, 250
 target of, see target of agreement
Agreement Hierarchy 28–30, 68
ambiguity 222, 223 n. 2, 226–7, 233
analysis problem 31–2
analytic form 8, 171
 see also periphrasis
anaphora 10, 224
 anaphor(a) resolution 224, 231, 234
animacy 1, 73 n. 9, 111, 114, 118, 125 n. 15, 129
 see also gender
Animacy Hierarchy 31
application, see computational linguistic application

application interface 222
Arc Pair Grammar 276
aspect 6, 8, 18, 69 n. 5, 76, 80, 83, 88–9, 94–5, 97, 100–1, 105, 149, 166, 168, 170, 201 n. 8, 225, 228
aspectual classes of verbs 224
assignment:
 of case 11, 68, 92, 100, 103, 242, 248, 261, 264
 of feature value 45, 65, 70–1, 80, 84, 105, 145 n. 1, 172, 176
 of nouns to genders/classes 7, 21, 76, 110, 112–42; see also gender assignment system
 of semantic role 266
assignment rule 33, 69, 82, 114–16, 120, 142
associativity 83
atomic formula 280–1, 283–4, 286
 see also feature, atomic
ATR contrast, see Advanced Tongue Root
AVM (Attribute Value Matrix) 196

bar level 272
 see also features: BAR
binarity 4, 18
 binary relation 277
 binary tree 279, 283–4, 289
 see also feature, binary
BNC (British National Corpus) 29, 231
borrowing 2, 60–1, 131
 see also loanword adaptation
branching diagram 47–8
broad-coverage processing; broad-coverage computational grammars 10, 221–4, 227, 230, 233, 235

Subject index

case:
  adnominal 89–92, 97, 103
  associative 90
  complementizing 89–91, 95–8, 103
  governed 6, 65, 98, 104, 258; *see also* case, structural
  modal 89–95, 97, 101–3
  relational 89–92, 97, 101–4
  semantic; semantically imposed 6, 69, 87 n. B, 99, 103–4
  structural 74, 104, 188, 191 n. 3
  verbal 90 n. 15
  verbalizing 90–2, 99, 101–4; *see also* case, verbal
case stacking 104, 264–6
case-stacking languages 6, 11, 65, 264
categorial features 199–200, 203–4, 206, 209, 217
CCG (Combinatory Categorial Grammar) 257
CG (Categorial Grammar) 247–8
characteristic variable 232
checking 28, 66, 189, 192, 203 n. 11
classifier 7, 85, 88, 117–20, 125, 128, 135–6, 141, 231
closure operator 231–4
collectivity 83
competition 109, 178, 258 n. 15
compositional semantics 10, 157, 161, 221–3
computational compositional semantics 222
computational linguistics 10, 221–2
computational linguistic application 4, 10, 17, 34–5, 64, 148, 222–3, 226–8, 230
concord 70, 164
  negative 70
conjoined noun phrases 29–30, 224
conjugation 82
consonant co-occurrence 63
construct state nominal (CSN) 8, 149–54, 157–64

construction 11, 24, 26–7, 94, 98, 100, 165, 226, 231, 233, 236, 248–55, 263, 269, 271
co-verb 102
expletive 262
filler-gap 270
genitive 8, 143, 148, 156, 161
'if-then' 228
periphrastic, *see* periphrastic construction
possessive 74, 158–9
predicate nominal 74
pseudo-partitive 224
reflexive 99, 259
resultative 99
serial verb 101–2
tag-question 251, 268
tough 217, 242–3, 247
Construction Grammar 11, 271
constructional mismatches 4, 29
context-free grammar 281
  context-free phrase structure grammar 12, 284
context-free subcategorization 245–6
contrastive hierarchy 5, 39, 46–8, 58–62
  see also feature hierarchy
control 11, 227, 236, 245, 259, 266
controller of agreement 6, 24–9, 68, 70 n. 7, 71–81, 84, 87, 92, 96, 100, 181–2
  hybrid 79–80; *see also* hybrid, lexical
copy raising 266, 268
correspondence problem 5, 31, 33, 275
  see also cross-linguistic identification of features
cross-linguistic identification of features 275
CSN, *see* construct state nominal

declensional class 82
default 4, 20, 24, 29, 29, 62, 75, 86, 96, 141, 191 n. 3
  emergency case 25
  general 23

default (cont.)
  identity function (IFD) 178
  normal case 25
  persistent 269–70
  ultimate 22–3
default class 120, 124–6, 129, 134–6
default condition 114
default interpretation 165
defective nouns 233–4
definability 12, 284
definite 143–4, 151–3, 157–62, 168, 188–94, 274
  definite article 75, 145–6, 150, 153 n. 9, 154–6, 161–3, 275
  see also indefinite
definiteness 2, 6–9, 69, 74–5, 83, 105, 143–65, 198
  definiteness spreading 8, 143, 151, 153, 156, 164–5
DELPH-IN grammars 10, 221, 224–9, 234
demonstrative 112, 122, 161
deponency 72
derivation; derivational 92, 99, 144, 164, 194, 205–8, 216, 227 n. 5, 250, 255, 272
determiner 1, 75, 147, 149, 151–2, 156–9, 162–3, 165–6, 234, 257, 258 n. 15, 259
diachronic development; diachronic motivation 38, 112, 117, 141
dichotomous scale 47
  see also feature hierarchy
domain 277–80
  domain union 254 n. 12
  of COLL (conditions on lexical licensing) 269 n. 25
  of extraction path 263
  of feature 3, 6, 68–71, 74, 78, 85, 87–91, 101 n. 18, 109
  of locality 11, 256, 271
  of subcategorization 237–9, 241, 245–8, 250, 253
  see also features: DOMAIN
downstep 262

EAGLES (Expert Advisory Group on Language Engineering Standards) 34
eliminability; eliminable 287, 289, 292
E-MELD (Electronic Metastructure for Endangered Languages Data) 35
emergency case default, see default
English Resource Grammar (ERG) 35, 224, 267 n. 24
entailment; entail 118, 159, 162, 193, 202 n. 9, 218, 223, 232–3, 264, 266–7
evidentiality 76, 80, 83
expletive 242, 262, 268
expressive power 11, 277, 284, 292
Extended Projections 197
External Merge, see Merge
extraction path 262–3

facultative value 4, 20
faithfulness constraints 49–50
feature:
  atomic 12, 187–8, 190–3, 196, 231, 253, 264, 278; see also atomic formula
  active 5, 46, 54, 57 n. 10, 62; see also phonological activity
  binary 12, 18–20, 25, 191–5, 218, 273–5, 286; see also feature, bivalent
  bivalent 8, 161–2, 164; see also feature, binary
  canonical 70 n. 6, 82
  contextual; contextually realized 2, 4, 6, 25–6, 71, 73–83, 85
  contrastive 5, 38–47, 50–1, 53, 55–63
  imposed 25, 69, 87 n. C, D, 98, 103, 104
  inert 5, 46
  inessential 12, 289–91; see also feature, redundant
  inherent; inherently realized 2, 4, 6, 25–6, 69 n. 4, 73–85, 125 n. 15, 159, 231, 258
  innate 45 n. 3
  interface 18

interpretable 26, 146, 211
lexical 82, 94, 286; see also feature value, fixed
monovalent 8, 161–4; see also feature, privative; feature, unary
morphological; *m*-features 1, 6, 18, 65, 67, 80, 82, 180
morphosemantic 5–6, 18, 65, 69–70, 80–5, 88, 94
morphosyntactic 5–6, 8–9, 12, 18, 27, 31, 64–7, 80–5, 98, 103–6, 143–52, 156–65, 166–9, 176, 180, 184, 198, 273, 291
multivalent 162 n. 12, 195, 197, 218; see also feature, *n*-ary
n-ary 273–4; see also feature, multivalent
non-autonomous 72, 73 n. 8, 75
non-interpretable, see uninterpretable
orthogonal 17
phonological 1, 5, 18, 37–63; see also phonological features
privative 45, 161, 187–94, 273; see also feature, monovalent; feature, unary
redundant 5, 38–9, 41–2, 58; see also feature, inessential
semantic 1, 7, 8, 10, 31, 69, 99, 103–4, 109–42, 144–56, 162–5, 229, 231, 233–4, 267 n. 24; see also noun class
syntactic, *s*-features 18, 180, 187, 190, 194–5, 242, 246, 275
unary 18 n. 2, 273; see also feature, monovalent; feature, privative
uninterpretable 3, 26, 146, 188–90
unvalued 9, 25, 164, 191, 194, 200–13, 216
feature co-occurrence restriction 26, 273, 286
feature declaration 252–3
feature geometry 11, 48, 236, 249, 251, 261 n. 18
feature hierarchy 5, 40–1, 44, 48–50, 57 see also contrastive hierarchy

feature inheritance 248
feature inventory 4, 6, 11, 31–2, 35, 40–1, 65–6, 72, 103, 105–6, 110, 144, 242–3
feature ordering 42, 45–6, 50, 61, 63
feature percolation 242, 267
feature sharing 144, 159–60
feature spreading 151
  see also definiteness spreading
feature structure 9, 10, 19–20, 26, 185, 195–7, 214, 225, 228–30, 242, 247–55
feature typing 26–7, 195–6
feature value; feature values:
  binary, see feature, binary
  facultative, see facultative value
  fixed 76–8, 81–2, 84
  formal properties of/criteria for/cues for the selection of 7, 75–85, 111, 116–22, 125, 128–36, 139–42, 144, 147–8, 163, 165, 174, 176, 181, 189, 275
  mismatch of, see mismatch of values
  multirepresentation of, see multirepresentation of feature value
  selected 6, 69, 76–82, 86, 92, 94–5, 100, 102–4
  semantic properties of/criteria for/cues for the selection of 5–8, 25, 29, 31, 64, 67–105, 111, 117–18, 122, 124, 128, 133, 135, 142, 190–1, 200, 275
features:
  AGR 245, 256, 257, 267 n. 23; see also agreement
  AUX 30, 243, 256, 272, 274, 291–2
  BAR 12, 196, 244, 272–3, 286, 290; see also bar level
  CASE 1, 12, 194, 196, 198, 210, 243, 256, 264–6, 272–4, 291; see also case
  CATEGORY (CAT) 196, 201–3, 206, 209–10, 212, 249, 254–70
  CONTEXT 251–3
  DOMAIN 250; see also domain
  DOOM 272–3
  EXTERNAL ARGUMENT (XARG) 250–1, 267–8, 271

features (*cont.*)
  FORM 250–3, 256–61, 263, 265, 267–8, 270
  GAP 263–4, 271
  HEAD 242–5, 249, 251, 254–7, 286–7; *see also* head
  LEXICAL IDENTIFIER (LID) 269–71
  LOCAL 249, 251
  MODALITY 175
  MODIFIED (MOD) 257
  MOOD 170, 177, 182, 195, 225; *see also* mood
  NFORM 243, 274
  NONLOCAL 249
  NUMBER (NUM) 1, 168–71, 177, 181, 183, 194–6, 198–203, 207, 218, 225, 230, 232, 272–4, 259; *see also* number
  PERSON (PERS) 1, 19, 168–70, 177, 181, 183, 207, 230, 271, 274; *see also* person
  PFORM 243, 256, 273–4
  PHONOLOGY 249, 251–2; *see also* feature, phonological
  PRED 243, 256
  RELATIONS (RELS) 225, 270
  SELECT (SEL) 257–9
  SEMANTICS (SEM) 251–3, 270; *see also* feature, semantic
  SLASH 12, 196, 217, 243–4, 264, 272–3, 288–90
  SPEC 158, 217, 257, 261
  SUBCAT 214, 249, 257, 272
  SYNTAX (SYN) 250–9, 261, 263, 265, 267–8, 290; *see also* feature, syntactic
  TENSE 167–73, 175, 182–3, 194, 196, 198, 211, 225, 229, 240–1, 272; *see also* tense
  VALENCE (VAL) 254–8, 261–2, 265–8, 270
  VFORM (VF) 243 n. 5, 244–5, 256–7, 261, 273–4
  WH 213, 272, 274

XARG, *see* features: EXTERNAL ARGUMENT
filler-gap dependency 11, 236, 248, 262–3, 270
finite-state languages 278, 288
first-order logic 277–8
focus 22 n. 5, 76, 80, 83
folklore 125–6, 137
formal semantics 231, 234
for/to clause 261
FUG (Functional Unification Grammar) 185, 195–6
Full Interpretation 189, 205, 207
functional category 197, 204

GB (Government and Binding framework) 28, 201 n. 8, 277
gender assignment system 71, 75–7
  see also gender system
gender system 2, 73, 111, 115, 117, 122 n. 12, 123, 125, 136, 141–2
  subgender 73
  see also feature value, formal properties/criteria/cues; feature value, semantic properties/criteria/cues
glossing 34, 36
  see also Leipzig Glossing Rules
GOLD (General Ontology for Linguistic Description) 35, 67 n. 2
governee 6, 67, 68, 74, 80
government 5–6, 64–89, 92–105, 206, 242, 248, 258–9, 265
  canonical 94, 105
  directionality of 88, 258
governor 68, 87, 94, 96, 258
GPSG (Generalized Phrase Structure Grammar) 12, 26, 195–6, 217, 242–9, 256–7, 263, 267 n. 23, 272, 277, 286, 288
Grammar Matrix 226–7
grammar signature 253

head 25–6, 29, 68, 69 n. 4, 92, 97–8, 102, 149 n. 4, 150, 153–4, 160, 179, 199, 202, 206, 212–13, 242–5, 255–9, 261, 286
  see also features: HEAD
Head-Driven Phrase Structure Grammar, see HPSG
Head Feature Principle (HFP) 11, 242, 245, 254, 256, 259, 264, 271
height contrast 43, 47, 51, 54, 56–7
heteroclisis 72
hierarchical classification 253
Hierarchy of Projection (HoP) 197–200, 203 n. 11, 204–5, 213, 215
honorific 70, 74–5
HPSG (Head-Driven Phrase Structure Grammar) 10–11, 27–8, 35, 160, 185, 195–6, 214, 221, 224–6, 245–57, 260–4, 267 n. 23, 272, 275–6, 288
hybrid, lexical 4, 28–9

Identity Function Default (IFD) 178
idioms 266, 269–71
ID rule 243
indefinite 8, 144, 147–8, 151–3, 155, 157–9, 161–3, 165
  indefinite article 75, 148, 150, 258 n. 15
inference 31, 222, 224, 231, 234
inferential form; inferential construction 174–6
infinitival form 166, 168
infinitival complement 207–8, 239, 261, 264 n. 21
inflection 6, 25, 73–5, 93–4, 97–102, 104, 147, 194, 206, 228
inflectional class 1, 18, 23, 82
information extraction (IE) 10, 222–3, 226
information management 222
insubordination 95
interaction of features 3, 76 n. 10, 114
interface 67
  morphology-semantics 6
  natural language 222, 224, 228
  Semantic (Sem-I) 229–30
  syntax-morphology 3, 18, 206–7
  syntax-semantics 7, 144, 148, 160–2, 165, 188–91, 195, 199, 205, 218
  syntax-prosody 149, 187
interface constraint 188, 205
interface feature 18
  see also feature
interpretability 146, 153, 155, 160
  uninterpretability 189
  see also feature, interpretable; feature, uninterpretable
inventory of features, see feature inventory
inversion:
  auxiliary 291
  locative 217
  stylistic 262
  verb-subject 262
IPI PAN corpus 36
ISO (International Organization for Standardization) 34

label 186, 199, 202, 286
  semantic label 125–40
language model 253
language-independent encoding 228
lattice 192, 230–1
learnability 7, 110, 112, 116, 122, 141, 195 n. 4
Leipzig Glossing Rules 25, 34, 36
lexeme 9, 72, 83, 166–70, 177–84, 255
lexical item 9, 71, 82, 86, 187–8, 197–8, 202–3, 210, 214–18
lexical licensing 269 n. 25
lexical markup framework (LMF) 34–5
lexical rule 229
lexical semantics 1, 147–8, 153, 158, 224
Lexical-Functional Grammar, see LFG
lexicalist theories 9, 197
Lexicality 290
lexicon 9, 11, 69, 82, 104–5, 195, 235, 254
  broad-coverage 10

lexicon (*cont.*)
  computational 34, 222, 224, 227
  Dyirbal nominal 112–13, 119 n. 7, 136, 141
LFG (Lexical-Functional Grammar) 27–8, 29 n. 9, 35, 160, 185, 195–6, 226, 257, 264, 277
liberation rules 250
linearization 187
  linearization theory 249
LinGO (LINguistic Grammars Online) 35, 224, 227
LKB (Lexical Knowledge Builder) 35
loanword 112, 124
  loanword adaptation 60, 63
locality 3, 218, 254–61
  of construction 11, 236, 248–51
  of selection 11, 236–7, 242, 246–8
  strict 237–9
locally threshold testable stringsets 278
logic, *see* first-order logic; modal logic; weak monadic second-order logic
logical redundancy 41–2
LOGON (machine translation demonstrator) 229
Longman Spoken American Corpus (LSAC) 29

markedness 24, 48
mathematical linguistics 276, 278, 292
maximality 159, 290
McCawley's Paradox 270–1
Merge 9, 186, 194–218
  External 212, 217, 251
  Internal 186, 194, 211–13, 217
  HoP-Merge 199–200, 203–5
  Sel(ect)-Merge 201–5, 208–9
metalanguage 11–12, 275–7, 280, 287, 292
Minimal Link Condition 212
minimal pair 40–1, 121
Minimal Recursion Semantics (MRS) 10, 225–32, 260 n. 17, 267 n. 24

Minimalism; Minimalist Program 3, 9–10, 26, 28, 145 n. 1, 146, 149, 160, 164, 185–8, 196–8, 201, 204 n. 12, 205, 209, 218, 251, 275
Mirror Theory 202, 212
mismatch of values 4, 8, 29, 31, 68, 72, 78–80, 146–7, 180
modal logic 12, 280–4
modal verbs 256
model-theoretic syntax 11, 276–8, 281
mood 6, 65, 69 n. 5, 76, 80, 83, 88–9, 94–5, 100, 105, 168, 215
  modal meaning 174–5
  see also modal verbs; features: MOOD
morpheme 58, 99, 168–9, 178, 189
morphology-free syntax 4, 18, 82
morphology-semantics interface 6
  see also interface
Move/Remerge 186–7, 208–9, 213, 218
movement transformation 10, 209, 212–13, 216–18, 288–9
multirepresentation of feature value 6, 65, 68–71, 85, 88–9, 95, 99–105
myths 114–16, 121, 123, 125 n. 15, 126, 137–9

nano-syntactic approach 198
natural language interface, *see* interface
No Complex Values Hypothesis 9–10, 197, 218
nominal classification, *see* noun class
nominalization 93, 97, 99–100, 103, 149
non-local dependency 10–11, 245, 249–51, 254, 261, 264, 271
normal case default, *see* default
noun class 109–42
  see also gender system
number 1–2, 6, 9, 17, 20–1, 24–7, 29 n. 8, 31, 33, 64, 67–9, 72–83, 105, 144–6, 149, 166–9, 172, 180, 188, 192–3, 228
  augmented 192–3
  plural, *see* plurality
  see also features: NUMBER

object marker 92, 147 n. 3
Optimality Theory (OT) 49
overriding; override 114, 147, 258 n. 15

pair nouns 233–4
  see also plurality
pairwise comparison 39–41, 62
palatalization 31, 47, 51, 57
paradigm, morphological 30, 72–3, 111, 168–9, 172–3, 177–83
Paradigm Function Morphology (PFM) 9, 167, 177
ParGram (Parallel Grammar Project) 35, 226
parse ranking 223
parsing 223, 226–7, 249
passive 99
pattern alignment 38–9
perceptual salience 7, 38, 119, 120
periphrasis 9, 167, 171, 176–7, 182
periphrastic construction 3–4, 8–9, 30–1, 95, 166–84
persistent default, see default
person 6, 9, 19–20, 64, 66–7, 72–5, 83, 105, 149, 164, 166, 168, 172, 180, 198, 228
  see also features: PERSON
philosophy of linguistics 292
phoneme 1, 4–5, 37–41, 44–5, 48–50, 54–5, 58–9, 62, 121
phonetic contrast 38, 62
phonological activity 46–7, 53, 63
  see also feature, active
phonological contrast 38–9, 50, 60, 62
phonological features:
  Advanced Tongue Root (ATR) 50–4
  back 39, 43–44, 46–9, 51–2, 54
  bilabial 40–2, 45, 48
  constricted 61–2
  continuant 45, 49, 61
  coronal 50–1, 54–7, 60–1
  dental 43–5, 62
  dorsal 62

  glottal width 61–2
  glottalic 59
  high 43–4, 53–4, 56–7; see also height contrast
  labial 41, 43–4, 49–51, 53–9, 61–2
  labiodental 45
  lateral 49
  low 43–4, 47, 49–51, 54–7
  nasal 22 n. 5, 40–2, 48–9
  round 38, 47, 49, 53–7
  sonorant 49, 61–2
  spread 61–2
  tense 42
  voiced 1, 40–2, 45, 48–9, 59–60
phonological redundancy 40–2
phonology-free syntax 4, 18
pied-piping 212–13
pivot 95–6
plurality 171, 190, 229–34
  see also number
polarity 6, 65, 70, 83, 89, 94, 98, 100, 105
portmanteau 95, 178 n. 4
possessive 26, 75, 147
possessive construction 74, 158–9
possessor 149 n. 4, 157–9, 256, 266–8, 271
precedence; immediate precedence 41, 44, 54, 280
privativity, see feature, privative
property co-occurrence restrictions 177, 286
prototype; prototypical 115–16, 152
pseudo-comitative 29

question answering (QA) 10, 223

radial category 115–16
Radical Interpretability, Thesis of 160
realization of feature value 67, 70–89
  distributive 85, 87 fn. B
realization rule 177–9, 182–3
realizational morphology 9, 72, 167, 171, 177, 184

recursion; recursive feature system 195–6
redundancy rule, *see* phonological redundancy
referential index 268
reflexive construction 99, 259
resolution rule 30
respect 6, 70, 74–5, 83, 88, 105
resultative construction 99
root 52, 168, 177–9, 182–3, 196
    root node 19, 251, 278–9, 284–5, 289–90
rule:
    assignment, *see* assignment rule
    grammar/syntactic 2, 11, 17–18, 65, 69, 75, 77, 86, 88, 98, 101, 188–90, 195–6, 206, 229, 236, 243, 247–9, 251, 256, 271
    ID, *see* ID rule
    lexical; rule for lexical items 187, 198, 229, 255
    phonetic 51
    realization, *see* realization rule
    redundancy, *see* redundancy rule
    resolution, *see* resolution rule

satisfaction relation 283
semiotics 116
scope of features 39, 42, 49, 91, 95, 104, 118
selection:
    of category 242, 256, 258–9
    semantic 215, 259–60
semantic index 225 n. 4, 229, 231, 234
Semantic Interface (Sem-I) 229–30
    see also interface
semantic plurality, *see* plurality
semantic representation 10, 221, 224, 226
serial verb construction 101–2
Set-theoretical School 5, 32
sharing, *see* feature sharing
Sign-Based Construction Grammar (SBCG) 11, 251–6, 260–1, 263, 269–71

Sign Principle, The 254
signature, grammar 253
similarity of sounds 61
sound pattern 38, 47–8
spreading, *see* feature spreading
star-free stringsets 278
statistical ranking 223
strings 12, 277–9
structure embedding 9, 185
Structured Specification theory 58, 60
subcategorization 214, 224, 238, 241, 243, 245–8, 272, 281
    bounds of 237–40
    locality of 242
    Subcategorization Principle 11, 254–5, 257, 259, 264, 271
    see also context-free subcategorization
subgender 73
subjunctive 241, 245
subsumption 173 n. 3
subtype 268
Succession 290
superclassing 4, 20–3
supertype 253
syllable 119, 128, 132–3, 141–2
syncretism 19–20, 23, 72
syntax-morphology interface, *see* interface
syntax-semantics interface, *see* interface
syntax-prosody interface, *see* interface
synthetic form 8, 166–84
    see also periphrasis

tag questions 250–1
tagging 36, 222
TAG (Tree-Adjoining Grammar) 246–7, 257
TAMP 6, 89, 92–5, 99–104
    see also tense; aspect; mood; polarity
target of agreement 6, 27–30, 67–87, 98
tectogrammatical structure 250

tense 6, 8, 18, 24, 31, 64–6, 69 n. 5, 73, 75–6, 80, 83, 85, 88–9, 92–5, 100–1, 105, 149, 162 n. 12, 166–76, 179, 181, 201 n. 8, 207, 212
  see also features: TENSE
Theta Criterion 187
topic 76, 80, 83
topicalization 263 n. 20
tough-adjective/construction 217, 242–3, 247
trace 194, 217, 262, 283
transformational grammar 242
transitivity 83
tree 9, 12, 204, 212, 237, 246–7, 251 n. 10, 277–92
  elementary 246
tree automaton 280, 288
trigger of harmony 51–7
type hierarchy 253
typing, *see* feature typing

unbounded dependency 283, 288
underspecification 10, 163–5, 227
underspecified representation 10, 144, 224, 232, 234
underspecifiability 10, 226
  underspecifiability theory 48

unification 28–9, 66, 160, 173, 185, 201, 207–9, 216, 218
  see also subsumption
Uniformity 290
uninterpretability 189
uniqueness 152, 156, 158–9
universality 4, 161, 177, 197
  of feature ordering/hierarchies 43, 44, 48

value of a feature, *see* feature value
variable 178, 228, 230, 232, 278
verbal complex; verbal group 69, 85, 95, 101–5
voice 76, 80, 83, 168, 170, 182
vowel harmony 50, 53, 60, 63
  ATR harmony 51–3
  labial harmony 51

Weak Maximality 290
weak monadic second-order logic 12, 278, 281, 287–8
word sense disambiguation 227
WordNet 224, 227

X-bar theory 281, 290, 291
XML 281

Ingram Content Group UK Ltd.
Milton Keynes UK
UKHW022351130323
418540UK00004B/269

9 780199 577743